RADIO PRODUCTION WORKTEXT
Fifth Edition

RADIO PRODUCTION WORKTEXT

Studio and Equipment

Fifth Edition

DAVID E. REESE

LYNNE S. GROSS

BRIAN GROSS

AMSTERDAM • BOSTON • HEIDELBERG • LONDON
NEW YORK • OXFORD • PARIS • SAN DIEGO
SAN FRANCISCO • SINGAPORE • SYDNEY • TOKYO

Focal Press is an imprint of Elsevier

Acquisitions Editor: Amy Jollymore
Project Manager: A. B. McGee
Assistant Editor: Cara Anderson
Marketing Manager: Christine Degon
Cover Design: Cate Barr
Composition: SPI Publisher Services
Cover Printer: Phoenix Color Corp.
Interior Printer: Maple-Vail Book Manufacturing Group

Focal Press is an imprint of Elsevier
30 Corporate Drive, Suite 400, Burlington, MA 01803, USA
Linacre House, Jordan Hill, Oxford OX2 8DP, UK

∞ Recognizing the importance of preserving what has been written, Elsevier prints its books on acid-free paper whenever possible.

Library of Congress Cataloging-in-Publication Data
Application submitted.

British Library Cataloguing-in-Publication Data
A catalogue record for this book is available from the British Library.

ISBN 13: 978-0-240-80690-7
ISBN 10: 0-240-80690-5

For information on all Focal Press publications
visit our website at www.books.elsevier.com

05 06 07 08 09 10   10 9 8 7 6 5 4 3 2 1

Printed in the United States of America

The transition to digital has brought broadcasting new technologies and techniques that hold the promise of greater quality, productivity, and creativity in radio production work. This text was written for anyone with a desire to embrace this changing face of audio production.

D.E.R.
L.S.G.
B.G.

CONTENTS

5 DIGITAL AUDIO PLAYERS/RECORDERS

6 DIGITAL EDITING AND MULTI-TRACK RECORDING

9   ANALOG AUDIO PRODUCTION

10   PRODUCTION SITUATIONS

11   INTERNET RADIO AND OTHER DISTRIBUTION TECHNIQUES

PREFACE

The fifth edition of *Radio Production Worktext* reflects the fast-paced change that digital technology has brought to the radio production studio and the techniques of audio production. As with previous editions, this edition offers a solid background for anyone who wishes to know more about audio equipment and production techniques. Some production texts seem to offer burdensome amounts of information and explanations that don't have practical applications in the day-to-day world of radio, and other texts wander into aspects of radio broadcasting that have only vague implications for radio production. This text sticks to the subject at hand, and although radio production can seem complex to the beginner, *Radio Production Worktext* simplifies the understanding of the radio production process.

Radio is more competitive than ever, and those with a firm understanding of the basics of the digital audio production process will stand the best chance of succeeding in this field. Like much in life, what you get from this text is largely up to you. As the title implies, this isn't a book just to read, but rather a text that will become an integral part of your study and practice of radio production. The fifth edition continues to utilize a worktext approach because it is our firm belief that this subject is best taught by a combination of theory and discussion *and* practical, hands-on use of broadcast equipment. Each chapter of the text is divided into sections of Information, Self-Study Questions and Answers, and Projects.

The Information sections for each chapter are divided into modular units so that all the primary concepts can be easily learned. These concepts are illustrated with drawings, photographs, and images that help the student grasp the specific ideas being presented.

Self-Study Questions include multiple choice and true/false questions covering the material presented in the chapter. Answers, as well as suggested procedures for those who don't answer correctly, guide the student through this section. These questions are not really test questions but rather are intended to be instructional so that by the time the student has read the Information section and answered all the questions correctly, he or she will feel confident about knowing the information.

The Projects sections of the chapters contain practical projects that should give readers a degree of expertise in equipment manipulation and, we hope, lead them on to further creative radio production work. It is assumed that the reader will have completed both the Information section and Self-Study Questions before beginning the various projects. The importance of practical production experience cannot be overemphasized, and these projects should be viewed as a starting point for a developing radio production person. Additional hands-on work in the production studio is never wasted time and is highly recommended.

The fifth edition is still primarily arranged by equipment, but it doesn't deal strictly with a nuts-and-bolts approach. Techniques as well as mechanics are included within each chapter. In fact, the book isn't intended to be that technical. It's written in an easy-to-read style that should enable people without technical training to understand the nature and makeup of the radio production process.

The book continues to refine its organization and content with expanded material on digital equipment and procedures throughout. For example, analog "cut and splice" editing has been moved to Chapter 9, "Analog Audio Production," and Chapter 6, "Digital Editing and Multi-Track Recording," now focuses on those two related subjects. Other chapters have been combined and repositioned in the text to reflect the importance of their content for modern audio production.

This edition of *Radio Production Worktext* includes an easy-to-navigate CD-ROM that illustrates many of the important concepts discussed in the text. For example, when the terms "crossfade" and "segue" are explained in Chapter 3, "The Audio Console," not only is there a definition of the terms and a diagram showing the concept, but there is also an audio clip that lets you readily hear the difference between these two basic sound transitions. Those sections of the text that include an audio clip are noted throughout the text with a small "compact disc" icon.

There are also files on the CD-ROM that provide material you can use to create audio production projects. Some of these files are for particular production projects in the text, but most of them are music and sound effects that can be used with a variety of projects. This is also denoted by the use of the CD icon next to the appropriate projects.

We've used the audio editing software program *Adobe Audition* to illustrate many digital production concepts in the text. To duplicate our demonstrations or create your own audio production projects, you can download a trial version of the program at their Web site, www.adobe.com. Demo versions of similar programs may also be available. For example, a free version of Pro Tools is available at www.digidesign.com/ptfree; however, not all computer systems are supported with this demo version.

Throughout the book, we have freshened and updated both the copy and artwork to reflect the modern production studio. Like in the previous edition, Chapter 1, "The Production Studio Environment," introduces the reader to the layout and design of the radio production studio—the environment in which you'll accomplish your production work—and describes briefly the equipment that's detailed in subsequent chapters.

The reader is quickly immersed in digital audio production in Chapter 2. In fact, some instructors may prefer to reverse the order of the first two chapters and start with this one. After a brief look at how audio is converted from analog to digital, this chapter introduces some of the digital equipment that can almost replace an entire studio. For example, once audio is recorded on equipment with audio editing capability, you can often edit, add signal processing, and work in a multi-track format with the audio, among other things. This chapter also discusses some basic concepts regarding sound that will help the production person to understand the raw material being worked with.

Chapter 3, "The Audio Console," introduces one of the key components of audio production work. Expanded material on digital consoles and "virtual" consoles keeps this chapter firmly in the digital age. A solid understanding of the material is important because most other broadcast equipment operates through the audio console. Having mastered the audio board, students should be ready to work with the sound sources that can serve as inputs or outputs for the console. One of these is covered in Chapter 4, "Microphones." Chapter 5, "Digital Audio Players/Recorders," deals with the players and recorders beyond those covered in Chapter 2. Compact discs, Minidiscs, DATs (Digital Audio Tapes), compact flash, and hard disk players and recorders are all considered here.

The first part of Chapter 6, "Digital Editing and Multi-Track Recording," looks at the tools and techniques of digital editing. Essentially all audio editing is now accomplished in this manner. Then, this chapter looks at the basics of multi-track production. Almost all digital-based production studios have multi-track capability, as do some analog-based studios, so it's important for the production person to learn

the basic techniques of multi-track recording and the creative possibilities that they open up. In this edition, Chapter 7, "Signal Processing Equipment," provides an introduction to the most popular signal processing equipment employed in radio production work. Once again you will learn that digital equipment can replicate most of the signal processing effects—usually faster and more easily.

Equipment that is often overlooked is included in Chapter 8, "Monitor Speakers, Cables, Connectors, and Studio Accessories." Monitor speakers and headphones are first discussed, and then the connectors, cables, and accessories that complement the major pieces of equipment in the production studio are surveyed. Chapter 9, "Analog Audio Production," is a survey of analog equipment and is an admission that some facilities haven't completely abandoned the equipment and techniques of this technology.

Chapter 10, "Production Situations," considers some production situations beyond basic spot production. Many of the techniques and skills used for regular commercial production are also employed for radio announcing, newscasting, interviewing, and sports play-by-play, to name a few. The final chapter in the fifth edition, Chapter 11, "Internet Radio and Other Distribution Techniques," explains how to develop an Internet radio station and briefly looks at some of the other distribution methods for getting radio production work to the listener. The Internet has changed the nature of the radio industry in certain ways. As an outlet for creative audio production, it has been of particular benefit to college radio stations.

Throughout the text, you'll also find Production Tips that provide interesting notes that are relevant to various audio production topics. Also, key terms are listed in **boldface** when they are first introduced; these terms are explained in the text, and/or they are included in the Glossary. A selected list of additional Suggested Readings is provided for students who wish to continue their study in this area.

This edition includes an additional author, Brian Gross. He developed and produced the CD-ROM for the previous edition, and, for this edition he undertook some additional writing as well as the updating of the CD-ROM.

At the request of some of our readers, the fifth edition of *Radio Production Worktext* will be available with an Instructor's Manual. It includes a sample syllabus, learning objectives, chapter summaries, pertinent Web sites, study questions, and more.

ACKNOWLEDGMENTS

We are indebted to many people for their help and encouragement while we put together this newest edition of *Radio Production Worktext*. Our colleagues at the University of Nevada, Las Vegas; John Carroll University, Ohio; and California State University, Fullerton, offered generous support for the fifth edition.

Many changes to this edition are a result of the helpful comments that came from the many instructors using previous editions. The authors would like to thank the following educations for feedback on the revision plan for this text:

- **Carla Gesell-Streeter,** Cincinnati State Technical and Community College,
- **Randy Ray,** Middle Tennessee State University,
- **Chris Pruszynski,** Instructor of Communication Arts, Mass Media, at Valdosta State University, and
- **Craig Breit,** Cerritos College.

Their comments and suggestions were very helpful throughout our revision process.

And once again, *Radio Production Worktext* is as good as it is because of the expert help and backing of the staff at Focal Press and its affiliates, especially:

- **Amy Jollymore,** Acquisitions Editor, Focal Press,
- **Cara Anderson,** Assistant Editor, Focal Press,
- **Anne B. McGee,** Project Manager, Elsevier, and
- **Christine Brandt,** Project Manager, SPI Publisher Services.

1

THE PRODUCTION STUDIO ENVIRONMENT

1.1 INTRODUCTION

The room that houses the equipment necessary for radio production work and in which a broadcaster's finished product is assembled is known as the **production studio.** What may initially appear to be merely a roomful of electronic equipment will become a comfortable environment, once you've become familiar with the space and components that make up the production facility. If your facility has several studios, they may be labeled "Production 1" or "Prod. B" or simply identified with a common abbreviation for the production studio, "PDX." Today, a streamlined digital "studio" may merely be a workstation desk setup in the corner of a room with a mix of computer and audio equipment as shown in Figure 1.1.

Traditionally, however, the radio production setting will be a full-blown studio and most radio facilities have at least two studios. One is usually delegated as the **on-air studio** and is used for live, day-to-day broadcasting. The others are production studios, used for putting together programming material that is recorded for playback at a later time. In other words, radio production is whatever isn't broadcast live. This includes such items as commercials, features, public service announcements (PSAs), and station promotional or image spots (promos). Regardless of the actual physical size or shape, the production facility is the creative center for a radio station or production house. Often the production studio mirrors the on-air studio with the same or very similar equipment configuration and serves as a backup for the on-air room. Some stations also have a studio that is considered a **performance studio** or **announce booth.** It usually is smaller than the other studios and houses nothing more than microphones, a table, and chairs. The output is normally sent to a production studio to be recorded, although sometimes it's sent directly to the on-air studio for live broadcast. A performance studio can be used for voice-over work, for taping interviews, for discussions involving several guests, or for putting a small musical group on the air.

Two of the biggest concerns for studio design looked at in this chapter are acoustics and ergonomics. Acoustics refers to how sound "behaves" within an enclosed space; and ergonomics refers to design considerations that help reduce operator fatigue and discomfort. While you may never build or remodel a broadcast studio, an understanding of the characteristics of the production room can help you assess your facility and suggest ways you can improve the surroundings you'll be working in.

1.2 THE AUDIO CHAIN

Figure 1.2 shows a simplified "map" of the typical radio production studio. Starting with various sound sources, such as an announcer's voice, a CD, or an audio recorder, it shows the routes that sound takes to ultimately be broadcast or recorded. This is often called an **audio chain** because the various pieces of equipment are literally linked together. The trip can be complicated since the sound can go through several changes along the way. For example, it can be dubbed, or copied, from CD to MiniDisc; or it can be **equalized,** which is a form of signal processing. The solid lines show sound being sent to the audio console from a variety of audio sources. Then it goes through **signal processing** equipment and finally to the transmitting system, which would be normal for an on-air studio. The broken line shows the sound being sent back to an audio recorder after signal processing, which would be common for a production studio. In both cases, the sound can be heard in the studio through monitor speakers or headphones. You'll learn more about all of this as you work your way through this text, but for now the diagram in Figure 1.2 provides a look at where you are headed.

The equipment shown is also representative of what is found in the typical radio production studio. A **microphone** transforms the announcer's voice into an audio signal. It is not uncommon for a production facility to have one or

1

FIGURE 1.1   Equipped with computer and broadcast equipment, a digital workstation desk can function as a complete audio "studio." (Image courtesy of Omnirax Studio Furniture.)

more auxiliary microphones for production work that requires two or more voices. Most production rooms also have two **CD players,** enabling different CDs to be played back-to-back or simultaneously. Many production studios still house a **turntable** so the occasional vinyl record can be played, but some have eliminated this piece of equipment. Audio recorder/player sources often include **reel-to-reel** or **cassette** recorders, although these analog devices, like the turntable, are becoming obsolete. Modern studios utilize **digital** gear, such as the **MiniDisc** recorder, personal audio editor, **CD-R** (compact disc recorder), or computer-controlled **digital audio workstation.** How many recorders or players are found in the production room depends on the complexity of the studio and the budget of the station. All of this equipment feeds into the **audio console,** which allows the operator to manipulate the sound sources in various ways. Signal processing equipment, such as an **equalizer, noise-reduction** system, or **reverb** unit, is usually put into the audio chain between the audio console and the transmitting or recording equipment. Monitoring the sound during production work is accomplished with studio **speakers** or **headphones.** Compare Figure 1.2 with Figures 1.4, 1.5, and 1.9 to see how the audio chain translates into the actual production studio.

1.3 THE STUDIO LAYOUT

Almost all radio production studios use a U-shaped layout (see Figure 1.3) or some variation of it because this allows

the operator to reach all the equipment control surfaces, and puts the operator immediately in front of the audio console. With the use of remote start/stop switches for any equipment that's out of arm's reach of the operator, all equipment manipulation can occur at the audio console once everything has been set up and cued. Today most radio work is done **combo;** that is, the announcer is also the equipment operator. Because of this, the equipment and operator are in a single studio, be it a production room or an on-air room. This type of studio layout facilitates working combo. In earlier radio days, the announcer was often located in a separate room or announce booth adjacent to the studio that housed the actual broadcast equipment. Visual contact and communication were maintained via a window between the two rooms. An engineer was required to manipulate the equipment, and the announcer merely provided the voice. Many larger-market radio stations still use a similar announcer/engineer arrangement, popularly known as "engineer assist" broadcasting.

One of the basic ergonomic considerations in putting the studio together is to decide whether it should be a sit-down or stand-up design. Sit-down studios would have countertops at desk height and would include a chair or stool for the announcer. As the name implies, stand-up operations have counter height set for the announcer to be standing while doing production work. If you're designing a stand-up studio, make sure even the shortest person can reach the equipment, especially gear in turrets or countertop modules. One approach isn't really better than the other, so it becomes a personal choice of the individual station.

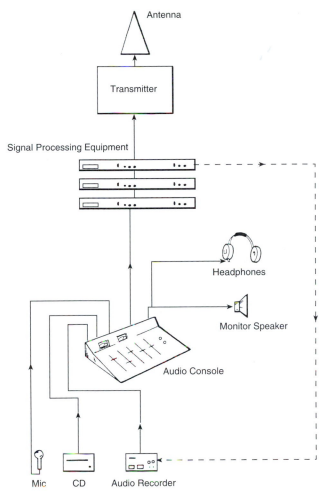

FIGURE 1.2 The audio chain shows how sound moves through the broadcast equipment that is linked together in the production studio.

1.4 PRODUCTION STUDIO FURNITURE

Studio furniture provides the foundation for the production studio because all the equipment in the room sets on it, mounts in it, or is wired through it. Studio equipment is often installed on and in custom-built cabinets and counters. While the cost can be high, such furniture can be built to the exact dimensions of the studio and for the exact equipment that will be housed in that studio. A less expensive but equally functional approach is to lay out the studio using modular stock components (review Figure 1.3). Radio studio furniture has been designed expressly for recorders, audio consoles, and other pieces of studio equipment. Using modular furniture and racks often makes it easier to reconfigure the studio or add additional equipment if the studio needs to expand.

Today's studio furniture systems also include space and cabinet modules for computer monitors and other computer equipment that's being integrated with traditional broadcast equipment in the radio studio, as shown in Figures 1.4, 1.5, and 1.9. A computer monitor should be

about 2 feet away from the announcer and the top-most screen line should fall slightly below eye level. Monitors that are placed too high, perhaps on top of a studio module, can cause neck strain. Some monitors can be kept off the studio furniture by using a special wall-mounted or ceiling-mounted TV boom. Flat screen monitors offer more mounting options, take up less space, and are aesthetically pleasing in the audio studio. If possible, the computer keyboard should be placed in line with the monitor rather than off to the side. Sometimes the keyboard can be placed on an under-counter drawer to accomplish this, but you have to watch the announcer's knee space in this situation. If possible, avoid putting a keyboard near hard counter edges that can cause a painful problem if the announcer's wrist strikes the counter edge, and make sure the computer mouse can be reached without stretching the operator's arm.

Most studio furniture is manufactured of plywood or particleboard with a laminate surface; however, a few modern radio counters are employing a solid-surface countertop of Corian or similar kitchen-counter type material as shown in Figure 1.5. Both custom-built and modular cabinets and counters are also designed to provide easy access to the myriad cables necessary to wire all the studio equipment together yet maintain an attractive image for the look of the studio. Digital equipment offers the advantage of better cable management, as linking equipment via digital inputs/outputs requires less cable than analog wiring. Other cabinets or storage modules are also available for CDs, records, tapes, and other material that's kept in the production studio. Furniture housing broadcast equipment may require cooling, but most digital equipment will operate fine with a passive air flow provided by back panel vents in the furniture. If a forced-air fan is required, be aware of the noise problem it could present.

Does stylish furniture make a studio sound better? Although that notion would be hard to quantify, a positive studio image does imply a commitment to high-quality professional production, and this often translates into more creativity, more productivity, and a better "sound" produced from that studio.

1.5 STUDIO SOUND CONSIDERATIONS

The radio production studio is a unique space in that the physical room will impact the sound produced in it. Because of this, several characteristics of sound need to be considered in designing the studio, including sound isolation, noise and vibration control, and room acoustics. When sound strikes a surface (such as a studio wall), some of that sound is reflected back, while some is absorbed within or transmitted through the material of the surface. Most of the sound that hits a hard, flat surface will be reflected back. However, if the surface is irregular, it will break up the sound wave and disperse the reflections—a phenomenon known as **diffusion**. Sound that's absorbed

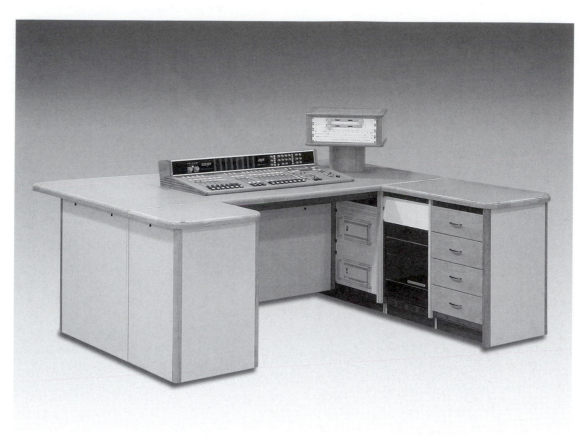

FIGURE 1.3 Many radio studios use modular furniture components arranged in a U-shaped design that allows the operator to easily see and reach the equipment. (Image courtesy of Wheatstone Corporation.)

into the surface is dissipated within it, but **penetration** occurs when sound goes through a surface and is transmitted into the space on the other side. Figure 1.6 illustrates that penetration, absorption, reflection, and diffusion are all characteristics that help determine the sound that is both produced and reproduced in the studio.

When a sound (such as an announcer's voice) is produced, the **direct sound** is the main sound that you hear. In a production situation, it is sound that goes from the announcer (the sound source) straight to the microphone. On the other hand, **indirect** or **reflected sound** reaches the microphone fractions of a second after the direct sound does because it has traveled a circuitous route. Reflected sound consists of **echo** and **reverberation**. This indirect sound has bounced off or been reflected from one surface (echo) or two or more surfaces (reverb) before reaching the microphone (see Figure 1.7). Since it's an early reflection, echo provides a distinct repetition of the sound, such as "hello—hello—hello." On the other hand, reverb's repeated later reflections provide a continuous decay of the sound, such as "hello—oo—oo." The components of direct and indirect sound make up what is commonly called the sound's "life cycle."

In designing the radio studio, the goal is to manipulate these sound characteristics to create a proper sound environment for production work. When considering reflected sound, we think in terms of reverb ring and reverb route, with the same concepts applying for echo but to a lesser extent. **Reverb ring** (or **reverb time**) is the time that it takes for a sound to die out or go from full volume to silence. **Reverb route** is the path that sound takes from its source to a reflective surface and back to the original source (or a microphone, if recording). Excessive reflected sound tends to accent high and midrange frequencies, which produces a "harsh" sound; to blur the stereo image, which produces a "muddy" sound; or to cause standing waves (see Section 1.7), which produces an "uneven" sound. Reflected sound can also be **reinforced sound,** which causes objects or surfaces within the studio to vibrate at the same frequencies as the original sound in a sympathetic fashion.

Both **absorption** and diffusion are utilized to control reflected sound. Part of the reflected sound can be absorbed within the carpeting, curtains, and walls of the studio. Absorption soaks up sound and shortens reverb time to prevent excessive reflection. Absorption provides a **dead studio,** which has a very short reverb ring (sound dies out quickly) and a long reverb route that produces a softer sound. Excessive absorption produces a totally dead studio, which provides a "dry" sound that is unlike any

FIGURE 1.4 Computer equipment must be integrated with traditional broadcast equipment in the modern production studio. (Image courtesy of WJCU, John Carroll University, Ohio.)

normal acoustic space and isn't really desirable. In contrast, a **live studio** has a longer reverb ring and a shorter reverb route that produces a harder, or more brilliant, sound. Diffusion uses irregular room surfaces to break up sound reflections. This decreases the intensity of the reflections, making them less noticeable, but doesn't deaden the sound as much because the sound reflections are redirected rather than soaked up. Most studio designs control reflections by a combination of absorption and diffusion techniques.

One common radio studio design is a **live end/dead end (LEDE)** approach. The front of the studio (where the announcer and equipment are located) is designed to absorb and diffuse sounds. This dead end quiets some of the equipment operation noise, picks up the direct sound of the announcer's voice, and absorbs the excess reflections that pass by the microphone from the live end. The live end, or back, of the studio adds a desirable sharpness to the sound by providing some reflected sound so the studio isn't totally dry. Other acoustic designs include early sound scattering (ESS), which uses a great deal of diffusion, and reflection free zone (RFZ), which uses a great deal of absorption to control unwanted reflected sound in the studio.

1.6 STUDIO CONSTRUCTION MATERIALS

Another design consideration involves the actual construction materials used for the studio. Ideally, you want to keep penetration to a minimum by keeping outside (unwanted) sound from entering the studio and inside sound from escaping from the studio, except via the audio console. Radio studios utilize **soundproofing** to accomplish this sound isolation. Doors are heavy-duty and tightly sealed; windows are often double glass with the interior pane slanted downward to minimize reflected sounds; and walls, ceiling, and flooring use special sound-treatment materials. For example, studio walls may be covered with acoustically treated and designed panels that both absorb and trap reflected sounds (see Figure 1.8). Some stations use carpeting on the studio walls, but this type of soundproofing doesn't absorb low frequencies very well. Some production studios have actually used egg cartons on the walls as a sound treatment. If you compare the design of an egg carton with the design of the acoustic panel shown in Figure 1.8, you'll see why some stations have gone the inexpensive egg carton route.

All materials absorb sound to some degree, but each material will have a different **absorption coefficient,** which

FIGURE 1.5   A solid-surface countertop on studio furniture provides the radio studio with a sleek, modern look. (Image courtesy of Mager Systems, Inc.)

is the proportion of sound that it can absorb. A coefficient of 1.00 indicates that all sound is absorbed in the material. On the other hand, a coefficient of 0.00 means no absorption occurs and that all the sound is reflected back. Hard, smooth surfaces like plaster or panel walls and hardwood floors have low absorption coefficients. Heavy, plush carpets, drape-covered windows, and specially designed acoustic tiles will have higher coefficients. For example, using a 1,000 Hz tone as the sound source, the absorption coefficient of a sheet rock wall would be .04 while a 2-inch Sonex foam tile would be .81; a glass window would be .12 while a window curtain would be .75; and a painted concrete block wall would be .07 while a carpeted concrete wall would be .37. The purpose of any soundproofing material is to help give the studio a dead sound. Soundproofing absorbs and controls excess reverb and echo and helps produce a softer sound.

1.7 STUDIO SIZE AND SHAPE

The size and shape of a production studio can also determine how reflective the studio is. As noted, the radio pro-

duction studio shouldn't be overly reflective because sound produced or recorded would be too bright and even harsh. Unfortunately, standard room construction often goes counter to good broadcast studio design. For example, studios with parallel walls (the normal box-shaped room) produce more reflected sound than irregularly shaped studios. Sound waves that are reflected back and forth within a limited area, such as between studio walls that are parallel, can produce standing waves. In basic terms, a **standing wave** is a combination of a sound wave going in one direction and its reflected wave going in the opposite direction. If the distance between the walls is the same as the wave length (or a multiple of it), the waves interact and produce an undesirable combined sound that tends to be uneven, as previously mentioned. To help prevent standing waves, adjacent studio walls can be splayed (joined at more than a 90-degree angle) to help break up reflected sound and control excessive reverb and echo.

The actual size of the production facility is partially determined by the equipment that must be housed in it. However, in constructing the radio production room, consideration should be given to the fact that when rooms are built with height, width, and length dimensions that are

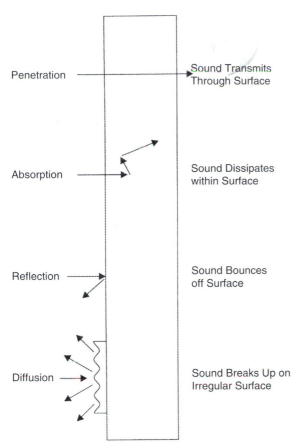

Penetration —————→ Sound Transmits
Through Surface

Absorption —————→ Sound Dissipates
within Surface

Reflection —————→ Sound Bounces
off Surface

Diffusion —————→ Sound Breaks Up on
Irregular Surface

FIGURE 1.6 Sound striking a studio wall will reflect off, penetrate through, be diffused by, or be absorbed by that surface.

FIGURE 1.8 Acoustic panels and tiles help control reflected sound through both absorption (by the foam material) and diffusion (by the irregular surfaces). (Image courtesy of Auralex Acoustics, Inc.—Photo by Erikk D. Lee.)

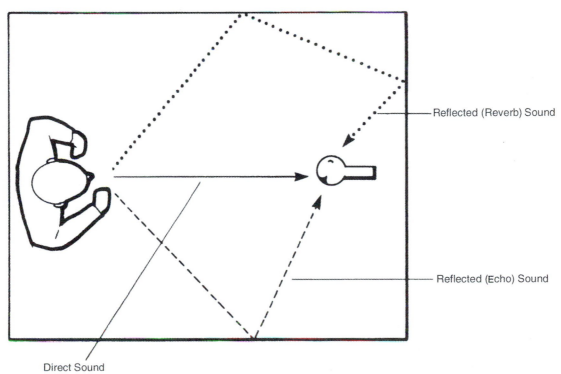

Reflected (Reverb) Sound

Reflected (Echo) Sound

Direct Sound

FIGURE 1.7 Direct sound takes a straight path from the announcer to the microphone, but reflected sound is also produced in the production studio.

equal or exact multiples of each other, certain sound frequencies tend to be boosted, and other sound frequencies tend to be canceled. Since this "peaks and valleys" sound is not desirable in the radio production room, cubic construction should be avoided when possible.

1.8 STUDIO AESTHETICS

There are some studio design considerations that can be categorized as the "aesthetics" of the production room. In general, the radio studio should be pleasant to work in; after all, the operator is confined to a rather small room for long stretches of time. For example, fluorescent lighting should be avoided when possible. Not only does it tend to introduce "hum" into the audio chain, it's also harsher and more glaring than incandescent light. If possible, the studio lights should be on dimmers so that an appropriate level of light can be set for each individual operator. If the lighting causes glare on a computer monitor, use an anti-glare shield or screen to diminish this problem or use track lighting that can be directed away from the screen.

Stools or chairs used in the radio studio should be comfortable and functional. User-friendly adjustments should allow the announcer to set the seat height so that the entire sole of the foot rests on either the floor or a footrest. Chairs must move easily because even though most of the equipment is situated close to the operator, he or she may have to move around to cue CDs or speak directly into the microphone. The production stool must also be well constructed so that it doesn't squeak if the operator moves slightly while the microphone is open. This may not be a factor for production studios designed for a stand-up operation in which there is no stool, and the counters are at a height appropriate for the operator to be standing while announcing. This stand-up operation allows the operator to be more animated in his or her vocal delivery and actually provides a better posture for speaking than a sitting position.

Many radio production rooms are decorated with music posters or radio station bumper stickers and paraphernalia. Not only does this keep the studio from being a cold, stark room, but it also gives the studio a radio atmosphere. Figure 1.9 shows the interior of a typical radio production studio.

PRODUCTION TIP #1
Static Electricity

Static electricity can be a problem in radio production studios because of the heavy use of carpeting. Most radio people don't enjoy getting shocked every time they touch the metal control surface of an audio console. Also, some modern audio equipment and computer systems have electronic circuits that can be disrupted by static discharges. There have been instances where audio recorders have switched into "play" mode when an announcer just "sparked" the faceplate of the machine. If design factors can't keep the studio static free, commercial sprays can be put on the carpeting or spray fabric softener can be used to provide an antistatic treatment at a modest cost. Dilute the fabric softener a bit or you'll build up a dangerous, slippery gloss on

FIGURE 1.9   The production studio should be a comfortable and functional environment for the announcer. (Image courtesy of Arrakis Systems, Inc.— www.Arrakis-Systems.com)

your carpets. A static touch pad could also be used in the studio—the operator merely places a finger on the pad to harmlessly discharge static buildup. Some studios have even been built with conductive laminate countertops connected to the studio's ground system to help keep static problems to a minimum.

1.9 ON-AIR/RECORDING LIGHTS

On-air lights (see Figure 1.10) are usually located outside the radio production room or studio. Normally they are wired so that whenever the microphone in that studio is turned on, the on-air light comes on. A light outside a production studio will often read "recording" instead of "on air." In either case, a lit light indicates a live microphone.

Good production practice dictates that when an on-air light is on, you *never* enter that studio, and if you're in the vicinity of the studio, you are quiet. *Inside* the studio, another alert light may come on when the microphone is turned on; the announcer often says "stand by" to alert others in the studio that he or she is preparing to turn on the microphone.

1.10 RADIO HAND SIGNALS

Radio **hand signals** don't play a major role in modern radio production; however, there are situations when vocal communication isn't possible and hand signals are necessary. For example, if an announcer and engineer are working an on-air show from adjacent studios with a window between them as mentioned earlier in this chapter, they must be able to communicate with each other. There are also times when two announcers must communicate in a studio, but an open or live microphone prevents them from doing so verbally. Because of situations like these, hand signals have evolved over the years to communicate some basic production information. Figure 1.11 shows some of the basic radio hand signals.

Often hand signals concern getting a program started or stopped. A **standby** signal is given just prior to going on air

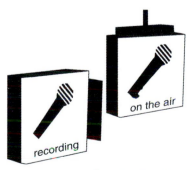

FIGURE 1.10 When lit, the on-air or recording light indicates that a microphone is "live" in that studio.

by holding one hand above the head with the palm forward. The standby signal is immediately followed by the **cue talent** signal. To convey "You're on," this signal is given by pointing your index finger (using the same hand that gave the standby signal) at the person who's supposed to go on air. The common hand signal for stopping a program is the **cut** signal, which is given by drawing the index finger across the throat in a slitting motion. This signal terminates whatever is happening at the moment and usually "kills" all live microphones and stops all recorders. Some hand signals are used to give directions to the announcer regarding the microphone. To get an announcer to **give mic level,** for example, hold one hand in front of you with the palm down and thumb under the second and third fingers. Open and close the thumb and fingers in a "chattering" motion to indicate that the announcer should talk into the microphone so that levels can be checked. Other hand signals are often used during a production to let the talent know how things are going or to convey some necessary information. Timing cues are given with the fingers. To indicate that 2 minutes are left in the program, you would hold up the index and second finger of one hand in front of you. Using both index fingers to form a cross in front of you means there are 30 seconds left. Timing cues always indicate how much time *remains* in the program because there is nothing you can do about the time that has already gone by. When everything is going fine, the radio hand signal is the traditional "thumbs up" given with clenched fist and extended thumb. There is no universal set of hand signals, so you may find that your facility uses some that are different, uses some not presented here, or doesn't use any at all. In any case, an understanding of radio hand signals should prove helpful in certain production situations.

1.11 NOISE AND DISTORTION

The next few chapters will deal with the equipment that's housed in the production studio. Inherent in any of this electronic equipment is noise. The term **noise** refers to any unwanted sound element introduced in the production process that was not present in the original sound signal. For example, a microphone that employs an extremely long cable might add noise to the audio signal. Turntables and recorders can introduce noise from mechanical gears or just through the electronic circuits used in amplifying or recording the signal. In broadcast production, the noise level should be kept as low as possible. Most radio production equipment is designed to produce a **signal-to-noise ratio (S/N)** of at least 60 to 1. S/N is an audio measurement, usually in decibels, that notes the amount by which a signal at a standard test level exceeds the level of noise produced by an electronic component. The higher the signal-to-noise level the better. For most analog equipment, an S/N of around 60 dB is considered good quality; modern digital equipment, such as a CD player, can show a signal-to-noise

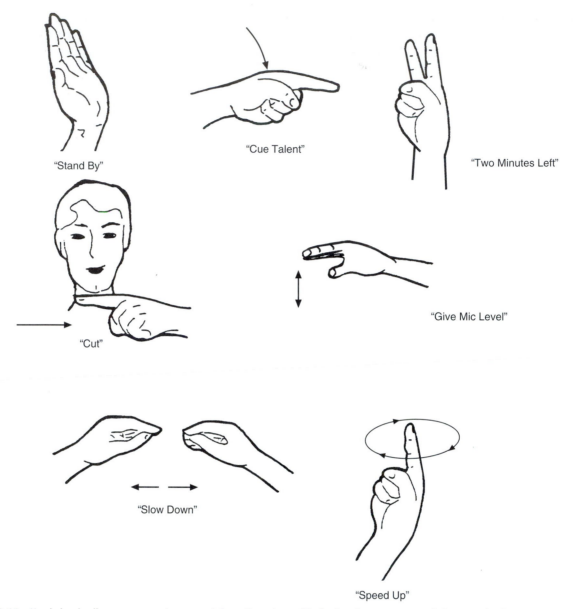

"Stand By"

"Cue Talent"

"Two Minutes Left"

"Cut"

"Give Mic Level"

"Slow Down"

"Speed Up"

FIGURE 1.11   Hand signals allow announcers to convey information when a "live" microphone prevents verbal communication.

ratio of 98 dB. The signal-to-noise ratio gives an indication of the equipment's ability to reproduce sound cleanly.

Distortion is an unwanted change in the audio signal due to inaccurate reproduction of the sound. One example is loudness distortion, which can occur when a signal is recorded at a level that is too loud for the equipment to handle. An overdriven or too loud signal sounds "muddy," and the reproduced signal does not have the same clarity or sharpness as the original. You should be aware of noise and distortion when working with audio equipment, especially analog equipment. Digital equipment frequently reduces the chance of introducing noise or distortion into your production work, but often your work will be accomplished using a combination of analog and digital.

1.12 PRODUCTION STUDIO SETUP

Before beginning any production work, you should set up the production studio. This means cleaning up any mess left behind from previous work. Theoretically, this shouldn't be an issue since good production routine dictates that each person cleans up the facility after each work session; but theory doesn't always translate into practice, so if necessary, put away background music CDs and clear some working space for yourself. Set all audio console controls to a neutral position—in other words, turn on only those pieces of equipment that you're going to use. Not only is it easier to keep track of and manipulate the volumes for just the equipment you need, but it also prevents audio noise from being introduced into your production work from a piece of equipment that you're not even using. If possible, use a **tone generator** to set reference levels for the audio recorders; some audio consoles have a built-in tone generator for this purpose. At the very least, read some copy into the microphone and set a good level on the audio board, and then balance that level with the input levels of the recorders. Do the same for the CD player and other sound sources you'll be using for your production work.

It's also good practice to keep notes while you're doing any production work. For example, if you're using any signal processing equipment, note the settings for the effect you're producing so that you'll be able to recreate it easily at another time. Also, write down the production music you use for music beds or the background music tracks for your production. That way you'll avoid using the same piece of music over and over. Make note of any sound effects or special recording techniques so you can duplicate what you've produced at some future time, if need be. Use a **track sheet** to keep notes regarding multi-track productions. The few minutes that you take now to set up the studio will make the production go more smoothly later. It will also save you time in the overall production process.

1.13 CONCLUSION

Unless you're building a radio facility from the ground up, you will probably have little control over the construction of the studio; sound treatment is an important consideration, however, and methods of improving the sound environment can be put into practice in almost any situation. While the radio studio may seem overwhelming at first, it is an environment you will become very comfortable in as you do production work. Completion of this chapter should have you in the radio production studio and ready to learn the procedures and techniques for operating all the equipment you see in front of you.

Self-Study

1. What does the radio expression "to work combo" mean?

   a) The announcer has an engineer to operate the studio equipment for him or her.
   b) The announcer operates the studio equipment and also announces.
   c) The announcer works at two different radio stations.
   d) The announcer is announcing in both the on-air and the production studio.

2. Which type of studio is least likely to contain an audio console?

   a) on-air studio
   b) production studio
   c) PDX studio
   d) performance studio

3. Which describes sound produced in the radio studio that causes objects or surfaces within the studio to vibrate sympathetically?

   a) absorbed sound
   b) reflected sound
   c) reinforced sound
   d) diffused sound

4. In the radio production studio, sound that has bounced off one surface before reaching the microphone is called what?

   a) echo
   b) reverberation
   c) direct sound
   d) indirect sound

5. What does "reverb ring" in the production studio refer to?

   a) the circular route reflected sound takes before it reaches the microphone
   b) the time it takes reflected sound to go from full volume to silence
   c) just another common name for echo
   d) a sound that has bounced off two or more surfaces

6. What is the use of carpeting on the walls of some radio production facilities an example of?

   a) an inexpensive way of decorating the studio
   b) producing reverb in the studio
   c) producing a live sound in the studio
   d) soundproofing the studio

7. Studios with parallel walls produce less reflected sound than irregularly shaped studios.

   a) true
   b) false

8. Why do most production studios use a U-shaped layout?

   a) This design places equipment within easy reach of the operator.
   b) This design uses incandescent lights rather than fluorescent lights.
   c) This design necessitates custom-built cabinets.
   d) This design uses the least amount of wire to connect the equipment.

9. Static electricity is not a problem in the modern production studio because state-of-the-art audio equipment is impervious to static.

a) true
b) false

10. Which hand signal almost always follows immediately after the standby hand signal?

a) 2 minutes to go
b) thumbs up
c) cue talent
d) give mic level

11. If you hold up the index, second, and third fingers of one hand in front of you, what are you telling the announcer?

a) There are 3 minutes left in the program.
b) There are 30 seconds left in the program.
c) He or she should move three steps closer to the microphone.
d) 3 minutes have gone by since the beginning of the program.

12. What does one call the linking of a CD player to an audio console, the console to an equalizer, and the equalizer to an audio recorder?

a) audio road map
b) audio linking
c) audio processor
d) audio chain

13. What do we call the uneven sound that is produced when sound waves are reflected between parallel walls in such a manner that a wave reflected in one direction is combined with an identical wave going in the opposite direction?

a) a diffused wave
b) a standing wave
c) an absorbed wave
d) a sympathetic wave

14. When a "recording" light is on outside a production studio, it means a microphone is "live" in that studio.

a) true
b) false

15. What is a tone generator used for in the audio production studio?

a) to set audio console controls in a neutral position
b) to bulk erase audio tapes
c) to set volume levels
d) to keep track of music played

16. When sound produced in the production studio strikes a hard, flat surface, which of the following does not happen?

a) reflection
b) absorption
c) penetration
d) diffusion

17. A production studio wall that has an absorption coefficient of .50 will absorb half the sound striking it and reflect back half the sound.

a) true
b) false

18. Posters and other radio station paraphernalia should not be put up in a production studio as they will distract the announcer from doing good production work.

a) true
b) false

19. Which term describes what happens when the irregular surfaces of acoustic tiles break up sound reflections?

a) absorption
b) reflection
c) penetration
d) diffusion

20. What is an unwanted change in the audio signal due to inaccurate reproduction of the sound called?

a) reverb
b) noise
c) distortion
d) diffusion

ANSWERS

If You Answered A:

1a. No. This is not working combo. (Reread 1.3.)
2a. No. An on-air studio needs an audio console for sending the mixed signal out. (Reread 1.1 and 1.2.)
3a. No. If anything, absorbed sound would be diminished. (Reread 1.5.)
4a. Yes. Echo is sound that has reflected off a single surface.
5a. No. This answer nearly (but not exactly) describes reverb route. (Reread 1.5.)
6a. No. Painted walls would be less expensive, so this can't be correct. (Reread 1.6 and 1.8.)
7a. No. Just the opposite is true. (Reread 1.7.)
8a. Right. The operator can reach around the "horseshoe."
9a. No. Just the opposite is true. (Reread Production Tip #1.)
10a. No. The two-minute signal would not come until the end of a program. It would not be right after a standby signal. (Reread 1.10.)
11a. Yes. This is the correct hand signal.
12a. No. Although you could map out this audio signal route, this is not the best answer. (Reread 1.2.)
13a. No. Diffused waves would be sound reflections that have been broken up. (Reread 1.5 and 1.7.)
14a. Right. On-air and recording lights usually come on automatically when a microphone is on in that studio.
15a. No. A tone generator does set something, but it has nothing to do with a neutral position. (Reread 1.12.)
16a. No. Most of the sound that strikes a hard, flat surface will be reflected. (Reread 1.5.)
17a. Yes. This would be a true statement.
18a. Wrong. Posters and other studio decorations aren't likely to cause poor production work, and they do add atmosphere to the studio. (Reread 1.8.)

19a. No. Absorption would be the soaking up of sound reflections. (Reread 1.5 and 1.6.)

20a. No. Reverb is a form of reflected sound. (Reread 1.5 and 1.11.)

If You Answered B:

1b. Correct. The announcer is also the equipment operator when working combo.

2b. No. A production studio needs an audio console for mixing. (Reread 1.1 and 1.2.)

3b. No. Reflected sound is sound that has bounced off a surface. (Reread 1.5.)

4b. No. Reverb is sound that has reflected off two or more surfaces. (Reread 1.5.)

5b. Yes. This is what we call reverb ring.

6b. Wrong. Carpeting absorbs sound and reduces reverb. (Reread 1.5 and 1.6.)

7b. Yes. This is the correct response.

8b. No. Lights have no relevance, so this can't be correct. (Reread 1.3 and 1.8.)

9b. Yes. Modern electronics, especially logic circuits, can be disrupted by static discharges.

10b. Wrong. You wouldn't know the production was going well if it hadn't started yet. (Reread 1.10.)

11b. No. Crossed index fingers indicate 30 seconds left. (Reread 1.10.)

12b. No. This is not correct. (Reread 1.2.)

13b. Correct. This is the right answer.

14b. No. This is exactly what it means. (Reread 1.9.)

15b. No. A tone generator has nothing to do with erasing tapes. (Reread 1.12.)

16b. This isn't a bad choice, but some sound will be absorbed and dissipated even with hard surfaces. (Reread 1.5.)

17b. No. A coefficient of 1.00 would mean total absorption and a coefficient of 0.00 would mean no absorption. (Reread 1.6.)

18b. This is the correct answer.

19b. No. Reflection would be sound that has bounced off a surface. (Reread 1.5)

20b. No. You're close because noise is an unwanted element introduced into the audio signal that was not present in the original sound, but there's a better response. (Reread 1.11.)

If You Answered C:

1c. No. This is not working combo. (Reread 1.3.)

2c. No. This is just another term for production studio. (Reread 1.1 and 1.2.)

3c. Right. This is the correct response.

4c. No. Direct sound doesn't bounce off any surface before reaching the microphone. (Reread 1.5.)

5c. No. Echo and reverb are both reflected sound but distinctly different. (Reread 1.5.)

6c. No. Just the opposite would happen. Soundproofing with carpeting would help produce a dead sound in the studio. (Reread 1.5 and 1.6.)

8c. No. In a cost-minded facility, this could be a negative. (Reread 1.3 and 1.4.)

10c. Correct. "Standby" and "cue talent" hand signals are always given one after the other.

11c. No. There is another hand signal to move the announcer closer to the microphone, and exact steps are never indicated. (Reread 1.10.)

12c. No. You are way off base with this answer. An audio processor is used to alter the sound characteristics of an audio signal. (Reread 1.2.)

13c. No. Absorbed waves would be sound reflections that have been soaked up. (Reread 1.5 and 1.7.)

15c. Correct. A tone generator is used to help set volume levels.

16c. No. Some sound will penetrate a hard surface and be transmitted to the adjoining space. (Reread 1.5.)

19c. No. Penetration would be sound that has been transmitted through a surface. (Reread 1.5.)

20c. Yes. You're correct.

1d. No. This seems improbable and is not working combo. (Reread 1.3.)

2d. Correct. A performance studio usually only has microphones that are fed to an audio console in either a production studio or an on-air studio.

3d. No. (Reread 1.5.)

4d. You're partly right, but echo and reverb are both indirect sound, and one is a better response to this question. (Reread 1.5.)

5d. No. While this describes reverb, there is a better response. (Reread 1.5.)

6d. Correct. Carpeting walls helps to soundproof, as would use of acoustic tiles designed for the production studio.

8d. While this may be true, it really is not the best reason. (Reread 1.3.)

10d. No. The "give mic level" signal, if used, would have been given before a "standby" signal. (Reread 1.10.)

11d. No. Time signals are usually given only to show how much time remains in a program. (Reread 1.10.)

12d. Correct. The term "audio chain" describes how broadcast equipment is connected together.

13d. No. Sympathetic waves would be sound reflections that have been reinforced. (Reread 1.5 and 1.7.)

15d. No. This would be a track sheet. (Reread 1.12.)

16d. Correct. Sound is diffused when it strikes an irregular surface.

19d. Correct. This is diffusion.

20d. No. Diffusion is sound that has been broken up by an irregular surface. (Reread 1.5 and 1.11.)

Projects

PROJECT 1

Tour a radio station and write a report describing its production facilities.

Purpose

To enable you to see a commercial radio production facility firsthand.

Advice, Cautions, and Background

1. Don't push a station that seems reluctant to have you come. Some stations (especially smaller ones) are happy to have you. Others are pestered to death by would-be visitors or aren't equipped to handle them.
2. Make sure that before you go you have some ideas about what you want to find out so that you can make the most of your tour.
3. Keep your appointment. Once you make it, don't change it, as this will breed ill will for you and your school.

How to Do the Project

1. Select a station that you would like to tour. (If the instructor has arranged a station tour for the whole class, skip to Step 4.)
2. Call the station. Tell them you would like to tour the station so that you can write a report for a radio production class, and ask if you may come.
3. If they're agreeable, set a date; if they're not, call a different station.
4. Think of some things you want to find out for your report. For example:
   a. How many production studios do they have?
   b. What types of equipment (CD player, audio recorder, etc.) do they have?
   c. What manufacturers (brand names) have they bought equipment from?
   d. How is the production studio soundproofed?
   e. How is the on-air studio different from the production studio(s)?
   f. Do the announcers ever use hand signals during a production?
   g. Are their studios designed for stand-up operation?
   h. What is the physical layout of the studios and the station?
5. Go to the station. Tour to the extent that they'll let you, and ask as many questions as you can.
6. Immediately after leaving the station, jot down notes so you'll remember main points.
7. Write your report in an organized fashion, including a complete description of the production studio and the other points you consider most pertinent. It should be two or three typed pages. Write your name and "Radio Facility Tour" on a title page.
8. Give the report to your instructor to receive credit for this project.

PROJECT 2

Redesign your production studio.

Purpose

To suggest improvements to your production facility, utilizing some of the concepts mentioned in this chapter.

Advice, Cautions, and Background

1. While you may initially feel your production studio is perfect just the way it is, almost every studio can be configured better.
2. You won't be judged on artistic ability, but make your drawings as clear as possible.
3. You may find it useful to complete Project 1 before attempting this project.

How to Do the Project

1. Draw a rough sketch of your production studio, showing approximate dimensions, door and window location, equipment placement, and so forth.
2. Draw another sketch of the studio, suggesting changes or improvements to it. For example, if there currently is a CD player on the left side of the audio console and another on the right side, you may suggest moving them both to one side. If you notice a paneled or painted sheet rock wall in the studio, you may suggest putting acoustic tile on that area. You may want to employ an idea for your studio that you noticed when you did Project 1. Just be creative, and try to design the best possible production studio.
3. On a separate sheet of paper, provide a reason for each change you suggest.
4. Write your name and "Studio Design" on a title page, and put your two sketches and reasons together.
5. Turn in this packet to the instructor to receive credit for this project.

PROJECT 3

Draw an audio chain flowchart for your production studio.

Purpose

To help you understand that the audio chain maps the route an electronic audio signal takes as it goes from one place to another in the production studio.

Advice, Cautions, and Background

1. It may be helpful to review Figure 1.2 before beginning this project.
2. Use simple shapes to represent equipment and arrowed lines to represent the sound signal.
3. You won't be judged on artistic ability, but make your drawings as clear as possible.

How to Do the Project

1. Pick a single sound source in your production studio, such as a CD player.
2. Draw a figure to represent the CD player toward the left side of a sheet of paper, and label it appropriately.
3. Determine where the sound goes as it leaves the output of the CD player. (Most likely, it goes to the audio console.)
4. Draw a figure to the right of the CD player to represent the audio console, and label it.
5. Draw an arrowed line going from the CD player to the audio console to represent the signal flow.
6. Now determine where the sound goes next. (It could go to a signal processor or maybe directly to an audio recorder.)
7. Continue in this manner until you've drawn all the possible signal paths that the CD player sound could take. (Don't forget to include the signal to the studio monitors!)
8. Pick another sound source, such as the studio microphone, and repeat the above steps. Do the same for all the other sound sources in your studio—audio recorders, turntables, and so forth.
9. Write your name and "Audio Chain" on your sketch, and turn it in to the instructor to receive credit for this project.

DIGITAL AUDIO PRODUCTION

2.1 INTRODUCTION

Over the past few years, digital technology has revolutionized how the radio production person can record, edit, and otherwise manipulate an audio sound signal. The days of pushing buttons to start a recorder have been all but replaced with manipulating a mouse or keyboard and viewing a computer monitor screen to accomplish the tasks of audio production. Audio tape cartridge machines and rotary pot consoles are almost obsolete, while turntables and reel-to-reel tape recorders sit idle in many studios. From the advent of the compact disc player in the early 1980s, to the total digital production studio of the early 2000s, radio has eagerly embraced digital technology. Not only has the equipment utilized in the typical audio studio changed, the physical setup may also be different as noted in the previous chapter.

Today, to complete the transition to digital, radio stations are beginning to broadcast digital signals, which you'll learn more about in Chapter 11, "Internet Radio and Other Distribution Techniques." This chapter introduces you to the world of digital audio production. First, some basic information is presented on how analog sound is now being converted to digital audio that can be stored and manipulated in any number of ways. Then the focus shifts to explore some of the digital audio equipment and basic production techniques used in the modern audio studio that have had this revolutionary impact on radio production. Finally, the chapter looks at some basic characteristics of sound—the raw material that all audio production centers around.

2.2 THE ANALOG AUDIO PROCESS BECOMES DIGITAL

Before digital technology was developed, audio recording relied on an **analog** process. An analog signal is a continuously variable electrical signal whose shape is defined by the shape of the sound wave produced (see Figure 2.1A). In the analog recording process, a duplicate, or electromagnetic representation, of the sound wave of the original sound source can be stored on magnetic tape. For example, a microphone converts sound pressure changes to changes in voltage that are sent down the microphone cable and recorded onto audio tape as changes in magnetic strength. Each time the analog signal is recorded or processed in some fashion, it is subject to degradation because the signal changes shape slightly. Analog encoding is similar to creating a line graph to show a statistical analysis. All measurements are on a continuous line that curves up and down with no discrete points. The recording process is like trying to retrace a curve on a graph; the reproduction is always slightly different than the original. In addition to this generation loss, because analog recording relies on magnetic pulses stored on tape, any defect or decrease in the magnetic properties of the tape means a loss of signal quality. Typical problems for analog recording have included noise and distortion, print-through and crosstalk, flutter and hiss, and limited dynamic range. You'll learn more about the limitations of analog recording in Chapter 9, "Analog Audio Production."

In today's production studio, computers and other equipment use a digital recording process. By digital technology, we mean the process of converting original audio waveform information into an electrical signal composed of a series of on and off pulses. In other words, the digital process is a conversion into **binary** numbers. All computers handle information in this manner by associating a binary number with each letter of the alphabet and each number, and then manipulating this binary data. Digital encoding is accomplished in a discrete fashion, similar to looking at individual numbers in a statistical analysis and writing them down in a set order. The audio signal starts out as analog, but it can be converted to digital by going through four basic stages: filtering, sampling, quantizing, and coding.

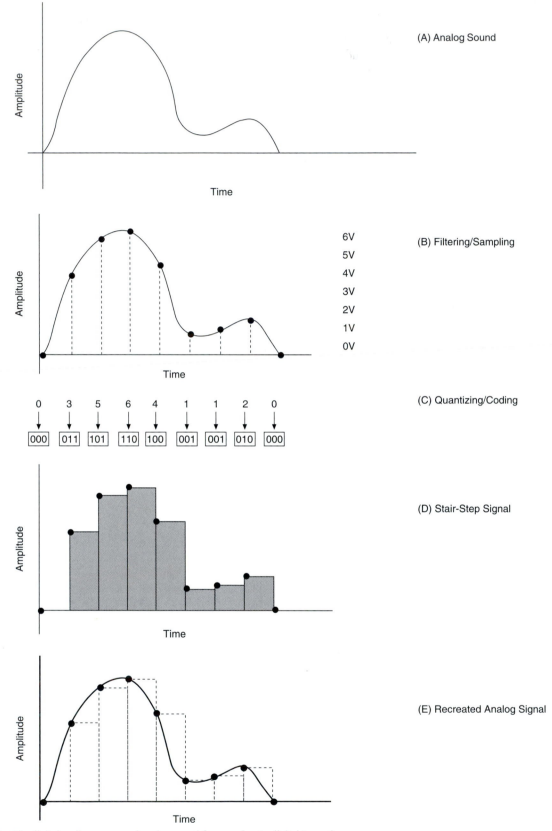

FIGURE 2.1   The digital audio process—changing sound from analog to digital to analog.

First, the original sound signal is sent through a low-pass **filter** that strips off frequencies that are above the range of human hearing. Although originally inaudible, these frequencies can be shifted, or **aliased**, into an audible range during recording and playback, so this process is known as **anti-aliasing**. The filtered analog signal is next divided many times a second in a process known as analog-to-digital conversion or simply, **sampling** (see Figure 2.1B). Each sample represents the amplitude of the audio signal at the moment the sample is taken. The more samples that are taken and converted to binary data, the more exact a reproduction of the original sound signal can be recorded onto tape or some other storage medium. The process is much like that of film, where 24 still photographs are taken per second. When these photographs are played back at the same rate, they create the illusion of movement. When audio samples are played back, they create the illusion of a contiguous sound. To do so, however, many more than 24 samples must be taken per second. Most digital audio equipment utilizes **sampling rates** of 32, 44.1, and 48 thousand samples per second. The sampling rate must be at least twice the highest frequency in the audio signal to enable high-quality and accurate encoding and decoding. Since we can't hear sounds above 20 kHz, the sampling rate should be slightly greater than twice 20 kHz, which is one reason why the most common digital sampling rate is 44.1 kHz. Lower sampling rates can be utilized for lower quality recordings. Higher sampling rates produce audiophile-quality sound, which, to be appreciated, must be played on the highest fidelity equipment and presently would be too bandwidth-intensive to broadcast.

Quantizing and coding are the stages that assign a numerical value to each individual sample. The samples taken of the amplitude of the audio signal can fall at any point within the range of amplitudes, from absolutely silent to very loud. Between these two extremes, or indeed between any two points as geometry tells us, there are an infinite number of other points. **Quantizing** breaks up these infinite points into a more manageable number, rounding samples up or down to the nearest value. The term "bit depth" references the quantizing levels; the more levels, the more accurate information you would have about the signal, as samples will be rounded up or down. For example, a 1-bit system would signify just two quantizing levels—either no amplitude or maximum amplitude—and that doesn't give us much information about the sound. Each additional bit doubles the number of levels—two bits gives four levels, three bits gives eight levels, and so on. The standard bit rate for most digital recording is 16 bits, with some compact disc and DVD recording now being done with 20-bit or 24-bit technology. Sixteen bits can represent 65,536 values. Higher bit depth equals lower noise and better fidelity of the digital recording. **Coding** involves putting 0s and 1s in a precise order corresponding to the values measured during the quantizing process. This binary, or digital, "word" (see Figure 2.1C) represents each individual sample's quantized

(rounded up or down) voltage level at that particular moment. The analog-to-digital (A/D) converter is the electronic circuit that accomplishes this task. Remember, it's the binary data that is actually recorded, not an analog representation of the signal. With digital technology, we can copy from tape to tape with no measurable loss of quality. Along with the improved frequency response, wide dynamic range, and drastically reduced noise and distortion, this ability to rerecord with no decrease in quality has contributed greatly to the acceptance of digital in radio production.

To transform the digital signal back to analog, the recorded numbers are sent to a digital-to-analog (D/A) converter where each sample is read and decoded. A signal of the corresponding analog amplitude is produced and "held" for the individual samples, producing a stair-step signal (see Figure 2.1D) that represents the analog signal. Finally, a filter employs an exact mathematical attribute for each sample to create a correct reproduction of the original analog signal, as shown in Figure 2.1E.

2.3 DESKTOP RADIO PRODUCTION— THE DIGITAL AUDIO EDITOR

One of the simplest ways to get into digital radio production is to put together an inexpensive digital audio editor that utilizes a standard off-the-shelf computer system, plus some specialized equipment, to make up an audio editing system. Often referred to as "desktop radio," this type of production system has the potential of replacing almost an entire production studio. There are two main types of audio editors: 2-track and multi-track. If you're going to just edit phone calls, a simple 2-track system might be more than adequate. If you plan on doing complex commercial production, however, you will want a multi-track system. As you'll see later, many audio editing software programs incorporate both types of editors in a single program.

Although some systems may run on a more basic computer setup, most will require one of the newer Windows platforms, a 400 MHz processor, 64MB of RAM, a mouse or similar pointing device, a high-resolution monitor, and a hard drive capacity of about 10 MB of memory for each stereo minute of audio. There are also Mac-based systems that would require a similarly configured computer. Even the most basic computer system today usually exceeds these specifications. In addition to the computer, the necessary specialized equipment includes a **DSP** (digital signal processing) **audio card**, normally a PCI-bus design, as shown in Figure 2.2. A standard computer audio card could be used, but professional audio hardware usually offers higher sampling rate capability, greater bit resolution, and broadcast-style connectors. The audio card functions as both the analog-to-digital and digital-to-analog converter, and the interface or I/O (input/output) device that moves the audio signal from its source in the production studio

FIGURE 2.2   The DSP audio card is an important component of any computer-based desktop audio editor. (Image courtesy of Digital Audio Labs.)

to the editing system, and then back into the production studio. In most radio production studios, an output from the audio console is fed into the audio card so that any equipment that runs through the audio board can be recorded into the desktop system.

The final component of a desktop radio system is a computer software program to perform the actual recording and editing of the audio. There are several software programs (see Figure 2.3) that can turn a PC into a powerful digital audio editor—*Pro Tools, SAW Studio, VoxPro e2, Sound Forge, Fast Edit,* and *Adobe Audition,* to name a few. Most professional programs used in the broadcast studio will fall within a range of $300 to $900—a relatively inexpensive investment. In addition, some bare bones audio editing software can be

found for less than $100, and at least one program is absolutely free. Audacity (www.audacity.sourceforge.net) offers a free audio editor with many of the key features of the professional programs. Check the end of the text for additional information on Audacity. With a budget of a few thousand dollars, any radio station should be able to build a desktop system and begin doing digital audio production work.

Basic editing programs allow you to set the sampling rate and bit depth using the sound card and software. Analog audio is accepted with a microphone or line level input on the audio card. The audio is sampled and converted to digitized audio as noted above. Each sample is recorded in order until recording is stopped. Using the software, the audio can now be edited, processed, or stored on the edi-

FIGURE 2.3 Audio editing software can transform an off-the-shelf computer into a desktop audio editor. (Left image from Audion Laboratories. Right image from Adobe Systems Incorporated.)

tor's hard disk as a **sound file.** Editing uses the mouse to define a **region** in a fashion similar to standard editing: that is, selecting a range (start point and end point) for each edit. In this case, the edit marks are made on the computer screen, which shows a "picture" of the audio (usually the actual waveform; see Figure 2.4) and can be easily moved, or trimmed, to the exact position desired. As shown in Figure 2.5, the portion of audio to be edited out is usually highlighted on the screen. Once edits have been made or the audio has been processed in another manner, the sound file can be saved on the computer's hard drive. These large audio files consist of an information header (noting sample rate, bit depth, channels, etc.) and the actual data (a long series of numbers; one for each sample). CD-quality audio at 44,100 samples per second times 16 bits of data adds up to around 10 MB for each minute of audio recorded.

One of the biggest advantages of this type of system is the *nondestructive* nature of the editing. The original audio isn't actually altered; edit information (where to start and stop

playing the audio) is recorded in an "edit decision list." Some systems execute editing that's *destructive* in that portions of the original audio are actually deleted or cut out; however, even these systems usually allow you to preview the edit before it's performed and undo it if it isn't marked properly. Most editing programs allow the recording of several "tracks" (just like a multi-track recorder) that can be manipulated individually, overlapped, and ultimately mixed together to provide a completely produced spot.

Although each program will utilize different techniques, you should find that they are similar in procedure. For example, to illustrate some additional digital production techniques, look at the *Adobe Audition* program. *Adobe Audition* has two main work areas. The "Edit View" screen (shown in Figure 2.6) puts the user in a single-waveform editor that is used to record, process, and edit mono and stereo audio segments. The "waveform display" shows the audio sound file and is utilized to edit or otherwise process the sound. The "transport" buttons control recording and playback functions of the audio. A "timeline display" shows

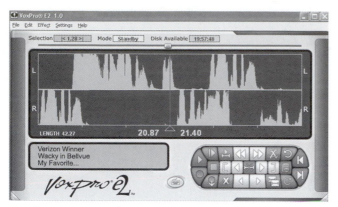

FIGURE 2.4 A sound file is pictured on the computer screen as the waveform of the audio, with the vertical axis indicating amplitude and the horizontal axis indicating time. (Image courtesy of Audion Laboratories.)

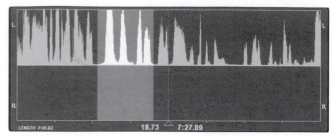

FIGURE 2.5 Audio editing can usually be accomplished with a simple mouse drag operation, with the area to be edited out highlighted. (Image courtesy of Audion Laboratories.)

timing information, and horizontal and vertical zooms allow you to scale the audio display to various sizes. Other options are available through either menu options or toolbar buttons.

Switching to the "Multi-track View" screen moves the operator to a multi-track hard disk recorder—capable of mixing and processing up to 128 tracks of audio—which shows the production being assembled, fine tuned, and ultimately finished. Other software programs will have similar screens and functions. Before you can record, you'll need to have an audio signal coming to the input of the audio card. In a radio studio, the output of the audio board is usually

sent to your audio editor so that *any* audio source in the studio can be plugged into the system. To start recording, mouse click on the "File" menu and select NEW. This will pop up a window (shown in Figure 2.7) that allows you to create settings that control the recording process. Key recording parameters include sample rate and bit resolution. As noted earlier, the higher the rate and resolution, the higher the quality of the recording. Most digital audio recording is done at 44.1 kHz (sample rate) and 16-bit (resolution), which is CD-quality audio.

You'll also need to select either mono or stereo recording. Click the OK button to set your recording parameters. To begin recording, click on the RECORD button on the "Transport" menu; click on the STOP button to discontinue recording. You can check recording levels by watching the "Record Level Meters" at the bottom of the "Edit View" screen. Double-clicking activates the meters if they

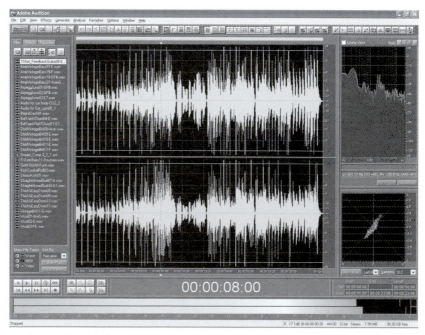

FIGURE 2.6 The main screen of an audio production software program shows various navigation and functional controls for manipulating the audio being worked on. (Adobe product screen shot reprinted with permission from Adobe Systems Incorporated.)

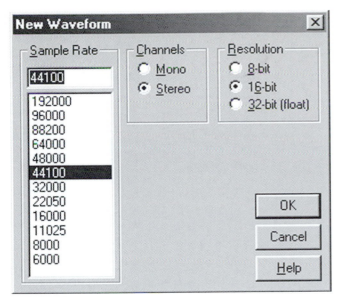

FIGURE 2.8 A personal audio recorder/editor has become a digital replacement for the two-track reel-to-reel recorder. (Image courtesy of 360 Systems. All rights reserved.)

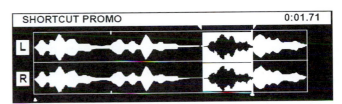

FIGURE 2.9 360 System's waveform display showing EDIT IN and EDIT OUT marks set; the highlighted area will be cut out when the edit is completed. (Image courtesy of 360 Systems. All rights reserved.)

FIGURE 2.7 Most audio editing software programs allow you to set the sample rate, bit depth, and other parameters prior to recording. (Adobe product screen shot reprinted with permission from Adobe Systems Incorporated.)

aren't already monitoring the audio amplitude. It's also probable that you can manipulate the source audio volume through an external control, such as the audio console noted previously. Once you've ended the recording session, you can immediately begin working on (editing) the audio. You'll find many additional recording features in the *Adobe Audition* software, but this should give you some familiarity with the basic recording techniques of a typical digital audio editor. Chapter 6, "Digital Editing and Multi-Track Recording," will further examine the techniques of manipulating audio with digital equipment or software programs.

2.4 THE PERSONAL AUDIO EDITOR

Another type of digital audio editor that *doesn't* need a computer, mouse, monitor, or special plug-in card enjoys a lot of use in the production studio. One example is 360 Systems *Short/cut*™ personal audio editor. This editor is configured in a compact, portable case (as shown in Figure 2.8) and records audio directly to its internal hard drive.

Beneath a small two-track waveform display are three distinct sections of controls. To the right are the basic transport controls (like play, pause, record, etc.); in the center are editing controls (like edit in, cut, erase, and a large scrub wheel); and to the left are the system controls (like hot keys, menu directory, and a QWERTY keyboard for labeling functions). Editing with *Short/cut* is as easy as recording or loading in a file, moving to the edit-in point, and then moving to the edit-out point (see Figure 2.9). The marked sec-

tion of audio will become highlighted and can then be removed, copied, or erased, or new material can be inserted. As with most digital equipment, if you make a mistake, an undo function will allow you to correct it. *Short/cut* has a selectable 44.1 kHz or 48 kHz sample rate, and the 360 Systems editor currently offers around 12 hours of recording time for stereo audio. Less complex than some of the PC-based audio editors, this type of audio editor has become a digital replacement for the reel-to-reel recorder and is becoming very commonplace in the digital production studio.

2.5 DIGITAL AUDIO WORKSTATIONS

A further extension of digital editing technology in the radio production studio is the development of the **DAW,** or **digital audio workstation.** These hard disk–based systems incorporate proprietary computer technology to convert the original sound signal to digital form, which can then be stored, manipulated, and recalled using the workstation. While some digital audio workstations are quite similar to the earlier mentioned desktop radio systems (see Figure 2.10), some do not physically look like computers at all (see Figure 2.11).

In either case, because the workstation has been developed as a dedicated audio recorder and editor, it often has

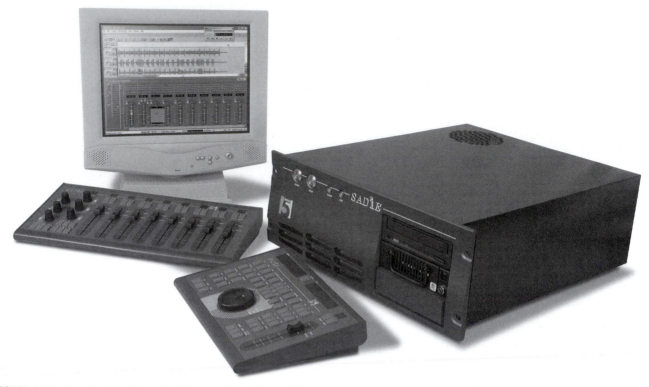

FIGURE 2.10 Some digital audio workstations resemble desktop radio systems but utilize specialized cards, customized boxes, and proprietary software. (Image courtesy of SADiE Inc.)

built-in specialized functions and features. The basic components of the DAW are similar to the elements that make up the simple digital audio editor mentioned earlier; however, DAWs are often packaged as a single unit similar to the one shown in Figure 2.11. A **frame** houses the computer chassis, power supply, and motherboard. An internal **hard disc drive** stores and manipulates the digital audio data. Remember, each stereo minute of audio will eat up about 10 megabytes; however, data compression techniques can greatly reduce the capacity requirements, and low-cost, high-capacity hard drives have made this almost a nonissue.

A **user interface,** such as a keyboard, touch screen, or mouse, is necessary to actually operate the workstation. However, many workstations have tried to be more user-friendly to radio production people by making the interface include typical radio production elements, such as faders, cue wheels, and tape transport buttons like rewind or play. Sometimes these interfaces are shown in graphics form on a computer screen, but other systems actually attach to a mini audio board (refer to Figure 2.11). A built-in audio card provides the connection between the workstation and the other audio equipment by converting analog audio into digital data and vice versa. Through the use of both serial and parallel ports, many workstations have the ability to net-

work with other workstations or interface with printers, modems, and other components.

But DAWs no longer hold a monopoly on innovative computer interfaces for audio technicians. There are now many USB devices, such as M-Audio's "Ozone," that provide user-definable control surfaces, such as faders, pan pots, and even a small keyboard, all packaged together with a quality sound card. Off-the-shelf software, such as Cakewalk's *Sonar*, provide integrated support for many third-party peripheral devices. Devices such as these have not only made professional audio production compact and affordable, they have also made it portable, as today's higher end laptop computers are more than capable of rising to the task of multi-track audio editing.

2.6 AUDIO SYNCHRONIZATION

With analog audio, the audio signals are constant streams with no specific demarcation points; however, digital audio has changed the audio environment. Digital audio signals are streams of digits broken up into digital words, as we noted earlier in this chapter. If two digital signals are out of sync, then one may just be beginning a new digital word when the other is in the middle of a word. Switching from

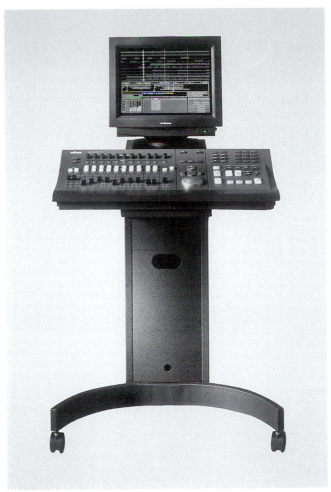

FIGURE 2.11 The swing to digital includes the use of the dedicated digital audio workstation, like Orban's *Audicy*. (Image courtesy of Orban.)

one to the other would result in an audible tick or pop. Synchronized audio signals start both new digital words at precisely the same time. Some digital production equipment is self-synchronizing, but digital audio consoles that accept many different types of digital inputs will need to synchronize audio to a common clock.

Most digital audio workstations and many other pieces of digital broadcast equipment also have the ability to incorporate MIDI and SMPTE synchronization. **MIDI (musical instrument digital interface)** is an interface system that allows electronic equipment—mainly musical instruments like synthesizers, drum machines, and samplers—to "talk" to each other through an electronic language. **SMPTE (Society for Motion Picture and Television Engineers) time code** is an electronic language developed for videotape editing that identifies each video frame with an individual address. The time code numbers consist of hour, minute, second, and frame. The frame digits correspond to the 30 video frames in each second. Both MIDI and SMPTE signals can be used to reference various indi-

vidual pieces of equipment and accurately start, combine, or stop them. Someone working in the production studio is more likely to make use of MIDI or SMPTE than someone in the on-air broadcast studio.

2.7 ADVANTAGES OF THE DIGITAL PRODUCTION STUDIO

One of the main advantages of digital equipment like the CD player or DAW is improved audio signal quality. The digital format offers superior technical specifications in the area of frequency response (see Chapter 3), dynamic range (see Chapter 7), and signal-to-noise ratio (noted in Chapter 1). **Wow, flutter,** and other forms of audio distortion are essentially nonexistent with digital technology. Not only does this provide an improved initial audio signal, but the digital process also doesn't build up any added noise during recording, dubbing, or transmitting.

Production people quickly realized that another advantage of digital editors like the DAW was the ability to utilize nondestructive editing. Not only does editing without using razor blades to physically cut audio tape provide a safer work environment in the production studio, it also allows you to preview the editing before it's finalized. Most DAW equipment has some type of undo button to put the sound back into its original form if you don't like the way the edit came out. Another operational advantage of the DAW is fast random access (the ability to immediately cue up at any point) to all the material stored in the system. Faster and easier operation of digital equipment should lead to less time spent on basic production functions and more time spent on the creative aspect of the production process. It is also easier to undertake many editing operations with digital editing than with traditional razor blade splicing. For example, if you must remove a very short segment, such as someone momentarily stuttering on a word, it's easy to do because you can both hear the problem and see the waveform of the audio. If necessary, you can zoom in to make the audio segment larger, and then remove the stuttering section accurately.

If you record something, but then need to make it slightly shorter or longer, you can do so easily with digital equipment. For instance, if you record what is to be a 15-second commercial and it turns out to be 17 seconds long, you can remove short bits of silence throughout the commercial to get it to 15 seconds. In fact, many digital audio software programs or workstations can do this time compression/expansion for you. You simply indicate how long you want something to be, and the program adjusts the material accordingly.

Digital equipment (see Chapter 5, "Digital Audio Players/Recorders"), such as the CD, minidisc, and digital audio cart recorders, offers a labeling function that's more convenient and comprehensive than paper labels. IDs and other types of label information can be encoded within the digital media. A table of contents can provide names, times, and other data through a front-panel window on the equipment or through the video monitor screen of a DAW.

Another technical advantage of digital is that there are fewer maintenance issues, such as dirty tape heads or alignment problems. Most digital equipment promises a longer interval between breakdowns than comparable analog equipment, and when there's a technical problem, digital equipment usually takes less time to repair. Since there are fewer internal operating parts, in many cases repair is a simple substitution of one circuit board or component for another. Often, digital equipment is smaller than the analog equipment it is designed to replace, offering a space savings that can be important in the smaller radio studio. For example, some minidisc recorders take up just a single rack space (a height of about 1¾ inches), and the 360 Systems *Short/cut* is smaller and more portable than the analog reel-to-reel recorder it was designed to replace.

On the other hand, when something goes wrong with a computer hard drive, for example, it's often not just the current project that is damaged or lost, but everything else contained on the hard drive can be corrupted as well. For this reason, the need for frequent backing up of hard drives cannot be overemphasized, especially if sensitive or long-labored-over material is contained on the drive. Computer programs also have a tendency to crash at exactly the wrong moment, erasing hours of work in an instant if the audio files you are editing or recording haven't been backed up. Most computer audio-editing software has an option to perform periodic automatic backups of files currently being worked on, either at timed intervals or after a set number of new edits. However, the automatic backup feature is not often turned on as a default after installation of the program, so it is worth looking in the index of the program's documentation for this feature so that you can enable it before you start working.

PRODUCTION TIP #2
Maintaining Digital Equipment

There are fewer mechanical elements in digital broadcast equipment than in older analog equipment, so maintaining that equipment is different. In addition to typical broadcast maintenance, computer knowledge is becoming more and more important. To keep your studio computers running in their most efficient manner, you will need to reboot every week to 10 days. Most computer programs, such as editing software, will cause the computer RAM to become fragmented as the program runs. You may not notice any problems with typical business

programs (like word processing) on computers that run during the normal workday and then are shut down until the next day. However, studio computers are often running 24 hours a day, every day of the week. RAM can become so fragmented that the computer will lock up, and that's a condition that you don't want to happen for a production or on-air computer. Set up a regular maintenance reboot during some station quiet time and you'll have fewer computer problems. In addition, memory management should become a regular part of your computer maintenance. As production work is accomplished, sound file fragments and completed productions may be left on the hard drive. But in a short period of time, hours of hard disc storage space will dwindle down to minutes unless old files are deleted from the system or archived onto a removable storage medium for later use.

Originally, the high cost of digital equipment was a definite drawback; however, the cost factor has decreased with continued development of digital technology, and today the majority of digital equipment is either less expensive or about the same price as the analog equipment it is replacing. Only the full-blown DAW systems or high-end digital multi-track recorders, at several thousands of dollars, would be considered expensive for some stations. The alternative—PC-based systems with consumer-grade equipment—offers the possibility of an entry-level approach to digital production, and many smaller market stations have taken this inexpensive direction.

2.8 DISADVANTAGES OF THE DIGITAL PRODUCTION STUDIO

The advantages of the digital studio far outweigh the disadvantages, but like any technology, there are a few minuses to go with all the pluses. One disadvantage of digital equipment is the learning curve tied to understanding the operation of various components. Although learning the basic editing functions of a minidisc recorder might be fairly straightforward, learning to operate a DAW in an expert manner can take longer, a factor that makes them somewhat user-unfriendly. Regardless of what manufacturers might claim, most digital equipment takes some time to learn, and production people must be willing to put in the time and effort necessary to pick up production techniques.

Most of the sound problems associated with analog recording are nonexistent with the digital process, but digital recording does have a unique, subjective problem of its own. The superior sonic quality of a digital signal is so clear and noise-free that some find it sounds harsh in comparison to the old "warmth" of analog distortion! It would be hard to argue against the superior sound quality that digital equipment provides, because it can be readily measured and compared to analog sound. Nonetheless, a criticism of digital sound still exists because, for some, the clear, brilliant sound has been likened to a "cold" or "mechanical" sound. For some people, the tremendous frequency response, dynamic range, and lack of noise and other forms of distortion add up to a sound that is just too stark. Of course, this judgment of sound quality is highly subjective, and for many if not most people, digital sound is just fine and highly superior to analog sound.

But there is a definite noise disadvantage of digital equipment—not audio noise, but noise from cooling fans in computers or disk drives. If this computer equipment has to be housed in a studio with live microphones, there could be a problem. Some production facilities solve this potential problem by putting the computer CPUs in a separate equipment room, leaving only the keyboard/mouse and monitor in the actual studio. If computer equipment must be in the studio, try to place it as far from the microphone as possible, and build it into studio furniture to minimize any noise. Laptop computers, though more expensive and not as powerful, are also an option to consider, as they cool their components through other means than potentially noisy fans. Another potential noise problem is the buzz or whine from the video monitor interfering with the speaker monitors or being picked up by the microphone. Shielding or creative placement might be necessary to make the digital studio workable in the normal studio environment. Flat panel LCD monitors, along with being more aesthetically pleasing and space-saving (and, of course, more expensive), also have little to no chance of producing any buzz or whine in studio components.

One advantage of the digital studio can, to a lesser extent, also show up as a disadvantage. It involves the space requirements of digital equipment. As we've noted, most digital equipment is smaller than the analog equipment it's replacing, but additional counter space for a video monitor and mouse might be necessary, along with additional rack space for hard drives and perhaps other digital equipment. For a time, digital hardware will have to coexist with some traditional broadcast equipment in most production studios. Of course, this will become less of a problem as older analog equipment is totally removed from the production studio.

2.9 THE ALL-DIGITAL RADIO FACILITY

The future of digital technology looks like more than just a very high-tech production studio. For example, most proponents of the DAW see it as part of an all-digital radio station (see Figure 2.12). Not only can the DAW-based system produce a radio commercial, but it can also store the commercial or several variations of it (while main-

taining digital quality), play the commercial on air by sending the signal to a digitized transmitter, and even send logging and bookkeeping information about the airing of the commercial to the appropriate station personnel. These types of systems are being used by more and more radio stations.

2.10 IS IT A SOUND SIGNAL OR AN AUDIO SIGNAL?

In the first chapter, we mentioned how sound acts in the audio studio. Before ending this chapter, it will be worthwhile to continue to look at sound since this will help you understand many aspects of the production process discussed in the rest of the text. Much of what happens in the production studio has to do with manipulating sound, whether it involves a sound signal or an audio signal. When sound is naturally produced (for example, when an announcer speaks into a microphone), we think of that sound (his or her voice) as a **sound signal**.

In radio production, when that sound signal is then manipulated electronically (such as recorded into a digital recorder), it's called an **audio signal**. Obviously, most radio production must start at some point with a sound signal, but during the actual production process, we are often recording and manipulating an audio signal. To further complicate things, these terms are sometimes interchanged when people talk about various radio production processes.

2.11 SOUND DEFINED

When something vibrates, sound is generated. For example, plucking a single guitar string causes a mechanical vibration to occur, which we can easily see by looking at the string. Of course, we can also hear it. The vibrating string forces air molecules near it to come together, slightly raising the air pressure and pushing those molecules into motion, which in turn sets neighboring air molecules in motion, and on and on. Thus sound develops waves (like a stone dropped into water), which vibrate up and down and set the air molecules in a push (**compression**) and pull (**rarefaction**) motion, causing an area of higher pressure to move through the air. So in addition to the vibration noted above, we need a medium for the sound to travel through. Of course, the medium we're usually concerned with is the atmosphere, or air. Sound can also travel through other materials, such as water or wood, but will often be distorted by the medium. Sound vibrations can't travel in a vacuum. Finally, for sound to exist technically, we need a receiver. Someone (a person) or something (a microphone) must receive it and perceive it as sound. The high-pressure area reaches receptors

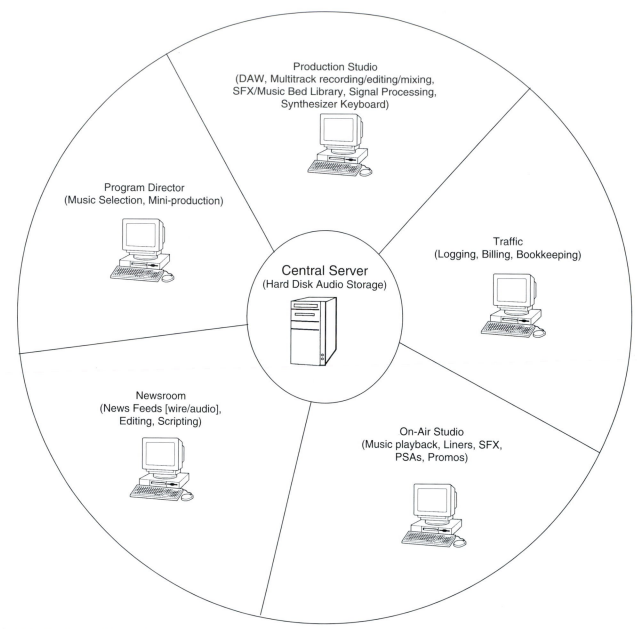

FIGURE 2.12   The all-digital station integrates digital audio production with other aspects of the facility's operation.

in our ear and we hear the vibrations as sound, or the pressure waves strike the diaphragm of a microphone, beginning the process of converting a sound signal into an audio signal.

Figure 2.13 shows a representation of sound being produced. We can't actually see sound waves, but they act very much like water waves as we've noted. The sine wave (shown in Figure 2.14C) is used to represent a sound waveform because it can readily show the wave compression (the higher pressure portion of the wave above the center line) and the wave rarefaction (the lower pressure portion of the wave below the center line).

2.12 KEY CHARACTERISTICS OF SOUND WAVES

There are four key characteristics of sound that help determine why one sound is different from another: amplitude, frequency, timbre, and the sound envelope. A sound wave's **amplitude** relates to its strength or intensity, which we hear as **volume,** or loudness. The loudness of a sound can be thought of as the height of the sound wave. The louder the sound is, the higher the amplitude as shown in Figure 2.14A. As a sound gets louder, greater compression and rarefaction of air molecules takes place, and the crest of

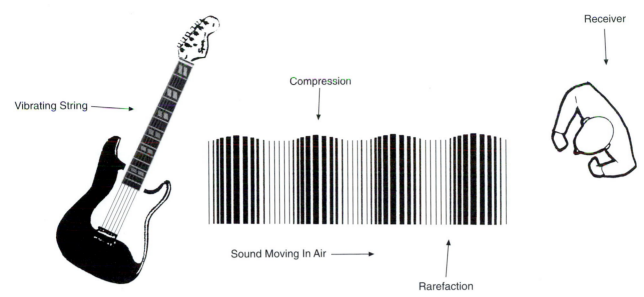

FIGURE 2.13 The production of sound requires vibrations, which are transmitted through a medium to a receiver.

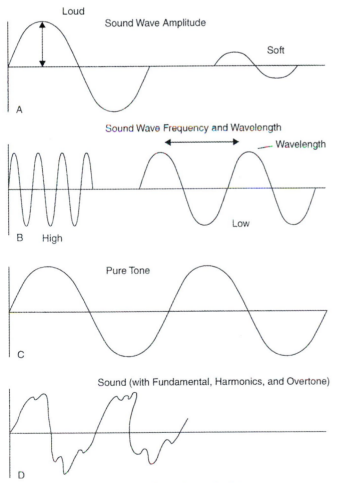

FIGURE 2.14 Characteristics of sound waves include volume, pitch, and tone, here visualized as sine waves.

the wave will be higher while the trough of the wave will be deeper. A sound wave's actual amplitude is readily measured; however, loudness is a subjective concept. What is loud to one person isn't necessarily loud to another person. Sound amplitude is measured in **decibels** (abbreviated dB). The human ear is very sensitive and can hear a tremendous range of sound amplitudes so the decibel scale is logarithmic. Near total silence is noted as 0 dB, a sound 10 times louder than this is 10 dB, a sound 100 times more powerful is 20 dB, and so on. Decibels represent the ratio of different audio levels and measure the relative intensity of sound. Sounds in the range of 0 Db (the threshold of hearing) to 120 dB (the threshold of pain) are detected by the human ear, but those sounds near and exceeding the high end can be painful and can damage your hearing. Any sound above 85 dB can cause hearing loss, but it depends on how close the listener is to the sound and how long he or she is exposed to it. The sound at many rock concerts has been measured around the 120 dB range, which explains why your ears often ring for a day or two after the show.

Frequency relates to the number of times per second that a sound wave vibrates (goes in an up-and-down cycle), which we hear as **pitch** (see Figure 2.14B). The faster something vibrates, or the more cycles it goes through per second, the higher the pitch of the sound. Like amplitude, frequency can be objectively measured, but like volume, pitch is subjective. In radio jargon, cycles per second are known as **hertz** (Hz). A sound wave that vibrates at two thousand cycles per second is said to have a frequency of 2,000 hertz. When the cycles per second gets higher, for example 20,000 hertz, the term **kilohertz** (kHz) is often used. It denotes 1,000 cycles per second, so 20,000 hertz could also be called 20 kilohertz. Humans hear frequencies that fall in the approximate range of 20 Hz to 20 kHz, but most of us do not hear sounds near the extremes of this range. A sound's **wavelength** is the distance between two compressions (crests) or two rarefactions (troughs). Sound wavelength can vary from around three-quarters of an inch for a treble sound near 16 kHz to around 36 feet for a bass sound near 30 Hz. There is an inverse relationship between wavelength and pitch, so higher pitched sounds have the shorter wavelength.

A sound's **timbre** (which is pronounced "TAM-bur"), or **tone,** relates to the **waveform** of the sound. It's the characteristic of sound that distinguishes one announcer's voice from another, even though both may be saying the same thing at the same volume and pitch. A graphic representation of a pure tone is shown as the shape of a sine wave, as in Figure 2.14C. Each sound has one basic tone that is its **fundamental;** most sound, however, is a combination of many tones with different strengths at different frequencies, so the waveform is much more complex, as shown in Figure 2.14D. These other pitches are either exact frequency multiples of the fundamental (known as **harmonics**) or pitches that are not exact multiples of the fundamental (known as **overtones**). For example, striking an A note (above middle C) on a piano would produce a fundamental tone of 440 Hz. In other words, the piano string is vibrating 440 times per second. The harmonics of this note will occur at exact (or whole number) multiples of the fundamental tone, such as 880 Hz (twice the fundamental) or 2,200 Hz (five times the fundamental). The interaction of the fundamental, harmonics, and overtones creates the timbre of any particular sound.

When sound waves combine, they will either be **in phase** or **out of phase.** If the peaks and troughs of two waves line up, they will be in phase and combine into one wave with twice the amplitude of the original waves. If the peaks of one sound wave line up with the troughs of another, they will be 180 degrees out of phase and will essentially cancel out, producing no sound or greatly diminished sound. Most sound (such as voice or music) is made up of a combination of sound waves that are out of phase, but less than 180 degrees off, thus producing the complex waveform mentioned above.

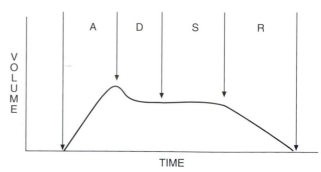

FIGURE 2.15 The sound wave envelope depicts the change in volume of a sound over a period of time.

A sound's wave **envelope** relates to its **duration,** or the change in volume of a sound over a period of time, as shown in Figure 2.15. Normally, a sound's wave envelope develops through four specific stages: **attack,** the time it takes an initial sound to build to maximum volume; **decay,** the time it takes the sound to go from peak volume to a sustained level; **sustain,** the time the sound holds its sustain volume; and **release,** the time it takes a sound to diminish from sustain volume to silence. In essence, decay, sustain, and release refer to the time it takes a sound to die out. Some sounds, like a percussive drum beat, have a very fast attack; other sounds, like a piano chord, have a long decay-sustain-release. Audio equipment must be able to accurately reproduce any sound wave envelope.

2.13 CONCLUSION

There seems to be little doubt that radio production has and will continue to change because of various developments in digital audio production. The whole industry is gravitating toward digital, and those who aren't embracing this technology will find they are left behind. Over the next few years, it's highly likely that digital radio will become the norm. A basic understanding of digital technology and the operation of digital-based equipment has become a prerequisite for success for the radio production person.

Self-Study

1. In which area is digital technology superior to analog technology?

   a) signal-to-noise ratio
   b) frequency response
   c) dynamic range
   d) all of the above

2. A standard off-the-shelf computer can be converted into a basic digital audio editor by adding appropriate software and what other component?

   a) an ESP audio card
   b) an ESPN audio card
   c) a DSP audio card
   d) an ASP audio card

3. In the digital recording process, an electromagnetic representation of the sound wave of the original sound source is stored on magnetic tape.

   a) true
   b) false

4. In general, a digital audio workstation's hard drive will require how many megabytes of memory for each stereo minute of audio the system is capable of handling?

   a) 5
   b) 10
   c) 15
   d) 20

5. Musical instruments (such as synthesizers or samplers) can interface with digital audio equipment through an electronic communications language known as what?

   a) Short/cut
   b) SAW
   c) MINI
   d) MIDI

6. Which stage of the digital recording process breaks down the analog signal into discrete values or levels?

   a) filtering
   b) sampling
   c) quantizing
   d) coding

7. Which of the following is one of the main advantages of the digital audio workstation in radio production?

   a) It's an inexpensive system to put together and maintain.
   b) It's easy to operate.
   c) It's capable of nondestructive editing.
   d) It offers better recording quality than a personal audio editor.

8. Digital audio workstations have the potential to introduce noise into the production process through cooling-fan noise picked up by a microphone and in what other way?

    a) video monitor interference picked up by a studio monitor speaker
    b) hiss picked up during the recording process
    c) clicks picked up at edit points during editing
    d) none of the above

9. The digital audio workstation has very little practical use outside the radio production studio.

    a) true
    b) false

10. Nondestructive editing is a feature of all desktop radio systems.

    a) true
    b) false

11. Why can digital recordings be copied over and over with no measurable loss of sound quality?

    a) The sound signal is a continuously variable electrical signal, the shape of which is defined by the shape of the sound wave produced.
    b) The original sound source is sampled over 44,000 times per second.
    c) It is binary data that is recorded, and this can be accurately copied.
    d) The laser beam is focused directly on the data track.

12. Most digital equipment promises a longer interval between breakdowns than comparable analog equipment; however, when there is a technical problem, repair time for the digital equipment will probably also be longer.

    a) true
    b) false

13. Which disadvantage of the digital production studio would be easiest to argue against?

    a) It can be difficult to learn digital equipment operation.
    b) The cost of digital equipment.
    c) The need for additional studio space for digital equipment.
    d) The sound of digital equipment.

14. Which digital sampling rate is used most frequently?

    a) 32 kHz
    b) 44.1 kHz
    c) 48 kHz
    d) 88.2 kHz

15. Which statement about sound is not true?

    a) Sound is generated when something vibrates.
    b) Sound, to technically exist, must be heard.
    c) Sound vibrations develop waves by setting adjacent air molecules in motion.
    d) Sound vibrations travel faster in a vacuum than in air.

16. Which of the following is not part of a sound wave's envelope?

    a) attack
    b) decay
    c) sustain
    d) rarefaction

17. The number of times a sound wave vibrates (goes in an up-and-down cycle) per second determines which characteristic of the sound?

   a) frequency
   b) amplitude
   c) wavelength
   d) wave envelope

18. What is the standard unit of measure to gauge the relative intensity of sound?

   a) signal-to-noise ratio
   b) hertz
   c) absorption coefficient
   d) decibel

19. Which digital audio editor has been touted as a replacement for the reel-to-reel recorder?

   a) Orban's *Audicy*
   b) Digital Audio Lab's *Card Deluxe*
   c) 360 Systems' *Short/cut*
   d) Adobe's *Audition*

20. Sound (such as an announcer's voice) that has been manipulated electronically (such as recorded on a digital recorder) is called a sound signal.

   a) true
   b) false

ANSWERS

If You Answered A:

1a. You're partially correct, but this is not the best response. (Reread 2.1 and 2.7.)

2a. No. You didn't "sense" the correct answer. (Reread 2.3.)

3a. No. This statement describes analog recording, not digital recording. (Reread 2.2.)

4a. No. Hint: This would work for a mono signal. (Reread 2.3 and 2.5.)

5a. No. 360 Systems' *Short/cut*™ is a personal audio editor, not a communications language. (Reread 2.6.)

6a. No. Filtering cuts off unwanted high frequencies before sampling begins. (Reread 2.2.)

7a. No. A DAW can be relatively expensive. (Reread 2.7.)

8a. Correct. This could be a problem with incorrectly positioned monitors.

9a. No. (Reread 2.9.)

10a. No. Some desktop radio systems have a destructive edit mode and actually delete the audio that has been edited, but usually only after a preview of the edit. (Reread 2.3.)

11a. No. This refers to an analog signal. (Reread 2.2.)

12a. No. Only half of this statement is true. Although digital equipment will probably break down less than analog equipment, repair time for digital equipment also promises to be shorter in many cases. (Reread 2.7.)

13a. No. Some digital equipment isn't very user-friendly and has a considerable learning curve. (Reread 2.8.)

14a. No. This is another sampling rate that some digital equipment is capable of utilizing. (Reread 2.2.)

15a. No. This is a true statement. (Reread 2.11.)

16a. No. Attack is the time it takes an initial sound to build up to full volume. (Reread 2.12.)

17a. This is the correct answer.

18a. No. While S/N is expressed in decibels, it measures the nominal output of audio equipment in relation to the equipment's noise level. (Reread 2.12.)

19a. No. The Orban *Audicy* is a full-blown, multi-track, digital audio workstation. (Reread 2.4 and 2.5.)

20a. No. This is not a true statement because once natural sound has been manipulated electronically, it is correctly called an audio signal; however, be aware that sometimes these terms are interchanged. (Reread 2.10.)

If You Answered B:

1b. You're partially correct, but this is not the best response. (Reread 2.1 and 2.7.)

2b. No. You might have just taken a "sporting" guess to get this answer. (Reread 2.3.)

3b. Correct. This is not digital recording, but rather analog recording.

4b. Yes. This is the correct answer.

5b. No. SAW is an audio editing software program, not a communication language. (Reread 2.6.)

6b. No. Sampling is when the signal is "sliced" into thousands of individual samples (voltages). (Reread 2.2.)

7b. No. A DAW is complicated and requires some time to learn to operate proficiently. (Reread 2.7.)

8b. No. Digital recording will add virtually no hiss. (Reread 2.8.)

9b. Yes. A DAW could well become the heart of a completely digital radio station.

10b. Yes. There are desktop radio systems that have both destructive and nondestructive edit modes.

11b. No. But you're heading in the right direction. Sampling rate is important for exact reproduction of the original sound, but it isn't really the reason why digital recordings can be copied over and over. (Reread 2.2.)

12b. Yes. Only part of this statement is true. Digital equipment repair time should be shorter than analog.

13b. No. While some digital equipment is costly, as more and more digital equipment hits the market, this is becoming less and less of a disadvantage. However, there is a better answer. (Reread 2.8.)

14b. Correct. This is the most common digital sampling rate.

15b. No. This is a true statement. (Reread 2.11.)

16b. No. Decay is the time it takes sound to go from peak volume to a sustain level. (Reread 2.12.)

17b. No. Amplitude relates to volume and the height of a sound wave. (Reread 2.12.)

18b. No. Hertz is another term for cycles per second and is a measure of frequency. (Reread 2.12.)

19b. No. The Digital Audio Labs Card Deluxe is an audio card that could be used with a desktop radio system. (Reread 2.3 and 2.4.)

20b. Correct. This is a false statement because once natural sound has been manipulated electronically, it is correctly called an audio signal; however, be aware that sometimes the terms are interchanged.

If You Answered C:

1c. You're partially correct, but this is not the best response. (Reread 2.1 and 2.7.)

2c. Correct. A DSP audio card is a standard audio interface for the PC platform.

4c. No. (Reread 2.3 and 2.5.)

5c. No. You're probably confusing this with the minidisc. (Reread 2.6.)

6c. Yes. This is correct.

7c. Yes. A DAW can offer nondestructive editing capability.

8c. No. DAW electronic editing is noiseless. (Reread 2.8.)

11c. Correct. Binary data can be accurately recorded over and over, making digital copies sound exactly like the original.

13c. No. It's true some digital equipment is smaller than comparable analog equipment, but usually additional studio space is required for keyboards, computer monitors, and so forth. (Reread 2.8.)

14c. No. This is another sampling rate that some digital equipment is capable of utilizing. (Reread 2.2.)

15c. No. This is a true statement. (Reread 2.11.)

16c. No. Sustain is the time a sound holds its volume. (Reread 2.12.)

17c. No. Wavelength refers to the distance between two wave compressions or rarefactions. (Reread 2.12.)

18c. No. Absorption coefficient measures the degree to which materials can absorb sound. (Reread 2.12.)

19c. Yes. This is correct. 360 Systems *Short/cut*™ two-track personal audio editor has often replaced the reel-to-reel recorder in radio production facilities.

If You Answered D:

1d. Correct. Digital technology offers all these technical improvements over analog.

2d. No. You got "bitten" on this answer. (Reread 2.3.)

4d. No. (Reread 2.3 and 2.5.)

5d. Yes. MIDI (musical instrument digital interface) is the correct response.

6d. No. Coding is when a series of binary digits are assigned to each individual sample. (Reread 2.2.)

7d. No. A personal audio recorder/editor and a DAW would both record with the same digital quality. (Reread 2.7.)

8d. No. There is a correct response, but this isn't it. (Reread 2.8.)

11d. No. While the use of a laser is an important part of CD technology, it is not the reason. (Reread 2.2.)

13d. Yes. This is the weakest disadvantage of digital equipment because in most ways, digital audio is obviously superior in quality to analog, and in other ways, it's a highly subjective judgment.

14d. No. This is not a common sampling rate. (Reread 2.2.)

15d. Correct. Sound vibrations can't travel in a vacuum.

16d. Correct. Rarefaction is not part of a sound's wave envelope.

17d. No. Wave envelope refers to a sound's duration. (Reread 2.12.)

18d. Right. The decibel is the standard unit or ratio used to measure a sound's volume.

19d. No. Adobe's *Audition* is a software program that could be used as part of a desktop radio system. (Reread 2.3 and 2.4.)

Projects

PROJECT 1

Using a digital audio editor or digital workstation, build a short music bed.

Purpose

To give you experience with digitally based recording and editing.

Advice, Cautions, and Background

1. Obviously, you can't do this assignment unless you have the hardware and software to complete it available to you.
2. CD music that you can use is provided on the CD-ROM that accompanies this text, but if you prefer, you can use your own music from some other source.
3. You'll be laying the same few seconds of music down several times, so select some music that will lend itself to this. Find a piece of music that won't sound like it has been cut off abruptly.
4. The project is written to make a music bed that is 60 seconds long.

How to Do the Project

1. Select music from the CD-ROM provided or from some other source and record a sound file of about 20 seconds onto your computer.
2. Activate your computer editing program.
3. Select a 10- to 15-second region of music from the sound file, and lay it down on one track made available through your computer editing program.
4. Lay the same material down again right next to the first region, and continue to do this until you have a 60-second segment.
5. Listen to the segment and improve upon it so that it could be used as a music bed under someone talking about a commercial product. You may want to change volume or edit to tighten it a bit. What you can do and exactly how you do it will depend on the computer program that you're using.
6. Record the music bed, labeling it with your name and "Digital Edited Music Bed."
7. Give the project to your instructor to receive credit for this project.

PROJECT 2

Record a basic "voice and music bed" commercial.

Purpose

To develop your skill in creating one of the most common types of radio spots.

Advice, Cautions, and Background

1. This project assumes you have enough familiarity with your studio equipment to accomplish basic recording and production techniques.
2. The production incorporates a single announcer voice and a music bed.
3. You will need to write a simple script that can be read in about 23 seconds. Write the copy about a desktop item, such as a ballpoint pen, stapler, or paperclip holder.
4. There are many ways to accomplish this project, so don't feel you must follow the production directions exactly.

How to Do the Project

1. Record the script (voice only) onto a recorder, such as a personal audio editor. Rerecord it to correct any vocal mistakes, to get the timing correct, or just to get it to sound the way you want.
2. Select a music bed that is appropriate for the style of the spot. You might use the bed you produced in Project 1, or you might find something on a production music CD, or on the CD-ROM that came with this text.
3. You can play back the music bed directly from a CD, or you may have to record it on another recorder.
4. Set correct playback levels for both the vocal track and the music bed. Both will start at full volume. Then cue both to the beginning sound.
5. Record your completed spot.
6. Start the music bed at full volume. Start the vocal track and simultaneously fade the music bed slightly so the vocal track is dominant.
7. As the vocal ends, bring the music bed back to full volume and then quickly fade it out as you approach 30 seconds.
8. It may take you several attempts to get the spot to come out correctly. If you need to do it over, just cue everything and try again.
9. Listen to the finished commercial. Make sure you've gotten a good balance between the music and the voice.
10. Label the project with your name and "Basic Radio Spot," and turn it in to your instructor to receive credit.

PROJECT 3

Write a report that compares various recording/editing software programs.

Purpose

To allow you to further investigate some of the computer software that is available for digital production systems.

Advice, Cautions, and Background

1. Prepare a list of questions that you want answered before you begin your research.
2. This project requires obtaining material through the Internet from various manufacturers.
3. The manufacturers shown below are not the only ones who produce audio editing software. You could also complete the project by looking at other programs.

How to Do the Project

1. Develop some questions that you want answered about audio editing software. For example:
   a. What are the computer system requirements for each software program?
   b. What exactly can each do in the area of radio production?
   c. How much do they cost?
   d. Are there any problems associated with these programs?
   e. What sample rate and bit depth does each program use?
2. Gather information by going to the web site of the manufacturers. (Some addresses are provided below.)
3. If your facility has this software or you know of a station in your area that does, try to talk with someone who uses it on a regular basis to further research the programs.

4. Organize your material into an informative report that compares the various software programs. It should be several pages long. Write your name and "Editing Software Programs Comparison" on a title page.

5. Turn in the report to your instructor for credit for this project.

Pro Tools

www.digidesign.com

Adobe Audition

www.adobe.com

SAW Studio

www.sawstudio.com

Sound Forge 7.0

www.mediasoftware.sonypictures.com

Sonar 3

www.cakewalk.com

Xtrack

www.digigram.com

Fast Edit

www.minnetonkaaudio.com

3

THE AUDIO CONSOLE

3.1 INTRODUCTION

In the modern studio, the spotlight is often on computer editing rather than the **control board**; however, the **audio console** is still a primary piece of equipment in most production facilities. It can be more difficult to understand than other equipment in the radio production studio, but most other pieces of equipment operate in conjunction with the audio console. Therefore, unless you can operate the audio console, you can't really utilize other studio equipment, such as a compact disc player or audio recorder. The broadcast, or on-air, consoles used in most radio stations are fairly straightforward in their construction and operation; however, some control boards used in audio production and music recording are much more complex with additional controls and features. Regardless of their complexity, all control boards have basic similarities. Even though you'll run across many different brands of audio consoles in your radio production work, a thorough knowledge of one control board will enable you to use any control board after a brief orientation.

Look at the audio console shown in Figure 3.1. Most boards, from the simplest to the most complex, include some method for input selection (such as A/B source selectors), and volume control (faders or pots) as well as some method for output selection (such as program/audition/auxiliary switches). They should also have some method of indicating to the operator the strength of the signal (through VU meters), and a way of allowing the operator to hear the mix of sources (through monitor/cue speakers or headphones). Boards also have amplifiers at various stages so that the signal is loud enough when it eventually goes to the transmitter or an audio recorder. These amplifiers are buried inside the board and are not something the board operator can usually control. In addition, audio consoles can have many other special features to help the board operator work more efficiently and creatively. The board may look intimidating because of all the buttons, knobs,

and levers, but most of these are repeats since the board has many different inputs and outputs. These will be explained in detail as we begin to explore the operation of the audio console.

3.2 THE DIGITAL AUDIO CONSOLE

Like most other audio production equipment, the audio console is facing transformation from analog to digital. The first generation of digital boards were quite a bit more expensive than the analog consoles they were designed to replace, which kept many stations from initially making the transition. Most current digital audio consoles are just slightly more expensive than their analog counterparts and often include additional features that justify any small extra expense. Some production facilities haven't felt the need for a digital board because many of their audio sources are still analog and a digital board wouldn't offer any particular advantage. However, as more and more studios become entirely digital, moving the console from analog to digital becomes the last step in building a totally digital audio chain. During this transitional stage, most digital boards have the capability to handle both analog and digital inputs with modular designs that include plug-in channels that can be easily updated from an analog to a digital format as the studio adds additional digital equipment.

There are several options for digital audio console design. Some boards emulate traditional audio consoles and are self-contained units as shown in Figure 3.2. The various audio sources are fed directly into the stand-alone console, which follows the most common wiring practice and allows console replacement to be a simple matter of "pick up the old, drop down the new." Other digital consoles are designed so that the "board" is merely an interface or control unit for an audio "engine" that can be installed in a rack in the studio or in an equipment room down the hall (see Figure 3.3). In this instance, the audio console works like

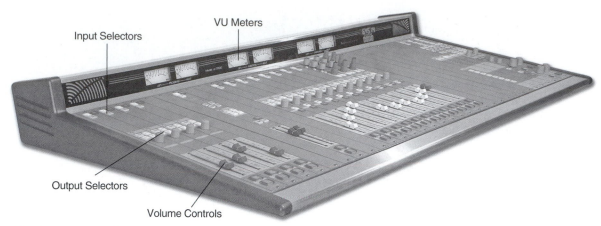

FIGURE 3.1 The audio console is important to the production studio because other equipment is manipulated through it. (Image courtesy of Wheatstone Corporation.)

the keyboard for your computer. The audio engine is essentially an router that accepts both analog and digital inputs with a capacity that greatly exceeds even the largest analog board. Generally, analog inputs are converted to digital signals, and digital signals with different sample rates are synchronized at the audio engine.

Rather than having a physical audio board containing individual input and output modules with multiple controls, the operator may also simply manipulate a "virtual console" on a computer screen, as shown in Figure 3.4. This is already common practice on digital audio workstations that include mixing functions and other audio software programs. Such virtual boards are often part of a digital audio storage and studio system, such as Broadcast Electronics' AudioVAULT, which is a complete suite of software modules. The primary sections include a control screen for live or automated announcer operation and a waveform editor, while additional sections incorporate traffic and music scheduling among other things.

Another feature of the new digital audio console is the inclusion of a touch screen interface (see Figure 3.5) or similar type of LCD (liquid crystal display) window. Because digital boards can be so readily customized to individual users, assigning different sources to different channels, a visual display helps with programming the board setup and operating the console.

3.3 AUDIO CONSOLE FUNCTIONS

Any control board has three primary functions: to mix, amplify, and route audio. First, the audio console enables the operator to select any one or a combination of various inputs. In other words, it must first be determined where the signal is coming from: a microphone, a CD player, or an audio recorder, for example. Audio consoles are sometimes referred to as mixing boards because of their ability to select and have several inputs operational at the same time. Much of the production work you do will be a mix of voice, music, and sound effects through the audio console.

The second function of the control board is to **amplify** the incoming audio signal to an appropriate level. Although all sound sources are amplified to a degree, some sound sources (especially microphones or turntables) produce such a small electrical current that they must be further amplified to be used. What is also meant by "amplify" is that the volume of an audio signal going through the console can be raised or lowered. You'll learn more about this

FIGURE 3.2 Some digital audio consoles feature a self-contained, modular architecture much like analog boards. (Image courtesy of Radio Systems.)

A

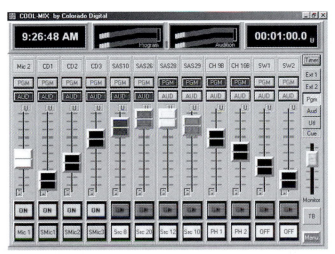

B

FIGURE 3.3 Many digital audio consoles can also feature the board as an interface (A) and a separate audio engine (B) that allows the electronics to be centralized in a rack or equipment room. (Image courtesy of Logitek Electronics Systems Inc.)

FIGURE 3.4 "Virtual" audio console controls emulate the functions of the traditional audio board. (Image courtesy of Arrakis Systems, Inc.— www.Arrakis-Systems.com)

FIGURE 3.5 Digital consoles also incorporate LCD panels. (Image courtesy of Klotz Digital America, Inc.)

level adjustment later in this chapter. The third function of the audio console is to enable the operator to route these inputs to a number of outputs, such as monitor speakers, the transmitter, or an audio recorder. This allows the operator to determine where the signal is going and to provide a means for listening to the signal.

3.4 BASIC AUDIO CONSOLE COMPONENTS

All control boards, whether digital or analog, operate in basically the same way. For the purpose of simplicity, let's consider a small audio console with just two channels; Figure 3.6 shows such a board. Each channel (M-1 and L-1) has two inputs (labeled A and B) so that, for example, a microphone could be assigned to channel M-1 (position A), while channel L-1 could have a CD player assigned to input A and an audio recorder assigned to input B. In general terms, a channel refers to the path an audio signal follows. On an audio console, a **channel** refers to a group of switches, faders, and knobs that are usually

associated with one or two sound sources (glance ahead to Figure 3.9). On the board in Figure 3.6, note the individual input selectors, output selectors, volume controls, and on/off switches associated with each individual channel. The cue, headphone, and studio monitor gain controls are associated with both channels, as are the VU meters.

3.5 INPUT SELECTORS

The **input selectors** on this particular audio console are pushbuttons that can be put in either an A or B position. This allows two different sound sources to be associated with each channel. Although channel M-1 and channel L-1 look identical, there is a major difference between them. Channel M-1 has been designed to accept only microphone-level inputs. Microphones generally do not have amplifiers built into them, whereas CD players and audio recorders have already put their signals through a small amount of amplification. When a signal from a sound source comes into channel M-1, it is sent through a

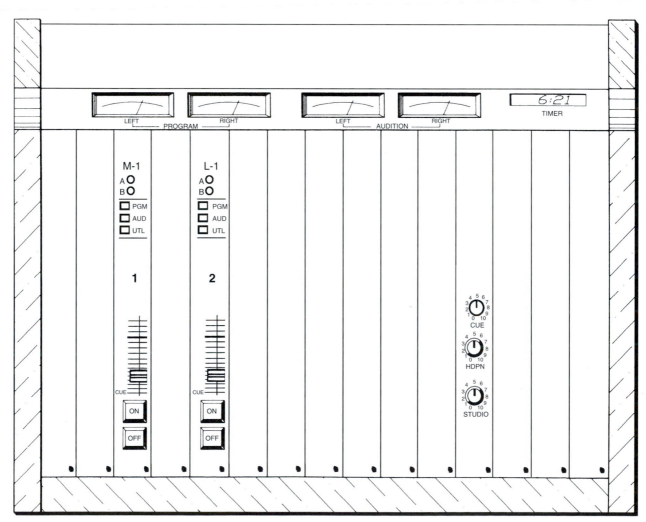

FIGURE 3.6   A simple two-channel audio console.

pre-amplification stage that is not present for signals coming into channel L-1. In other words, a microphone-level input allows a signal to catch up to a stronger signal coming into the line position in terms of amplification. Then both signals often go through additional amplification.

The way the input selector switches in Figure 3.5 are arranged, a microphone comes into the M-1 channel (A input), a CD player comes into the L-1 channel (A input), and an audio recorder comes into the L-1 channel (B input). Nothing is assigned to the B input of channel M-1. Wiring the equipment to the board involves running a cable from the microphone, CD player, and audio recorder to the back (or bottom) of the audio console. Such wiring is usually done in a semipermanent way by the engineer.

Not all audio boards have input selector switches. Some radio production boards have only one input per channel that must be at the microphone level, or other inputs that can only accommodate equipment that has been pre-amplified and is ready for a line level. On boards of this type, usually only microphones can be patched into the first two inputs, and only CD players, audio recorders, and other line-level equipment can be patched into the remaining inputs.

On the other hand, some boards have input selector switches that have three or more positions for one input. For these boards, it's possible to patch a CD player at position A, a turntable at position B, and an audio recorder at position C all into the same input. The use that the facility is going to make of the various pieces of equipment has to be carefully studied because, of course, no two pieces of equipment could be used at the same time on a single channel. Regardless of the configuration of an audio board, the first two channels (from the left) are often utilized as microphone-level channels. Channel 1 is normally the main studio microphone, and channel 2 is often an auxiliary microphone.

Digital audio consoles are changing the concept of input selection somewhat. Most digital boards allow the user to assign *any* audio source to *any* channel using a type of audio router, as shown in Figure 3.7. In other words, the console configuration can be personalized to each individual user, so that channel 3 can be associated with a CD player for one person, a DAT recorder for another person, and a microphone for the next person. Once the source is selected for any of the console's channels, the source name is usually displayed on an alpha display for that channel module.

3.6 INPUT VOLUME CONTROL

The input **volume controls** shown in Figure 3.6 are called **sliders,** or **faders.** They are merely **variable resistors.** Although they are called volume controls, or **gain controls,** they don't really vary the amount of amplification of the

FIGURE 3.7 On most digital audio consoles, any available audio source can be assigned to any one of the console's input channels. (Image courtesy of Wheatstone Corporation.)

signal. The amplifier is always on at a constant volume. Raising the fader (moving it from a south to a north position) decreases the amount of resistance to this signal. When the fader is raised and the resistance is low, a great deal of the signal gets through. The dynamic is like that of a water faucet. The water volume reaching the faucet is always the same, even when the faucet is closed. When you open the faucet (decrease the resistance), you allow the water to flow, and you can vary that flow from a trickle to a steady stream.

Some older boards have rotary knobs called **potentiometers,** or **pots,** instead of faders. These provide the same function. As the knob is turned clockwise, the resistance is decreased and the volume is increased. Some production people feel the fader is easier to work with. For one thing, the fader gives a quick visual indication of which channels are on and at what level. This is much harder to see with a rotary knob.

The numbers on both rotary knobs and faders may be in reverse order on some audio consoles to show their relationship to resistance. For example, if a knob is turned completely counterclockwise, or off, it may read 40; at a 12 o'clock position it may read 25; and completely clockwise, it may read 0. These figures represent decreasing amounts of resistance and thus higher volume as the knob is turned clockwise. Modern boards with fader volume controls often use a range of numbers from −55 to 0 to +10 or +15. While the same relationship to resistance is true (the more the fader is raised, the less resistance), these numbers actually relate to decibels and the VU meter. If the board has been set up properly, a 0 setting of the fader will produce a 0 reading on the VU meter. Some boards avoid using any numbers at all and merely use equally spaced indicator lines to provide some kind of reference for various knob and fader settings.

Of course, most boards have more than the two channels of our example board. In most radio production studios, boards have 10 to 20 channels, but there are smaller and larger boards. Each channel has its own gain control and with two inputs per channel, more than 30 individual pieces of audio equipment can be manipulated through the console. In professional audio production facilities, consoles with more than 20 channels are not uncommon. With the digital board's ability to assign various sources to channels, the trend is for smaller boards since you usually only work with two to four channels active at any one time.

In addition to the gain controls just mentioned, some boards have a **gain trim,** or **trim control,** that fine-tunes the volume of each input. For example, if the sound signal coming from a CD player has the left channel louder (stronger) than the right channel, a stereo trim control can decrease the left level or increase the right level until the sound signal is equal for both channels. Each input channel on an audio console usually has a gain trim feature, and often there is a similar trim adjustment for the program and audition output of the audio board. While these trim controls may be on the face of the audio board, they are often an internal adjustment that is taken care of by the engineer when the control board is initially set up.

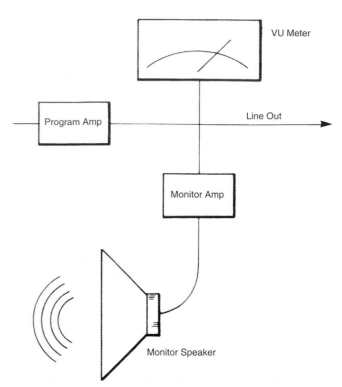

FIGURE 3.8 A block diagram of the monitor amplifier section of an audio console.

3.7 MONITORING—SPEAKERS AND HEADPHONES

Once the signal is through the input gain controls, it's amplified in a program amplifier and then sent several places (see Figure 3.8). One of these is a **monitor amplifier.** This amplifies the signal so that it can be sent into a **monitor speaker** to enable the operator to hear the signal that is going out. Boards usually contain a simple potentiometer to control the gain of the monitor speaker. For instance, our example board has a pot labeled STUDIO, which controls the volume of the monitor speakers. This control in no way affects the volume of the sound being sent out to an audio recorder (or transmitter, etc.). It only controls the volume for the person listening in the control room. A common mistake of beginning broadcasters is to run the studio monitors quite loud and think all is well, while in reality they have the signal going through the audio board (and therefore to a recorder or on the air) at a very low level. It's important for the operator to be aware of the level of sound going out the line.

Most audio consoles also have provision for listening to the output of the board through **headphones.** Since live microphones are often used in production work, the monitor speakers are muted when the microphone is on so that **feedback** doesn't occur. To be able to hear an additional sound source, such as a CD, headphones are necessary. Audio consoles often allow you to monitor any of the outputs with headphones by selecting an appropriate switch. There is usually a volume control to adjust the signal level going to the headphones. On our example board, this control is labeled HDPN.

3.8 CUE

Another function found on most audio boards is called **cue,** which allows you to preview an input sound source. Both rotary pots and fader controls go into a cue position, which is below the off position for that control. If you turn the rotary pot all the way counterclockwise to off, it will reach a detent, or stop. If you keep turning the knob (with a little extra pressure) it will click into the cue position. Faders are brought down, or south, until they click into cue (see Figure 3.6 again). Some faders can be put into cue with a separate pushbutton (see Figure 3.9) that, when depressed, puts that channel into cue regardless of where the fader control is set. Cue position is usually marked on the face of the audio console.

In the cue position, the audio signal is routed to a cue amplifier and then to a small speaker built into the control board. Since the quality of this small internal speaker is usually marginal at best, the cue signal is often sent to a small, but better quality, external speaker located near the audio console. Some audio consoles send the cue signal to the

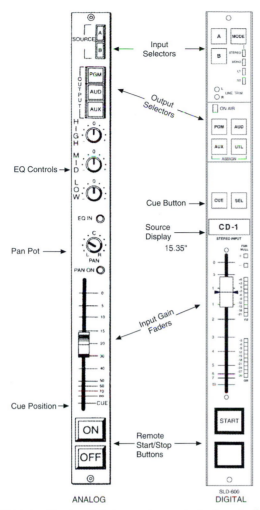

FIGURE 3.9 Whether digital or analog, a single channel of an audio console consists of a group of switches, pushbuttons, and a fader that can be used to manipulate a sound source assigned to that channel. (Image courtesy of Wheatstone Corporation.)

main studio monitor speakers. The program signal is automatically turned down, or dimmed, when a channel is put into cue and the cue signal is heard on top of the program signal. On our example audio console, the cue volume level is controlled with the pot labeled CUE.

As the name implies, this position is designed to allow the operator to cue up a sound source. For example, an audio recording can be cued to the exact beginning so that the sound will start immediately when the recorder is turned on. If an input is in cue, the signal doesn't go to any other output such as the transmitter or an audio recorder. Its only purpose is to allow off-air cueing. Many beginning announcers and production people forget to move the volume control out of the cue position after cueing up the sound source. If the control is left in the cue position, the signal won't go out on the air or be routed to an audio recorder. It will only play through the cue speaker.

3.9 VU METERS

Another place the signal is sent after program amplification is the volume unit indicator, or VU meter (see Figure 3.10). This is a metering device that enables the operator to determine what level of sound is going out the line.

One common type of VU meter has a moving needle on a graduated scale. Usually the top position of the scale is calibrated in **decibels (dB)**, and the lower portion of the scale is calibrated in percentages. In audio engineering, a reading of 0 dB is 100 percent volume, or the loudest you want the signal to go. The VU meter is important for consistent audio production work. As noted in Chapter 2, "Digital Audio Production," how loud something sounds is very subjective. What is loud to one announcer may not be deemed loud by another, especially if they each set the monitor speaker volume differently. The VU meter gives an electronic reading of volume that is not subjective.

The accuracy of VU meters is sometimes questioned in two areas. First, VU meters have trouble indicating transients—sudden, sharp, short increases in volume of the sound signal. Most VU meters are designed to indicate an average volume level and ignore these occasional sound bursts. Second, VU meters tend to overreact to the bass portion of the sound. In other words, if a sound signal is heavy in the bass frequencies, it will probably show a higher VU reading than it would if the total sound signal were being accurately read. In spite of these concerns, the VU meter remains the best indicator of volume levels in broadcast production.

Generally, an operator should control the signal so that it stays approximately between 80 percent and 100 percent. When the needle swings above 100 percent, we say the signal is **peaking in the red** because that portion of the VU meter scale is usually indicated with a red line. This is a warning to the operator to lower the gain of the fader or pot. Occasional dips into the red portion of the scale are likely, but having the needle consistently above 0 dB should be avoided. Sound signals above 100 percent are over-

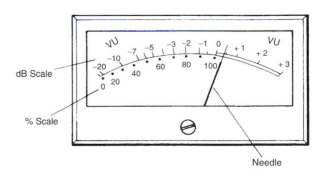

FIGURE 3.10 The standard VU meter incorporates both a percent and decibel scale.

modulated and can cause a distorted sound. Users of digital production equipment will quickly find that, unlike analog equipment, digital equipment is very unforgiving in regard to recording "in the red." Most digital equipment will not tolerate recording at any level above 100 percent and will distort or add "pops" to any recorded signal that exceeds it. Good production practice would be to record everything around −10 dB when using digital equipment.

Often there is a metal peg at the far end of the VU meter to prevent the needle from going off the dial. Allowing the gain to become so high that the needle reaches the upper peg is called **pegging the meter,** or **pinning the needle,** and should be avoided to prevent damage to the meter as well as distortion of the signal.

When the signal falls below 20 percent consistently, we say the signal is **under-modulated** or **in the mud,** and the operator should increase the volume. If it's necessary to adjust the level during the program, we say that the operator is **riding the gain** or **riding levels.** Gain is an audio engineer's term for loudness or volume. This is why a radio operator is often called a disc jockey. He plays record "discs" and "rides" the gain.

Our example audio board (review Figure 3.6) has a set of VU meters that indicates the left and right volume of the program sound going out and another set of meters that shows the audition output. Most boards have multiple VU meters. For example, they might have separate meters for each individual channel. Boards that have multiple outputs also have multiple meters. For example, a board that is stereo, like our example board, will have one meter for the right channel and one for the left.

On some boards, the VU meter isn't an electromagnetic meter at all, but rather is a succession of digital lights (LEDs, or light-emitting diodes) that indicate how high the volume is. Other electronic meters replace the LEDs with liquid crystal or fluorescent displays, and the advantage of these over mechanical meters is that they can indicate volume changes more quickly and accurately (see Figure 3.11).

FIGURE 3.11 VU meters with fluorescent or liquid crystal displays can indicate volume changes more quickly and accurately than electromechanical meters. (Image courtesy of Dorrough Electronics.)

3.10 OUTPUT SELECTORS

The most common arrangement for the **output selectors** on a radio production board is a bank of three buttons for **program, audition,** and **auxiliary** outputs. The example board in Figure 3.6 has this type of configuration except the auxiliary output is labeled UTL for utility. When no button is pushed in, the output is stopped at this point. When the program button is pushed (PGM), the signal normally goes to the transmitter if the board is in an on-air studio, or to an audio recorder if the console is in a production room. The program position would be the normal operating position when using an audio console.

If the audition button is depressed (AUD), the signal is sent to an audition amplifier and can then be sent to the monitor speakers, an audio recorder, another studio, and so on. The audition signal will *not* normally be sent to the transmitter. The purpose of the audition switch is to allow off-air recording and previewing of the sound quality and volume levels of a particular signal. For example, you could be playing a CD on one CD player through channel 3 of the audio console (in the program position) and at the same time be previewing another CD on a different CD player through channel 4 in the audition position. Each channel of the audio console can be used either in the program or audition position.

The auxiliary (**aux**) or utility (**utl**) position is just like either the program or audition position and is another output for the audio board (see Figure 3.6). For instance, some studios are set up so that the aux position of one control board feeds another studio and becomes an input on the audio console in the other studio. Unlike most input selectors, which allow only one input to be selected at a time, output selectors usually allow more than one output to be active. If all output buttons were depressed, you could send the same audio signal to three different locations at the same time.

The configuration of output selector buttons varies from board to board. If there are a large number of outputs—six, for example—then there may be six output buttons for each input. The input signal will be sent to whichever buttons are depressed, or selected. For instance, the microphone could be sent to the transmitter; the turntable, to a DAT recorder; and the CD, to a minidisc recorder. Sometimes there are no output selectors; every input either goes out or it doesn't, depending on the master volume control. Other boards have buttons labeled SEND that determine where the signal goes. Some boards just use a single toggle switch in place of push buttons. The functions are exactly the same, depending on which way the toggle is switched; if the toggle is in the middle, or neutral position, the signal stops at that point (just like having no button pushed in a three-button bank).

Audio boards are often referred to by their number of inputs and outputs. A 16-in/4-out board has 16 inputs and 4 outputs.

3.11 OUTPUT VOLUME CONTROL

There is no output volume control on our example board in Figure 3.6 that can be adjusted by the operator. Some audio consoles include a **master fader** that controls the volume of the signal leaving the board. Even if an input sound source is selected, program output is selected, and fader volume is up, if the master fader is all the way down, no signal will go from the console. Many boards have more than one output gain control. Again, a stereo board requires two masters, one for the right channel and one for the left. If there are multiple volume controls, then there's usually a master gain control that overrides all the other output volume controls. In other words, if the master is down, the signal won't go anywhere, even though one or more of the output volume controls are up.

3.12 REMOTE STARTS, CLOCKS, AND TIMERS

Other bells and whistles that frequently appear on audio boards include **remote start switches** (see Figures 3.6 and 3.9). These are usually located below each individual channel fader, and if the equipment wired into that channel (such as a CD player or audio recorder) has the right interface, it can be turned on, or started, by depressing the remote start. This makes it easier for the announcer to start another sound source while talking into the microphone without having to reach off to the side and possibly be pulled off microphone. For most consoles, these switches also turn that channel on and off. In other words, even if you have the fader for that channel turned up, no sound signal will go through the channel until it has been turned on. However, some consoles are set up so that they will automatically turn the channel on when the fader is moved upward.

Many control boards include built-in clocks and timers. Digital clocks conveniently show the announcer the current time (hours, minutes, and seconds), and timers (see Figure 3.1, 3.2, or 3.6) can be reset at the start of a CD or tape to count up the elapsed time or count down the remaining time. Many timers will begin automatically when an "on" or remote start button is pressed.

3.13 FREQUENCY RESPONSE

In radio production, we often mention the frequency response of equipment or, for that matter, the frequency response range of human hearing. In very general terms, we can think of the human ear as able to hear frequencies within the range of 20 to 20,000 cycles per second. For most of us, it's not quite that low or that high. In any case, radio production equipment, such as an audio console, should be able to reproduce an audio signal in that range, and most modern equipment is measured by how well it does so. For example, a monitor speaker may have a frequency response of 40 Hz to 18 kHz, meaning that that speaker can accurately reproduce all frequencies within that range. An inexpensive broadcast microphone may have a frequency response of only 80 Hz to 13 kHz. It would not be able to pick up any of the higher frequencies—those above 13,000 Hz. This may not be a problem if the microphone were used primarily to record speech because the human voice usually falls in a frequency range of 200 to 3,000 Hz. Obviously, if you wanted to record a musical group (which often produces sounds in the full range of frequencies), you would want to use a microphone with a wider frequency response. A frequency response curve is often used to indicate the level of frequency response because some equipment may not pick up or reproduce certain frequencies as well as others. Broadcast equipment is designed to pick up all frequencies equally well, so its response curve is considered to be **flat** if the equipment can't pick up certain frequencies, although few components have a truly flat frequency response curve.

Although there are no standard figures, the audio frequency spectrum is often divided into three regions: bass, midrange, and treble. The low frequencies (bass) are those between 20 and 250 Hz and provide the power, or bottom, to sound. Too little bass gives a thin sound, and too much bass gives a boomy sound. The midrange frequencies fall between 250 and 4,500 Hz. These frequencies provide a lot of sound's substance and intelligibility. Too little midrange gives a lack of presence, but too much midrange gives a harsh sound. High frequencies (treble) are those from 4,500 Hz to 20,000 Hz. The treble frequencies provide the sound's brilliance and sharpness. Too little treble gives a dull sound, and too much treble gives excess sparkle as well as increasing the likelihood of hearing noise or hiss in the sound.

As frequencies change, we think in terms of the musical interval of the **octave,** or a change in pitch caused by doubling or halving the original frequency. For example, a sound going from bass to midrange to treble frequencies by octave intervals would go from 110 Hz to 220 Hz to 440 Hz to 880 Hz to 1,760 Hz to 3,520 Hz to 7,040 Hz and so on. As humans, we are subject to an awkwardly named **equal loudness principle.** That is, sounds that are equally loud will not be *perceived* as being equally loud if their pitch is different—we hear midrange frequencies better than either high or low frequencies. In radio production (and other forms of sound manipulation), we often compensate for this by equalization of the signal.

3.14 EQUALIZERS AND PAN POTS

Many sound boards include simple equalizers (EQ). These increase or attenuate certain frequencies, thus altering the sound of the voice or music by changing the tonal quality of the sound. In some instances they help eliminate unwanted sound. For example, scratches in records are heard mainly on high frequencies. By filtering out these frequencies, the record could sound scratch-free. Likewise, a low rumble can be removed by eliminating or turning down low frequencies. Equalizers can also be used for special effects, such as making a voice sound like it is coming over a telephone. It's important to note that when you equalize a sound, you affect both the unwanted and wanted sound; equalization is usually a compromise between eliminating a problem and keeping a high-quality, usable audio signal.

Usually the equalizers are knobs or switches that increase or attenuate a certain range of frequencies. They are placed somewhere above each input volume control. In Figure 3.9, the input signal of the analog channel is split into three frequency ranges: high, midrange, and low. Turning the control clockwise increases the volume of that range of frequencies; counterclockwise rotation of the control will decrease its level. The "EQ in" button on this channel is actually a bypass switch that allows the operator to hear and compare the signal with and without equalization. Equalizers and other similar equipment will be discussed in further detail in Chapter 7, "Signal Processing Equipment."

Audio console channel inputs that are **monaural** (such as a microphone channel) often have a **pan pot,** or **pan knob.** By turning (panning) this knob to the left or right, you can control how much of the sound from that input goes to the right channel and how much goes to the left channel output. In other words, if the pan pot of a microphone channel is turned toward the L position, the vocal would sound stronger, or louder, from the left speaker. Normally, the pan pot would be in the center position and the input sound would be directed equally to the left and right outputs of that channel. **Stereo** input channels may have a **balance control,** which serves a similar purpose.

3.15 OTHER FEATURES

Some boards have a built-in **tone generator.** This reference tone is usually placed on a recording before the actual program material. The tone generator sends out a tone through the board that can be set at 100 percent, using the board VU meter. The VU meter on the source to which the signal is being sent (e.g., an audio recorder) is simultaneously set at 100 percent. After the two are set, any other volume sent through the board will be the exact same volume when it reaches the recorder. Having a tone generator allows for this consistency. Otherwise, sounds that register at 100 percent coming through the board might peak in the red and be distorted on the recorder. The tone on the recording is also used during playback. The audio engineer or board operator listens to the tone and sets the recorder VU meter to 100 percent. That way the recording will play back exactly as it was recorded.

Some audio consoles have a **solo switch** above each input. When this switch is on, only the sound of that particular input will be heard over the monitor. Other boards have a **mute switch** for each channel, which prevents the signal from going through that channel when it's depressed. A mute switch acts just like an on/off switch.

A few boards have a **talk-back switch,** which is a simple intercom system consisting of a built-in microphone and a push-button control that turns the microphone on or off. The normal position of this switch is "off" so that the button must be pushed in to activate the microphone. The signal from the talk-back microphone is sent to a speaker in another studio—for example, a performance studio—which would allow the operator at the audio console to communicate with the announcer in a studio at a separate location.

PRODUCTION TIP #3
Manipulating Faders

The type of transition you are planning to have can affect how you are operating the faders of your board. If you know you will be doing a segue, you can set the faders for the new sound you will be bringing in ahead of time by using the cue function. Then when it's time to take out one sound and bring in the other, you can simply hit the appropriate off and on buttons below the faders. That way you don't need to be concerned about getting the fader to the right position in order to have the new sound at the right level.

Working with the on/off buttons instead of the faders is also a good idea if you are doing a program where people are speaking. You can set the faders for each person's speaking level ahead of time and then, when the program begins, you can just push the "on" buttons and all the levels will be correct. This mode of operation is also advantageous if you are both talking and playing music. Set your microphone level ahead of time and then each time you will be talking, you can simply push the "on" button and not have to look down to make sure you have set the fader in the right position.

Of course, if you need to do a fade-in, fade-out, or cross-fade, this method won't work. For these transitions, you will want to have the "on" buttons already pushed and then bring the faders up or down to execute the fade.

3.16 SOUND TRANSITIONS AND ENDINGS

As mentioned early in this chapter, one of the functions of the audio console is to mix two or more sound sources together. Often this mix is really a sound transition, or the merging of one sound into another. In radio production, one basic transition is the **fade** (gradually increasing or

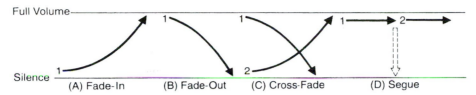

FIGURE 3.12	Sound transitions are used frequently in radio production work.

decreasing volume), where you mix one sound with silence. For example, to **fade in** a CD means to slowly increase the volume from silence to the desired level (see Figure 3.12A). A **fade-out** accomplishes just the opposite, as the CD goes from full volume to silence (see Figure 3.12B). Most compact discs are recorded so that they fade out at the end naturally, but in production work it's sometimes necessary to end a song early, and the production person can do so with a manual fade-out.

The other common transitions are the cross-fade and segue. As the name implies, a **cross-fade** occurs when one sound is faded down as another sound is faded up (see Figure 3.12C). There is a point as the two sounds cross when both sounds are heard. Because of this, care should be taken in choosing music to cross-fade. Some combinations of songs can sound extremely awkward. The speed of a cross-fade is determined by the board operator and depends on the type of effect desired; however, most cross-fades are at a medium speed to give a natural, brief blending of the two sounds. A **segue** is quite different; it is the transition from one sound to the next with no overlap or gap (see Figure 3.12D). A segue can best be accomplished when the first song ends cold. Music with a **cold ending** doesn't fade out, but rather it has a natural, full-volume end. Unlike fades of any kind, segues are accomplished with both sounds at full volume. Most disc jockey work is

a mixture of cross-fades and segues, but all the sound transitions are used frequently in radio production work.

In addition to the fade-outs and cold endings, one other music ending that should be noted is the **sustain ending.** Songs with a sustain ending will hold the final chord or notes for a short period of time and then very gradually fade out. This is distinctly different from either a normal fade-out or a cold ending. Music that is specifically designed for radio use will often have an indication of the ending—F (fade-out), C (cold ending), or S (sustain ending)—as part of the timing information about the song, found on the label or liner material.

3.17 CONCLUSION

If you have followed the descriptions and explanations offered in this chapter, the audio console should be a less frightening assemblage of switches, knobs, and meters than it was when you began. You should begin to have a good idea of how to operate each board and feel comfortable working with the controls of the board in your own studio.

You should also be aware that the audio console is becoming a digital board—one that you might manipulate very similarly to older analog boards, or it may be a virtual audio console that you maneuver with a few mouse clicks or a touch screen.

Self-Study

1. It's possible to have music from an audio recorder go into a control board and then come out and be recorded on another recorder.

   a) true
   b) false

2. In Figure 3.9, according to the pan pot position on the analog channel, what is the relationship between the sound signal going to the left channel and the signal going to the right channel?

   a) Left channel volume would be less than right channel volume of the same signal.
   b) Left would be the same as right (similar change).
   c) Left would be greater than right (similar change).
   d) There would be no signal going to the right channel.

3. If the digital fader in Figure 3.9 was at 3 and you moved it to 7, what would you have accomplished?

   a) amplified the signal
   b) put the channel in cue
   c) decreased the resistance
   d) decreased the volume

4. In Figure 3.6, sound on channel L-1 would not get to program out to be broadcast or recorded unless what happened?

   a) The fader is at 0.
   b) The PGM output selector switch is on.
   c) The HDPN volume control is at 3.
   d) The A input selector switch is set to CD.

5. Audible sound comes from what in Figure 3.8?

   a) the VU meter
   b) the monitor amplifier
   c) the program amplifier
   d) the monitor speaker

6. In Figure 3.10, a reading of 50 percent on the scale is roughly equivalent to which reading on the dB scale?

   a) −6 dB
   b) −4 dB
   c) 50 dB
   d) −10 dB

7. Which expression describes a 20 percent reading on the VU meter in Figure 3.10?

   a) peaking in the red
   b) turning up the pot
   c) being in the mud
   d) riding the gain

8. Which expression describes a +3 dB reading on the VU meter in Figure 3.10?

   a) riding the gain
   b) broadcasting in stereo
   c) peaking in the red
   d) pegging the meter

9. A line-level channel of an audio console would have what type of equipment assigned to it?

   a) CD player and audio recorder
   b) microphone and CD player
   c) microphone and audio recorder
   d) only microphones

10. Which choice most accurately describes the monitor/speaker?

    a) an input
    b) a mix
    c) an output
    d) an equalizer

11. Look at Figure 3.6. What happens if the PGM/AUD/UTL output selector switch of channel M-1 is in the audition position?

    a) sound will not reach the input A switch
    b) sound can be going to an audio recorder
    c) sound can be going to the transmitter
    d) sound will go to the cue speaker

12. Which statement about the master volume control on an audio board is true?

    a) must be up for sound to leave the board
    b) is required only if the board is stereo
    c) controls only the volume of the line inputs
    d) controls only the volume of the microphone inputs

13. Which control found on an audio console might be used to help eliminate scratches on records?

    a) the pan knob
    b) the gain trim
    c) the solo button
    d) the equalizer

14. Which statement about the cue position on a fader is true?

    a) allows sound to go to the transmitter
    b) sometimes substitutes for the trim control
    c) sends sound to a small speaker in the audio board
    d) allows sound to fade from the left to right channel

15. Which of the following can help assure that the level that's being recorded on an audio recorder is the same as that coming from the audio board?

    a) tone generator
    b) remote switch
    c) digital timer
    d) pan pot

16. Which of the following statements about digital audio consoles is *not* true?

   a) Digital consoles are more expensive than analog consoles.
   b) Digital consoles include some type of display screen.
   c) Digital consoles do not accept analog inputs.
   d) Digital consoles offer several design architectures.

17. Which sound transition occurs when a disc jockey fades down one CD at the same time as another CD is faded up?

   a) fade-in
   b) fade-out
   c) segue
   d) cross-fade

18. On an audio console, which term refers to a group of switches, faders, and knobs that are usually associated with one sound source, such as a CD player?

   a) input selector
   b) remote start switch
   c) channel
   d) output selector

19. A segue is the basic sound transition in which one sound is mixed with silence.

   a) true
   b) false

20. Most audio consoles used in radio broadcasting are identical to the consoles used in music recording.

   a) true
   b) false

21. Which feature of an audio console would allow the operator to alter the tonal quality of a sound going through the board?

   a) mute switch
   b) gain trim control
   c) equalizer control
   d) talk-back switch

22. How can a channel of the digital audio console shown in Figure 3.9 be put into cue?

   a) by moving the fader up to 0
   b) by moving the fader down to 7
   c) by depressing the START button
   d) by depressing the CUE button

23. Which feature of an audio console is a simple intercom system?

   a) talk-back switch
   b) tone generator
   c) pan knob
   d) output selector

24. Because of the complexity of the numerous buttons, switches, and knobs associated with the audio console, this is one piece of production equipment that is *not* likely to be moving from an analog to a digital configuration.

    a) true
    b) false

25. If you were attempting to segue from one song to another, how should the first song end?

    a) fade-out
    b) cold ending
    c) fade-in
    d) sustain ending

ANSWERS

If You Answered A:

1a. Right. A tape recorder can be both input and output and an audio console can link two recorders.

2a. No. Check the setting of the pan pot. (Reread 3.14.)

3a. No. The fader never actually amplifies the signal. This is done with preamp or amplifier circuits. (Reread 3.6.)

4a. No. When a fader or pot is at 0, it is usually on. (Reread 3.6 and 3.10.)

5a. No. This indicates level, but you hear nothing from it. (Reread 3.7 and 3.9.)

6a. Right. You read the scale correctly.

7a. No. The needle would be at the other end of the scale for this. (Reread 3.9.)

8a. No. "Riding the gain" means to keep the volume at proper levels, and this is not being done. (Reread 3.9.)

9a. Correct. Both a CD player and an audio recorder are line-level inputs.

10a. No. You're at the wrong end. (Reread 3.3, 3.4, and 3.7.)

11a. No. The input selector switch is before the output selector switch and really has nothing to do with it. (Reread 3.5 and 3.10.)

12a. Right. The purpose of the master volume is to allow all appropriate sounds to leave the audio console.

13a. No. This controls how much sound is going to the left and right channel. (Reread 3.14.)

14a. No. When a channel is in cue, sound will not go to the transmitter. (Reread 3.8.)

15a. Right. If the board VU meter and the tape recorder VU meter are both set at 100 percent tone, the levels should be the same.

16a. No. While the difference between the price of an analog board and a digital console is becoming less and less, many digital boards are slightly more expensive than their analog counterparts. (Reread 3.2.)

17a. No. This is a different sound transition. (Reread 3.16.)

18a. No. This is one of the switches involved, but this is not the correct term. (Reread 3.4 and 3.5.)

19a. No. You've confused this with the fade. (Reread 3.16.)

20a. No. While there are similarities between all audio consoles, those most often found in radio are more basic than those used in the music recording studio. (Reread 3.1.)

21a. No. This control turns off a console channel. (Reread 3.14 and 3.15.)

22a. No. This will turn the volume of the channel up. (Reread 3.6 and 3.8.)

23a. Correct. The talk-back feature allows a board operator to talk with an announcer in another studio via a simple intercom system.

24a. No. Digital consoles are already a part of production room equipment. (Reread 3.1 and 3.2.)

25a. No. A segue should happen with both songs at full volume with no overlap or silence between songs; if the first song fades out, this won't happen. (Reread 3.16.)

If You Answered B:

1b. Wrong. A tape recorder can be fed into an audio console and another tape recorder can be placed at the output. (Reread 3.3 and 3.4.)

2b. No. Check the setting of the pan pot. (Reread 3.14.)

3b. No. Cue would be even below the "infinity" mark. (Reread 3.6 and 3.8.)

4b. Right. When the PGM output selector switch is in the "on" position, normally sound would be sent to the transmitter or an audio recorder.

5b. No. This amplifies so that the sound can come out, but you don't hear the sound from it. (Reread 3.7.)

6b. No. You went in the wrong direction. (Reread 3.9.)

7b. No. If anything, the pot is being turned down. (Reread 3.9.)

8b. No. This is not correct. (Reread 3.9.)

9b. No. A microphone should come into a microphone input because it needs to be amplified to reach the line level of amplification. A CD player would be plugged into the line position. (Reread 3.3 and 3.5.)

10b. No. This is incorrect. (Reread 3.3, 3.4, and 3.7.)

11b. Yes. The purpose of the audition position is to send the sound somewhere other than the transmitter. Sound would not necessarily have to go to an audio recorder, though it could.

12b. No. A master volume control functions the same for both mono and stereo. Stereo boards, however, usually have two master volume controls, one for each channel. (Reread 3.11.)

13b. Wrong. This allows fine-tuning of input or output levels on an audio board. (Reread 3.6 and 3.14.)

14b. No. The two have nothing to do with each other. (Reread 3.6 and 3.8.)

15b. No. This will turn on the recorder remotely but will do nothing about levels. (Reread 3.12 and 3.15.)

16b. No. Whether it's a simple alpha display on the channel module or a full LCD screen, because they can be readily reconfigured, all digital boards have some type of display screen. (Reread 3.2.)

17b. No. This is a different sound transition. (Reread 3.16.)

18b. No. This is one of the switches involved, but this is not the correct term. (Reread 3.4 and 3.12.)

19b. Correct. The basic sound transition that mixes one sound with silence is the fade, not the segue.

20b. Yes. This is false because radio consoles are usually not as complex as the boards used in music recording.

21b. Wrong. This control varies the input level of a sound source of a console channel. (Reread 3.6 and 3.14.)

22b. No. While some consoles are put into cue by moving the fader down, it would have to go all the way down and usually "click" into a cue position. (Reread 3.6 and 3.8.)

23b. Wrong. The tone generator provides a reference level for setting correct recording levels. (Reread 3.15.)

24b. Yes. This is a correct response because digital audio consoles are readily available now.

25b. Yes. The first song should have a cold ending if you're going to segue into the next song.

If You Answered C:

2c. Right. The pan pot is set so that more of the sound from the input goes to the left channel.

3c. No. Changing the level from 3 to 7 would increase resistance. (Reread 3.6.)

4c. Wrong. The HDPN volume control only controls the volume of the headphone's audio. (Reread 3.7 and 3.10.)

5c. No. This amplifies sound, but you don't hear sound from it. (Reread 3.7.)

6c. There is no such reading on a VU meter. (Reread 3.9 and review Figure 3.10.)

7c. Right. "In the mud" is the term for an extremely low reading.

8c. No. It is worse than that because the needle is all the way to the end of the scale. (Reread 3.9.)

9c. No. A microphone should come into a microphone input because it needs to be amplified to reach a useable level. An audio recorder would be plugged into the line position. (Reread 3.3 and 3.5.)

10c. Right. Sound comes out to the monitor/speaker.

11c. No. The audition position is not normally used to send the sound to the transmitter. (Reread 3.10.)

12c. No. It controls all the sound that is set to leave the board. Line and microphone positions have no bearing on it. (Reread 3.5 and 3.11.)

13c. No. This allows you to hear one input channel by itself. (Reread 3.14 and 3.15.)

14c. Right. Cueing is just for the person operating the board.

15c. No. This is simply a type of clock. It has nothing to do with levels. (Reread 3.12 and 3.15.)

16c. Yes. Digital boards have modules that accept analog signals and convert them to digital.

17c. No. This is a different sound transition. (Reread 3.16.)

18c. Yes. This is the correct term.

21c. Right. EQ controls increase or decrease certain frequencies of the sound, thus changing the tone.

22c. No. If the fader was up, this would let us hear audio, but not in cue. (Reread 3.8 and 3.12.)

23c. Wrong. Pan pots control the amount of sound that goes to the left or right output of a channel. (Reread 3.14 and 3.15.)

25c. No. You're confused here; a fade-in isn't a way a song ends. (Reread 3.16.)

If You Answered D:

2d. No. That would not be correct. (Reread 3.14.)

3d. Right. This is an increase in resistance to the signal; not as much of the signal gets through, and it's at a lower volume.

4d. Wrong. It wouldn't matter if the A input was assigned to a CD, audio recorder, or some other piece of equipment. (Reread 3.5 and 3.10.)

5d. Right. You hear sound from the monitor speaker.

6d. You might be thinking of half of the dB scale, but that isn't correct. (Reread 3.9.)

7d. No. If anything, the operator is not properly riding the gain. (Reread 3.9.)

8d. Right. "Pegging" the meter is correct. We could also have used the term "pinning the needle."

9d. Wrong. Microphone signals must be amplified to reach line level and should only come into a microphone input. (Reread 3.3 and 3.5.)

10d. No. An equalizer affects frequencies. (Reread 3.3, 3.4, 3.7, and 3.14.)

11d. Wrong. The cue speaker will be activated when a channel is put into cue, regardless of where the PGM/AUD/UTL switch is. (Reread 3.8 and 3.10.)

12d. No. It controls all the sound that is set to leave the board. Microphone and line positions have no bearing on it. (Reread 3.5 and 3.11.)

13d. Right. This can help eliminate high frequencies where scratches reside.

14d. No. You're confusing this with a pan pot. (Reread 3.8 and 3.14.)

15d. No. This allows sound to fade from the left to right channel. (Reread 3.14 and 3.15.)

16d. Wrong. Digital boards have more than one design approach, for example, the mainframe and control-surface system. (Reread 3.2.)

17d. Yes. This is the correct response.

18d. No. This is one of the switches involved, but this is not the correct term. (Reread 3.4 and 3.10.)

21d. Wrong. This control is a form of studio intercom. (Reread 3.14 and 3.15.)

22d. Yes. On this console, any channel can be put into cue merely by pressing the cue button associated with that channel, regardless of where other switches or buttons are set.

23d. Wrong. Output selectors determine where sound goes when it leaves the audio console. (Reread 3.10 and 3.15.)

25d. No. A segue should have no overlap or silence between songs; if the first song has a sustain ending, this won't happen. (Reread 3.16.)

Projects

PROJECT 1

Learn to operate an audio console.

Purpose

To make you somewhat proficient at some of the functions of the audio console, and to practice basic sound transitions.

Advice, Cautions, and Background

1. Audio boards are generally one of the more complicated pieces of equipment in a radio station. It may take you a while to master a board, but don't despair. Take it slowly, and don't be afraid to ask for help.
2. Audio boards all have the same general purpose. Sounds come into the board, are mixed together, and are sent out to somewhere else.
3. The actual exercise should be done as quickly as possible. You won't be judged on aesthetics. In other words, when you're fading from one source to another, do it quickly. Don't wait for the proper musical beat, phrase, or pause.

How to Do the Project

1. Familiarize yourself with the operation of the audio console in your production studio. Learn the inputs, the outputs, the method for changing volume, and other special features of the board.
2. As soon as you feel you understand the board, do the following exercise as rapidly as possible while recording it on an audio recorder. Practice as much as you like first.
   a. Cue up a CD, play part of it, and fade it out.
   b. Using the studio microphone, announce your name and the current time.
   c. Begin a second CD.
   d. Cross-fade to another CD, and then fade it out.
   e. Bring in an auxiliary microphone, and ad-lib with another announcer.
   f. Fade in either a record or a CD, segue to another CD, and fade it out.
   g. Announce something clever on the studio microphone.
3. Listen to your recording to make sure it recorded properly.
4. Label your recording "Audio Console Operation" and include your name. Hand the assignment in to your instructor to receive credit for the project.

PROJECT 2

Diagram and label an audio board.

Purpose

To familiarize you with the positioning of the various switches and controls so that you can access them quickly.

Advice, Cautions, and Background

1. Some boards are very complicated and have more functions than are discussed in this chapter. Usually, this is because they're intended to be used for sound recording of music. If you have such a board, you only need to label the parts that you will be using frequently.

2. If you can't find controls for all of the functions given in this chapter, ask for help. Because there are so many different brands and types of boards, sometimes functions are combined or located in places where you cannot identify them easily.
3. You don't need to label each switch and knob. If your board has 10 inputs, it will obviously have 10 channel-volume controls. You can circle them all and label them together, or make one label that says "Input Volume Controls" and draw arrows to all 10.
4. You will be judged on the completeness and accuracy of your drawing. You won't be graded on artistic ability, but be as clear as possible.

How to Do the Project

1. Sketch the audio console in your production studio.
2. Label all the basic parts: input selectors, channel gain controls, VU meters, output selectors, and master gain controls (if your board has them).
3. Also label any other parts of the board that you will be using frequently, such as equalizers, cue positions, and headphone connections.
4. Label your sketch with your name and the title, "Audio Console Diagram." Give your completed drawing to the instructor for credit for this project.

PROJECT 3

Record a two-voice commercial.

Purpose

To develop your skill in creating a radio spot while working with another announcer.

Advice, Cautions, and Background

1. This project assumes that you have enough familiarity with your studio equipment to accomplish basic recording and production techniques.
2. The production incorporates two announcer voices and a music bed.
3. You will need to write a dialogue script that can be read in about 23 seconds. You might write copy about a restaurant you eat at frequently or some cosmetic or health product you are familiar with.
4. There are many ways to accomplish this project, so don't feel you must follow the production directions exactly.

How to Do the Project

1. Record the script (voices only) onto a recorder, such as a reel-to-reel or digital recorder. Make sure both voices are close to the same volume level. Rerecord to correct mistakes or just to get it to sound the way you want.
2. Select a music bed that is appropriate for the style of the spot. You might find something on the CD-ROM that accompanies this text.
3. You can play back the music bed directly from a CD, or you may have to record it on another recorder.
4. Set correct playback levels for both the vocal track and the music bed. Both will start at full volume. Then cue both to the beginning sound.
5. Record your completed spot onto an audio cassette, so set your cassette recorder to record mode.
6. Begin recording. Start the music bed at full volume. Start the vocal track and simultaneously fade the music bed slightly so the vocal track is dominant.
7. As the vocal ends, bring the music bed back to full volume and then quickly fade it out as you approach 30 seconds.

8. It may take you several attempts to get the spot to come out correctly. If you need to do it over, just cue everything and try again.

9. Listen to the finished commercial. Make sure you've gotten a good balance between the music and the voice and all recording levels are proper.

10. Label the assignment with your name/s and "Two-Voice Radio Spot." Turn it in to your instructor to receive credit for this project.

4

MICROPHONES

4.1 INTRODUCTION

In radio production, the studio microphone (see Figure 4.1) takes on an important role because it's the first element in the audio chain. It's the piece of equipment that changes the announcer's voice into an electrical signal that can then be mixed with other sound sources and sent to a recorder or broadcast over the air. Because the purpose of the microphone is to change sound energy into electrical energy, it's called a **transducer,** which is a device that converts one form of energy into another.

Unlike much of the other studio equipment, microphones are generally analog based, although some digital microphones are now on the market. Putting an A/D (analog-to-digital) converter in an external microphone preamplifier or immediately after the microphone in the audio chain could quickly transform *any* microphone's electrical output to a digital signal. One manufacturer, beyerdynamic, offers a digital microphone with the preamp and analog-to-digital converter built into the microphone housing. In both instances noted above, the sound signal is changed to an analog signal by the microphone, and then that signal is changed into a digital signal. Another manufacturer, National Semiconductor, has developed an integrated circuit that converts a microphone sound signal *directly* into a digital bit stream output signal. Used in conjunction with an electret condenser microphone, it would truly be a digital microphone. While such microphones are not yet in general use in the broadcast studio, it's highly likely we'll see more digital microphone developments in the not-too-distant future.

4.2 CLASSIFYING MICROPHONES

There is no one correct microphone to use in radio production work, but specific types of microphones will work better than others in certain situations. For example, a microphone that is perfect for voice-over work in the studio may not work well for recording a sound effect in the field. Microphones are usually described by two key specifications—their electrical operation and their pickup pattern. Categorized by their internal, sound-generating element, there are two types of microphones commonly used in radio: the dynamic microphone and the condenser microphone. When considering their pickup patterns, there are also two main types: omnidirectional and cardioid. In both instances, as you will see, these are not the only types.

There are two schools of thought in selecting microphones for the radio studio. One is to use a standard microphone throughout the facility. The other approach is to have multiple microphones available. One method isn't necessarily better than the other, but you'll probably find more studios use multiple microphones than a single standard microphone for the entire facility.

4.3 DYNAMIC MICROPHONES

The **dynamic microphone** is sometimes known as the **moving-coil microphone** or occasionally as the **pressure microphone.** This microphone's sound-generating element is constructed of a diaphragm, a magnet assembly, and a voice coil, as shown in Figure 4.2. The flexible diaphragm (usually thin plastic), which responds to the pressure of the sound, is positioned so the attached small wire coil is within the field of a permanent magnet. Movements of the diaphragm caused by sound waves result in a disturbance of the magnetic field, and this induces a small electric current into the coil of wire, which is the audio output signal. In Chapter 8, "Monitor Speakers, Cables, Connectors, and Studio Accessories," you'll see that the basic loudspeaker consists of similar elements and works much like a dynamic microphone in reverse when changing electrical energy into sound energy.

FIGURE 4.1 The studio microphone changes the announcer's voice into an electrical signal. (Image courtesy of Neumann USA.)

The dynamic microphone is very commonly used in radio and has many advantages that make it so popular. Because of its relatively simple construction, it is a modestly priced microphone that produces very low self-noise and has excellent **frequency response** so that both highs and lows reproduce accurately. But the main reason it has seen such acceptance by broadcasters is its sturdy design. The dynamic microphone can withstand a moderate amount of abuse, which often occurs in the broadcast setting. Dynamic microphones can handle extremely high sound

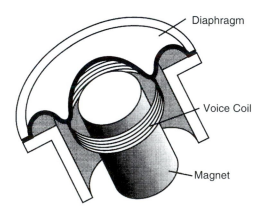

FIGURE 4.2 The internal components of a dynamic microphone include a diaphragm, magnet, and voice coil. (Image courtesy of Shure Incorporated.)

levels, making it almost impossible to overload them. This style of microphone is also fairly insensitive to wind, and this, along with its ruggedness, makes it an excellent remote microphone. The dynamic microphone can be used in most broadcast situations—as a stand microphone, a hand-held microphone, or a lavalier (a small microphone hung around the neck or clipped to clothing below the neck).

The main disadvantage of the dynamic microphone is that it does not satisfactorily reproduce certain voices. With some announcers, the microphone exaggerates plosives (popping on *p*) and sibilance (hissing on *s*). Dynamic microphones also can lose some light, delicate sounds because the mass of the diaphragm requires a fairly high sound level to move it. Even though the dynamic microphone is fairly rugged, all microphones are fragile to some extent and should be handled with care like any other piece of audio production equipment.

Beginning announcers often misuse a microphone by blowing into it to see if it's live or to set a level. This is the worst way to test a microphone and can result in serious damage to the microphone. In fact, the higher the quality of the microphone, the more likely that it *will* be damaged in this manner. The best way to set a microphone level is to read several sentences of your script or ad-lib some material into the microphone. If you just count (such as saying, "Testing . . . 1 . . . 2 . . . 3 . . .") or simply say "check" over and over, you're really not getting enough constant sound to set an accurate level. Also, most people don't count or say a single word in quite the same tone and volume as when they speak several sentences.

4.4 CONDENSER MICROPHONES

The other common type of broadcast microphone is the **condenser microphone.** Also known as a **capacitor microphone,** it uses an electronic component—the capacitor—to respond to the sound. The sound-generating element consists of a charged conductive diaphragm and an oppositely charged metallic backplate separated by an insulating material that creates an air space between them and forms a sound-sensitive capacitor (see Figure 4.3). The thin metal, or metal-coated, plastic diaphragm responds to sound waves, changing the distance between the diaphragm and the backplate; this alteration changes the capacitance (resistance to electrical voltage build-up) and generates a small electrical signal that is further amplified within the electronics of the microphone. This fluctuation of electrical current is the audio output signal.

The condenser microphone requires a power supply, such as a battery, to charge the backplate and diaphragm and related electronic components. Because batteries used to be large and cumbersome, early condenser microphones were both inconvenient and expensive. Today's condenser microphones utilize small internal power supplies or **phantom power** supplies. The latter usually comes from a recorder or an audio board through the microphone cable and back to the microphone. Because all condenser

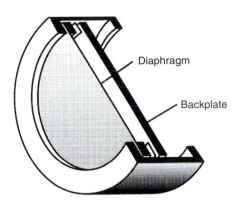

Condenser Microphone

FIGURE 4.3 The internal components of a condenser microphone include two oppositely charged plates—a moveable diaphragm and a fixed backplate. (Image courtesy of Shure Incorporated.)

microphones are powered, the electronics of the microphone can produce a little noise, and there is a limit to the sound level signal the microphone can handle. Still, the condenser microphone is an excellent radio microphone because it's fairly rugged and produces excellent sound quality and wide frequency response. Although the dynamic microphone is the most used radio production microphone, the condenser microphone is also frequently found in the modern radio production studio. In addition, the built-in microphone on many portable audio recorders is often a condenser microphone that provides fairly good quality on both consumer and professional models.

Another form of condenser microphone is the **electret microphone.** Its capacitor is permanently charged during manufacture, but it still needs a power supply (albeit much less power) for its electronic circuit. The lower power requirement offers some flexibility in usage, but the electret microphone possesses less dynamic range than the regular condenser microphone, so you may not find an electret microphone in many radio production studios.

4.5 OTHER MICROPHONES

There are other types of microphones, but they are less likely to be encountered in the broadcast studio. For many years the **ribbon microphone** was common in broadcasting. Another form of a dynamic microphone, the ribbon microphone contains a sound-generating element that consists of a thin, corrugated metallic ribbon suspended in the field of a magnet. Sound waves vibrating the ribbon generate an electrical output signal. The ribbon microphone has an excellent warm, smooth sound, but it is bulky and fragile and has been largely replaced by the condenser microphone, which has a similar high-quality sound.

A **regulated phase microphone** can be thought of as part dynamic and part ribbon microphone. A wire coil is attached

to or impressed into the surface of a circular diaphragm. The diaphragm is suspended between two circular magnets that are designed to be acoustically transparent. In other words, the magnets don't impede the sound waves striking the diaphragm in any way. An electrical current is generated as sound waves vibrate the diaphragm. Because of its design, the regulated phase microphone exhibits some of the qualities of a ribbon microphone with some of the ruggedness of the dynamic microphone. This microphone is used more in the recording industry than in radio, but you may run across one in some production studios.

4.6 SPECIAL-PURPOSE MICROPHONES

There are other microphone types, but these are not based on internal sound-generating elements. In fact, these microphones usually employ one of the basic designs mentioned in the previous sections; however, they are often designed for a specific usage and are frequently considered to be another variety of microphone. For example, the **lavalier microphone** (see Figure 4.4) mentioned previously is a tiny microphone that can be unobtrusively clipped to an announcer's lapel or tie. There are both dynamic and condenser models, and although the lavalier microphone is occasionally used in a radio remote situation, its small size makes it more appropriate for television than radio.

A **stereo microphone** like the one shown in Figure 4.5 incorporates small, multiple sound-generating elements as part of a single microphone housing that can duplicate the various stereo microphone techniques. You'll learn more about these methods later in this chapter.

FM microphones—also known as **RF** (radio frequency), **wireless,** and **radio microphones**—are used occasionally in radio production situations when a microphone cable might hinder the recording or production. A wireless microphone is really a system—a microphone, a radio

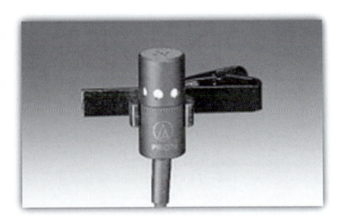

FIGURE 4.4 Because of their unobtrusive design, lavalier microphones are more appropriate for television than radio. (Image courtesy of Audio-Technica U.S., Inc.)

FIGURE 4.5 Stereo microphones often employ multiple sound-generating elements as part of a single microphone. (Image courtesy of RODE Microphones.)

transmitter, and a radio receiver (see Figure 4.6). The audio signal generated (employing either a dynamic or condenser element) is sent out from the microphone by a low-power transmitter rather than a microphone cable. This transmitter is either in the microphone housing or contained in a small pack designed to be worn by the announcer. The transmitted signal is picked up by a receiver located nearby and converted from a radio frequency signal back into an audio signal at that point. One problem associated with wireless microphones is interference. Since they broadcast on specific FCC-assigned frequencies that are not exclusive to FM microphones, they sometimes pick up interference from VHF TV, cordless telephones, and other radio frequency users.

The **pressure zone microphone**, or the **PZM** (also known as a **boundary**, **plate**, or **surface-mount microphone**), is a small microphone capsule mounted next to a sound-reflecting plate (or boundary), as shown in Figure 4.7. Designed to be used on a flat surface, such as a tabletop, the microphone picks up sound from all directions above the table surface. Boundary microphones offer

exceptional microphone sensitivity because both direct sound and reflected sound reach the microphone at the same time, since the microphone is so close to the reflective surface. This boosts the incoming sound signal, which improves the clarity of the sound.

Figure 4.8 shows that the **shotgun microphone** is appropriately named. A microphone capsule is at one end of a tube (or barrel) that is "aimed" like a gun toward the sound source. The design of the microphone rejects sound from the side and rear but picks up a very narrow angle of sound from the front of the microphone's barrel. The highly directional nature of the microphone makes it good at picking up sound from a considerable distance from the sound source; however, sound quality is somewhat less than microphones designed to pick up only nearby sounds. There are other specialized microphones available, but in typical radio production work you aren't likely to run across them. In fact, even the microphones mentioned in this section will only be useful on occasion, but an understanding of them may prove helpful from time to time.

4.7 MICROPHONE PICKUP PATTERNS

The other way of classifying microphones is by their pickup patterns. Microphones can be constructed so that they have different directional characteristics. In other words, they pick up sound from varying directions, as shown in Figure 4.9. Sound picked up at the front of the microphone, or at 0 degrees, is said to be on-axis. Sound picked up from the microphone's side is 90 degrees off-axis, and sound picked up from the rear of the microphone is 180 degrees off-axis. The microphone housing, through the use of small openings and ports, can be designed so that unwanted sound (often off-axis sound) is canceled out or attenuated as it enters the microphone. The on-axis sound received directly from the front of the microphone fully impacts the microphone's diaphragm. An understanding of the microphone pickup patterns helps the user place the microphone relative to the sound source to maximize the pickup of desired sound and minimize the pickup of unwanted background noise.

The three basic sound patterns are omnidirectional, bidirectional, and cardioid. Although most microphones will have one fixed pickup pattern, **multidirectional microphones** have switchable internal elements that allow the microphone to employ more than one pickup pattern—most commonly cardioid and omnidirectional.

4.8 THE OMNIDIRECTIONAL PICKUP PATTERN

The **omnidirectional** microphone is also known as a **nondirectional** microphone. These two terms may seem to contradict each other—*omni* (all) and *non* (no). Both terms

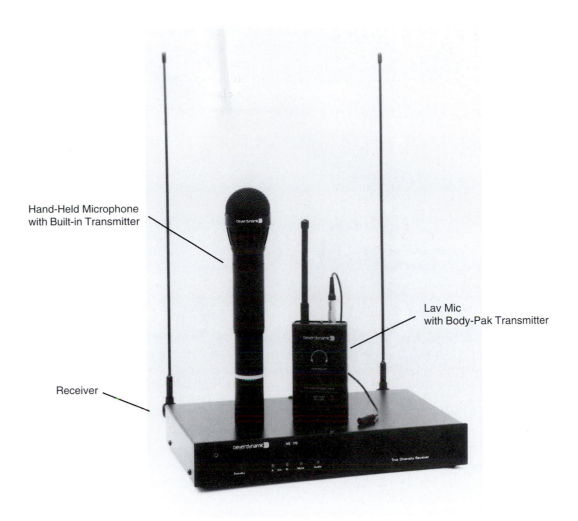

Hand-Held Microphone
with Built-in Transmitter

Lav Mic
with Body-Pak Transmitter

Receiver

FIGURE 4.6 Since it's wireless, the FM microphone can be used when the microphone cable would get in the way. (Image courtesy of beyerdynamic.)

FIGURE 4.7 The PZM microphone is designed to be used on a flat surface, such as a tabletop. (Image courtesy of Crown Audio, Inc.)

FIGURE 4.8   A shotgun microphone has a long tube or barrel that is "aimed" at the sound source. (Image courtesy of Sennheiser Electronic Corporation.)

are correct, however. The microphone picks up sound in all directions, but it also has no particular pickup pattern. Omnidirectional microphones pick up sound equally well in just about any direction. Think of an orange with a microphone right in the middle. No matter where the sound comes from, the microphone responds to it equally well.

Figure 4.10 illustrates the pickup pattern for a typical omnidirectional microphone.

Omnidirectional microphones are used whenever it is desirable to pick up sound evenly from all sides of the microphone, including above and below it. Omnidirectional

microphones are commonly used in broadcast situations outside the studio when the ambience of the location needs to be picked up along with the announcer's voice. Of course, the fact that they pick up sound equally well from all directions can also be a disadvantage. You may pick up unwanted background noise (such as traffic noise) in addition to the announcer when recording in a remote situation. Omnidirectional microphones used in a highly reflective room may also produce a "hollow" sound, since they tend to pick up more reverb than other types of microphones.

4.9 THE BIDIRECTIONAL PICKUP PATTERN

As the name implies, the **bidirectional** microphone picks up sound mainly from two directions: the front and the rear of the microphone, or on-axis and off-axis (see Figure 4.11). Its pickup pattern can be visualized as a figure 8, with the microphone located at the intersection of the two circles, or, to maintain the fruit analogy, think of two grapes sitting side by side. It was often used for radio dramas so that actors could face each other, but it is not a common pickup pattern for today's broadcast microphones. Although you may not utilize it in many radio production situations, it's a good microphone for the basic two-person interview and is sometimes used, in combination with other microphone types, for stereo recording.

4.10 THE CARDIOID PICKUP PATTERN

The **cardioid** microphone is sometimes referred to as **unidirectional** because it picks up sound coming mainly from one direction—the front of the microphone. Its pattern is actually heart shaped, hence the name cardioid (refer to Figure 4.12). Another way to visualize this pickup pattern is

OFF-AXIS

180°

150°   150°

120°   120°

90°   90°

60°   60°

30°   30°

0°

ON-AXIS

FIGURE 4.9   On-axis sound, picked up directly from the front of the microphone, fully impacts the microphone's diaphragm.

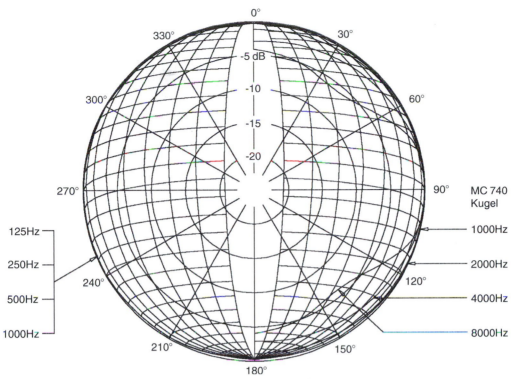

FIGURE 4.10 The omnidirectional pickup pattern shows that the microphone picks up sound equally well from all directions. (Image courtesy of beyerdynamic.)

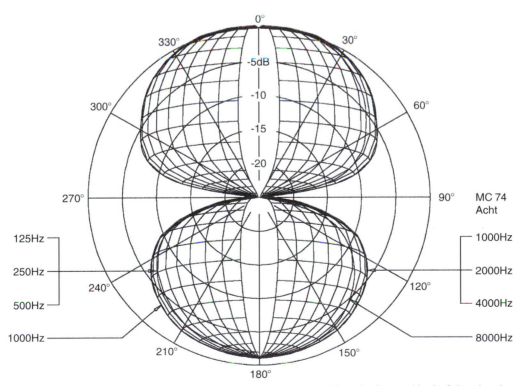

FIGURE 4.11 The bidirectional pickup pattern shows that the microphone picks up sound from the front and back of the microphone. (Image courtesy of beyerdynamic.)

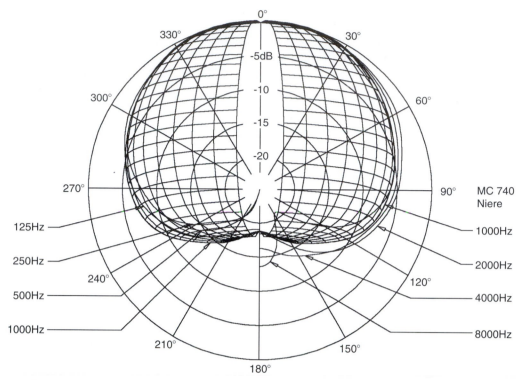

FIGURE 4.12 A cardioid pickup pattern shows the microphone picks up sound from the front and sides, but not from the back. (Image courtesy of beyerdynamic.)

to think of an upside-down apple, where the stem represents the microphone and the rest of the apple approximates the cardioid pickup pattern. Although the microphone picks up sound from the front and sides, the level of pickup from the sides is only about half that of the front. The microphone doesn't pick up sound well from the rear at all—less than one-tenth the sound it can pick up from the front.

Variations on the basic cardioid design include the **super-cardioid, hyper-cardioid,** and **ultra-cardioid** microphones. They continue to offer great rejection of the sound from the sides, but each microphone also picks up a narrower scope of on-axis sound. In other words, these microphones are even more directional in nature. All cardioid microphones are popular because they do reject unwanted sounds (excessive reverb, feedback, background noise), but the announcer must be careful to stay "on mic" and not move too far off-axis, especially when using super-, hyper-, or ultra-cardioid microphones. Cardioid microphones are often employed in remote sports broadcasts; the sportscaster talks into the live side (front) of the microphone, and the crowd and action sounds coming from the rear and sides are limited.

4.11 POLAR RESPONSE PATTERNS

The diagrams shown in Figures 4.10 to 4.12 indicate pickup patterns. One of the concepts that you need to understand

is the difference between **pickup pattern** and **polar pattern.**

We have already described a microphone's pickup pattern as the area around the microphone in which it best "hears" or picks up the sound. This is actually a three-dimensional shape (see Figure 4.13), as demonstrated by the orange, grape, and apple analogies. When a microphone's pickup pattern is shown by a two-dimensional

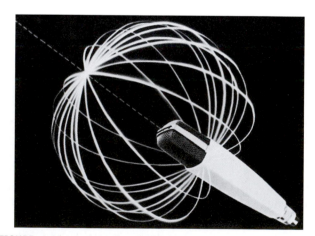

FIGURE 4.13 A three-dimensional view of the cardioid microphone pickup pattern. (Image courtesy of Sennheiser Electronic Corporation.)

drawing, we call that drawing the microphone's polar pattern or polar response pattern, as shown in Figures 4.10 to 4.12. Compare the cardioid pickup pattern shown in Figure 4.13 with the cardioid polar response pattern shown in Figure 4.12.

A polar pattern is drawn around a full circle, or 360 degrees. As noted earlier, the line from 0 to 180 degrees represents the microphone's axis, and sound entering the microphone from the front (0 degrees) is on-axis. The concentric circles show decreasing dB levels and allow us to see how the sound will be attenuated as it is picked up off-axis. For example, Figure 4.12 shows that sound picked up directly in front of the microphone will experience no attenuation. On the other hand, sound picked up from either side (90 degrees off-axis) will be attenuated about 5dB, and sound coming directly from the rear of the microphone (180 degrees) will be attenuated almost 20 dB. The lines labeled at various frequencies show that microphone patterns usually vary somewhat by frequency. In most cases, lower frequencies are picked up in a less directional fashion.

4.12 IMPEDANCE OF MICROPHONES

Another factor sometimes used to categorize microphones is **impedance,** a characteristic similar to resistance and common to audio equipment. Impedance is expressed in ohms, and microphones can be either high-impedance (10,000 ohms or higher) or low-impedance (600 ohms or less). Most broadcast microphones are low-impedance, as they provide the best frequency response, and most broadcast equipment is designed to accept this type of microphone. High-impedance microphones are also quite limited in the length of microphone cable that can be used with them before hum and severe signal loss occur. High-impedance microphones should not be plugged into audio recorders or other equipment designed for low-impedance; similarly, low-impedance microphones should not be used with high-impedance equipment, although the negative effects aren't as noticeable with this combination. If impedance is mismatched, sound will be distorted. There are impedance converters that can convert one type of impedance to the other.

4.13 SENSITIVITY OF MICROPHONES

Sensitivity refers to a microphone's efficiency or ability to create an output level. For the same sound source (say, one particular announcer's voice), a highly sensitive microphone produces a better output signal than a less sensitive microphone. To compensate for this, the gain control (volume) must be increased for the less sensitive microphone; this increased gain produces more noise. Although different sensitivity-rating systems can be employed, condenser microphones generally have high-sensitivity specifications, and dynamic microphones have medium sensitivity. Obviously, if you're trying to pick up a loud or close-up sound, a microphone with a lower sensitivity rating would be desirable.

4.14 PROXIMITY EFFECT AND BASS ROLL-OFF

Announcer use of microphones sometimes produces a sound phenomenon known as the **proximity effect.** This is an exaggerated bass boost that occurs as the sound source gets closer to the microphone. The effect should be noticeable as the announcer gets about 2 or 3 inches from the microphone and is especially noticeable with microphones that have a cardioid pickup pattern. Although it could help deepen a normally high voice, the proximity effect is usually compensated for by a **bass roll-off switch** on the microphone. This switch, when turned on, will electronically "roll off," or turn down, the bass frequencies that would be boosted by the proximity effect, thus leaving the desired flat response. Bass boost can also be controlled at the audio console, using the equalizer controls associated with the microphone channel as noted in the previous chapter.

4.15 MICROPHONE FEEDBACK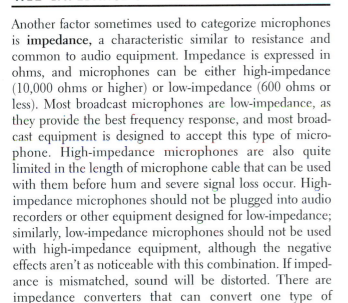

Feedback is a "howling" signal generated when a sound picked up by a microphone is amplified, produced through a speaker, picked up again, amplified again, and so on. Generally, reducing the volume or turning off the microphone ends the feedback. Feedback is a common microphone problem in public address situations but not usually in radio production, since the speaker is muted when the microphone is switched on, as was mentioned in Chapter 3. Occasionally, announcers can produce feedback in the production studio by operating their headphones at an excessive volume or accidentally picking up a stray speaker signal from an outside source, such as another studio speaker.

4.16 MULTIPLE-MICROPHONE INTERFERENCE

Sometimes when two or more microphones receiving the same sound signal are fed into the same mixer, the combined signal becomes **out of phase.** What happens is that the sound reaches each microphone at a slightly different time so that while the sound wave is up on one microphone, it's down on the other. Under these circumstances, the resulting sound will have frequency peaks and cancellations causing very poor sound quality. This situation is known as **multiple-microphone interference** and can be avoided by remembering a 3-to-1 ratio. That is, if the microphones are about 1 foot from the announcer (sound

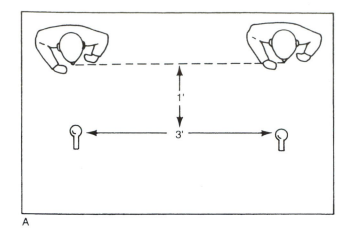

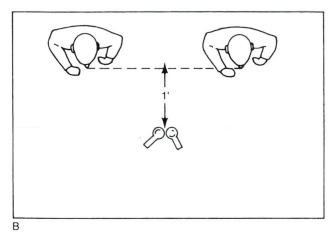

FIGURE 4.14 Avoid multiple-microphone interference by keeping the distance between the two microphones three times the microphone-to-source distance (A) or by keeping the microphones head-to-head (B).

source), they should be at least 3 feet apart from each other. In this way the signals won't overlap (see Figure 4.14A). Another solution to this problem is to place microphones that must be close together head-to-head, so they will receive the signal at the same time (see Figure 4.14B). Although multiple-microphone interference isn't usually a problem in the studio, it can occur in some radio remote situations.

4.17 STEREO

We hear sound in stereo because most sounds arrive at one ear before the other. In other words, the right ear hears a slightly different sound perspective from the left ear. This allows us to locate sound by turning our head until the sound is "centered." Most modern production work is done with stereo equipment. For example, the audio console has two master channels—a left and a right channel—and often we can pan the audio signal in such a fashion that more of it is assigned to the left or right channel. When we compare

stereo sound to monophonic sound, we quickly realize that stereo adds both "depth" and "imaging" to the sound.

Imaging is the apparent placement of the sound between the left and right plane and, as noted, provides location of the sound in space. *Depth* is the apparent placement of the sound between the front and back plane and often provides the ambience of the space where the sound is produced. Good stereo sound allows us to record and reproduce sound as it is in real life.

4.18 STEREO MIKING TECHNIQUES

Much radio production work is done with a mono microphone. Even in stereo studios, usually the same mono microphone signal is simply sent to the left and right channels.

However, there may be times when you will want to employ true stereo microphone techniques. Using traditional microphones, there are several common stereo methods: **A-B** (or **spaced pair** or **split-pair**) **miking**, **X-Y** (or **cross-pair**) **miking**, **ORTF miking**, **stereosonic miking**, and **M-S** (or **mid-side**) **miking**. All of these techniques, except spaced pair, are a form of **coincident miking** because they simultaneously employ two microphones whose pickup patterns overlap.

Since the ultimate goal of stereo recording is to have separate sound signals come from the left and right speakers, one common way to accomplish this is to split a pair of omnidirectional or cardioid microphones to the left and right of center about 18 to 36 inches apart. This A-B technique uses one microphone to feed the left channel of the stereo signal and another one to feed the right channel. As long as phase problems are watched and the sound source is kept a relatively equal distance from the microphones, a true stereo signal will be obtained. However, when using this technique, the sound is often "spacious," with a great deal of separation, especially if you separate the microphones further (8 to 10 feet), which some people do. Room ambience may be overbearing, with individual sounds seeming to "wander" in the stereo image.

Another stereo miking technique requires placing two cardioid microphones faced left and right like crossed swords forming an X- and Y-axis, as shown in Figures 4.5 and 4.15. The angle formed between the heads of the microphones is somewhere between 90 and 140 degrees, with the right microphone facing the left side of the announcer and the left microphone facing the right side of the performance area. This angle has an impact on the stereo effect and requires some experimenting to get it right. If the microphones become too parallel, the stereo effect is minimal; if the angle is too wide, there will seem to be a "hole" in the stereo image. If the heads of the microphones are close together, this X-Y miking allows the sound signal to reach both microphones at the same time and there will be no phase problems. Although this solves some of the

FIGURE 4.15 Cardioid microphones arranged for stereo (X-Y) miking look like crossed swords. (Image courtesy of Shure Incorporated.)

split-pair arrangement problems, it can cause a loss of "focus" on the image because the microphones are off-axis to the center of the stereo image.

The ORTF technique comes from a microphone placement developed by the French broadcasting organization, l'Office de Radiodiffusion-Television Francaise. Similar to X-Y miking, two cardioid microphones are crossed so that the heads are 17 centimeters apart (6.7 inches) and form an angle of 110 degrees. Unlike X-Y miking, the right microphone provides the right channel output, and the left microphone provides the left channel output. ORTF miking provides a very natural stereo sound with an "openness" that surpasses typical X-Y placement.

A lesser known stereo miking technique, stereosonic miking, involves placing two bidirectional microphones, one on top of the other. The front of each microphone faces the announcer at about a 45-degree angle, and the rear of each microphone faces the back of the performance area.

Mid-side miking, or M-S miking, offers superior imaging by using microphones arranged in an upside-down "T" pattern. The mid microphone (often a super-cardioid, but sometimes an omnidirectional) is aimed at the sound source, and the side microphone (usually a bidirectional) is placed parallel to the sound source and at a 90-degree angle to the mid microphone to pick up the sound to the left and right. Both microphones must be fed into a mixer designed to matrix, or decode, the incoming signals into a stereo signal.

Variations of these techniques, using different types of microphones and microphone placements, are also employed to achieve stereo miking. Furthermore, stereo microphones can duplicate X-Y or M-S techniques using a single microphone with specially designed internal sound-generating structures (review Figure 4.5).

4.19 SURROUND SOUND

Surround sound is more difficult to record than stereo sound and generally isn't recorded for radio. If it is used at all, it is most likely to be put together in a postproduction environment. This is because of the number of channels involved. Surround sound, in its most common form, provides a 5.1-channel sound, that is, six separate audio channels. To accomplish this, a center channel is added to the stereo left and right channels (to the front of the listener), and left and right surround channels are added (to the rear of the listener). These are all full-frequency response main channels. The sixth channel, designated as ".1" is a limited-response channel for bass frequencies only, often reproduced by a powered subwoofer.

It is possible to record audio so that it can accommodate all these channels. One way involves placing cardioid and/or supercardioid microphones in a circle, each pointing at a different place on the circumference of the circle. Another method is to use a surround sound microphone (see Figure 4.16), such as the Holophone. Its elliptical shape emulates the characteristics of the human head. Sound waves bend around the microphone as they do around the head, providing sound spatiality and

FIGURE 4.16 A microphone designed specifically for surround sound recording. (Image courtesy of Holophone, a Division of Rising Sun Productions Limited.)

directionality. The microphone can be particularly effective and convenient for recording live music concerts.

As with stereo recording, however, it is often easier to send a mono signal to all the channels than to try to record all of them. The problem with making realistic surround sound is that there are so many channels, front and rear, that the mono signal often needs to be altered so that it conveys the characteristics people expect as they hear sound coming from different directions. This is best undertaken in postproduction where the sounds can be manipulated in a more leisurely, technical fashion.

Although surround sound isn't currently used much for radio, it is fairly standard for motion pictures and DVDs where the dialogue is mostly handled by the left-center-right speakers, ambient sounds and some special effects are handled by the rear surround speakers, and big explosive sounds are handled by the subwoofer. Surround sound helps convey "movement" of sound as effects and other sounds can swirl around the listener. If radio broadcasting gets more involved with surround sound, it may become a more important microphone issue, but that appears to be many years away at this time.

In addition to the basic microphone, the radio production person will find one or more of the following accessories necessary for proper audio production work: windscreens, shock mounts, and stands or booms.

4.20 WINDSCREENS

The most common **windscreens** (sometimes referred to as **blast filters** or **pop filters**) are ball-shaped foam accessories that can be placed over the head or front of the microphone (as shown in Figure 4.17) to help reduce the chance of a plosive sound. Not only do they prevent popping, but they also help keep dust out of the internal elements of the microphone and can provide some cushion if the microphone is accidentally dropped. Windscreens can also be built into the grill of the microphone. Another design consists of a porous, film-like material that is suspended within a circular frame. This windscreen apparatus is then attached to the microphone stand and positioned in front of the microphone rather than placed on the microphone itself.

Announcing words that emphasize the *p*, *b*, or *t* sounds naturally produce a sharp puff of air and can produce a pop or thump when hitting the microphone (especially when a dynamic microphone is closely worked). The pop filter, however, eliminates or reduces this problem.

4.21 SHOCK MOUNTS

A **shock mount** is often employed to isolate the microphone from any mechanical vibrations (or shocks) that may be transmitted through its stand. The microphone is physically suspended (usually by an arrangement of elastic bands) and isolated from the stand or boom to which it is attached (see Figure 4.18). If the microphone stand is accidentally bumped, the sound of this thud will not be passed on and amplified by the microphone.

FIGURE 4.17 Windscreens help reduce plosive sounds. (Image courtesy of Shure Incorporated.)

microphone in a workable relationship to him or her. A **boom arm** (see Figure 4.19C) is a microphone stand especially designed for use in the radio studio. It consists of metal rods and springs designed somewhat like a human arm; the microphone attaches to one end, and the other end goes into a mounting base. The whole unit can then be attached to the countertop or other production studio furniture so that the microphone can be placed in close proximity to the audio console.

4.23 MICROPHONE USAGE

An understanding of the microphone types, pickup patterns, and other microphone characteristics is only useful if you can apply this knowledge to everyday radio production use. It seems reasonable to assume that the microphone in a broadcast studio will be a dynamic microphone because that's the one most commonly used in broadcasting, but it could also be a condenser microphone. Perhaps the more important consideration is its pickup pattern. In the studio, we mainly want to pick up the announcer's voice and some studio ambience. A cardioid pickup pattern, with its pickup of front and side sounds, works best to accomplish this but not pick up unwanted sounds from the rear, such as the announcer moving papers or turning on and off various switches.

FIGURE 4.18 The microphone shock mount isolates the microphone from the microphone stand. (Image courtesy of beyerdynamic.)

PRODUCTION TIP #4
Microphone-to-Mouth Relationship

You see it every day on MTV—your favorite singers practically "eating" the microphone as they perform their latest hits. *Don't emulate this!* "Swallowing" the microphone is *not* good microphone technique. When using a microphone in the standard studio setup, keep in mind two basic rules concerning distance from the microphone and position of the microphone. First, the announcer's mouth should be about 6 inches away from the microphone. That's about the length of a dollar bill—a good way to remember mic-to-mouth distance. This is a good starting point for using a microphone. You may find that you need to be closer or farther away because of the strength of your voice or the vocal effect that you're trying to achieve. Second, position the microphone so that you are not talking directly into it. Position the microphone level with your nose and tilted down toward your mouth, and talk beneath the front of the microphone, or place the microphone below your mouth with the front of it tilted up toward your mouth, allowing you to talk across the top of it.

4.22 MIC STANDS AND BOOMS

Some microphone stands consist of two chrome-plated pipes, one of which fits inside the other. A rotating clutch at one end of the larger diameter pipe allows the smaller pipe to be adjusted to any height desired. At the other end of the larger pipe is a heavy metal base (usually circular) that supports the pipes in a vertical position. Other microphone stands utilize a single pipe that's at a fixed height. In either case, the microphone is attached to the top of the pipe by a standard thread and microphone-stand adapter (see Figure 4.19A). **Floor stands** adjust for the announcer in a standing position, and **desk stands** are used for the seated announcer. A **boom stand** is a long horizontal pipe that attaches to a large floor stand (see Figure 4.19B). One end of the boom is fitted with the standard thread (for the microphone), and the other end is weighted to balance the microphone. The horizontal pipe allows the boom stand to be away from the announcer and positions the

In radio production work, it's not uncommon to leave the studio to record an interview. Certainly the radio news person does this frequently. In a remote-location interview, the

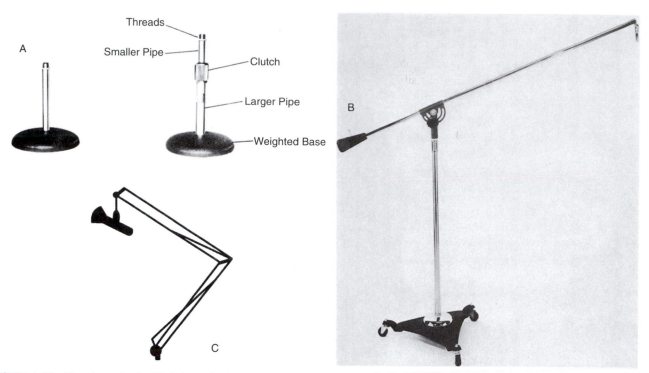

FIGURE 4.19 Microphone stands: (A) desk stands; (B) boom stand; (C) boom arm. (Images courtesy of Atlas Sound.)

dynamic microphone would probably be used because of its ruggedness, good quality, and the fact it does not need a power supply. In most cases, at a remote site you *want* to pick up the ambiance of the location and various voices (particularly the announcer and the interviewee). The omnidirectional pickup pattern, with its ability to pick up sound equally well in all directions, provides a solution for this situation. If there's likely to be a great deal of background noise, a cardioid microphone might be better, but it will have to be carefully placed so that it picks up both voices well.

Interviews (and some other broadcast situations) may require you to mic a group of people in the studio seated around a table. You could use a single omnidirectional microphone in the center of the table, or you could use a separate cardioid microphone for each individual at the table. Another option is to use the PZM, or pressure zone microphone.

Sportscasters are commonly out of the studio to broadcast games and other sports events. The sportscaster's headset provides both earphones and a microphone in a single unit, leaving the announcer's hands free (see Figure 4.20). The microphone is usually a dynamic with either a cardioid or an omnidirectional pickup pattern. If a cardioid microphone is employed, the sportscaster may want to have an additional microphone for picking up crowd and sports action noise.

FIGURE 4.20 The sportscaster's headset combines headphones and a microphone. (Image courtesy of Sennheiser Electronic Corporation.)

4.24 CONCLUSION

We said earlier that there is no one correct microphone to use in radio production. When using microphones, don't be afraid to experiment in each particular situation. The bottom line in any production should be how it sounds. It's good to be flexible in radio production because often you won't have a wide variety of microphones available. If you use what you've learned in this chapter, you should be able to obtain clear, appropriate sound under a variety of circumstances.

Self-Study

1. What is another name for the dynamic microphone?

   a) condenser
   b) pressure
   c) capacitor
   d) PZM

2. The dynamic microphone's sound-generating element is constructed of a diaphragm, a permanent magnet, and a voice coil. Into which of these is a small electrical current induced during use?

   a) diaphragm
   b) magnet
   c) coil
   d) none of the above

3. In what way does the condenser microphone differ from the dynamic microphone?

   a) The condenser microphone needs a power supply, and the dynamic microphone doesn't.
   b) The dynamic microphone has a diaphragm, and the condenser microphone doesn't.
   c) The dynamic microphone has better sound quality than the condenser microphone.
   d) The condenser microphone is bidirectional, and the dynamic microphone is omnidirectional.

4. True 5.1 surround sound is accomplished by adding what to the basic stereo setup of left and right front channels?

   a) a single rear or surround channel
   b) both left and right rear or surround channels
   c) both left and right rear or surround channels plus a center front channel
   d) both left and right rear or surround channels plus a center front channel plus a bass channel

5. Which microphone pickup pattern picks up sound on all sides?

   a) hyper-cardioid
   b) cardioid
   c) omnidirectional
   d) bidirectional

6. Which microphone would be most appropriate for conducting an interview on the sidelines at a football game?

   a) unidirectional
   b) omnidirectional
   c) bidirectional
   d) hyper-cardioid

7. Which microphone would be most appropriate for picking up a sportscaster announcing at a baseball game?

   a) cardioid
   b) nondirectional
   c) bidirectional
   d) omnidirectional

8. Which characteristic is true of most broadcast-quality microphones?

   a) low cost
   b) high impedance
   c) low sensitivity
   d) low impedance

9. Which of the following is most likely to exaggerate the bass sounds of a person's voice?

   a) feedback
   b) proximity effect
   c) multiple-microphone interference
   d) bass roll-off

10. What is the purpose of a shock mount?

   a) to reduce plosive sounds
   b) to keep the announcer's head at least 12 inches away from the microphone
   c) to isolate the microphone from mechanical vibrations
   d) to prevent static electricity discharges

11. Which type of microphone stand can be farthest away from a person and still allow the person to be close to the microphone?

   a) boom stand
   b) floor stand
   c) desk stand
   d) shock mount

12. Which stereo miking technique uses two microphones crossed (like swords) at a 90-degree angle to each other?

   a) split-pair miking
   b) mid-side miking
   c) M-S miking
   d) X-Y miking

13. Which type of microphone uses small, multiple sound-generating elements within a single microphone housing?

   a) ribbon mic
   b) wireless mic
   c) stereo mic
   d) boundary mic

14. A microphone's pickup pattern is exactly the same thing as a microphone's polar response pattern.

   a) true
   b) false

15. Which microphone has a permanently charged capacitor as part of its sound-generating element?

   a) condenser mic
   b) regulated phase mic
   c) electret mic
   d) ribbon mic

16. Which microphone would be best at picking up sound when the sound source is a considerable distance from the microphone?

   a) lavalier microphone
   b) PZM microphone
   c) RF microphone
   d) shotgun microphone

17. Sound picked up from the rear of a microphone is 90 degrees off-axis.

   a) true
   b) false

18. Which microphone pickup pattern describes a microphone with the narrowest scope of on-axis sound pickup?

   a) cardioid
   b) ultra-cardioid
   c) hyper-cardioid
   d) super-cardioid

19. Microphone impedance refers to a microphone's ability to create an output signal.

   a) true
   b) false

20. Which term describes a "screech" that occurs when sound is picked up by a microphone, amplified, fed back through a speaker, and picked up again, over and over?

   a) proximity effect
   b) multiple-microphone interference
   c) feedback
   d) bass roll-off

21. Which of the following is *not* a way that microphones are commonly classified?

   a) a microphone's sound-generating element
   b) a microphone's size
   c) a microphone's pickup pattern
   d) a microphone's impedance

22. Which stereo miking technique requires exact placement of two cardioid microphones?

   a) ORTF miking
   b) stereosonic miking
   c) X-Y miking
   d) A-B miking

23. Which microphone has a wire spiral embedded in a circular diaphragm as part of its sound-generating element?

   a) dynamic microphone
   b) electret microphone
   c) moving coil microphone
   d) regulated phase microphone

24. Multiple-microphone interference can be avoided if the microphones employed are at least three times as far from each other as they are from the sound source.

   a) true
   b) false

25. Which of the following is *not* another term for a wireless microphone?

    a) FM microphone
    b) RF microphone
    c) radio microphone
    d) PZM microphone

ANSWERS

If You Answered A:

1a. No. This is a different type of microphone. (Reread 4.3 and 4.4.)

2a. Wrong. The diaphragm feels the pressure. (Reread 4.3.)

3a. Right. The condenser microphone power supply is needed to charge the backplate and diaphragm.

4a. No. This would not provide surround sound. (Reread 4.19.)

5a. No. Hyper-cardioid microphones pick up mainly from the front. (Reread 4.7 to 4.10.)

6a. Wrong. As a cardioid microphone, it picks up in mainly one direction, so it would not pick up much of the crowd ambience. (Reread 4.7 to 4.10.)

7a. Yes. It would pick up the sportscaster without much of the background noise.

8a. No. Most broadcast studio microphones cost $300 to $500. Although remote microphones may be less, they are usually not inexpensive. (Reread 4.12.)

9a. No. Feedback is a howling noise caused by having open microphones near speakers. (Reread 4.14 and 4.15.)

10a. No. A pop filter is used to reduce plosive sounds. (Reread 4.20 and 4.21.)

11a. Right. This is the best selection.

12a. No. This is a different stereo miking technique. (Reread 4.18.)

13a. No. As the name implies, a ribbon microphone employs a thin metallic ribbon as part of a single sound-generating element. (Reread 4.5 and 4.6.)

14a. Wrong. A pickup pattern is the three-dimensional shape of the area around the microphone in which it hears the sound best; a polar response pattern is the two-dimensional representation of this. (Reread 4.11.)

15a. You're close to the correct response, but normal condenser microphones require a power supply to charge the capacitor. (Reread 4.4.)

16a. Wrong. Lavalier microphones are designed to be attached to the announcer's clothing. (Reread 4.6.)

17a. No. Sound that is 90 degrees off-axis would be coming from the side of a microphone. (Reread 4.7.)

18a. All cardioid microphones pick up sound mainly from the front, but this is not the correct answer. (Reread 4.10.)

19a. No. Impedance is an electrical characteristic similar to resistance. (Reread 4.12 and 4.13.)

20a. No. Proximity effect is a characteristic of microphones that accents the bass response. (Reread 4.14 and 4.15.)

21a. No. Microphones are categorized by their sound-generating elements. (Reread 4.2.)

22a. Correct. The microphone heads are spaced 6.7 inches apart and form a 110-degree angle.

23a. Wrong. Dynamic microphones do have a wire coil as part of their sound-generating element, but it's not configured like this. (Reread 4.3 and 4.5.)

24a. Yes. This is a true statement.

25a. No. FM microphone is another term for a wireless microphone. (Reread 4.6)

If You Answered B:

1b. Correct. The dynamic microphone is also called a pressure or moving-coil microphone.

2b. Wrong. The magnet sets up the field. (Reread 4.3.)

3b. No. Both microphones have a diaphragm. (Reread 4.3 and 4.4.)

4b. No. This would not provide surround sound. (Reread 4.19.)

5b. Wrong. The cardioid picks up sound on all but one side—usually the one right behind the microphone. (Reread 4.7 to 4.10.)

6b. Correct. It would pick up from all sides, thus easily miking the interview and some crowd noise.

7b. No. The crowd noise would tend to drown out the announcer. (Reread 4.7 to 4.10.)

8b. No. Consumer-quality microphones are usually high-impedance, but not broadcast quality. (Reread 4.12.)

9b. Right. When an announcer gets too close to the microphone, the bass may be exaggerated.

10b. No. For one thing, the announcer's head should be about 6 inches away, not 12 inches away. (Reread 4.21.)

11b. No. A person must stand right beside a floor stand. (Reread 4.22.)

12b. No. This is a different stereo miking technique. (Reread 4.18.)

13b. No. Wireless microphones employ a transmitter (often part of the microphone) and a receiver, but this is not a description of this system. (Reread 4.6.)

14b. Right. This is the correct response.

15b. No. The regulated phase microphone doesn't require phantom power, nor does it have a capacitor as part of its sound-generating element. (Reread 4.4 and 4.5.)

16b. Wrong. PZM microphones are designed to be placed on a flat surface, such as a tabletop. (Reread 4.6.)

17b. Yes. This statement is false. Sound that is picked up from the rear of a microphone is 180 degrees off-axis.

18b. Yes. This is the correct response.

19b. Correct. Microphone sensitivity refers to a microphone's ability to create an output level.

20b. No. This is not correct. Multiple-microphone interference is a phase problem that creates peaks and cancellations in the sound. (Reread 4.15 and 4.16.)

21b. Correct. While microphones come in a wide variety of sizes, they are not usually *categorized* *by size.

22b. Wrong. For one thing, stereosonic miking utilizes bidirectional microphones, not cardioid microphones. (Reread 4.18.)

23b. No. The electret microphone is a type of condenser microphone that uses a capacitor as its sound-generating element. (Reread 4.4 and 4.5.)

24b. No. The statement is true. (Reread 4.16.)

25b. No. RF microphone is another term for a wireless microphone. (Reread 4.6.)

If You Answered C:

1c. No. This is another name for the condenser microphone. (Reread 4.3 and 4.4.)

2c. Correct. The current is in the coil.

3c. No. The condenser microphone usually has slightly better sound quality than the dynamic microphone. (Reread 4.3 and 4.4.)

4c. No. This wouldn't provide true surround sound although you're getting close. (Reread 4.19.)

5c. Yes. An omnidirectional microphone picks up on all sides.

6c. No. It could pick up the interview, but wouldn't get much crowd noise. (Reread 4.7 to 4.10.)

7c. No. A bidirectional microphone picks up on two sides, and the sportscaster would only be on one side. (Reread 4.7 to 4.10.)

8c. No. Condenser microphones have a high sensitivity, and dynamic microphones have medium sensitivity. Neither has low sensitivity. (Reread 4.12 and 4.13.)

9c. No. This will create a distorted signal. (Reread 4.14 and 4.16.)

10c. Yes. This is a special type of microphone holder that suspends the microphone.

11c. No. A desk stand has to be right in front of the person. (Reread 4.22.)

12c. No. This is a different stereo miking technique. (Reread 4.18)

13c. Yes. This is the correct answer.

15c. Yes. A type of condenser microphone, the electret microphone, has a capacitor that is charged during manufacture.

16c. No. RF microphones are wireless, but they don't have exceptional distance pickup characteristics. (Reread 4.6.)

18c. While the hyper-cardioid microphone does have a narrow, unidirectional pickup pattern, this is not the best response. (Reread 4.10.)

20c. Correct. That screeching, howling sound is feedback.

21c. No. Microphone pickup patterns are used to categorize microphones. (Reread 4.2.)

22c. Wrong. This is a similar miking technique, but there are distinct differences. For example, the angle formed by crossed microphones can vary from 90 to 140 degrees with X-Y miking. (Reread 4.18.)

23c. No. The moving coil microphone is just another name for the dynamic microphone. (Check the response to 23a; reread 4.3 and 4.5.)

25c. No. Radio microphone is another term for a wireless microphone. (Reread 4.6.)

If You Answered D:

1d. No. A PZM microphone does not indicate a type of construction. (Reread 4.3 and 4.6.)

2d. Wrong. (Reread 4.3.)

3d. No. Both dynamic and condenser microphones can have omnidirectional or bidirectional pickup patterns. (Reread 4.3, 4.4, and 4.8 to 4.10.)

4d. Yes. These components when added to the stereo left and right front channels make up 5.1 surround sound.

5d. No. A bidirectional microphone picks up sound from the front and back of the microphone. (Reread 4.7 to 4.10.)

6d. No. This is a type of cardioid microphone with a very narrow one-direction pickup pattern. Although it might be useful for picking up one specific section of the crowd, it wouldn't provide full background crowd noise. (Reread 4.7 to 4.10.)

7d. No. This is another term for nondirectional. (Reread 4.7 to 4.10.)

8d. Right. Low-impedance is what most broadcast equipment is.

9d. Wrong. Bass roll-off is an electronic "turn down" of bass frequencies. (Reread 4.14.)

10d. No. This is not the correct answer. (Reread 4.21.)

11d. No. Although this is often used in conjunction with a microphone stand, it won't determine the distance between announcer and microphone stand. (Reread 4.22.)

12d. Correct. This is a description of X-Y stereo miking technique.

13d. No. Boundary microphones employ a single sound-generating element in conjunction with a sound-reflecting plate. (Reread 4.6.)

15d. No. The ribbon microphone doesn't require a power supply, nor does it have a capacitor as part of its sound-generating element. (Reread 4.4 and 4.5.)

16d. Right. Shotgun microphones are designed with a narrow tube that can be aimed at, and will pick up sound from, a point some distance away.

18d. While the super-cardioid microphone does have a narrow, unidirectional pickup pattern, this is not the correct response. (Reread 4.10.)

20d. No. Bass roll-off is a switch on some microphones that electronically turns down the lower frequencies. (Reread 4.14 and 4.15.)

21d. No. Microphone impedance is used to categorize microphones. (Reread 4.2 and 4.12.)

22d. Wrong. For one thing, A-B miking uses omnidirectional microphones. (Reread 4.18.)

23d. Yes. This is the correct response.

25d. Yes. The PZM is a type of boundary microphone that is designed to be placed on a flat surface, such as a tabletop.

Projects

PROJECT 1

Position microphones in various ways to create different effects.

Purpose

To enable you to experience proximity effect, feedback, multiple-microphone interference, and the differences in sound quality that occur when a microphone is placed at different distances and angles from an announcer.

Advice, Cautions, and Background

1. You have not yet read Chapter 5, "Digital Audio Players/Recorders," or Chapter 9, "Analog Audio Production," so you may need some help from your instructor or the engineer in setting up the equipment.
2. For the proximity effect, try to find a microphone that doesn't have a bass roll-off switch, or make sure it's switched off if it does.
3. Don't allow feedback to occur for too long. It can be damaging to all the electronic equipment—and your ears. You may have to plug the microphone into something other than the audio board if the board automatically shuts off the speakers when the microphone is turned on.
4. For multiple-microphone interference, make sure the microphones are closer than 3 feet apart. Omnidirectional microphones will demonstrate the effect the best.
5. Use a cardioid microphone for the distance and angle experiments because it will demonstrate the points better.

How to Do the Project

1. Set up an audio board so that two microphones are fed into it and so that the sound of those two microphones can be recorded on an audio recorder.
2. Put the recorder in record mode and activate one of the microphones. Start talking about 2 feet away from the microphone, and keep talking as you move closer until you are about 2 inches from it. As you talk, say how close you are to the microphone, and mention that you're experimenting with the proximity effect. Stop the recorder.
3. Position a microphone so that it's close to an activated speaker. Turn on the audio recorder and talk into the microphone. Record a short amount of the feedback and turn off the recorder.
4. Position two microphones in front of you that are less than 3 feet apart. Put the audio recorder in record mode and talk into the microphones, saying that you're testing for multiple-microphone interference. Turn off the recorder.
5. Position one microphone in front of you. Put the audio recorder in record mode. Position yourself 12 inches from the microphone and talk into it. Then position yourself 6 inches from the microphone and talk directly into it. Then talk across the top of the microphone. Move 6 inches to the side of the microphone, and talk into it with your mouth positioned to speak across the top of it. Get behind the microphone, either by moving behind it or by turning it around, and talk from about 6 inches away. Describe each action as you do it.
6. Listen to the recording to hear the various effects and to see that you have, indeed, recorded all the assignments. If some of them didn't turn out as well as you would have liked, redo them.
7. Turn in your recording to your instructor to receive credit for the project. Make sure you put your name on it and label it "Microphone Placement."

PROJECT 2

With several other students, make a recording using stereo miking techniques.

Purpose

To give you experience utilizing standard microphones to employ various stereo miking techniques.

Advice, Cautions, and Background

1. Which technique you employ will depend on the microphones that are available at your facility.
2. Since this project requires several people, your instructor may assign it as a class project.
3. The "How To" section that follows uses X-Y techniques for illustration purposes; you can adjust it for any of the other techniques.

How to Do the Project

1. At one end of your studio (or room) arrange at least three students in a left–center–right configuration. This could also be three groups of students or even a small musical group, as long as they're arranged so that specific sections can be identified as left, center, or right.
2. Set up two cardioid microphones to record onto an audio tape recorder.
3. Arrange the microphones in an X-Y position as described in the text, in line with the "center" of the students or group.
4. Begin recording and have the students or group do the following:
   a. have the left say something
   b. have the right say something
   c. have the center say something
   d. have all three sections say something different, but at the same time
   e. have just the center say something
   f. have the left and right say something
   g. have all three sections say something
5. As you are recording the above, make sure to identify each segment by having one student say something like, "This is just the 'left' group," before the group says anything.
6. Play back your recording. Are you able to "hear" the stereo image correctly? Does the left group "appear" to be located left? Make some observations about the recording results and write them down.
7. Repeat the same recording, but use a single microphone; that is, record in mono.
8. Listen to the second recording. What differences do you hear between the two recordings? Write down your observations again.
9. Turn in your recording and the observation sheet labeled with your name and "Stereo Miking" to your instructor to receive credit for this project.

PROJECT 3

Compare sound from different types of microphones.

Purpose

To learn the differences between dynamic and condenser microphones and between cardioid and omnidirectional pickup patterns.

Advice, Cautions, and Background

1. You have not yet read Chapter 5, "Digital Audio Players/Recorders," or Chapter 9, "Analog Audio Production," so you may need help from your instructor or engineer in setting up the equipment.
2. Don't be concerned if you can't discern differences between the dynamic and condenser microphones. The pop and hiss effect doesn't occur for all voices.
3. If your facility has microphones with other sound-generating elements (such as ribbon or regulated phase) or other pickup patterns (such as bidirectional or ultra-cardioid), add those to the exercise.

How to Do the Project

1. Select a dynamic and a condenser microphone from those at your facility.
2. Attach the microphones to an audio recorder. You can put both microphones through an audio console and use them one at a time, or you can attach each microphone to the recorder in its turn.
3. While you're recording, say the following into the dynamic microphone: "Peter Piper picked a peck of pickled peppers," and "She sells seashells by the seashore." Turn the recorder off.
4. Repeat Step 3, but use the condenser microphone.
5. Select a microphone with a cardioid pickup pattern and another microphone with an omnidirectional pickup pattern from those at your facility.
6. Attach the microphones to an audio recorder as in Step 2.
7. Position the cardioid microphone on a stand and, while recording, walk totally around the microphone, saying where you are as you move: for example, "Now I'm right in front of the microphone; now I'm 90 degrees to the right of the front of the microphone." Turn the recorder off.
8. Repeat Step 7, using the omnidirectional microphone.
9. Listen to the recording, and write down any observations you have about the differences among the various microphones.
10. Turn in the paper and your recording to your instructor to receive credit for the project. Be sure to include your name on both and call the assignment "Microphone Comparisons."

5

DIGITAL AUDIO PLAYERS/ RECORDERS

5.1 INTRODUCTION

Digital technology continues to replace conventional technology in various applications around the radio production studio. For example, since the advent of the compact disc, turntables have steadily lost favor as a necessary piece of production equipment. Other analog mainstays, such as reel-to-reel tape recorders and cart machines, are also found in fewer and fewer production facilities. This chapter looks at some of the digital studio equipment that is both increasing the choice of available formats to work with and, in many cases, bringing on the demise of older analog equipment. While it is not intended to be a comprehensive survey, most of the equipment noted is playing a prominent role in digital playback and recording in many production studios today.

5.2 THE CD PLAYER

The compact disc player was the first piece of digital equipment to be embraced in radio production and broadcast work, and today the CD player is one of the main sources for playing back prerecorded material. Because CDs are often aired one right after the other, there are usually at least two CD players in each production room or on-air studio. This way, one can be cued while the other is playing on the air or recording.

The CD player shown in Figure 5.1 is typical of a unit designed specifically for broadcast use. Many radio stations and production facilities just use consumer CD players, but these often require special interfaces to be compatible with other broadcast equipment and are not really designed for day-in and day-out use. Good production practice dictates the use of rugged, broadcast-quality CD players rather than consumer models.

One of the main operational features of many broadcast-quality units is a **cue wheel** that allows the operator to "rock" or "scrub" the CD back and forth. In this manner, the exact start point of the music can be found, and then the player can be paused at that spot, ready for play. Most CD players will also automatically cue to the start of the music when you cue up to any specific track on the CD or cue to an index point within an individual track. Other normal CD controls include a play button to start the CD, several controls to select or program specific tracks on the CD, and an open/close control to load the CD into the machine. Regardless of the exact design, the CD ends up in a **tray** or **well,** where it spins so the laser can read it.

The internal structure of the CD player centers around three major components: a drive motor, a **laser** and lens system, and a tracking mechanism. The drive motor spins the disc at a variable rate between 200 and 500 RPM (revolutions per minute). To keep the data on the disc read by the laser at a constant rate, the drive motor slows down as the laser moves to the outside of the disc. In the laser and lens system, a **laser diode** generates a laser light beam, and a **prism system** directs it toward the disc surface. Different types of lenses focus the laser beam exactly on the pits of data encoded on the disc. Reflected light is directed back through the lens and prism to another wedge lens and a **photodiode,** which provides the data signal that will be converted to an audio signal. The tracking mechanism moves the laser assembly so that it follows the spiral track of data on the disc.

A different design approach to CD players has been to build them so that the CD must be put into a plastic housing before it can be played in the unit (see Figure 5.2). Special broadcast features of this type of CD player include the ability to select one track while another is playing (so two songs can be played back-to-back from the same CD) and a countdown timer (so the operator knows exactly how much time remains on the song currently playing). The plastic cartridge increases the cost of this system, but it also affords the CD extra protection from dirt and damage.

FIGURE 5.1 The professional-quality CD player is built for rack-mounting, heady-duty use, and may have features not available on consumer units. (Image courtesy of Denon Professional.)

Another type of player is the **multi-play** CD player. With the ability to hold up to 300 CDs and with interfacing capability, this type of unit has been used as a music source in some automation systems. Not only does the operator have random access to thousands of individual songs, but also all the CDs can be secured under lock and key. However, since the advent of digital hard-disc storage systems, this type of CD player has seen little use in the broadcast studio.

As noted earlier, regardless of the type of CD player utilized, some compact discs seem to display an overly bright, metallic, or even harsh sound—a distinctive "digital sound." The problem actually has nothing to do with the CD player or even the CD process. It occurs with some CDs because the original recording was intended for vinyl playback. Engineers often added equalization to compensate for sonic limitations of vinyl recording. Many early CDs were mastered with this same equalization applied rather than removed for transfer to the CD medium, thus the bright or shiny sound. Material that has been recorded essentially for CD use does not display this problem, nor should older material that has been carefully prepared or remastered for transfer to CD.

5.3 ADVANTAGES OF THE CD PLAYER

The advantages of the CD player far outweigh any perceived problems. The CD player offers the superior sound quality of any piece of digital equipment—greater frequency response, better signal-to-noise ratio, improved dynamic range, and almost no distortion—when compared to an analog component. In addition, there is no physical contact between the player and the actual CD so little wear or degradation takes place.

The CD format also offers the convenience of random access to the material stored on the disc. Unlike tape-based formats that require winding through the tape to move from one point to another, CD players can instantly move from one track to another track anywhere on the disc in a second or two. Another plus of the CD player, from a production viewpoint, is its ability to "cue to music." Whether using a cue wheel or an auto-cueing feature, CD players allow the announcer to find the exact beginning of the music and start the CD instantly at that point. CD timing information (elapsed/remaining time and track length) is helpful for production work, and the ability to select and play segments of music or to automatically fade in at any point in the music can be a creative production tool. The ease of cueing and the consistently high quality obtained make the use of CDs and the CD player an important part of the production process in the modern studio.

FIGURE 5.2 A compact disc must be put into a plastic housing before it can be played in a cart-style CD player. (Image courtesy of Denon Professional.)

5.4 COMPACT DISCS

The **compact disc (CD)** is a small plastic disc, 12 centimeters (about 4.7 inches) in diameter. On one side of the disc, the music is stored as a single spiral of microscopic pits and lands (or flat areas) that contain the encoded information about the sound. In addition to music information, data encoded on the disc tells the CD player where each track begins and ends, how many tracks are on the disc, and other timing and indexing information.

A CD stores music as 16-bit digital words, going from the center hole to the outside rim of the disc. With the standard digital sampling rate, 44,100 of these digital "words" are required for each channel every second! In fact, there is around 650 MB (megabytes) of data stored on a standard 74-minute CD. A thin aluminum reflective coating (some CDs use a gold-coated reflective surface) makes it possible for the laser light to read the encoded data, and a layer of clear polycarbonate plastic protects the encoded information. The reverse side of the CD is made up of the label and a protective lacquer coating (see Figure 5.3).

CDs were originally designed to hold 60 minutes of recorded material; however, about 74 minutes of music has become the standard CD length, with 80-minute lengths also being used. CD singles (3-inch CDs) were developed that are capable of holding about 20 minutes of music, but these never really caught on and are not frequently seen today.

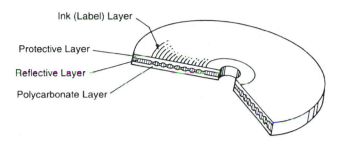

FIGURE 5.3 A compact disc is made up of several layers as this cutaway view shows.

Labels: Ink (Label) Layer, Protective Layer, Reflective Layer, Polycarbonate Layer

5.5 CARE OF CDS

The compact disc is not as indestructible as it was once promoted to be. Practical use in the radio studio has shown that CDs do require some care. When removing a CD from its jewel box case, put your thumb on the center spindle of the jewel box and your index or middle finger on the rim of the disc. Press down with your thumb and gently pull up on the disc until it is free of the case. When handling a disc, continue to hold only the outer edges or the edges of the hole, and avoid bending the CD in any manner. Never touch the surface of the disc.

Some CD players will not track properly with dust or fingerprints on the CD surface, and serious scratches can also render the CD unplayable. CDs can be cleaned by gently wiping the aluminum side (the side without the label) with a lint-free cotton cloth from the center hole of the CD directly toward the CD rim. Do *not* use a circular cleaning motion because this could cause a scratch that follows the spiral data on the disc, causing the disc to not properly track. Use a special CD-cleaning solution, isopropyl alcohol, or methanol to remove dirt or other material from the disc.

Flexing a disc or touching it with oily fingers can damage the CD's protective coating and ultimately allow oxidation of the aluminum layer, which can ruin the CD. If your CD player has a tray that opens and closes, be sure to stop the CD *before* you open the tray. Hitting the open (eject) button while the CD is still playing can cause damage to the CD as it continues to rotate while the tray is opening.

If you must mark the disc, do not use pen, pencil, fine-tip markers, or adhesive labels; rather, use a non solvent-based felt-tip permanent marker on the label side of the disc. To get the maximum life span out of a compact disc, it should be stored in its plastic jewel box in an upright position, like a book.

5.6 THE CD RECORDER

CD recorders are finding a home in the broadcast studio. Although the first CD players were merely "turntables" for

---

prerecorded CDs, shortly after their development, manufacturers produced a recordable CD. The high price of first-generation CD recorders kept broadcast studio use to a minimum, but falling costs over the years have made the CD recorder (see Figure 5.4) very affordable now. Broadcast companies like Tascam, Marantz, Denon, and HHB all offer CD recorders that work in the CD-R and/or CD-RW format.

CD-R (CD-recordable) is a WORM (write once, read many) design. The CD consists of a photosensitive dye layer and a reflective layer, encased in the normal protective polycarbonate. When heated by high-power laser pulses, the dye melts or "burns." This creates bumps (and pits) that have a different reflective nature, similar to those of a regular CD. The data is read off the disc by a lower powered laser. The recording laser follows a preformed spiral track so the data can be played back on any standard CD player. Actually, the CD-R recorder allows you to record during several different sessions or until the disc is full (99 separate tracks, up to 80 minutes total); however, you may not be able to play the disc on a regular CD player until you "finalize" the disc and permanently write the Table of Contents of the disc. Partially recorded CD-Rs *will* play on the CD-R recorder at any time. The biggest drawback to the WORM design is the inability to record over old material; if you make a mistake in the recording process, you have ruined that disc or at least a section of it, and once you finalize the disc you cannot add any new material to it.

The **CD-RW** (CD-rewritable) disc is used in a similar fashion; however, the last track recorded can be erased (before the disc has been finalized), and the space on the disc can be reused for recording other material. CD-RW discs that have been finalized can also be totally erased and rerecorded. The CD-RW format uses a phase-change technology; the material in the recordable CD surface goes from crystalline to amorphous when heated during the recording process, which changes its reflectivity. During playback, the laser light is reflected differently from opposite-phase areas, allowing the player to distinguish binary zeros and ones and thus reproduce a digital signal. An audio CD recorded in the CD-RW format may not play back correctly on all CD players, although it will play on its own recorder, which will also play standard CDs.

Another development in the CD recording area is a small, digital workstation component (see Figure 5.5) that combines a CD recorder with a small mixing console to provide recording, editing, and mixing features. The mixer section can handle up to eight tracks of simultaneous recording with built-in EQ and effects, such as reverb or delay. The recorder section uses 16-bit or 24-bit recording at a 44.1-kHz sampling rate. Other features include an internal hard drive (usually at least 40 GB), up to 24 playback tracks, and stereo mastering to the built-in CD-RW drive. Similar digital workstations use a minidisc or compact flash as the recording medium.

Even though there is intense competition with other digital recording media (such as the minidisc or hard disk recorder), the CD recorder is finding a place in the digital production studio. Some stations record jingles, commercials, custom sound effects, and other production elements on CD. Other stations might prerecord a block of programming onto CD for later playback, perhaps through an automation system. In addition, most sound effect and production music libraries that used to be available on vinyl records are now produced on compact disc.

5.7 SACD (SUPER AUDIO CD)

The CD format has seen around 25 years of use in audio production and still appears to have a long life ahead of it. However, there are "new and improved" audio formats that have offered some competition to the venerable compact disc. The two most similar to CD, but offering higher quality, are DVD-audio and the SACD. Developed by the orig-

FIGURE 5.4   Most CD recorders found in the broadcast production studio can record in both the CD-R and CD-RW format. (Image courtesy of Tascam®.)

FIGURE 5.5 This multi-track recorder can function as a portable mini-studio and record on compact disc. (Image courtesy of Roland Corporation)

inators of the compact disc, Sony and Philips, the **SACD** employs a new digital process rather than standard PCM digital technology. Direct Stream Digital ™ uses a simplified 1-bit, 2.82-MHZ digital method that touts increased resolution and clarity while providing a warmer, more natural sound. SACDs can hold more information, so multiple mix capabilities are usually provided—often a stereo mix and a 5.1 surround sound mix. (Review the section on surround sound in Chapter 4.) Most, but not all, SACDs are backward compatible because they offer a hybrid disc (see Figure 5.6) with a standard CD layer and the SACD layer. The bottom layer contains data for both a stereo mix

and 5.1 channel mix of the audio, along with video or graphic information, if employed. The separate top layer contains standard CD data. Standard CD players would read this information and reproduce CD-quality sound. Players with SACD capability would read the high-density layer and reproduce the higher quality audio. At the moment, there are only a limited number of titles available in the SACD format and there are no recorders for this format. The main competitor for the SACD is DVD-audio as noted in the next section.

5.8 DVD-AUDIO

The next generation of audio disc may well be the **digital versatile disc (DVD)** or a variation of it. Originally called a digital *video* disc, the DVD was designed to hold a feature-length movie on a compact disc-sized medium. Primarily a video format, it also has applications for computer data and music. Physically, the DVD is the same size as a compact disc; however, it can have two data layers that can both be read from one side of the disc by refocusing the laser in the DVD player. The data information is spaced much closer together than on a compact disc, so by using a data compression scheme (around 2:1) and a two-sided, dual-layer disc, the DVD could hold up to 17 gigabytes of data, or the content of about 25 current compact discs! Even a standard, single-sided DVD-audio disc holds more data than the CD—about 4.7 gigabytes.

In addition to greater storage capacity, the DVD-audio specifications offer a wide variety of possible formats of equal or better quality than the CD. An audio-only DVD can have sampling rates of 44.1, 48, 88.2, 96, 176.4, and 192 kHz, plus 16-, 20-, and 24-bit quantizing compared to the CD's 44.1 kHz/16-bit standard. Most broadcasters prefer a DVD-audio standard of 96 kHz/24-bit, and this has

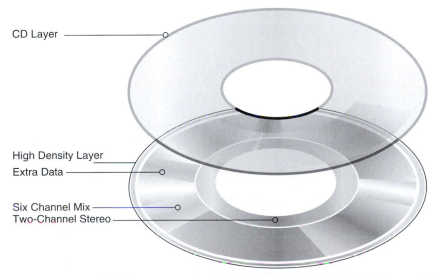

CD Layer

High Density Layer
Extra Data

Six Channel Mix
Two-Channel Stereo

FIGURE 5.6 The high-density layer of a hybrid SACD can contain stereo and multi-channel mixes along with video or graphic information.

become the most popular format. Like the SACD, DVD-audio also offers the advantage of multi-channel sound—from a simple mono mix, up to a maximum of 6 channels (5.1 surround sound). In addition to musical content, DVD-audio discs can also offer text, still images, and short video clips.

While there are DVD recorders, they are primarily for recording video, or as the data storage medium of choice on personal computers. DVD-RW discs and drives also exist, with the same advantages as the CD-RW. Veteran users of CD-RW and DVD-RW discs, however, will point out that the medium is not as stable as the CD-R or DVD-R medium, so they are hesitant to put any vital or one-of-a-kind data on an RW disc.

To what degree consumers or the broadcast industry will embrace either of the enhanced DVD audio technologies is subject to speculation. Competing audio formats and even new technologies are also appearing that could bypass both SACD and DVD-audio before they have time to become mainstream formats.

5.9 THE MD RECORDER/PLAYER

Minidisc (MD) recorders and players of different styles and applications have seen moderate success for a number of years in the radio production studio. Originally developed by Sony as a digital replacement for the cassette, the minidisc can be a handheld, tabletop, or rack-mounted (see Figure 5.7) system and has become a replacement for the audio cart in some broadcast studios. Employing a small disc, the MD can still hold up to 80 minutes of music because of a data compression scheme. The minidisc is *not* actually CD quality, but still an extremely high-quality audio medium. The MD also features a "shock absorber" system that uses a memory buffer to store music that can continue to play for a few seconds if the player mistracks, until the pickup can return to its correct position.

The portable MD recorder as shown in Figure 5.8 is a serious competitor for standard cassette and DAT recorders

when it comes to news gathering or any production situation that requires recording in the field. The stand-alone unit offers recording, playback, and editing tracks on the move.

5.10 THE MINIDISC

The minidisc is permanently sealed in a plastic cartridge (see Figure 5.9), so it can be handled without worrying about dust, dirt, or fingerprints getting on the disc. The MD comes in both a prerecorded and recordable format. The actual disc is much smaller than a compact disc—about 2.5 inches in diameter—but otherwise shares many of the CD characteristics, including its digital data in a spiral of microscopic pits. The minidisc, like a computer disk, has a sliding protective shutter that automatically opens when the disc is put into a recorder/player.

Recordable MDs utilize a **magneto-optical design**. A magnetically active layer of the disc is heated (by a laser) to the point where its magnetic orientation can be changed by a magnetic recording head. As the heated spot moves out of the laser beam, it rapidly cools, "freezing" its magnetic polarity according to the data applied to the recording head corresponding to a digital zero or one. During playback, the laser senses variations in reflected light in relation to the magnetic orientation. New material is recorded directly over the old with the minidisc format.

5.11 DATA COMPRESSION

In order for the minidisc to record the large amount of necessary digital data and still employ its small disk-recording medium, the MD recording process uses a data **compression** system developed by Sony known as **ATRAC (Adaptive Transform Acoustic Coding)** to provide digital-quality sound. Like any other data compression scheme, data compression occurs because only audible sounds are encoded. In other words, sound below the threshold of

FIGURE 5.7 The minidisc recorder in a rack-mount configuration (and combined with a CD player) can be found in many production studios. (Image courtesy of Tascam®.)

FIGURE 5.8 A portable MD allows recording and editing on the move, as well as all the other features of the minidisc format. (Image courtesy of Superscope Technologies, Inc.)

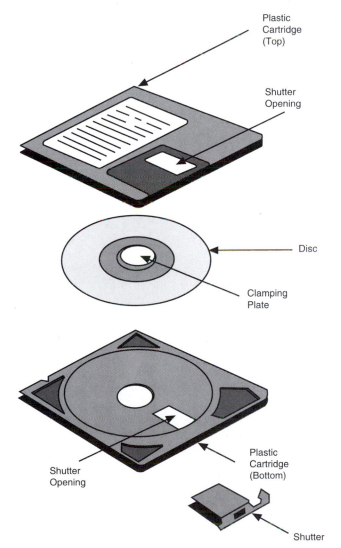

FIGURE 5.9 The minidisc is housed in a plastic case to keep it free from scratches, dust, and fingerprints.

hearing or too soft to hear, and sounds masked by louder sounds heard at the same time, are excluded, according to a "perceptual coding" model. In addition, those sounds that are encoded use only the number of data bits necessary for near-CD-quality sound. This allows the minidisc recording to cut down the amount of data that must be recorded by about one-fifth, with no apparent sound-quality change or loss.

There is no standard method of data compression, and other digital equipment utilizes other types of audio data reduction schemes. There has been some concern about the audible effects on sound that has been compressed more than once. For example, a minidisc could be played through a signal processor that also uses data compression. Some tests have shown a degradation of the audio signal with some combinations of data compression; however, this doesn't appear to be a major problem.

Data compression can also be used with any of the digital media mentioned above, thus making their audio capacities even greater. A CD-R or -RW can hold a maximum of 80 minutes of uncompressed audio, but were those audio tracks to be compressed into, for example, the very popular MP3 format, 10 to 12 times that amount of audio could be stored on the same disc, or around 800 minutes. A standard DVD, with 4.6 GB of space, could store nearly 4000 minutes of compressed, CD-quality audio. Looking at these numbers, storage space is obviously not a problem anymore. Ease of organization and utilization then becomes the issue. Here many compressed formats, such as MP3, also provide great flexibility, as the files can contain text and other data that can help to categorize and identify the files. Much of this additional data is user-definable. If you think a song fits better in the Bluegrass genre than the Country genre, switching this is a snap and will be reflected in all future searches of the content.

In addition to being playable in computers, MP3 and other popular audio compression formats are increasingly playable in CD and DVD players, as well as minidisc players and, of course, stand-alone MP3 players.

5.12 COMPACT FLASH AND OTHER DIGITAL RECORDERS

Over the years, broadcast audio manufacturers have developed numerous other digital recorders designed to replace the old analog cart machines. Instead of an analog audio cart, MD, CD, or DVD as the recording or storage medium, these machines have used 2-MB computer floppy disks, 100-MB zip disks, or gigabyte-capacity Magneto-Optical disks. Depending on the configuration, recording time could range from about a minute to many hours. Most **digital cart recorders** offer selectable sampling rates, the usual operational controls, and can easily add an electronic "label" (through the use of a keyboard), which can show the cart name and timing information on an LCD (liquid crystal display) screen. The only such recorders that still have a presence in the audio studio are 360 Systems Digicart/II Plus or their Digicart/E. Both units are actually hard disk recorders, but both use removable zip disks to move audio from one location to another or to archive projects.

The digital recorder that now enjoys a prominent place in audio production work is the **solid-state recorder** that records on a compact flash or PCMCIA (Personal Computer Memory Card International Association) card. Portable, rack-mount, and mixer/recorder workstation units have all found their way into audio production work. A 2-GB compact flash card allows up to six hours of uncompressed .wav recording at a 48-kHz sampling rate. The portable recorder shown in Figure 5.10 is designed to mimic the typical cassette or minidisc recorder. The front panel of the unit shows an LCD screen and typical recorder controls. One-button recording is featured, as well as EDL marking during recording or playback. Additional controls are used to set various digital parameters, such as sample rate or data compression. There are both analog and digital I/O options, featuring XLR inputs with phantom power.

Once recording is complete, basic nondestructive editing can be accomplished by manipulating a waveform display on the LCD screen, or the audio files can be fed to a laptop or desktop PC for editing or archiving. While a long battery life is important for any portable unit, perhaps the biggest plus for the compact flash recorder is that the recording system does not rely on moving parts and, once recorded, files can be directly downloaded into an editing system via USB cable rather than having to wait on "real-time" transfers. Whether the compact flash recorder replaces the cassette in

broadcast production work remains to be seen, but it must be counted as one of the current main contenders.

As noted above, some production recorders combine an internal hard disk drive and a removable storage drive (see Figure 5.11). In addition to providing multi-track capability and normal transport controls, these recorders often feature a large LCD screen for file manipulation and editing, and a jog wheel for scrubbing and marking edit points. Hard drives offer the greatest amount of storage space, extremely quick access time, and low maintenance. However, if a hard drive device "crashes," a huge amount of audio can be lost, which can disrupt a production or on-air studio.

Another type of portable recorder is Edirol Corporation's handheld digital audio recorder. The R-1 (shown in Figure 5.12) records in .wav or .mp3 formats. A standard 64-MB compact flash card provides a maximum recording time of over two hours and can be upgraded to 512 MB or 2 GB for higher quality or longer recordings. A single button initiates recording with built-in omnidirectional, electret microphones or external line/mic inputs. Since the unit is entirely solid-state, there is no internal noise generated that often plagues built-in microphones on portable units. The recorder also has a USB interface to import or export audio files and an effects circuit to add EQ, reverb, and other effects to the recording. The immediate advantage of this type of recorder is its "palm of your hand" size and its rugged design. Such portable recorders are becoming less expensive, as are the flash card media. Radio reporters, or anyone recording in the field, can look forward to the further development of these types of devices.

FIGURE 5.10 One of the biggest advantages of the compact flash recorder is the ability to bypass real-time file transfers by utilizing USB direct downloads. (Image courtesy of Marantz Professional.)

FIGURE 5.11 Some digital recorders utilize both an internal hard-disk drive and a removable storage drive. (Image courtesy of Mackie®.)

5.13 DIGITAL REEL TAPE RECORDERS

DASH stands for **digital audio stationary head**, a reel-to-reel standard for Sony PCM digital multi-track recorders. A ¼-inch format that was available for two-track is no longer in production, but a ½-inch format for multi-track recorders is still in use. A redesigned 48-track system is backward compatible with the original 24-track system. Although other parameters are possible, most recording is at 30 inches per second (IPS) with a sampling rate of 48 kHz. The multi-track systems have found frequent use in the recording studio, but a very high price tag (even the audiotape for the DASH format is very expensive) has kept almost all broadcast stations away from the DASH machines.

FIGURE 5.12 Some compact flash recorders are designed to be held in your hand with all functional controls at your fingertips. (Image courtesy of Edirol Corporation.)

5.14 THE DAT RECORDER

One tape-based digital format that has found some broadcast application is **DAT**; however, it has never been widely used. The DAT (**digital audio tape**) recorder, also known as **R-DAT** (**rotary head digital audio tape**), uses technology that is based on the VCR, traditional cassette recorder, and CD player. As shown in Figure 5.13, although a DAT recorder has normal audio tape recorder controls (play, record, rewind, etc.), the DAT tape goes into a slide-out drawer (operated with an open/close control) like many CD players.

The DAT unit, like the CD, has several controls for selecting specific songs on the tape. An **AMS** (**Automatic Music Sensor**) button allows the operator to skip forward or backward to the start of the next or previous recorded track. Subcodes can be recorded along with the audio on a DAT tape so that the operator can select any individual track by entering that track's "start ID" or "program number." A DAT system records with rotating heads, putting digital data on ⅛-inch tape in a series of diagonal tracks similar to

FIGURE 5.13 The DAT recorder has never gained the wide use that some of the other digital recorder formats have. (Image courtesy of Tascam®.)

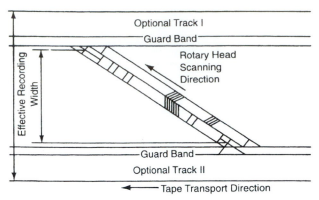

FIGURE 5.14 Digital data is put on the DAT audio tape in a diagonal track configuration.

FIGURE 5.15 The DAT cassette is similar in design to a VCR tape. (Image courtesy of TDK Electronics Corporation.)

VCR recording (see Figure 5.14). This is unlike the analog cassette or reel-to-reel systems, which record with a stationary head that puts data on the tape in a straight-line (linear) fashion.

Tape speed for the DAT recorder is not a factor in the quality of the recording, since only binary data is recorded on the tape; however, with its rotary head drum spinning at 2,000 RPM, the DAT records at an effective tape-to-head speed of over 120 IPS. This high recording speed makes it possible to get all the necessary binary data on the tape. The result is the usual outstanding digital sound quality.

5.15 DAT CASSETTES

The actual DAT cassette tape is designed similarly to a VCR tape and consists of two small tape reels encased in a plastic housing about the size of a pack of playing cards (see Figure 5.15), with the ends of the audio tape permanently attached to the internal reels. The longest DAT tapes are capable of recording about 2 hours. DAT recording is 16-bit at sampling rates of 32, 44.1, or 48 kHz.

While cueing time for any track on a CD player is only 1 to 2 seconds, cueing time from one end of the DAT tape to the other is about 40 seconds. This slower access time is of some concern to broadcasters and would probably necessitate more available DAT sources than CD sources in practical use. On the other hand, cueing a DAT deck from any position to another position 10 minutes either side of the current position can be done in 10 seconds or less, which compares with the normal run-out time on the audio tape cartridge. This made DAT another possible replacement for the analog cart machine, but it never really developed; however, DAT is often used in field recording and also finds a home as another digital recorder in the audio production studio.

5.16 ADVANTAGES OF THE DAT RECORDER

The DAT recorders have the same superior sound quality associated with CDs—exceptional frequency response and signal-to-noise ratio; wide dynamic range; and virtually no wow, flutter, hiss, hum, or distortion. In addition, the DAT has been developed with recording capability, and the material recorded can be dubbed almost endlessly without degradation of quality. Even with recordable CDs now available, the DAT has the advantage of a longer recording time. Perhaps the biggest advantages of the DAT format are convenience of handling (similar to working with a cassette) and the relative compactness of its portable units. However, future use of the DAT in the broadcast studio is unsure because it faces stiff competition from the newer digital recording equipment noted earlier in this chapter.

5.17 CONCLUSION

With the advent of digital equipment and the advantages in quality and convenience it offers, the use of older analog equipment continues to diminish. Being comfortable working with various kinds of digital equipment will be a necessary skill for most radio production people. It's also probable that new types of digital-based equipment will continue to be developed, and equipment not yet thought of will find a home in future radio production facilities.

Self-Study

QUESTIONS

1. Digital cartridge recorders use the same audio carts as the older analog machines, but record in a digital format.

   a) true
   b) false

2. What does the minidisc recorder use as its recording and storage medium?

   a) standard audio cassette
   b) 2.5-inch computer-type disk
   c) 3.5-inch computer-type disk
   d) DAT cassette

3. What is one reason for using a professional-quality CD player rather than a consumer model in the radio production studio?

   a) Professional-quality players use a higher powered laser than a consumer model.
   b) Professional-quality players offer a better signal-to-noise ratio and less distortion than consumer models.
   c) Professional-quality players offer a greater frequency response and better dynamic range than consumer models.
   d) Professional-quality players are built for heavy-duty, continuous operation, and consumer models are not.

4. The lacquer coating on a compact disc makes it virtually indestructible in normal broadcast use.

   a) true
   b) false

5. The DASH format is used in many radio production studios because it is one of the least expensive digital formats.

   a) true
   b) false

6. Which of the following is true of the DAT recorder?

   a) uses a stationary head
   b) places data on the tape in a linear fashion
   c) cues up any track in two seconds
   d) uses an AMS function to skip forward or backward to the next track

7. What is ATRAC (Adaptive Transform Acoustic Coding) used for?

   a) auto-reverse on a DAT recorder
   b) synchronization of CD-R and CD-RW discs
   c) data compression
   d) recording audio on a DVD

8. Which format allows a CD recorder to record a blank CD only once?

   a) CD-RW
   b) DASH
   c) WORM
   d) DVD

9. Compact discs are best cleaned with a cloth wiped in a circular motion over the playing surface of the disc.

   a) true
   b) false

10. Most digital recorders allow the user to add to the recording an electronic label that can show track name, timing, and other information on an LCD screen.

    a) true
    b) false

11. The DVD-audio disc can utilize music encoded at each of the sampling rates and bit lengths shown. Which one is also shared with the CD?

    a) 44.1 kHz/16-bit
    b) 48kHz/24-bit
    c) 96kHz/24-bit
    d) 192kHz/16-bit

12. Once a CD-RW disc has been "finalized" it cannot be erased and rerecorded.

    a) true
    b) false

13. The MD is one type of digital player featuring a memory buffer that helps prevent mistracking if the player is bumped during playback.

    a) true
    b) false

14. Which of the following is *not* an advantage of the CD player?

    a) random access to material on the CD
    b) lack of physical contact between player and CD
    c) large signal-to-noise ratio
    d) ability to hold more information than a DVD

15. Which recording medium would provide the longest recording time under normal stereo recording conditions?

    a) MD
    b) DAT
    c) CD-R
    d) CD-RW

16. You know a compact disc should only be marked on the label side, but which type of writing instrument should you use to mark a CD?

    a) ball-point pen
    b) No. 2 lead pencil
    c) felt-tip permanent marker
    d) none of the above; use an adhesive label

17. Which of the following is *not* one of the main internal components of the compact disc player?

   a) drive motor
   b) laser and lens system
   c) compact flash card
   d) tracking mechanism

18. The DVD Direct Stream Digital™ recording process promises increased resolution and a more natural sound than other digital recording methods.

   a) true
   b) false

19. In the production studio, which of the following would be considered a playback-only medium?

   a) CD
   b) MD
   c) SACD
   d) DASH

20. Digital recorders that employ a compact flash card have the ability to dub recordings using USB direct downloading rather than having to wait for real-time dubs.

   a) true
   b) false

ANSWERS

If You Answered A:

1a. No. Some digital cart machines use compact flash cards or zip disks, but none utilize the old analog carts. (Reread 5.12.)

2a. Wrong. The audio cassette is the recording and storage medium for the analog cassette recorder that the minidisc was designed to replace. (Reread 5.9 and 5.10.)

3a. No. Both professional and consumer-model CD players use a similar laser system. (Reread 5.2 and 5.3.)

4a. No. Although the lacquer coating helps protect the CD, it is far from indestructible—fingerprints, dust, and scratches can damage CDs. (Reread 5.4 and 5.5.)

5a. Wrong. Just the opposite is true; DASH is an expensive digital format rarely used in radio production. (Reread 5.13.)

6a. No. The DAT recorder uses a rotary head. (Reread 5.14.)

7a. No. This is not a feature found on DAT recorders. (Reread 5.11 and 5.14.)

8a. No. This is a recordable/erasable format. (Reread 5.6.)

9a. Wrong. CDs should only be wiped in a straight line from the center hole toward the outer rim. (Reread 5.5.)

10a. Correct. This is a feature of most digital recorders.

11a. Yes. This is the standard CD recording format that can also be used by DVD-audio.

12a. Wrong. CD-RW discs can be completely erased and rerecorded even after they have been finalized. (Reread 5.6.)

13a. Yes. This is true of the minidisc as well as many other digital players.

14a. No. Being able to instantly move from one track to another on the CD is a big advantage. (Reread 5.2 and 5.3.)

15a. Wrong. MD is limited to 80 minutes of stereo recording time in normal mode. (Reread 5.9 and 5.15.)

16a. No. You should not use a ball-point pen to label a CD. (Reread 5.5.)

17a. Wrong. The internal structure of a CD player centers around a drive motor. (Reread 5.2.)

18a. No. This is a false statement because Direct Stream Digital™ is associated with SACD, not DVD. (Reread 5.7 and 5.8.)

19a. No. CD recorders are readily found in the production studio. (Reread 5.2 and 5.7.)

20a. Correct. This feature is one of the main advantages of the compact flash recorder.

If You Answered B:

1b. Correct. There are several formats of recording media for various digital cart machines, but none are the same as the old analog carts.

2b. Yes. Minidisc recorders utilize a small CD-type disc encased in a plastic housing similar to a computer disk.

3b. Wrong. All CD players have similar S/N and distortion characteristics. (Reread 5.2 and 5.3.)

4b. Yes. CDs require careful handling even though the lacquer coating helps prevent problems.

5b. Correct. This is false statement because the DASH digital format is very expensive and rarely found in the radio production studio.

6b. Wrong. The recording tracks on a DAT are diagonal. (Reread 5.14 and 5.15.)

7b. No. This answer doesn't really make any sense. (Reread 5.6 and 5.11.)

8b. No. DASH is a digital reel-to-reel system. (Reread 5.6 and 5.13.)

9b. Correct. While a circular cleaning motion works for vinyl, it can damage a CD.

10b. Wrong. Most digital recorders do offer this operational feature. (Reread 5.12.)

11b. No. This is a DVD-audio format, but it is not used by CDs. (Reread 5.8.)

12b. Correct. CD-RW discs can be erased even after they have been finalized.

13b. No. This is a true statement. The MD (and other digital players) offers this feature. (Reread 5.9.)

14b. No. Since the CD is read by laser, there is no wear on the CD and this is a big advantage. (Reread 5.2 and 5.3.)

15b. Yes. DAT tapes are available that can record about two hours.

16b. No. You should not use a pencil to label a CD. (Reread 5.5.)

17b. Wrong. The internal structure of a CD player centers around a laser and lens system. (Reread 5.2.)

18b. Yes. Direct Stream Digital™ is associated with SACD, not DVD, making this a false statement.

19b. No. MD recorders are readily found in the production studio. (Reread 5.7 and 5.10.)

20b. Wrong. This is a true statement and this feature is one of the main advantages of the compact flash recorder. (Reread 5.12.)

If You Answered C:

2c. No. The regular computer disk has been used in another type of digital "cart" recorder, but not the minidisc. (Reread 5.9, 5.10, and 5.12.)

3c. No. All CD players have similar frequency response and dynamic range characteristics. (Reread 5.2 and 5.3.)

6c. Wrong. It takes longer than that to cue, especially if you're moving from one end of the tape to the other. (Reread 5.15.)

7c. Correct. This is Sony's data reduction scheme, which allows a long recording time on a small recording medium.

8c. Yes. This is the write once, read many format used by CD-R machines.

11c. No. This is a DVD-audio format, but it is not used by CD. (Reread 5.8.)

14c. No. The larger the S/N ratio the better, so this is an advantage. (Reread 5.2 and 5.3.)

15c. No. CD-R, like CD-RW, is limited to 80 minutes of recording time in normal recording mode. (Reread 5.6 and 5.15.)

16c. Yes. If you must label a CD, use a soft, felt-tip permanent marker.

17c. Correct. The compact flash card is a removable recording medium for other digital recorders.

19c. Yes. A super audio compact disc recorder would not likely be found in the typical production studio.

If You Answered D:

2d. No. DAT tapes are only used in DAT recorders and players. (Reread 5.9, 5.10, and 5.15.)

3d. Yes. Most consumer-model CD players can't stand up long to the constant use of a broadcast facility.

6d. Correct. AMS stands for Automatic Music Sensor and allows the operator to skip to the beginning of tracks.

7d. Wrong. Although there are different data compression schemes for recording onto digital media, ATRAC is associated with the minidisc. (Reread 5.8 and 5.11.)

8d. No. DVD is a different type of format. (Reread 5.6 and 5.8.)

11d. No. This is a DVD-audio format, but it is not used for CDs. (Reread 5.8.)

14d. Correct. A DVD can hold more information that a CD.

15d. Wrong. CD-RW, like CD-R, is limited to 80 minutes of recording time in normal recording mode. (Reread 5.6 and 5.15.)

16d. No. You should not use adhesive labels to mark a CD. (Reread 5.5.)

17d. Wrong. The internal structure of a CD player centers around a tracking mechanism. (Reread 5.2.)

19d. No. A DASH reel recorder could be found in a production studio, although it is too expensive for most broadcast stations. (Reread 5.7 and 5.13.)

Projects

PROJECT 1

Play and record several compact disc selections.

Purpose

To familiarize yourself with the operation of CD players.

Advice, Cautions, and Background

1. For this exercise you will need to work with a microphone, audio board, and audio recorder, so you may need help from your instructor to operate the pieces of equipment that you haven't yet learned.
2. Different brands of CD players have slightly different features, so you will need to learn the particular characteristics of your player.
3. You can play several selections from one CD or use several CDs. If you only have one CD player, you would be advised to use three cuts from one CD as you will probably not have time to change discs. If you have two CD players, you would be better off playing selections from at least two CDs.

How to Do the Project

1. Make sure your CD player is connected so that it can be faded out and will record onto an audio recorder.
2. Make sure a microphone is available so that you can announce the title of the selections you choose.
3. Examine the CD player and practice with it so that you can cue, play, and pause it with ease.
4. When you feel familiar with the player and have decided on three selections to play, start the recorder.
5. Complete the project by doing the following:
   a. Announce the name of the first musical selection, bring it in, and then fade it out after about 30 seconds.
   b. Announce the name of the second selection, bring it in, and fade it out after about 30 seconds. (If you have two CD players, you can cue the second one while the first is playing. If not, you'll need to cue a second selection while you are introducing it. This is not particularly difficult because most CD players enable you to cue easily.)
   c. In the same manner, announce the name of the third selection, bring it in, and then fade it out.
6. Label the assignment with your name and "CD Recording."
7. Turn in the assignment to your instructor to receive credit for the project.

PROJECT 2

Prepare a report on a digital player/recorder that is not discussed in this chapter.

Purpose

To keep you up-to-date on what is happening in this field.

Advice, Cautions, and Background

1. Technological developments in this field are changing rapidly. Undoubtedly there will be new products available by the time you read this text that were not available when it was written. It behooves anyone in the audio production field to keep up-to-date. However, audio

equipment also comes and goes, so don't be surprised if the player/recorder you write about today is no longer available a year from now.

2. You can select equipment that does more than play and/or record. For example, some of the current recorders also allow for editing or mixing.

3. The Internet is an excellent place to find this information. The major manufacturers place a great deal of material about their products on their web sites. Companies that are particularly active in this field include 360 Systems, Sony, Marantz, Roland, and Tascam. Use a search engine, such as Google, to find their Internet addresses.

How to Do the Project

1. Find a piece of equipment that qualifies as a digital player/recorder. As suggested, you can do this on the Internet or you can write to companies for their catalogues.

2. Research the characteristics of the piece of equipment. If you know a facility that has this equipment, talk with the engineer or an operator who uses it. You could also call a distributor who sells the equipment for additional information.

3. Organize your report, taking into consideration some of the following points:
   a. What is the primary purpose of the piece of equipment?
   b. How does it operate—with regular transport controls (play, record, stop, etc.); attached to a computer; with the use of a rotary dial?
   c. Is it designed to replace an older piece of equipment or is it designed for a new application?
   d. What compression format does it use, if any?
   e. What type of recording medium does it use—tape, computer disk, flash card, specially designed material?
   f. When was it introduced to the market? Are there optional features of this equipment?
   g. What does it cost?
   h. What is your assessment of whether or not this will be a successful product?

4. Write your report; remember to include your name and "Digital Player/Recorder" as a title on it.

5. Turn in the report to your instructor to receive credit for this project.

PROJECT 3

Record a public service announcement that uses a sound effect.

Purpose

To develop your skill in creating a radio spot that incorporates a sound effect to provide a transition.

Advice, Cautions, and Background

1. This project assumes you have enough familiarity with your studio equipment to accomplish basic recording and production techniques.

2. The production incorporates a single announcer voice, two distinct music beds, and a sound effect to provide a transition between the music beds.

3. You will need to write a simple script that can be read in about 20 seconds. Write the copy about an environmental concern, such as water pollution, littering, or forest fire prevention. The spot should follow a "problem–solution" format.

4. There are many ways to accomplish this project, so don't feel you must follow the production directions exactly.

How to Do the Project

1. Select music beds that are appropriate for the style of the spot. You should use a more somber-sounding bed for the "problem" and a more upbeat sound for the "solution." The CD-ROM that came with this text contains a variety of musical styles that may provide what you need, or you can find your own music on another CD.

2. You can play back the music beds directly from the CD.

3. Record the music bed and script (voice) onto a recorder. First record the "problem" part of the spot, using a serious tone of voice and mixing the appropriate music bed with it. Then record the "solution" with a lighter vocal delivery, slightly faster pace, and more up-tempo music.

4. Begin recording the music bed at full volume. Start the vocal track and simultaneously fade the music bed slightly so the vocal track is dominant while you record the rest of the script.

5. Now, find an appropriate sound effect. It will be used to separate the two music beds and provide a transition between the "problem" and "solution" parts of the spot.

6. Record the sound effect onto another recorder.

7. Set correct playback levels for the vocal/music bed tracks and the sound effect. Then cue both to the beginning sound.

8. It may take you several attempts to get the spot to come out correctly. If you need to do it over, just cue everything and try again.

9. On the finished commercial, write your name and "Sound Effect Radio Spot," and turn it in to your instructor to receive credit for this project.

6

DIGITAL EDITING AND MULTI-TRACK RECORDING

6.1 INTRODUCTION

From creating a music bed to adding sound effects to editing out vocal mistakes, audio editing is a day-to-day part of radio production work and it's one of the more important skills you need to know as a production person. Because of the use of digital equipment, the techniques for audio **editing** have changed. The beginning of this chapter is concerned with digital audio editing, but if you'd like an understanding of old-fashioned audio tape splicing, you'll find sections in Chapter 9, "Analog Audio Production," that will provide it. And lest you think you're learning outdated skills, you'll see that many of the basic procedures of audio tape editing are the same, whether you're using "cut and splice" methods or manipulating a mouse.

Closely related to audio editing is multi-track production work. Even though some larger facilities have had multi-track reel-to-reel recorders in their production studios for years, the majority of radio production work was done in either mono or 2-track stereo. Now, as digital equipment has found its way into almost all production studios, more and more of the production that's done is multi-track. In this chapter, you'll learn some of the basic techniques of multi-track production; however, these should merely suggest new ways to approach your future production work. You'll quickly learn that the biggest advantage of multi-track recording is that it opens the door to faster, easier, and more creative production work.

6.2 REASONS FOR EDITING

Why do you even need to edit audio in the first place? The answers are relatively obvious. For example, rarely will you produce the vocal track for a commercial exactly the way you want it on the first try. While you could record the script over and over until you got it perfect, editing gives you the ability to eliminate mistakes. Now you can just record a few takes and it's more likely you'll get part of it great on one take, part of it great on another, and so on. The best recording will probably be bits and pieces from various takes that you edit to take out fluffs and bad segments and keep only the exact words and phrases you want. Other production work may require you to edit out excessive pauses or "uhs" from a piece of news tape or language not allowed by the FCC from an artist interview.

In addition to eliminating mistakes, editing allows you to decrease the length of production work. Radio requires exact times for commercials, news stories, and other programs, and editing can keep your work to the exact lengths required. You can either manually edit out excessive pauses in a vocal track or, in some instances, utilize digital audio editing software to automatically "time compress" a vocal segment to the exact length you need. Many half-hour interview programs are really edited down from an actual interview that went on much longer. Entire questions that didn't get a good response can be edited out, or long, rambling responses can be cut down to a more concise reply.

Audio editing also gives you the freedom to record out of sequence. For example, you might be putting together a commercial that uses the testimonials of several customers that you've recorded. It's probable that the one you want to use first in your commercial may not have been recorded first. Editing allows you to easily rearrange the order or, again, just use a portion of what you originally taped in the final production.

6.3 TYPES OF EDITING

Digital audio editing is presently the most common form of editing. However, two other forms, splicing and dubbing, were used in the past and are still used in some facilities today. **Splice editing** normally refers to physically cutting audio tape, taking a portion out, and splicing the remaining pieces back together. It's almost always done with a reel-to-reel recorder because the tape in other recorders, such as a cassette, is for all practical purposes inaccessible for editing. **Dub editing** refers to editing in which portions of one recording are copied onto another. **Digital audio editing** refers to any system that uses computer software to manipulate audio with either a PC computer or proprietary editing equipment. Before continuing this chapter, you may want to review Chapter 2, "Digital Audio Production," to refresh your memory on the digital process and various types of editing equipment, from desktop editing systems to digital audio workstations.

PRODUCTION TIP #6
Destructive vs. Nondestructive Editing

The two most common methods for manipulating audio once it has been brought into a digital or computer system are **linear** and **nonlinear**. The linear mode is a destructive form of editing because the software makes physical changes to the data as the editing is accomplished. Each editing action is performed on the original sound file in sequential order, writing the processed data to a new sound file that represents the edited audio. The linear mode was somewhat based on the analog splicing technique and is becoming less common. With a linear or destructive system, the edited audio can be heard only after the audio has been processed and written to the hard drive. Destructive is a little misleading, for although the original audio data is ultimately altered, most of these editing systems do have an "undo" feature that lets data be restored until you save the edited sound file. To do so, however, requires copying and saving large amounts of the original data during the editing process. This not only eats up lots of computer storage space on the hard drive, but also requires more time to accomplish the edits.

Nonlinear or nondestructive systems use pointers to tag the original audio and mark where the edits take place. To edit out a portion of an audio sound file, a pointer at the beginning and end of the edit would instruct the software program to skip the deleted section of audio during playback. Essentially, you manipulate the pointers that are linked to the original data. Playback can occur immediately without waiting for the audio to be rewritten to the hard drive, and the original audio on the hard drive remains intact. Most modern editing systems are nonlinear and therefore nondestructive, although many software programs employ both destructive and nondestructive editing methods.

6.4 DIGITAL AUDIO EDITING

Editing normally begins after you've recorded some audio into whichever type of system you're using. You might also be able to import a previously recorded audio file, or some programs may allow you to directly "rip" audio from a CD into a file. There are many different systems currently available for digital editing; however, there is no one standard technique. To gain an understanding of digital audio editing, we'll look at one system (see Figure 6.1) that uses a PC-compatible computer, digital sound card, and a digital editor program—*Adobe Audition*.

To illustrate the basic audio edit, let's first record three words—*dog, cat, banana*—into our system. To begin recording, click on FILE from the Options menu, select NEW, click the appropriate recording specifications (for example, sample rate = 44,100, channels = stereo, resolution = 16-bit), and then click on OK. We'll assume you have a microphone plugged directly into your sound card or the output of your audio console feeds into the sound card. Click on the RECORD button (red circle) on the Transport controls and speak the three words into the microphone, pausing slightly between each word. Finally, click on the STOP button (gray square) on the Transport controls. The audio you recorded will appear as a green waveform (see Figure 6.2) on the black background in the Waveform Display area of the screen. Silence (the pauses) will be shown as a flat green line. (These are the default screen colors, so you may see something different depending on the settings for your system.) Even though some procedures and terminology will be different, many of the basic principles would apply to any equipment that's capable of digital audio editing. Much like dealing with the audio console, an understanding of one editing program will give you a good idea about the operation of most of the other available programs.

If you wanted to edit out the word *cat*, you would click an edit point just to the left of the waveform for the word *cat* and then drag the mouse to the right, stopping just before the waveform for the word *banana*. Including the pause after the word maintains the natural pacing of the audio. Selecting edit points just before and immediately after the word *cat* would increase the pause between *dog* and *banana*. In a similar manner, selecting edit points just after the word *dog* and just before the word *banana* would eliminate any pause between those words, creating an unnatural flow to the words. The area you have selected will become highlighted in white (refer to Figure 6.2). You can hear the audio segment you've highlighted by clicking on the PLAY button (single green forward triangle). If you need to adjust either edit point, hold down the SHIFT key and click on the edit point. Move the edit point left or right as required. Most editor programs have a function to zoom in on the segment of audio you're working on to fine-tune any adjustments and get the mark exactly where you want it. To complete the edit, click on EDIT on the Options menu and select CUT or click on the appropriate toolbar icon. The selected audio will be cut to a clipboard and the remaining audio will automatically "heal" or be joined together, leaving the words *dog* and *banana*. It takes a lot longer to

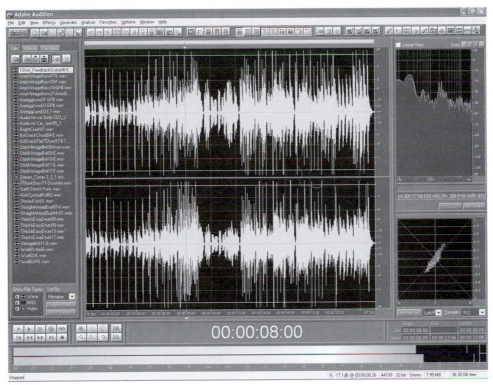

FIGURE 6.1 With the digital audio editor you can instantly cut, paste, copy, and otherwise manipulate audio with a few mouse clicks. (Adobe product screen shot reprinted with permission from Adobe Systems Incorporated.)

explain this process than it does to accomplish it—as you'll quickly learn!

Suppose you now want to paste the word *cat*, which we just edited out, in front of the word *dog*. Simply click a single edit point just to the left of the waveform of the word *dog*, then click on EDIT on the Options menu and select PASTE. The audio from the clipboard will be edited back in at that point so the word order is now *cat*, *dog*, and *banana*. Should you decide you don't really want to do this, you can click on FILE and select UNDO, which will cancel or undo your last action. Normally, UNDO can be repeated to back out of several actions if necessary.

To copy a word, you'd follow a similar process. Click an edit point just after the word *dog* and drag to the end of the word *banana*. The word *banana* and the pause before it should now be highlighted. Once again go to EDIT and select COPY. Click an edit point right at the end of the word *banana* and go to EDIT and select PASTE. The word order should be *cat, dog, banana, banana*.

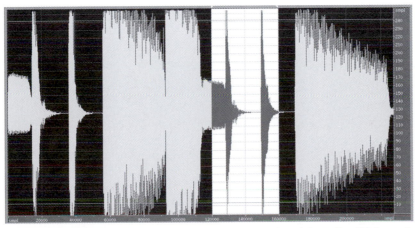

FIGURE 6.2 The waveform display of the digital audio editor shows a visual representation of the audio. (Adobe product screen shot reprinted with permission from Adobe Systems Incorporated.)

In most cases and with most audio editing programs, you'll want to both export and save your project when you're done editing. You want to export your file when you are finished editing it and would like to write it to a CD or other medium to play later on the air. Most programs give you the option to export in various file formats, but the most popular are .wav (which gives you high quality, but uses lots of hard drive space) and .mp3 (which saves you space, but can sacrifice sound quality). How the audio will ultimately be used may well determine what sound format you want to employ if you have that option.

Saving the project creates a file that only your audio editing software can open. You would reopen this file either if you weren't finished with your project when you saved it last and wanted to work on it more, or if later you wanted to re-edit the material. Unlike the exported file, which exports a single mono or stereo file, the saved file keeps intact multiple tracks, if you used them in your project, making it possible to separate them again. This is especially helpful if, for example, you have created a project with dialogue or narration and an underlying music bed. Perhaps when you were creating it, you were using headphones and the mix between dialogue and music sounded balanced, so you exported it to play on the air. Later, however, when playing it on monitor speakers, you found that the music was too loud or not loud enough and distracted from the voice or didn't support it enough. If you had only exported the audio, not saved the file, all you would have would be the file with the audio elements out of kilter, irretrievably mixed together. With the saved file, however, you have the music on one track and the voice on another. You can therefore turn up or down the voice or music to readjust the balance and then export the corrected audio again.

You'll find that regardless of what audio editor you're using, it's capable of a lot more than these few simple operations. We've only touched the surface of what a digital audio editor can do, but it should be obvious, when comparing this procedure with the steps involved in traditional splicing explained in Chapter 9, "Analog Audio Production," that digital audio editing is the more accurate, quicker, and easier technique. The best way to learn what an editor can do is to try different things and, of course, reading the manual or Help screens doesn't hurt either. You should also check the software manufacturer's web site as many offer tutorials or hints on how to get the most out of their programs. Most digital audio editors also feature multi-track and signal processing capabilities, which we'll look at next as well as in the following chapter.

6.5 THE DIGITAL MULTI-TRACK RECORDER

From the desktop audio editor to the complex workstation, most digital systems have multi-track capability. Figure 6.3 shows the multi-track view screen from *Adobe Audition*. In this view, the first few tracks of the system are shown with

FIGURE 6.3 Most digital audio editing software also incorporates a virtual multi-track recorder. (Adobe product screen shot reprinted with permission from Adobe Systems Incorporated.)

some of the controls associated with those tracks. Multi-track recorders are merely a number of 2-track recorders combined, but that gives the production person a tremendous amount of creative flexibility. Each production element, such as a vocal track or music bed, can be recorded on a separate track. Once recorded, they can be individually manipulated (such as changing volume or adding some signal processing effect), but also played back simultaneously to hear the mix of the whole production.

Like the editing portion of the program, pull-down menus provide access to all the multi-track functions, and tool bar icons also can be used to select the most commonly used functions. The audio data in each track is graphically displayed as a waveform block as shown in Figure 6.4. The bottom of the waveform display window, along the horizontal axis, shows a time line. In the multi-track mode, audio can easily be mixed, moved, copied, or deleted, and information can be displayed on the screen in different sizes with a "zoom" control. Each track has various virtual faders and pan controls that allow for level setting and balance control during the mix of the production.

All the production techniques mentioned in the rest of this chapter can be utilized with any multi-track system, but you'll probably find that actually manipulating the audio is much easier digitally. For example, to move a waveform block with *Adobe Audition*, right mouse click on it and continue to hold down the mouse button. You can now "drag and drop" that audio from one track to another, from one part of a track to another part, or, with other simple mouse moves, mix, copy, divide, or delete the audio.

From a simple combining of a music bed and voice-over track to a complex production using hundreds of audio blocks, digital multi-track recorders offer ease of operation and new creative possibilities for the modern production person. Remember, when you copy or otherwise manipulate the audio in digital form, the sound doesn't degrade as it can with dubbed analog generations.

6.6 OTHER MULTITRACK RECORDERS

In addition to the DAW or audio editing software already mentioned, some production facilities have a digital multi-track recorder, like the one shown in Figure 6.5, that employs built-in and removable hard drives as the recording and storage medium. Analog, multi-track, reel-to-reel recorders (shown in Figure 6.6) may also be found in some production facilities, but like all analog-based equipment, their presence is becoming less and less likely.

Any machine that can record more than one track is technically a multi-track recorder. However, in radio production, multi-track generally means recorders that have four, eight, or more tracks. The recording studio often employs recorders with 16, 24, 32, and more tracks. In any case, at some point in the production process the multi-track signal is mixed down to stereo or mono.

The multi-track recorder is often part of a system that contains the recorder, an audio mixer, input sources and output devices, and signal processing equipment. Several elements may be combined; for example, a multi-channel mixer with equalization capability and a multi-track recorder with noise-reduction capability may be combined in a single unit. The audio mixer may be the production room board or a dedicated mixer that is associated only with the multi-track recorder like the one shown in Figure 6.7. In either case, it will need a good number of inputs and outputs—although a microphone is usually assigned to just one channel, stereo sources (such as a CD player) are usually assigned to two channels. In general, the mixer should have at least one input/output channel for each track of the multi-track recorder. In other words, an 8-track recorder should have an audio mixer with at least eight channels associated with it. In addition, the mixer must be able to input each of the tracks of the multi-track recorder so that monitoring and mixing can take place. One arrangement might put all the normal inputs (microphones, CDs, etc.) on the "program" mode of the mixer and all the tape inputs on "audition" or "auxiliary."

Signal processing usually includes equalization, noise reduction, and reverb effects at the least, and it can be much more elaborate. Some signal processing is usually associated with individual channels of the mixer; for example, each channel may have some EQ adjustment. In other cases, the output of a channel (such as a microphone) may be sent to a signal processing device (such as a digital reverb), and then the output of the device is sent back to

FIGURE 6.4 Audio segments are shown as waveform blocks that can be manipulated with drag-and-drop mouse clicks. (Adobe product screen shot reprinted with permission from Adobe Systems Incorporated.)

FIGURE 6.5 A digital multi-track recorder that uses built-in and removable hard drives as its recording and storage medium. (Image courtesy of Tascam®.)

another input on the mixer, where the "processed" signal can be routed to the multi-track recorder.

The input sources are normal production inputs, such as microphones, CD players, or other audio players, and the output devices are either headphones or monitor speakers that allow for listening to the mix of all the tracks.

The multi-track recorder operates like any other audio recorder. Some multi-track recorders employed in radio production use audio tape that is ½-inch or 1-inch wide; however, there are a few recorders that use standard ¼-inch tape, cassette tape, various videotape formats, and hard disk drives. Recorders that use 2-inch tape, such as those found in recording studios, record on 24 (or more)

FIGURE 6.6 No longer available, one of the first multi-track recorders used in the radio production studio was a 4-track reel-to-reel recorder. (Image courtesy of Studer Revox America, Inc.)

tracks. The tape track configuration in Chapter 9, "Analog Audio Production," shows that a 4-track recorder would have four separate tracks being recorded on the audio tape in one direction. Each track can be recorded and played back separately so that you can record one track while listening to another; this is a primary advantage of multi-track recording. Regardless of the actual type of multi-track used, you'll find that you're employing a handful of multi-track techniques as you begin your production work.

6.7 OVERDUBBING TRACKS

One of the most basic techniques used in multi-track work is **overdubbing,** or the process of adding new tracks to existing tracks. Refer to Figure 6.3 as you follow the steps of a basic overdub using the multi-track function of *Adobe Audition.* Assume the correct device settings have been made; then to begin recording click on FILE and select NEW SESSION. A window will pop up that allows setting the recording characteristics for this session, so choose the sample rate and bit resolution you want. Now click on the small red **R** button (to enable recording) for Track 1. Then when you click on the master RECORD button on the Transport Controls, you can record, for example, an announcer's voice onto this track. Click the Transport STOP button when you're done recording. To accomplish the overdub, click on the **R** button for Track 1 again, which will now make this track play back. Click on the **R** button for Track 2. This time, when you click on the master RECORD button, you will record another voice on Track 2. Click on the STOP button when you're done recording. Remember to click on the Track 2 **R** button when you've finished recording the vocal track to disable recording on this track. With a few other mouse clicks, you can adjust the volume levels between the two tracks. You could also import a musical .wav or .mp3 file into Track 3, providing a music bed for your production. With

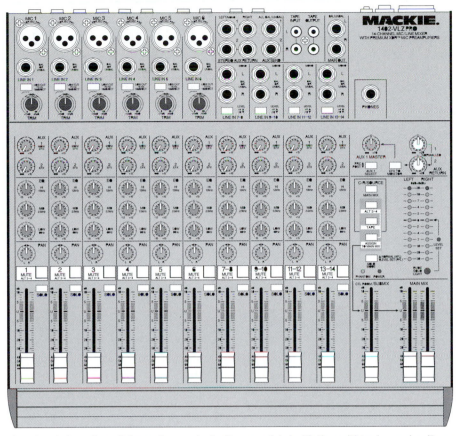

FIGURE 6.7 A small audio mixer, independent of the studio console, is often associated with the multi-track recorder. (Image courtesy of Mackie®.)

Adobe Audition, you can "rip" music into the system by clicking on FILE and then selecting the EXTRACT AUDIO FROM CD option. There are a number of parameters you can choose, but the main options will be to select the TRACK you want to import into the system or select the TIME to import just a portion of a track. Once you've set the various components and clicked on OK, the audio will be ripped into the system. The exact steps described are unique to this software, but most systems will employ a similar type of process.

A comparable procedure would be followed if you used a multi-track, analog, reel-to-reel recorder. This time, record the music bed on two separate tracks: Track 1 for the left channel and Track 2 for the right channel. Then cue the recorder to the beginning of the music bed. Now, while you listen to the playback of the music bed (usually through headphones) on Tracks 1 and 2, you record a vocal on Track 3. All multi-track recorders have a **sel-sync** feature that lets you listen to one track and record on a different track in synchronization.

Overdubbing allows you to build a production in layers, because you don't have to record everything at the same time. If you decided later to add a sound effect to the production, you could just record it on another track, move it to the appropriate spot where you want it to occur, and set

the proper volume. Playing back all the tracks at the same time would let you hear how all the elements fit together.

6.8 PUNCHING IN TRACKS

If you've recorded a vocal on one track, but a portion of the vocal contains a mistake, a multi-track recording technique known as the **punch in** allows you to record over just the part that contains the mistake, and leave the rest of the track undisturbed. To punch in using *Adobe Audition*, first highlight the section of audio you want to rerecord by clicking and dragging. Click EDIT on the menu, select the PUNCH IN option, and put the track into the record-enabled mode. Place the cursor a bit before the section where the punch in will occur. Click RECORD and you will hear the audio up to the point of the punch in where you begin your rerecording. You can record several different "takes," and the program will allow you to select the one you feel is best.

It's important not to change volume levels or microphone position of the original setup so that the rerecording is consistent with the original recording.

Most multi-track recorders can be put in "record" mode by pressing a record button for the individual track you want to record on or putting that track into a "record ready" mode, then pressing a master record button on the multitrack. The technique is a punch in because you play back the track to the point where you want to rerecord, punch in the record button, and record over the portion of the track that you wish to correct. You punch out of record mode at an appropriate point after you've fixed the mistake. Essentially you're doing an edit on the fly with a punch in; in fact, it's also known as an **insert edit**. You might need to practice a few times so you know exactly where you want to punch in and punch out. Try to choose logical spots, such as the end of a sentence or at a pause between words; otherwise the punch in may be noticeable.

6.9 BOUNCING TRACKS

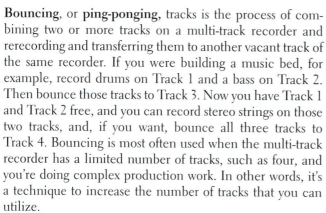

Bouncing, or **ping-ponging**, tracks is the process of combining two or more tracks on a multi-track recorder and rerecording and transferring them to another vacant track of the same recorder. If you were building a music bed, for example, record drums on Track 1 and a bass on Track 2. Then bounce those tracks to Track 3. Now you have Track 1 and Track 2 free, and you can record stereo strings on those two tracks, and, if you want, bounce all three tracks to Track 4. Bouncing is most often used when the multi-track recorder has a limited number of tracks, such as four, and you're doing complex production work. In other words, it's a technique to increase the number of tracks that you can utilize.

However, bouncing tracks brings with it two disadvantages that the production person must be aware of. First, once several tracks are combined, they can't be uncombined. You can't change the balance of the mixed tracks, and if you equalize or otherwise process the track, it impacts all elements on the track. Second, each "bounce" causes a degradation of the sound quality of the track if the recorder is analog. It's just like dubbing from one tape to another; once you've bounced to one track, that track is a second-generation recording. If you bounce that track again, it's become a third-generation recording with resulting lower audio quality. Careful planning can help keep the number of tracks that you must bounce to a minimum.

Digital editing software has a function to bounce tracks even though many programs allow you to add as many tracks as you like, limited only by the hard drive space you have available. Even with a large number of tracks, there are two main reasons for bouncing several tracks to one. First, at the end of the production you will want to create a final stereo mix. For many programs, including *Adobe Audition*, this is simply a menu item selection to "mix down" all files. Second, you may need to bounce some tracks together to reduce the hard disk space and processing time needed to manipulate the audio. If you have a large number of tracks, making a "sub-mix" of some of them will speed up CPU processing. Again, you can just highlight the

tracks you want to combine and choose a "mix down" option for selected files.

Live bouncing is a similar technique, but at the same time that you're mixing several tracks onto a vacant track, you add a live track to the mix. Again, it's a technique to get a maximum number of sources onto a minimum number of tracks and is therefore primarily useful with limited-channel analog systems.

6.10 TRACK SHEETS

As you can tell just by reading about the various techniques above, multi-track recording can become complicated. Good production practice dictates that you keep notes of what material is recorded on which track. Although there is no standard form, Figure 6.8 shows one possible **track sheet**, or format, for keeping notes regarding a multi-track production. The top of the page indicates the number of tracks the recorder has, the edge of the page indicates the various takes, and the boxes show what was put on each track during each take. As shown, during the first take, an announcer vocal was put on Track 1, a sound effect was put on Track 2, a music bed was put on Tracks 3 and 4, and Track 5 was left open. This doesn't mean that these elements were all recorded at the same time; most likely they were put down separately, but these were the first elements assigned to those tracks.

During the second take, the announcer vocal was not changed, but the sound effect on Track 2 and the music bed on Tracks 3 and 4 were all bounced to Track 5. On the third take, Tracks 1 and 5 did not change; however, a new music bed was put on Tracks 3 and 4, and the announcer vocal was rerecorded on Track 2. You could also put any signal processing settings, music bed cuts used, or special notes regarding the production on the track sheet.

With digital software, most programs allow you to simply name the tracks directly in the program, so that these track labels are saved along with the file and there is no need for a hard copy. When using nondestructive signal processing, the equalization and other settings are automatically saved as part of the file and can be edited later. If you are using destructive editing, it's a good idea to make a note of the settings used, in case you want to duplicate effects later. Most programs have a "file information" or "notes" section where you can type in whatever information you might want to maintain, and it will be saved when the file is saved.

6.11 MIXING TO STEREO/MONO COMPATIBILITY

As noted, regardless of how many tracks you work with in a multi-track production, you will ultimately mix the production down into a stereo mix with just a left and right channel. Certain tracks from the multi-track master may be

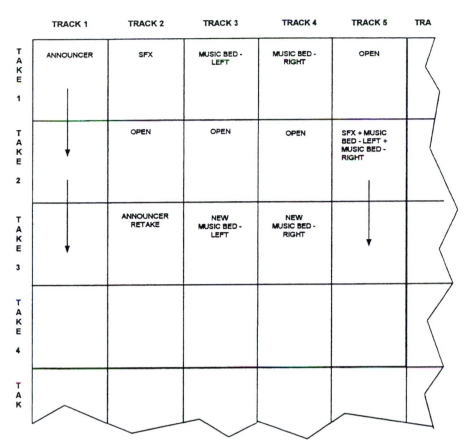

FIGURE 6.8 A track sheet shows what material is recorded on which track during a multi-track recording session.

panned to the right channel, some tracks may be panned to the left channel, and some tracks may be balanced to both left and right. This is where the production person needs a good monitoring system and some good judgment to create just the right mix.

Most likely you're working in stereo and hearing the final mix in stereo; however, you need to hear the same mix in mono because sometimes a mix sounds great in stereo, but not in mono. Often by listening in cue (assuming the cue signal is in mono), you can tell if a stereo mix is not going to be compatible with mono. It's possible that portions of the audio signal will be out of **phase** when the left and right channels are combined for the mono signal, causing a cancellation and diminishment of the sound at different spots. A fine-tuning of some track equalization, a slight volume change, or minor panning adjustment will usually correct the mono signal, but it's always important to make sure the stereo and mono signals are compatible.

6.12 THE MULTI-TRACK COMMERCIAL SPOT

There is no "standard" way to record using multi-track techniques, but let's look at the production of a commercial spot that includes two announcer voices, a background music bed, and two sound effects. In most cases, the music bed

would begin first at full volume for a few seconds, and then fade under the vocals and hold at a background level. The first announcer begins his or her voice-over on top of the music bed, probably trading lines with the other announcer until the end of the copy. Sound effects are added at the appropriate points, and the music bed is brought up to full volume at the end of the voice-over. The music bed ultimately ends cold or may fade out. Of course, all of this takes place in a 30- or 60-second time frame. Assuming a production studio setup with an 8-track recorder (or eight tracks on an audio editing software program), refer to Figure 6.9 to help visualize what is happening during this "typical" production.

Each sound source (microphone, CD, etc.) should be assigned a channel on the mixer and a corresponding track on the recorder. Let's put announcer #1 on Track 1, announcer #2 on Track 2, a CD sound effect on Tracks 3 and 4, a CD music bed on Tracks 5 and 6, and a minidisc sound effect on Tracks 7 and 8. The first track you record is extremely important because it's often the reference for all the other tracks. In radio production, the music bed or vocal track is often put down first. In this case, the music bed is a preproduced and timed music bed from a CD production library. We just have to dub it or rip it from the CD into our recorder, either by importing it or setting the multi-track recorder to record on Tracks 5 and 6 only (the music

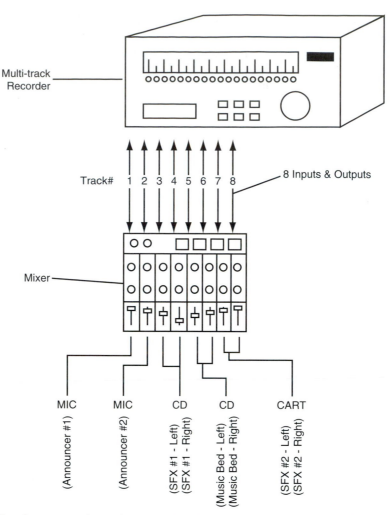

FIGURE 6.9 Multi-track recording often routes various audio sources through a mixer and to individual tracks of the recorder, which can also play back those tracks through the mixer.

bed). In either case, you want to have the entire music bed at full volume in the recorder, even though you'll be fading it under the announcers. The various levels can be balanced during the final mix.

Next, put the recorder Tracks 5 and 6 into a "safe" and "sync" mode. This allows you to overdub on the other tracks at the same time that you monitor the music bed tracks. Set Tracks 1 and 2 into the record position. Since the announcers "trade" lines throughout the commercial, you should record them at the same time, which will provide a more natural feeling of interplay and continuity than if they were recorded separately. While monitoring Tracks 5, 6, 1, and 2, record the vocals on Tracks 1 and 2. You should fade the music at the appropriate place, so the announcers get the proper feel of reading the spot, but remember the actual blend of all the elements will take place later. At this point, if the vocal tracks came out okay, the announcers could leave, and a production person would finish the spot. That makes sense to do if the announcers are high-priced talent, and that's why many multi-track productions are started by

putting down the vocal tracks. Suppose announcer #2 misspoke the final line in the spot. Depending on the complexity of the spot, it would be possible to set up Tracks 5, 6, and 1 to play, and have announcer #2 rerecord a portion of Track 2 to correct the mistake with a punch in.

By additional overdubbing, the various sound effects would be added by playing back the tracks that were previously recorded and recording only those tracks that were assigned to sound effects, doing one effect at a time. If you miscue a sound effect, you don't have to reset every element and start all over again. You would merely rerecord the track that had the mistake on it or click and drag the misplaced element to the desired location. Once you have all eight tracks recorded, you can begin to "mix down" the final spot. Since most commercials are played on a stereo format, they are usually mixed down to a 2-track (stereo) master. You'll probably play back all eight tracks several times now (through the mixer, monitoring the multi-track recorder outputs) to adjust the levels. For this commercial, you can get the announcer and sound effect levels balanced and leave them set, but you'll have to fade the music bed up and down manually at the appropriate points as you record onto the 2-track. With a more complex spot, you might have to manipulate more than one fader during the final mix, and that's where practice and experience come in to produce the perfect spot! If you're using digital multi-track software, you can often adjust volume levels and pans so they will automate during playback and you don't have to manipulate a bunch of faders during the mix. Also, most digital software allows for stereo tracks. Instead of having to set both Tracks 5 and 6 for the music bed and manipulate both volume controls, a single stereo track can be set up that contains both the right and left channels. In the case of music or sound effects, usually there is no need to adjust the volume of the left and right channels discretely, so this saves on tracks and trouble.

6.13 VOICE DOUBLING, CHORUSING, AND STACKING

Multi-track techniques open the door to many special effects that can turn a basic production into a creative masterpiece. Voice doubling, chorusing, and stacking are three forms of overdubbing that can give your next production a unique sound. They are often used to add a "thickness" to the vocal by making it seem like several voices speaking at the same time. **Voice doubling** is exactly what the name implies. Record your voice on Track 1. Now, while monitoring Track 1, record your voice again on Track 2. Even though you read the same script, it's impossible to record both tracks exactly alike. The effect, also known as "voice

dubbing," will be closer to two people reading the same script at the same time.

Chorusing is taking voice doubling one step further. Record at least two additional tracks in sync with the original track, creating a "chorus" effect. The more additional tracks you record, the larger your chorus will sound. It's a way for one announcer to become a group of announcers. **Stacking** is a similar multi-track technique in which an announcer "sings harmony" to a previously recorded track. Since it is actually a form of delay, chorus effects are often included on audio editing software (see Figure 6.10). In this case, up to 12 voices can simulate various chorus effects, and even though only one voice recorded the script, the program will slightly change timing, intonation, and vibrato of the original audio to give each voice created a distinct sound.

6.14 DOVETAILING

One announcer can appear to be two different announcers trading lines using a technique referred to as **dovetailing**. On Track 1, the announcer records the *odd* lines of the script, while reading the even lines silently. This leaves space between the odd lines on Track 1. Now, record on Track 2 the *even* lines of the script while mentally reading the odd lines to keep the timing correct. When both tracks are played back, you get the effect of two announcers reading a dialogue script. Obviously, you must slightly change one of the voices so that it sounds like two different announcers, and you'll probably need to practice a few times to get the timing correct. Remember, you usually

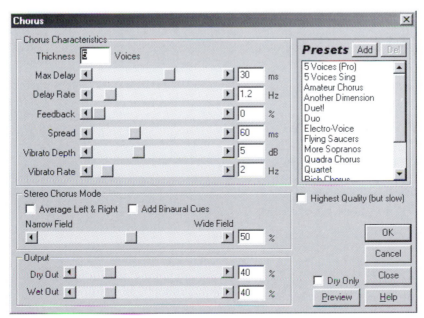

FIGURE 6.10 The chorus effect adds richness or thickness to sound by making it seem as though several voices are being played at the same time. (Adobe product screen shot reprinted with permission from Adobe Systems Incorporated.)

"mentally" read lines slightly faster than you do when you actually speak them. It can take a little time to perfect this technique, but it can be well worth the effort.

The same effect can be produced using editing software without having to mentally leave pauses. Just record the lines for each announcer on the appropriate track of the multi-track, changing one voice slightly. Now cut, move, and paste the lines to create the dialogue. You can create the natural pacing of two announcers by slightly overlapping the end of one line with the beginning of the next line. This is very easy to do since you can move the audio around on the tracks with drag-and-drop commands.

6.15 SLAPBACK ECHO

To produce a slapback echo with a multi-track recorder, record your voice on Track 1. Now, dub Track 1 to another track, but without synchronization. Play back both tracks, and you'll get a unique echo effect. If you do the recording at a higher recorder speed, you'll get a "closer" echo effect. Since this is another form of delay, look for this special effect to be a menu item on your editing software's special effects section (see Figure 6.11).

6.16 CONCLUSION

As we've noted, much of the digital equipment that has made its way into the radio production studio has both editing and multi-track recording capability. This chapter is a significant one in your development as a radio production person. Audio editing is a very important concept as more emphasis is being placed on sound bites and ear-catching commercials. The modern production person must also be skilled in working in the multi-track environment to be successful. Although this chapter is only designed to give you some basic familiarity with the equipment and techniques, it should serve as a good starting point. Like most everything about radio production, the real learning comes when you go into the studio and try out different concepts. You'll only become really skilled in multi-track production work or audio editing if you spend time in the studio to understand the creative possibilities it offers. The type of equipment or particular software that is used is not nearly as important as *how* this equipment is used to convey information in a meaningful way.

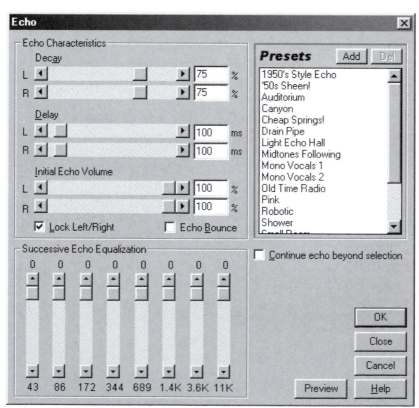

FIGURE 6.11 Various echo effects can be created with both a multi-track recorder and editing software that features effects options. (Adobe product screen shot reprinted with permission from Adobe Systems Incorporated.)

Self-Study

1. Which of the following is a reason to edit audio?

   a) to eliminate mistakes
   b) to record out of sequence
   c) to cut to exact length
   d) all of the above

2. What is the purpose of the UNDO function of a digital audio editing program?

   a) to clear all the Transport controls
   b) to bring up the Options menu
   c) to cancel the last action you undertook
   d) to bring up the Help screen

3. An audio sound file that has been edited with a destructive system has been permanently altered so the original audio cannot be restored.

   a) true
   b) false

4. Which type of audio tape editing is the most accurate and the easiest?

   a) splicing
   b) dubbing
   c) digital audio editing
   d) analog audio editing

5. Where would you place the edit marks to edit out the word *one* from the phrase *one . . . two . . . three*?

   a) just after letter *e* of *one* and just before letter *t* of *three*
   b) just before letter *t* of *two* and just before letter *t* of *three*
   c) just before letter *t* of *two* and just after letter *o* of *two*
   d) no correct way to mark this edit is shown here

6. How many tracks is a multi-track recorder found in the radio production studio likely to have?

   a) 1
   b) 2
   c) 4
   d) 6

7. Which term describes the process when two or more tracks of a multi-track recording are combined and rerecorded on another vacant track?

   a) overdubbing
   b) bouncing
   c) punching in
   d) combo-cording

8. Which of the following is *not* part of a stand-alone multi-track recorder system?

   a) audio mixer
   b) multi-track recorder
   c) DSP audio card
   d) microphone

9. Which type of tape is *not* used as a recording medium in multi-track recording systems?

   a) cassette tape
   b) videotape
   c) reel-to-reel tape
   d) all of these are multi-track recording media

10. In multi-track recording, what is the process of adding new tracks to existing tracks called?

    a) bouncing tracks
    b) overdubbing tracks
    c) punching in tracks
    d) ping-ponging tracks

11. One announcer can appear to be two different announcers reading a dialogue script using which multi-track recording technique?

    a) voice doubling
    b) chorusing
    c) dovetailing
    d) stacking

12. The main reason announcer voices are often recorded first on a multi-track recording is because vocal sources are usually assigned to Track 1 and Track 2.

    a) true
    b) false

13. Most audio editing software can save files in a number of different audio formats. Which are the two most common?

    a) .wav and .wma
    b) .mp3 and .aif
    c) .voc and .pcm
    d) .wav and .mp3

14. A track sheet is a manufacturer specification sheet that lists the number of tracks that a multi-track recorder has.

    a) true
    b) false

15. Multi-track productions are usually mixed down to a 2-track stereo master. If the stereo master is slightly out of phase when combined into a mono signal, it can be corrected by all but which of these adjustments to one of the stereo tracks?

    a) change track equalization
    b) move track to a vacant track
    c) change track volume
    d) change track panning

16. During multi-track recording, which technique allows you to rerecord just a portion of a track to correct a mistake, while leaving the rest of the track undisturbed?

    a) punching in
    b) overdubbing
    c) voice doubling
    d) bouncing

17. What is another term for "bouncing tracks" on a multi-track recorder?

    a) chorusing
    b) overdubbing
    c) ping-ponging
    d) dovetailing

18. Which of the following is true on an analog, 4-track, reel-to-reel tape recorder?

    a) all the tracks go the same direction
    b) two tracks go left and two go right
    c) only Tracks 1 and 3 can be used
    d) you can record eight tracks of sound

19. What is one advantage of digital multi-track over analog multi-track?

    a) Digital multi-tracks have six tracks, but analog can have no more than four tracks.
    b) The sel-sync feature is in better synchronization on digital than analog.
    c) You can punch in on digital, and you can't on analog.
    d) You can manipulate sounds easier with digital because you can move them with the mouse.

20. The "drag-and-drop" function of a multi-track audio editor would allow you to move audio segments from one part of a track to another, but not from one track to a completely different track.

    a) true
    b) false

ANSWERS

If You Answered A:

1a. Although this is one reason for editing audio, there is a better answer. (Reread 6.2.)
2a. Wrong. If you chose this answer, you don't understand the function of either the Transport control or UNDO. (Reread 6.4.)
3a. You're not quite right with this answer. While audio edited with a destructive system is ultimately physically changed, most editing systems provide an UNDO function that can restore the original audio. (Reread 6.4 and the Production Tip for this chapter.)
4a. No. Splicing can be very accurate when done by a skilled operator, but it really isn't the easiest method. (Reread 6.3 and 6.4.)
5a. No. This would leave no space or pause between the words *one* and *three*. (Reread 6.4.)
6a. No. One would not be "multi." (Reread 6.5 and 6.6.)
7a. Wrong. Overdubbing is the normal technique for multi-track recording. (Reread 6.7 to 6.9.)
8a. No. This is part of the multi-track setup. (Reread 6.5.)
9a. No. There are multi-track recorders that use cassette tapes. (Reread 6.5 and 6.6.)
10a. No. This is another multi-track recording technique. (Reread 6.7 to 6.9.)
11a. Wrong. While this is a "voice doubling" technique, it's another multi-track trick. (Reread 6.13 and 6.14.)
12a. No. It really doesn't matter what sources are assigned to what tracks. (Reread 6.12.)
13a. No. While audio editors might use both of these formats to save files, only one of them is very common. (Reread 6.4.)
14a. No. A track sheet is a way of keeping notes during a multi-track production. It usually lists track numbers and what is recorded on each track. (Reread 6.10.)
15a. Wrong. This will often correct the mono signal. (Reread 6.11.)
16a. Yes. The punch in is also known as an insert edit because you can just rerecord a portion of a track.

17a. No. This is a different multi-track technique. (Reread 6.7 to 6.9 and 6.13 to 6.14.)

18a. Yes. All the tracks must go in the same direction, so you can listen and record at the same time.

19a. No. Both can have a varying number of tracks. (Reread 6.5 and 6.6.)

20a. Wrong. You would be able to move the audio from track to track as well as anywhere on an individual track. (Reread 6.4.)

If You Answered B:

1b. Although this is one reason for editing audio, there is a better answer. (Reread 6.2.)

2b. No. It is possible that on some programs UNDO might be under the Options menu, but generally these two things have nothing to do with each other. (Reread 4.4.)

3b. Yes, because most destructive editing systems have an UNDO function that enables edited audio to be restored.

4b. Wrong. Dubbing is neither a very accurate nor a very easy method of audio tape editing. (Reread 6.3.)

5b. Yes. This would edit out the word *two,* but it would maintain the natural pause between *one* and *three.*

6b. You're close because 2-track recorders are usually found in the production studio, and technically they are multi-track, but this is not the best answer. (Reread 6.5 and 6.6.)

7b. Correct. Bouncing or ping-ponging tracks is the multi-track technique described here.

8b. No. This is an obvious part of the multi-track setup. (Reread 6.5.)

9b. No. There are multi-track recorders that use S-VHS videotape. (Reread 6.5 and 6.6.)

10b. Yes. This is a primary advantage of multi-track recording and one of the most basic techniques used in multi-track production.

11b. Wrong. Although this is a technique for adding voices, it's another multi-track technique. (Reread 6.13 and 6.14.)

12b. Yes. It doesn't really matter what sources are assigned to what tracks, but announcers are often recorded first because it's easier to lay down other tracks to the vocals, and high-priced talent can be finished with their part of a production once their tracks are recorded, even if the entire spot isn't completed.

13b. No. While audio editors might use both of these formats to save files, only one of them is very common. (Reread 6.4.)

14b. Yes. This is a false statement. A track sheet is a way of keeping notes of what is recorded on each track of a multi-track production.

15b. Correct. Just moving a track's location won't help.

16b. No. This technique allows you to add additional tracks to a production. (Reread 6.7 to 6.9.)

17b. No. This is a different multi-track technique. (Reread 6.7 to 6.9 and 6.13 to 6.14.)

18b. No. This would be very confusing. (Reread 6.5 and 6.6.)

19b. No. You are incorrect. (Reread 6.5 and 6.6.)

20b. Correct. This is false because you can move audio from track to track as well as anywhere on an individual track.

If You Answered C:

1c. Although this is one reason for editing audio, there is a better answer. (Reread 6.2.)

2c. Right. It cancels the last action, and can often "undo" several *layers* of actions if the function is activated repeatedly and before any other actions are performed.

4c. Correct. Digital audio tape editing is extremely accurate and easy to accomplish.

5c. No. This would lengthen the pause between *one* and *three* and sound unnatural. (Reread 6.4.)

6c. Yes. Of the answers offered, this is the most likely configuration of a multi-track recorder in the production studio.

7c. Wrong. To punch in is a technique that allows you to record a segment of a track without affecting the material before or after that segment. (Reread 6.7 to 6.9.)

8c. Correct. A DSP audio card is part of an audio editing system, and although the system may have multi-track recording capability, it's different from a multi-track recorder system.

9c. No. Some multi-track recorders use reel-to-reel audio tape. (Reread 6.5 and 6.6.)

10c. No. This is another multi-track recording technique. (Reread 6.7 to 6.9.)

11c. Correct. By reading even lines of a script on one track and then odd lines on another track, one announcer can sound like he or she is talking to another person with this technique.

13c. No. While audio editors might use both of these formats to save files, neither of them is very common. (Reread 6.4.)

15c. Wrong. This will often correct the mono signal. (Reread 6.11.)

16c. No. This technique is a form of overdubbing that allows you to "voice double." (Reread 6.7 to 6.9.)

17c. Yes. This is another term for bouncing tracks.

18c. No. This would limit the usefulness of the recorder. (Reread 6.5 and 6.6.)

19c. No. You can punch in on analog. (Reread 6.5 and 6.6.)

If You Answered D:

1d. Right. All of these are good reasons for editing audio.

2d. No. UNDO, like other functions, will probably be defined in the Help portion of the program, but it won't bring up the Help screen. (Reread 6.4.)

4d. No. Analog audio editing uses splicing and dubbing techniques. They are no longer the most accurate or easiest methods for editing. (Reread 6.3.)

5d. No. One of the other answers is the correct way to mark this edit. (Reread 6.4.)

6d. No. This is not a common number of tracks for a radio production multi-track recorder. (Reread 6.5 and 6.6.)

7d. Wrong. There is no such thing. (Reread 6.7 to 6.9.)

8d. No. This is a possible input source for a multi-track recorder system. (Reread 6.5.)

9d. Yes. This is the correct answer.

10d. No. This is another multi-track recording technique. (Reread 6.7 to 6.9.)

11d. Wrong. Although this is a technique for adding voices, it's another multi-track technique. (Reread 6.13 and 6.14.)

13d. Yes. These are the two most common formats that audio editors might use to save files.

15d. Wrong. This will often correct the mono signal. (Reread 6.11.)

16d. No. This technique allows you to combine tracks and transfer them to a vacant track. (Reread 6.7 to 6.9.)

17d. No. This is a different multi-track technique. (Reread 6.7 to 6.9 and 6.13 to 6.14.)

18d. No. It's only a 4-track recorder. (Reread 6.5 and 6.6.)

19d. Yes. A few clicks of the mouse can easily move sounds with a digital multi-track system.

Projects

PROJECT 1

Digital audio editing.

Purpose

To gain practice editing a vocal audio tape using a digital editing system.

Advice, Cautions, and Background

1. If you're not sure of what you're doing, ask the instructor for assistance.
2. Remember, you're to do several edits, not just one.
3. You'll be judged on how clean your edits are, so be sure you make your edit marks accurately.

How to Do the Project

1. Familiarize yourself with the operation of the digital editing system in your production studio. If you have questions, ask your instructor.
2. You may use the material on the CD-ROM enclosed with the text, or you may be allowed to record your own. If you can record your own, select some news copy or a weathercast from a news wire service, or write something similar and record it into your editing system. Label this sound file as required by your system.
3. Do your edits as follows:
   a. Press the "play" button, and listen to what is recorded.
   b. Select something you wish to edit. Write down on a piece of paper the part you plan to edit, with a few words before and after it. Put parentheses around what you plan to take out. For example: "This is Mary Anderson (broadcasting from KZXY) bringing you the latest news."
   c. Stop playback so that it's at the exact place you wish to edit—in our example, just in front of "broadcasting."
   d. Make your beginning edit mark.
   e. Continue playing the audio until you get to the end of your edit—in our example, just before "bringing."
   f. Make your end edit mark.
   g. Preview the edit. You can probably adjust either edit mark so that it is accurately positioned. If necessary, do so.
   h. Perform the actual edit, and listen to it. If you've made some type of error, "undo" the edit, and start again.
4. Repeat the above steps for another edit. Do a few more similar edits.
5. When you've done several edits, record them all.
6. Label your recording with your name and "Digital Audio Editing."
7. Turn in the recording to your instructor to receive credit for the project.

PROJECT 2

Record a 60-second "concert commercial."

Purpose

To develop your skill in creating a spot for a concert by a recording artist, a type of commercial frequently heard on radio.

Advice, Cautions, and Background

1. This project assumes you have some type of digital audio editor in your studio; however, it can also be accomplished with analog equipment.
2. The production incorporates two announcer voices, a music bed, and several "clips" from the artist's songs.
3. You can write the actual script as you want it, but follow the basic concept given below.
4. Exact production directions aren't given in this project because there are many ways to accomplish the recording and editing.

How to Do the Project

1. Record four or five segments of songs from the artist's biggest hits. Each clip should be about 10 seconds long, but some may be longer and others shorter.
2. You should pick segments of the song that are readily identifiable, usually the chorus or "hook" of the song. Try to end the clip at the end of a phrase so that it isn't just cut off in the middle of a word. Make sure the last clip doesn't fade out, as you want to finish the spot with a strong, natural ending.
3. Start recording each segment a bit before the point you actually want and record a bit beyond the actual end. Mark the true start point and end point using your audio editor and then label and save each segment.
4. Record the announcer lines with both announcers "trading lines." However, the announcers should read the last line together. If your editor has effects capability, add some reverb or a flanging effect to the voices.
5. Your script should use lines similar to this:

   Announcer 1: "Appearing live at the Rock Arena, (Artist Name)!"

   Announcer 2: "Join (Artist Name) on June 25th for (his/her/their) first-ever concert in (Your City)!"

   Announcer 1: "Here's the summer concert you've been waiting for!"

   Announcer 2: "Tickets are just $50 and can be purchased at the Rock Arena Box Office or at www.rockarena.com!"

   Announcer 1 & 2: "Don't miss this chance to see (Artist Name) in concert at the Rock Arena, June 25th!"

6. Using your audio editor, assemble the spot in a sequence that alternates between announcer tracks and song clips, beginning with Announcer 1's first line.
7. Now, add a background music bed that will pull the whole spot together. You might edit an instrumental segment from one of the artist's songs to do this, or you might find a music bed from the CD-ROM that fits the style of the other music used in the spot.
8. When you mix the music bed in, you should start with the bed at full volume for a couple of seconds and then fade it under the announcer segments. When the music clips are playing, the music bed should be faded out entirely.
9. Listen to the finished commercial. If it's good enough, prepare it for the instructor.
10. Write your name and "Concert Commercial" on the recording and turn it in to your instructor to receive credit for this project.

PROJECT 3

Use multi-track recording to create a chorusing effect.

Purpose

To practice the multi-track techniques of chorusing and bouncing while keeping a track sheet.

Advice, Cautions, and Background

1. This project assumes you have a multi-track recorder or an editing software system with at least four tracks.
2. Your system should be set up so that you can record from a microphone as well as a source (such as a CD player) that can play music.
3. You can use any dialogue you want, but the first line of "Mary Had a Little Lamb" works well.
4. You may find music appropriate for this project on the CD-ROM that came with this text.

How to Do the Project

1. Record your selected dialogue on Track 1.
2. While playing back Track 1, overdub the dialogue again on Track 2.
3. As you're doing your recording, keep a track sheet similar to the one depicted in Figure 6.8 that shows what you did.
4. Bounce Tracks 1 and 2 onto Track 3.
5. While listening to Track 3, overdub the dialogue again on Track 1.
6. Bounce Tracks 3 and 1 onto Track 4.
7. Listen to Track 4. It should sound like a chorus of four voices.
8. Record a music bed on Track 1.
9. Mix down Track 1 and Track 4 so you have a spot with a vocal track over a music bed.
10. Dub the finished project and turn in the recording to your instructor to receive credit for this project. Make sure you include the track sheet with your name and label it "Chorusing Production."

7

SIGNAL PROCESSING EQUIPMENT

7.1 INTRODUCTION

Signal processing, or audio processing, is nothing more than altering how audio, such as an announcer's voice or a CD, sounds. We've already seen a few forms of audio processing in the equalization capabilities of some audio consoles and the bass roll-off feature of some microphones, but most signal processing is accomplished by the use of separate audio components. Most digital equipment, especially audio editing software and digital audio workstations, also includes features that allow for processing the sound signal.

Usually signal processing involves the manipulation of the frequency response (tonal balance), stereo imaging, or dynamic range of the sound signal. As noted in Chapter 3, "The Audio Console," frequency response refers to the range of all frequencies (pitches) that an audio component can reproduce and we can hear, that is, around 20 Hz (low bass) to 20 kHz (high treble). **Imaging** refers to the perceived space between, behind, and in front of monitor speakers and how we hear individual sounds within that plane. Dynamic range refers to the audible distance between the softest sounds that can be heard over noise and the loudest sounds that can be produced before distortion is heard.

Several signal processing devices will refer to the terms "wet" and "dry." The incoming, or unprocessed, audio signal is considered a *dry* signal, and the outgoing audio signal that has been processed is considered the *wet* signal. This chapter focuses on the capability of audio editing software to signal process, and it will also look at other electronic audio processors commonly used in radio. However, the amount of equipment available for signal processing in any production facility can vary widely, from essentially none to a veritable smorgasbord of electronic black boxes.

7.2 EQUALIZERS

One of the most commonly used signal processors is the equalizer. An equalizer allows for manipulation of frequency response by adjustment of the volume of selected frequencies and can be thought of as a fancy **tone control**. You're familiar with bass and treble tone controls because most home and car stereo systems have them. When you turn up the treble, you increase the volume of the higher frequencies. Unfortunately, a treble control turns up *all* the higher frequencies. An equalizer, on the other hand, offers greater flexibility and allows the operator to differentiate, for example, between lower high frequencies and upper high frequencies, and to make different adjustments to each.

Most equalizers found in the radio production studio are **unity-gain** devices. The sound signal that has passed through the equalizer's circuits is no stronger or weaker overall than the input sound signal was. In other words, if the processor's controls are set at zero, they should have no processing effect on the incoming audio signal. Of course, if the signal is processed by increasing the level of several different frequencies, then the overall volume of the outgoing signal will be louder than the unprocessed signal.

7.3 THE GRAPHIC EQUALIZER

The two main kinds of equalizers found in radio production are the graphic equalizer and the parametric equalizer. The **graphic equalizer** is more common and derives its name from the rough graph of a sound's altered frequency response formed by the slider control settings on the equalizer's front faceplate (see Figures 7.1 and 7.2). A digital graphic equalizer may have a "select" button for each band and "raise" and "lower" buttons to adjust the volume of each band. As shown in Figure 7.1, you'll still see the frequency response curve formed by your settings, but on

FIGURE 7.1 The graphic equalizer, whether digital or analog, can boost or cut the audio signal at various frequencies and provide a visual representation of the equalization being applied. (Image courtesy of Alesis.)

multiple LED bar-graph meters instead of the positions of the slide controls.

Graphic equalizers come in different designs, but all of them divide the frequency response range into separate frequency bands. A complex design would be a stereo ⅓-octave equalizer with 31 controls; while a simple mono 10-band octave equalizer would feature 10 controls on 1-octave intervals. If the first band of a full-octave equalizer was at 31 hertz, the second would be at or near 62 hertz, the third at 125 hertz, and so on. Obviously, the more bands you have to work with, the greater tone control you have, but it also becomes harder to correctly manipulate the equalizer. Most broadcast-quality graphic equalizers feature 15 or 31 band channels. Each band has a volume control that's "off" in a middle or flat position and can move up to increase ("boost") or down to attenuate ("cut") the volume at that particular frequency. This volume range varies, but +12 to −12, or 12 decibels of boost or cut, is a common configuration.

To understand equalization techniques, look at the simple 5-band equalizer shown in Figure 7.2. You might have a similar equalizer in your car radio system. Note how the slider setting would demark a frequency response graph, indicating how the original sound was being manipulated. Typical equalizing procedure starts with all bands set "flat" or at the mid-position. Then each band is adjusted by increasing or decreasing the volume of various frequencies. If we were playing rock music through this equalizer, the boost at 60 hertz would give the drums extra punch; while cutting back at 250 hertz would help minimize bass boom. The increase at 1 kilohertz would add brilliance to the

voices and the slight decrease at 4 kilohertz would minimize the harshness of the sound. Finally, the boost at 8 kilohertz would add presence to the highs. There is no one correct setting for an equalizer, and we could just as easily have had all different settings and yet produced an excellent sound. There are, however, settings that could make the sound very poor, and the production operator needs to beware of altering any sound too much. By adding a little here and taking away a little there, you can usually improve any poor-sounding audio.

As previously noted, audio editing software often includes signal processing capability. Figure 7.3 shows the screen for *Adobe Audition*'s graphic equalizer, which allows you to select a 10-, 20-, or 30-band unit. Clicking on the virtual slider control lets you cut or boost the volume of the specific frequency. The position of the sliders and the top portion of the screen give a visual representation of what is happening to the audio signal. Equalization procedures are exactly the same as with any other graphic equalizer. Clicking on the PREVIEW button lets you hear the equalized or "wet" signal and actually change settings as it is playing back. When you have the sound you're looking for, click on the OK button and the original audio will be changed according to the EQ settings.

7.4 THE PARAMETRIC EQUALIZER

The **parametric equalizer** gives the operator even greater control over the sound because it allows not only volume control of specified frequencies, but also control over the actual frequency and bandwidth selected. In other words, the parametric equalizer is used for finer control of the frequencies within a sound than the broad control offered by graphic equalizers. For example, the 5-band graphic equalizer mentioned above had fixed frequency bands at 60, 250, 1000, 4000, and 8000 hertz, but a parametric equalizer allows the operator to select an exact frequency. For example, instead of a set band at 1000 hertz, you might choose a band at 925 hertz or 1200 hertz. If the graphic equalizer were increased at 1 kilohertz, not only would that frequency get a boost, but so would the adjacent frequencies according to a preset bandwidth determined by the manufacturer, (perhaps from 500 to 1500 hertz).

Many parametric equalizers also allow the operator to adjust that bandwidth. For example, still using the 1-kilohertz frequency, the parametric equalizer operator could select

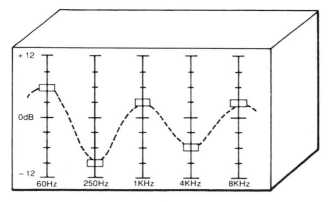

FIGURE 7.2 A simple 5-band graphic equalizer.

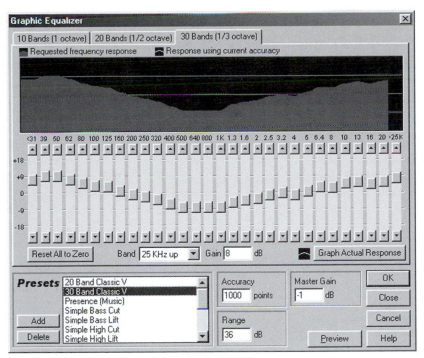

FIGURE 7.3 The graphic equalizer screen from an audio editing software package. (Adobe product screen shot reprinted with permission from Adobe Systems Incorporated.)

a bandwidth of 800 to 1200 hertz or a narrower bandwidth of 950 to 1050 hertz to be equalized. Most equalizers also have a switch that allows the sound signal to pass through the equalizer unaffected, or not equalized at all, so you can compare the original sound with the equalized sound. Figure 7.4 shows one type of parametric equalizer.

7.5 EQUALIZER USES

Whether a feature of an audio editing program or a stand-alone unit, the general use of an equalizer is to alter or change the sound character of an audio signal. The term **EQ** refers to the general process of equalization when an equalizer is used to cut or boost the signal level of specific frequencies. Specifically, equalizers are often used in the production studio to alter recordings to suit individual taste, to create special effects, and to cut down on various forms of audio noise.

Equalization is often employed for altering the sound of a CD (or any music) or an announcer's voice to suit an individual's taste. For some production work, you may need to accentuate the bass of an announcer's vocal track. Boosting the frequency settings between 50 and 100 Hz certainly would help to do so. Perhaps a background music bed seems overly "bright," so you attenuate frequencies in the 10 to 18 kHz range to lessen their impact. Remember, equalizing anything is a subjective process and what sounds great to one listener may not to another. However, some specific adjustments like those mentioned above would usually be noticed as a positive improvement. The key to good EQ technique is to use any effect moderately and experiment to find just the right sound you're looking for.

Another reason for using equalization is to achieve a special audio effect. For example, cutting down most of the lower frequencies below 1 kHz leaves a very tinny-sounding vocal that might be perfect as a robot voice for a particular commercial or radio drama. You could create an effect that approximates an old-fashioned, poor-quality telephone

FIGURE 7.4 A parametric equalizer offers greater control of various frequencies within a sound than the graphic equalizer. (Image courtesy of Rane Corporation.)

sound by boosting the frequency bands at 640 and 800 Hz and cutting the frequency bands on either side of this range. Many such effects are achieved by experimenting with various settings for the equalizer.

EQ is also often used to deal with hiss, one of the common forms of noise in production work. **Hiss** describes a high-frequency noise problem inherent in the analog recording process. Hiss sounds exactly as you would imagine and is heard by the human ear within the frequency range of 2 to 8 kHz. Using an equalizer to cut or turn down the frequency settings closest to this range can attenuate hiss to a less noticeable level. EQ is sometimes used to combat hum, which is another form of noise in production work. **Hum** is a low-frequency problem associated with leakage of the 60-hertz AC electrical current into the audio signal. A poor or broken ground in any part of the electrical circuit can cause hum, and it, too, sounds exactly as you would imagine. Attenuating frequencies right around 60 Hz would lessen the problem.

However, even with careful adjustment, it's often impossible to eliminate noise entirely. Remember, you also affect the program signal as you equalize, so EQ is usually a compromise between less noise and a still-discernible signal. Digital recording technique has lessened hiss and hum problems, but in radio production you are often working with prerecorded audio that already has such inherent problems.

7.6 AUDIO FILTERS

Filters are less likely to be found in the radio production room, but since they are a type of equalizer, a short discussion of them may prove useful. Instead of manipulating a specific frequency, filters affect a whole range of the audio signal. For example, a **low cut filter** cuts, or eliminates, frequencies below a certain point, say 500 hertz. Instead of a normal frequency response of 20 to 20,000 hertz, once the signal goes through this filter, its response is 500 to 20,000 hertz. A **low pass filter** works in the same fashion but lets frequencies below a certain point pass or remain unaffected. In other words, a cut filter and a pass filter are opposites in their actions. A **band pass filter** eliminates frequencies except for a specified band. It has a low cut point (maybe 1,000 hertz) and a high cut point (maybe 3,000 hertz). When a signal is sent through this filter, only that portion of the signal between the two cut points is heard. A **band reject (or cut) filter** is just the opposite of the band pass filter in that it allows frequencies to pass except for a specified frequency range. A **notch filter** is a special filter that completely eliminates an extremely narrow range of frequencies or one individual frequency, such as AC hum at 60 Hz.

Usually filters are used to correct a specific problem. For example, a vinyl recording may have a scratch that shows up around 11 kilohertz, and a notch filter is used to eliminate that frequency. Of course, filters eliminate both the problem *and* the actual program signal, so careful use is necessary to maintain a good audio signal after filtering has taken place. Figure 7.5 shows a digital audio editing program that has a filtering function. This screen illustrates the use of a low pass filter so that low frequencies are allowed to pass through the filter unaltered. The cutoff point has been set at 661.5 hertz, so the high frequencies above this point are rejected or removed from the original audio. The graph gives a visual representation of what is happening to the audio.

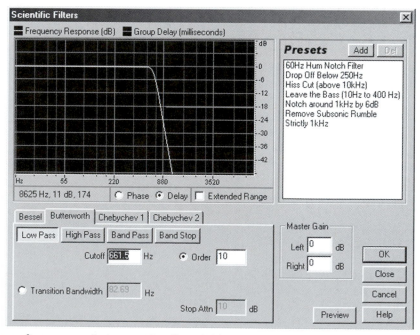

FIGURE 7.5 Digital editing software can replicate an analog filter. (Adobe product screen shot reprinted with permission from Adobe Systems Incorporated.)

7.7 NOISE REDUCTION

We've mentioned the problem of noise inherent in the production process, especially with recording. Signal processing devices, known as noise-reduction systems, have been devised to help prevent noise. Note that these electronic devices can't get rid of noise that already exists; their job is to prevent noise from being *added* to a recording. Digital recording does not need to use noise-reduction devices because the noises they are meant to eliminate are ones inherent in the analog recording process. There are two systems commonly used with analog recording: Dolby and dbx®. Dolby noise reduction is commonly built into cassette and reel-to-reel recorders. Many of the dbx® stand-alone noise-reduction systems have been discontinued, but their Type III circuitry can be found in some of their newer EQ products. Both systems are **companders**—their general operation is to compress (reduce the dynamic range of) an audio signal during recording and then expand the signal during playback—but they are not compatible systems.

There are several **Dolby** noise-reduction systems in use in recording studios, broadcast stations, home stereo equipment, and movie theaters, but the Dolby B, C, S, and SR noise-reduction systems are most likely to be found in production equipment. The two-part Dolby process consists of encoding the program signal before recording begins and noise can be introduced into the recording. The volume of soft sounds (especially at the upper end of the frequency spectrum, where the signal is most likely to be lost to noise) is made louder than normal. Loud elements, which actually hide noise, aren't altered by the Dolby encoding process. In the second part of the process, during playback decoding, levels that were increased are decreased to their original levels, and any noise introduced during the recording process is also reduced so it now seems much lower in relation to the program level. Depending on the system employed, 10 to 25 decibels of noise reduction can be attained using the Dolby process. As with all other signal processing equipment, careful use is required to achieve the results the operator wants. Setting proper levels prior to recording with Dolby is important so that both encoding (recording) and decoding (playback) of the audio signal are at the same level. Dolby SR (for spectral recording) and Dolby S are more sophisticated noise-reduction systems from Dolby Laboratories. Dolby S (derived from the SR system) is designed to be an improved version of the Dolby B and Dolby C systems.

Unlike Dolby, dbx® compresses the signal over the entire frequency range during recording. The audio signal is compressed during recording by a 2-to-1 ratio (in other words, the dynamic range is cut in half), with the loud levels greatly reduced and the soft levels boosted by a carefully designed frequency response preemphasis. During playback, the signal is expanded by a 1-to-2 ratio, with de-emphasis, so that the original dynamic range is restored.

Noise buildup usually introduced in the recording process is dramatically reduced (noise reduction of 40 decibels can be attained); however, as with all noise-reduction systems, any noise present in the original audio signal is not reduced.

Although digital audio recording will not generally introduce noise, most software programs have features for noise reduction so that audio recorded outside the system and then brought into it can be improved. For example, a sound effect or piece of music from a vinyl record may contain pops and clicks from excessive use. Some software programs include a feature that would eliminate this noise by first analyzing the audio to determine where the pops are and then repairing or reconstructing the audio at that point. There may be several parameters to set, and a bit of trial and error is usually required to get the correct settings, but salvaging just the right piece of music may be critical to a specific production project. Other noise-reduction features may help eliminate or reduce tape hiss, 60-cycle AC hum, microphone background noise, or other noise problems heard in the audio. However, since the noise is embedded in the audio you want to keep, noise reduction is a trade-off between how much noise level you can decrease and how much loss of audio quality you can afford. Still, depending upon the sophistication of the software program you may have available, there is a great deal that can be done to improve a noisy audio signal.

Generally speaking, the more consistent the noise you want to remove is, the easier it will be to dispose of. For example, the consistent hum of a refrigerator is easier to remove than the sound of traffic going by, as each engine will have its own frequency. Some noise-reduction software allows you to sample a short section of unwanted background noise, and then remove the sound from a longer section of audio. Using this process, the hum of a refrigerator behind a conversation can virtually be eliminated very simply, automatically, and without having to experiment with frequencies. But there is always the chance that parts of the desired signal will be mistaken for refrigerator noise and be eradicated as well.

7.8 REVERBERATION

A signal processor that affects the imaging of sound is the reverberation unit, probably the second most common type of processor. It manipulates the sound signal to artificially produce the sound of different acoustic environments. As we've mentioned, reverb is reflected sound that has bounced off two or more surfaces. Sound heard (or produced) in a small studio "sounds" different than sound produced in a large hall or auditorium, and reverb is the main characteristic that audibly creates the difference.

The modern production studio is likely to have a **digital reverb** unit that is either an electronic device (see Figure 7.6) or a feature of an audio editing program. The original signal is fed into the unit and electronically processed to

FIGURE 7.6 A digital reverb unit can simulate various acoustic environments altering the "image" of the sound. (Image courtesy of Yamaha Corporation of America.)

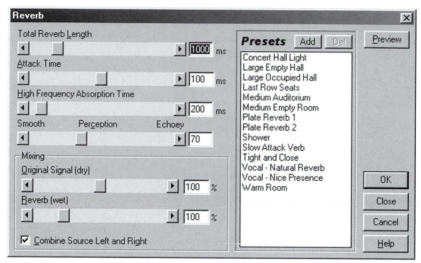

FIGURE 7.7 A digital reverb program, within audio editing software, can have various preset acoustic environments, ranging from a coat closet to a concert hall. (Adobe product screen shot reprinted with permission from Adobe Systems Incorporated.)

achieve the reverb effect; then the altered signal is sent out of the unit. Besides a black box digital reverb, audio editing software may also have reverb, echo, or delay functions. Figure 7.7 shows a reverb screen from one audio editing program. In addition to building your own reverb sound by setting various parameters, note that several preset acoustic environments can be chosen, such as a medium-sized auditorium or a tiled bathroom shower. Merely selecting the appropriate preset and clicking on OK button will transform the original audio so that it sounds as if it had been recorded in that environment with the corresponding reverb effect.

PRODUCTION TIP #7
World Wide Web Effects

The Internet can be a source for some interesting Digital Signal Processing (DSP) effects. This isn't pirated software, but legitimate programs that are available for free or nominal cost. Most are plug-ins you can add to your digital audio software program, but some you can just install on your computer. One free program you might want to check out is Izotope's *Vinyl 1.61*. It's a DirectX plug-in that works fine with *Adobe Audition*, but it's also available in a few other Windows-based formats. Best of all it's free. You'll need to go to their Web site at www.izotope.com and click on the "Vinyl" icon. Then you'll have to supply some registration information that will allow them to e-mail you back the necessary install information. Once you've completed the download, you'll need the install information the first time you use the plug-in with your audio software. *Vinyl 1.61* is a vinyl record simulation. It lets you take an audio file and process it so it sounds like it is being played back on a record player. While there are several presets, you can make a number of parameter adjustments including adding hum (electrical noise) or turntable rumble (mechanical noise). You can add dust and scratches to your recording, as well as warp to give you that great off-speed or off-center "wow" sound. Like with most signal processing devices, you'll have to experiment to find the right sound you're looking for, but Izotope provides a handy "10 Steps to Lo-Fi" help screen to get you started. There are, no doubt, other programs on the Web so some search time might be beneficial. However, remember that one small effect used as part of a production can be very effective, but too many special effects take away from their uniqueness.

7.9 DIGITAL DELAY

A **digital delay** unit can be used in both the production studio and the on-air control room. As its name implies, this signal processor actually takes the audio signal, holds it, and then releases it to allow the signal to be used further. The time the signal is held or delayed can be varied from fractions of a second to several seconds. Although there are analog delay units, most systems are digital, and the incoming signal is converted from its analog form to digital for processing and back to analog after processing. In the on-air studio, a delay unit (see Figure 7.8) is often used in conjunction with a phone-in radio talk show. The program signal is sent through the delay unit to provide approximately a 7-second delay before it is sent to the transmitter. If something is said by a caller that should not be broadcast, the operator has time to "kill" the offending utterance before it is actually broadcast. The delay system will dump the delayed signal and revert to the live signal to do this. Listeners who call a program using a delay system are asked to turn their home radio down if they're talking to an announcer on-air, because the sound they hear on the radio is the delayed sound and not the words they are actually saying into the telephone. It's extremely difficult to carry on a conversation when you can hear both the live and delayed sounds.

In the production studio, delay units are used to create special effects similar to reverb. Set for an extremely short delay, the units can create an effect that sounds like a doubled voice or even a chorus of voices. These types of effects are most commonly included in a multi-effects processor, which will be mentioned below, but also may be available as one of the special effects of digital audio software programs.

7.10 DYNAMIC RANGE

When we mention **dynamic range** in a radio production context, we're referring to the range of volumes of sound that broadcast equipment can handle. This intensity of a sound is measured in decibels (dB). One **decibel** represents the minimum difference in volume that we can hear, but a change of 3 decibels is often necessary before we actually do perceive a difference in volume. The dynamic range goes from 0 decibels at the **threshold of hearing** to 120+ decibels at the **threshold of pain.** A whisper is around 20 decibels, normal conversation is near 60 decibels, and shouting is about 80 decibels. Average music-listening lev-

els are between 30 and 80 decibels, but some rock concerts have been measured above 110 decibels. Dynamic range also relates the volume of one signal to another, such as signal to noise or input to output.

We should note that dynamic range is measured on a logarithmic scale. For example, to hear one audio signal twice as loudly as another, you would have to increase the volume of one by 10 decibels in relation to the other. A 60-decibel dynamic range was once considered quite adequate for high-quality broadcast production equipment; today's digital equipment, however, offers an increased dynamic range and a 90-plus decibel range is now common.

Why would you want to reduce dynamic range? Even modern broadcast equipment can have trouble handling extremes in dynamic range. If equipment is set to handle typical volume levels, when extremely loud levels are encountered the equipment overloads. If everything is set to handle extremely loud levels, when you hit a quiet section nobody can hear it. Radio announcers do a certain amount of gain-riding at the audio console, but signal processing can do it a lot more reliably.

7.11 COMPRESSORS, EXPANDERS, AND NOISE GATES

The compressor is one of the two most common signal processing devices used to affect the dynamic range of the audio signal; the limiter is the other. Although they are most often used to process the signal between the studio and the transmitter and therefore aren't pure production room devices, they were the first processing devices used in radio, and virtually every radio station uses them. They are also occasionally used in the production room to process the signal before it's sent to an audio recorder.

The **compressor** operates as an automatic volume control and reduces the dynamic range of an audio signal put through the unit. In the contemporary production studio, the compressor is used if the audio signal is too loud to automatically lower it. Several adjustments on the compressor determine its actual operation. The threshold of compression is the setting of the level of signal needed to turn on the compressor. As long as the audio signal stays below this point, the compressor doesn't do anything, so the compressor really needs to work only some of the time. If the input is too low, the threshold of compression will never be reached, and if the input is too high, the compressor will severely restrict the dynamic range. The compression ratio

SIGNAL PROCESSING EQUIPMENT

FIGURE 7.8 A delay unit is often used in conjunction with radio talk shows to prevent material that should not be broadcast from going out over the air. (Image courtesy of Eventide.)

determines how hard the compressor works or how much it will turn down audio above the threshold. A ratio of 5 to 1 means that if the level of the incoming signal increases to 10 times its current level, the output of that signal from the compressor will only double.

Compressors also have settings for attack time (how quickly volume is reduced once it exceeds the threshold) and release time (how quickly a compressed signal is allowed to return to its original volume). The release time adjustment is very important because too fast a setting can create an audible pumping sound as the compressor releases, especially if there is a loud sound immediately followed by a soft sound or a period of silence.

An expander is essentially the opposite of a compressor and is used to expand the dynamic range of an audio signal. Today's expanders are set to operate only below a threshold level on low-volume audio so they make quiet passages quieter. As was noted earlier, the process of noise reduction uses compressor and expander technology. A **noise gate** is a type of expander used to reduce noise by turning the level of an audio signal that falls below a set threshold point way down. For example, it could be set so that pauses in a piece of music would be attenuated to "zero" volume so that background noise would not be recorded. Audio editing software often includes some type of dynamics processor that can emulate stand-alone compressors, limiters, expanders, and noise gates.

7.12 LIMITERS

A **limiter** is a form of compressor with a large compression ratio of 10:1 or more. Once a threshold level is reached, a limiter doesn't allow the signal to increase anymore. Regardless of how high the input signal becomes, the output remains at its preset level. If they're adjustable, attack and release times on limiters should be quite short. Both the limiter and the compressor can be rather complicated to adjust properly. Too much compression of the dynamic range makes an audio signal that can be tiresome to listen to, and pauses or quiet passages in the audio signal are subject to the pumping problem mentioned earlier.

Since they're often associated with the transmitter only, compressors and limiters are usually the domain of the engineer. If you do have access to them in the production facility, it may take some experimenting to get the kind of processing that you're looking for because there are no standard settings for signal processing devices. Figure 7.9 shows a system that combines both a compressor and limiter in a single unit.

FIGURE 7.9 The compressor/limiter is used to process the dynamic range of an audio signal. (Image courtesy of Symetrix, Inc.)

7.13 OTHER SIGNAL PROCESSORS

A **flanger** is another processor for producing a specific special effect. This unit electronically combines an original signal with a slightly delayed signal in such a way as to cause an out-of-phase frequency response that creates a filtered swishing sound. Flanging, also called phasing, was originally accomplished by sending an audio signal to two reel-to-reel tape recorders and then physically slowing down one of the reels by holding a hand on the flange, or hub, of the reel. As the two signals went in and out of sync with each other, the audio would cancel and reinforce, creating a psychedelic phase-shift effect. Figure 7.10 shows the flanger screen from *Adobe Audition*'s audio editing software. The Original–Delayed slider on the top left side of the screen controls the mix between the dry (original) audio and the wet (flanged) signal. Portions of both must be mixed to achieve the effect of slightly delaying and phasing the signals. Like with many of the other signal processing effects using audio software, there are several other adjustments that can be made to create just the effect you're looking for, or you can just choose a preset effect by clicking on one of the descriptive names on the right side of the screen.

A **de-esser** is an electronic processor designed to control the sibilant sounds without affecting other parts of the sound signal. A **stereo synthesizer,** as the name implies, is a processor that takes a mono audio signal (input) and simulates a stereo signal (output). Some processors use a form of delay to provide separation between the left and right channel outputs; others use a form of filtering to send certain frequencies to one channel and other frequencies to the other channel to provide a synthetic stereo effect.

7.14 MULTI-EFFECTS PROCESSORS

Rather than using several individual signal processor "boxes," many signal processing devices are designed so that they perform more than one function—that is, more digital effects can be created from a single black box. For example, Eventide, Yamaha, and Lexicon are all manufacturers who provide popular signal processing tools for the production studio (see Figure 7.11). These devices offer a variety of audio effects in one unit, including the ability to alter the pitch of an incoming audio signal, time compression and expansion, delay, natural reverb effects, flanging, time reversal, and repeat capabilities. Any production person should find it enjoyable to experiment with the variety of creative effects that can be produced with a multi-effects processor.

As we've noted throughout this chapter, another form of multi-effects processor is the digital audio workstation or audio editing software. In addition to offering improved editing capabilities, most workstations or software programs have provisions for adding special effects to the audio signal. Often you can add an effect to the audio by mouse-clicking on a preset effects button. Otherwise, you may have to set

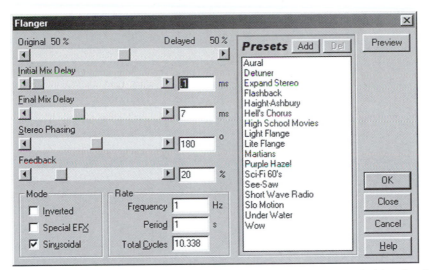

FIGURE 7.10 Flanging—a psychedelic, swooshing sound—is a phase-shifted, time-delay effect easily created with audio editing software. (Adobe product screen shot reprinted with permission from Adobe Systems Incorporated.)

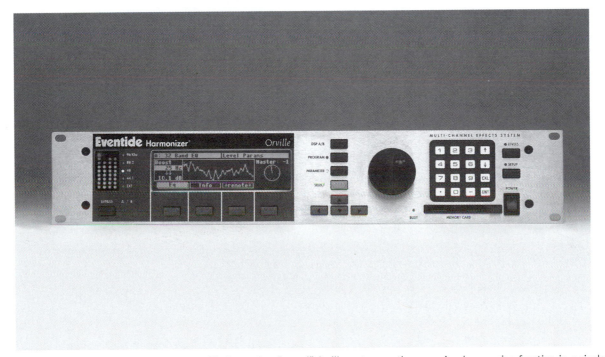

FIGURE 7.11 This multi-effects processor, an Eventide Harmonizer "named" Orville, puts more than one signal processing function in a single "black box." (Image courtesy of Eventide.)

various parameters to create the signal processing effect that you desire, and that can range from being fairly easy to extremely complex. Regardless of this fact, editing software or workstation systems are still, in many cases, simpler to set up and operate than their black box counterparts.

7.15 CONCLUSION

This chapter is not intended as a complete guide to signal processing equipment. There are other units in use in radio production facilities, and there are other effects available through audio editing software programs. Nor is this chapter designed to make you a professional operator of such equipment. What is intended is that you become aware of a number of the more common processors and that you have an understanding of their basic purpose. The actual operation of most of this equipment will take some trial-and-error work in your production facility. Use signal processing in moderation, and bear in mind that a lot of great radio production has been produced using no signal processing equipment at all.

Self-Study

1. The equalizer processes an audio signal by altering which of the following?

   a) volume
   b) imaging
   c) dynamic range
   d) frequency response

2. An audio signal that has been equalized would be called a "dry" signal.

   a) true
   b) false

3. Which type of equalizer can select an exact center frequency and bandwidth as well as alter the volume at that frequency and bandwidth?

   a) graphic
   b) parametric
   c) dielectric
   d) full-octave, 10-band

4. What type of filter would most likely be used to attenuate or eliminate a 60-hertz hum in a recording?

   a) low pass filter
   b) band pass filter
   c) notch filter
   d) low cut filter

5. The 60-hertz hum mentioned in question 4 could also have been eliminated by the use of either Dolby or dbx® noise reduction.

   a) true
   b) false

6. Which signal processor affects the imaging of a sound?

   a) equalizer
   b) noise-reduction unit
   c) de-esser
   d) reverb unit

7. How could you create a tinny voice using signal processing equipment?

   a) Cut out most of the lower frequencies.
   b) Cut out most of the higher frequencies.
   c) Eliminate the EQ.
   d) Increase compression.

8. Which noise-reduction system is most likely to be found in the radio production studio?

   a) Dolby A
   b) Dolby S
   c) Type I
   d) Flanger

9. Which is a true statement about the Dolby system of noise reduction?

    a) Volumes of certain frequencies are increased during recording and decreased during playback.
    b) The dbx® is increased with a calibrated tone so that it attains the level of 30 decibels.
    c) All frequencies pass through, except ones that have been preset by the notch filter.
    d) Once a threshold level is reached, the signal isn't allowed to increase any more.

10. A noise gate is which type of signal processing equipment?

    a) limiter
    b) equalizer
    c) expander
    d) imager

11. Which is true about a compressor?

    a) usually has a compression ratio of 10 to 1
    b) lowers a signal that's too loud and raises one that's too soft
    c) doesn't operate unless it's connected to a digital delay unit
    d) produces an out-of-phase, filtered, swishing sound

12. Any signal processing equipment that's labeled a unity-gain device would amplify all frequencies of the signal going through that equipment an equal amount.

    a) true
    b) false

13. Which of the following is *not* a type of Dolby noise reduction?

    a) Dolby S
    b) Dolby B
    c) Dolby C
    d) Dolby D

14. Which signal processing device is most likely to offer a variety of effects, such as pitch change, time compression, reverb, and flanging?

    a) dbx® Graphic Equalizer
    b) Eventide Broadcast Delay
    c) dbx® Compressor/Limiter
    d) Eventide Harmonizer

15. Which signal processing device inputs a mono signal and outputs a simulated stereo signal?

    a) digital delay
    b) band cut filter
    c) flanger
    d) stereo synthesizer

16. Today's digital equipment offers an increased dynamic range, and a range of how many decibels is now common?

    a) 153
    b) 90
    c) 60
    d) 3

17. A digital audio workstation usually includes digital reverb and delay effects but rarely any other type of signal processing capability.

    a) true
    b) false

18. Which graphic equalizer setting would most likely be used to add "brilliance" to an announcer's voice?

    a) boost at 60 Hz
    b) cut at 250 Hz
    c) boost at 1 kHz
    d) cut at 8 kHz

19. Which signal processor is designed to help control sibilance in an announcer's voice?

    a) compressor
    b) limiter
    c) de-esser
    d) digital reverb

20. Which of the following is the opposite of a compressor?

    a) equalizer
    b) expander
    c) flanger
    d) limiter

ANSWERS

If You Answered A:

1a. No. You're headed in the right direction. Equalizers do increase or attenuate volumes at specific frequencies, but they do this to alter another sound characteristic. (Reread 7.1 and 7.2.)

2a. No. A dry audio signal is an unprocessed signal. (Reread 7.1.)

3a. No. Center frequencies and bandwidths are usually preset on graphic equalizers. (Reread 7.3 and 7.4.)

4a. No. This type of filter allows lower frequencies to pass and would not eliminate noise at 60 hertz. (Reread 7.6.)

5a. No. Noise-reduction units, regardless of brand name, can't eliminate noise that already exists in a recording. They only prevent noise during the recording process. (Reread 7.7.)

6a. No. Equalizers affect frequency response. (Reread 7.2 and 7.8.)

7a. Correct. Cutting the bass will give a tinny sound.

8a. No. (Reread 7.7.)

9a. Correct. It's a two-step process.

10a. No. In a way it is the opposite. (Reread 7.11 and 7.12.)

11a. Wrong. That's a limiter. (Reread 7.11 and 7.12.)

12a. No. A unity-gain device doesn't amplify the overall level of the incoming signal at all. (Reread 7.2.)

13a. Wrong. This is one of the newest and most sophisticated Dolby noise-reduction systems. (Reread 7.7.)

14a. No. This doesn't really exist. It's a mixture of signal processing. (Reread 7.3, 7.7, and 7.13.)

15a. No. You may be thinking about a stereo synthesizer that uses a form of delay. (Reread 7.9 and 7.14.)

16a. No. You may be getting this confused with the threshold of pain. (Reread 7.10.)

17a. No. Most digital audio workstations have multi-effect capability. (Reread 7.1 and 7.13.)

18a. No. This would punch up the bass. (Reread 7.3.)

19a. Wrong. This is a form of automatic volume control used to affect dynamic range. (Reread 7.11 and 7.14.)

20a. No. You might be confusing frequency response and dynamic range. (Reread 7.2 to 7.5 and 7.10 to 7.11.)

If You Answered B:

1b. No. Imaging can be affected by other signal processors. (Reread 7.1 and 7.2.)

2b. Correct. This is the right response.

3b. Yes. The parametric equalizer gives the operator the greatest control over the EQ process.

4b. No. This type of filter is usually used to allow a range of frequencies to pass, not to eliminate a single frequency. (Reread 7.6.)

5b. Yes, because you can't eliminate existing noise with noise-reduction units.

6b. No. Noise-reduction units affect dynamic range. (Reread 7.7 and 7.8.)

7b. No. That is where the tinny sound would be. (Reread 7.5.)

8b. Correct. It's one of the newer common ones.

9b. No. (Reread 7.7.)

10b. No. A noise gate has nothing to do with frequencies. (Reread 7.2 and 7.11.)

11b. Yes. It lowers and raises signals in that manner.

12b. Yes. Unity-gain devices don't amplify the overall level of the incoming signal.

13b. Wrong. Dolby B is a common noise-reduction system found on cassette recorders. (Reread 7.7.)

14b. No. This isn't correct. Delay is a single type of audio processing, often used with radio talkshows. (Reread 7.9 and 7.13.)

15b. No. You may be thinking about a stereo synthesizer, which uses a form of filtering. (Reread 7.6 and 7.14.)

16b. Correct. This is the right response.

17b. Yes. Most digital audio workstations have multi-effect capability.

18b. No. This would minimize bass boominess. (Reread 7.3.)

19b. Wrong. This is a form of automatic volume control used to affect dynamic range. (Reread 7.12 and 7.14.)

20b. Correct. Since the expander increases dynamic range, it is the opposite of a compressor.

If You Answered C:

1c. No. Dynamic range can be affected by other signal processors. (Reread 7.1 and 7.2.)

3c. Wrong. There's no such thing. (Reread 7.3 and 7.4.)

4c. Correct. This type of filter allows all frequencies to pass except a specified one, which we could specify at 60 hertz to eliminate the hum.

6c. Wrong. A de-esser is an electronic processor designed to control sibilant sounds. (Reread 7.8 and 7.14.)

7c. Wrong. That wouldn't really be possible. (Reread 7.5.)

8c. No. (Reread 7.7.)

9c. No. You are confusing this with filters. (Reread 7.6 and 7.7.)

10c. Correct. A noise gate is a type of expander.

11c. No. They have nothing to do with each other. (Reread 7.9 and 7.11.)

13c. Wrong. Dolby C is a common noise-reduction system found on cassette recorders. (Reread 7.7.)

14c. No. This isn't correct. (Reread 7.7 and 7.11 to 7.13.)

15c. No. You're thinking about another signal processing device. (Reread 7.14.)

16c. Wrong. You may be getting this confused with the level of normal conversation. (Reread 7.10.)

18c. Yes. This would add brilliance to a voice.

19c. Right. This is the correct answer.

20c. No. Flanging concerns phase-shift and time delay, but not dynamic range. (Reread 7.10, 7.11, and 7.13.)

If You Answered D:

1d. Correct. Equalizers allow you to adjust selected frequency volumes and thus alter the audio signal's frequency response.

3d. No. This would be a type of graphic equalizer. (Reread 7.3 and 7.4.)

4d. Although it could eliminate a 60-hertz hum, low cut filters normally are designed to eliminate *all* frequencies below a certain point. There's a better response. (Reread 7.6.)

6d. Yes. This is what reverb units do by electronically changing the apparent acoustic environment in which we hear the sound.

7d. No. A compressor acts as an automatic volume control affecting the dynamic range of an audio signal. (Reread 7.5 and 7.11.)

8d. No. This is not a noise-reduction unit. (Reread 7.7 and 7.13.)

9d. Wrong. This happens in a limiter, but not during noise reduction. (Reread 7.7 and 7.12.)

10d. No. A noise gate does not deal with imaging. (Reread 7.1 and 7.11.)

11d. No. You're thinking of a "flange" effect. (Reread 7.11 and 7.14.)

13d. Right. This is not a current Dolby noise-reduction system.

14d. Yes. This is a multi-effect processor.

15d. Correct. As the name implies, a stereo synthesizer makes a mono signal into a "fake" stereo signal.

16d. Wrong. You're thinking about the amount of change in volume that's usually necessary before we actually hear a difference in level. (Reread 7.10.)

18d. No. This would decrease the highs, if anything. (Reread 7.3.)

19d. Wrong. This is a type of processor used to affect imaging of an audio signal. (Reread 7.8 and 7.14.)

20d. Wrong. A limiter is a type of compressor, not the opposite of it. (Reread 7.10 to 7.12.)

Projects

PROJECT 1

Record a radio commercial that uses a signal processing effect.

Purpose

To develop skill in incorporating a signal processing effect into a radio spot.

Advice, Cautions, and Background

1. This project assumes you have enough familiarity with your studio equipment to accomplish basic recording and production techniques.
2. The production incorporates a single announcer voice, a music bed, and some type of signal processing technique.
3. You will need to write a simple script that can be read in about 20 seconds. Write the copy about a department store and use the phrase, "One Day Sale!" several times in the script.
4. There are many ways to accomplish this project, so don't feel you must follow the production directions exactly.

How to Do the Project

1. Record the script (voice only) onto an audio recorder. Each time the "sale" phrase is read, add some type of signal processing effect (reverb, flanging, echo, EQ, etc.). Depending on your studio, you may be using a "black box" processor or a signal processing effect available in your audio editing software.
2. Select a music bed that is appropriate for the style of the spot. You might find one on the CD-ROM that came with this text.
3. You can play back the music bed directly from a CD, or you may have to record it on another recorder from the CD-ROM.
4. Set correct playback levels for both the vocal track and the music bed. Both will start at full volume. Then cue both to the beginning sound.
5. Mix the vocal track and music bed to complete the spot.
6. Start the music bed at full volume. Start the vocal track and simultaneously fade the music bed slightly so the vocal track is dominant.
7. As the vocal ends, bring the music bed back to full volume and then quickly fade it out as you approach 30 seconds.
8. It may take you several attempts to get the spot to come out correctly. If you need to "do it over," just cue everything and try again.
9. On the completed project, write your name and "Signal Processing Radio Spot," and turn it in to your instructor to receive credit.

PROJECT 2

Visit a radio station or recording studio, and learn about the signal processing equipment used there. Write a report about what you learn.

Purpose

To give you more familiarity with signal processing equipment.

Advice, Cautions, and Background

1. Find a place that has enough signal processing equipment to make your trip worthwhile. Your instructor may arrange a trip for the entire class.
2. Find someone at the facility willing to spend some time with you explaining how the equipment works.
3. Prepare the questions that you want to ask so that you can guide the visit to some extent.
4. If possible, experiment with some of the equipment yourself. If the facility is unionized, you won't be able to do this. Don't push on this particular point because some people are very sensitive about who touches their equipment, but don't back away from any opportunity.
5. Once you have an appointment, keep it, and arrive on time.

How to Do the Project

1. Call various radio stations and recording studios until you find one that's both willing to let you visit and has sufficient signal processing equipment.
2. Visit the facility, and talk with someone who can give you information for your report. Make a list of all the equipment you are shown, and take notes regarding it. Some of the things you may want to find out are:
   a. Is the equalizer graphic or parametric?
   b. Do they have band pass or notch filters or both or none?
   c. Do they use Dolby or dbx® and if so, which system?
   d. Do they have digital audio workstations with signal processing features?
   e. Is there a digital delay unit, and if so, how many seconds of delay does the station use?
   f. Do they have a compressor? A limiter?
   g. Do they have any multi-effects signal processing equipment?
   h. What other signal processing equipment do they have, and what does it do?
3. As soon as you leave the facility, organize your notes so that you remember the main points.
4. Write a report. It should be several pages long, preferably typed. Write your name and "Signal Processing Equipment Tour" on a title page.
5. Turn in the report to your instructor to receive credit for this project.

PROJECT 3

Record and play back material using Dolby noise reduction.

Purpose

To make you aware of some of the characteristics of noise-reduction signal processing.

Advice, Cautions, and Background

1. You'll need a recorder with Dolby noise-reduction capability to complete this project.
2. You'll also need a prerecorded tape that has been encoded with Dolby.
3. Other configurations can be used, but this project will assume that a cassette recorder with Dolby B is being used.

How to Do the Project

1. Set up the cassette recorder to play back the prerecorded cassette tape with Dolby B. Make sure the packaging of the cassette indicates that it was recorded with Dolby.
2. Listen to the tape for several minutes. Stop the tape and rewind it to the start point.
3. Turn the Dolby B switch to the "off" position, and play the tape again, listening for a comparable amount of time.
4. Note any differences in the sound quality of the recording as it's played back with and then without Dolby.

5. On a blank cassette tape, record several minutes of an announcer talking. Make sure the Dolby B switch is in the "on" position.

6. Listen to this recording. Then make a similar recording with the Dolby B switch in the "off" position.

7. Listen to this recording, and note any differences in the sound quality between the recording with and without Dolby noise reduction.

8. If your recorder also has Dolby C, repeat Steps 5 to 7 with the Dolby C switch on.

9. Write a short paper that describes any differences you noted. Label the paper "Dolby Differences."

10. Turn in this paper and the tape you made to your instructor to receive credit for this project.

8

MONITOR SPEAKERS, CABLES, CONNECTORS, AND STUDIO ACCESSORIES

8.1 INTRODUCTION

This chapter looks at production studio items that are often treated as passive devices that simply exist in the studio, but they are actually quite significant. Monitor speakers (see Figure 8.1) are used to listen to the program (and also the audition or auxiliary) sound in the radio studio. The speakers convert the audio signal, stored on recording media like CDs and minidiscs, back into sound we can actually hear. The sound that comes from them is the final product, so they are important in determining the quality of that product. What you hear on the monitor speakers is an accurate gauge of what you recorded and what the listener will hear.

The various pieces of equipment used in the radio production studio, including monitor speakers, are all interconnected. This chapter also looks at the **cables** and **connectors** used for this interconnection, as well as some of the accessories that make work in the production studio easier. Some accessories have been previously mentioned: microphone windscreens and audio cassettes, among others.

8.2 TYPES OF SPEAKERS

You may want to review the sections on sound in Chapter 2, "Digital Audio Production," as it will help you understand how speakers work. **Speakers** are transducers. They work in a manner opposite to that of microphones. Instead of converting sound waves into electrical energy, speakers produce sound from an electrical signal by converting the signal into mechanical energy that produces sound waves or audible sound.

The most common type of monitor speaker found in the broadcast studio is a **dynamic speaker**. Also known as a **moving coil** or an **electromagnetic speaker**, its transducing element, called a driver, produces sound by moving a flexible cone or diaphragm in and out very rapidly. The paper diaphragm, which also may be plastic or metal, is sus-

pended in a metal frame. Attached at the narrow end of the cone is a voice coil (a cylinder wound with a coil of wire), which is located between powerful circular magnets (see Figure 8.2). When an electrical current is generated in the voice coil, it creates another magnetic force that moves the coil (and cone) back and forth, according to the electrical signal entering the coil. The cone vibration causes the surrounding air to move in a like manner, which our ears pick up as sound. Instead of a cone, some speakers use a dome, which is just another type of diaphragm that bulges out rather than tapers in. Other speaker drivers, such as **electrostatic** or **planar-magnetic,** are usually considered too exotic for radio use, and you aren't likely to run across them in the production studio.

With the radio production facility becoming an all digital environment, at least one manufacturer now offers a digital monitor speaker (see Figure 8.3). The speaker has S/PDIF digital inputs, in addition to analog inputs, which can identify a 16- to 24-bit digital signal with a sampling rate between 22 kHz and 55 kHz. When a digital signal is detected, the speaker's internal D/A (digital-to-analog) converter becomes activated. Does the digital speaker sound better? There really is no monumental sound difference between an analog and a digital input; however, the convenience of attaching directly to the digital output of an audio console or digital audio workstation will become more important in the future.

8.3 BASIC SPEAKER SYSTEM COMPONENTS

The basic components of the typical speaker system (see Figure 8.4) are the woofer, tweeter, crossover, and speaker enclosure. **Woofer** and **tweeter** are names given to drivers or individual speakers used in a speaker system. Since no one speaker design can reproduce the entire frequency range adequately, different speakers were developed to

FIGURE 8.1 Studio monitor speakers help you judge the sound quality of your audio production. (Image courtesy of JBL Professional.)

both. However, this bulk prevents the speaker from adequately reproducing the higher frequencies that require rapid cone movement. The tweeter uses a lighter and smaller design; often a convex dome (1 inch or less in diameter) replaces the cone. There are also midrange speakers with cones from 3 to 5 inches in diameter that are designed to reproduce higher-bass and lower-treble frequencies.

An individual speaker is really a speaker system in that most modern speakers use at least a woofer and a tweeter driver. To divide the audio signal and send the proper frequencies to the proper driver, another element of the speaker is used: the **crossover.** A crossover is a network of filters (mainly capacitors and inductors) between the input to the speaker and the individual speaker drivers. In the two-way system, an inductor would pass all audio *below* a certain frequency, sending it to the woofer. A capacitor would pass all audio *above* a certain frequency, sending it to the tweeter. Although there is no universal design for the crossover, most dividing points between the bass and treble frequencies are between 500 and 1,500 hertz. A speaker that has just a woofer, a tweeter, and a crossover is a **two-way speaker system,** like the one shown in Figure 8.4. A speaker that employs another driver (such as a midrange) is a **three-way system.**

8.4 SPEAKER SYSTEM ENCLOSURE DESIGNS

The speaker drivers and crossover are encased in a box (enclosure) that also plays a role in how the speaker sounds. Although there are different speaker system designs, each is intended to handle the rearward sound wave. Every speaker produces sound both behind and in front: The back sound wave is exactly opposite to the one that goes into the forward listening space. If the two sound waves are allowed to combine naturally, they would be acoustically out of phase (see section 8.7) and cancel each other out, producing no sound or greatly diminished sound in a good portion of the frequency range, especially the bass part of the range.

The two most widely used speaker enclosure designs are the acoustic suspension and bass reflex systems shown in

handle different portions of it. A woofer is designed to move the large volume of air necessary to reproduce lower frequencies. The cone should be large in size (usually anywhere from 8 to 12 inches) or be able to make large movements, and often a woofer utilizes a combination of

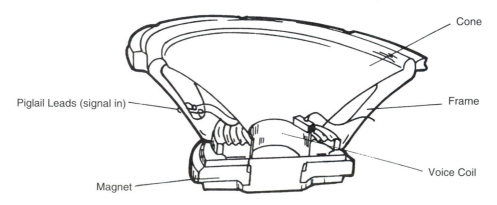

FIGURE 8.2 The most common type of speaker driver is the dynamic cone driver.

FIGURE 8.3 Digital monitor speakers offer a digital input for direct patching into a digital audio console or workstation. (Image courtesy of Genelec, Inc.)

Figure 8.5. The **acoustic suspension** (or **sealed-box**) design puts the speaker drivers (and crossover) in a tightly sealed enclosure that produces an accurate, natural sound with a strong, tight bass. By containing and absorbing the back wave in the enclosure, the acoustic suspension design prevents the rear sound from radiating and disrupting the main sound of the speaker. Because half the sound energy is trapped and absorbed in the box, acoustic suspension speakers are less efficient than other designs and require a more powerful amplifier to drive them. The acoustic suspension design also demands a rather large, sturdily built physical enclosure to ensure accurate reproduction of the lowest bass notes.

On the other hand, the **bass reflex** (or **vented box**) design is quite efficient and produces a strong bass sound with less power required. The bass reflex speaker enclosure is designed with a vent, duct, or port—an opening that is tuned to allow some of the rear sound (mainly the lower frequencies) to combine in phase and reinforce the main sound from the speaker. Some bass reflex design speakers have been criticized for not having tonal accuracy that is quite as good as the acoustic suspension design and for even adding a "boomy" quality to the sound. These problems, however, are often the fault of a particular speaker's tuning and construction and not caused by the bass reflex design. There are many different vented box designs, and most modern bass reflex speakers produce a clean, wide-ranging bass.

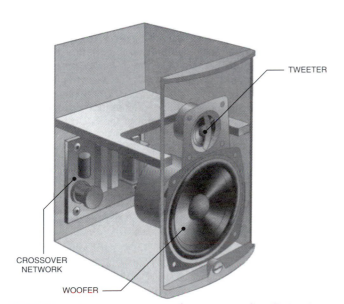

TWEETER

CROSSOVER NETWORK

WOOFER

FIGURE 8.4 The basic two-way speaker system consists of a tweeter, a woofer, and a crossover housed within an enclosure.

8.5 SPEAKER SOUND QUALITIES

There's a wide variety of speaker systems to choose from, and, as with some other radio production equipment, the differences between various models may be minimal. One of the important qualities that a good monitor speaker must have is excellent frequency response. As we've already noted, we are able to hear sounds or frequencies in the range of 20 hertz to 20 kilohertz, although most of us don't hear quite that low or that high. Top-line broadcast monitors often provide a frequency response range from 35 to 45 hertz, to 18 to 20 kilohertz. Increased use of digital equipment will make it necessary to have speakers that produce as much of this range as possible.

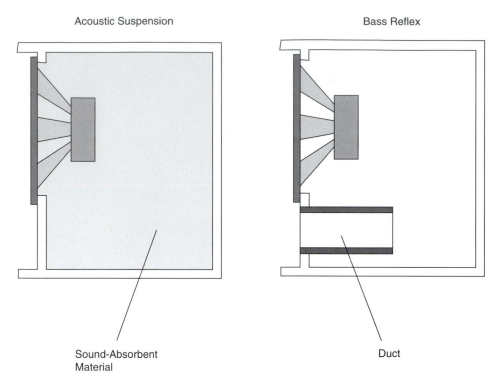

Acoustic Suspension   Bass Reflex

Sound-Absorbent   Duct
Material

FIGURE 8.5 The two most widely used speaker enclosure designs are the acoustic suspension and bass reflex systems.

Another important quality for the broadcast monitor speaker is its ability to produce a **flat frequency response.** The speaker should be able to reproduce low, midrange, and high frequencies equally well to produce a natural sound. The speaker itself shouldn't add anything to the audio signal, such as a boosting of the highs. Perhaps what is most important is merely how a speaker sounds. Among the combinations of driver types, speaker enclosure design, and crossover frequencies, there is no one speaker configuration that produces the "best sound." It is agreed, however, that a good speaker sound doesn't depend only on the speaker itself. How a speaker sounds is also dependent on the program (what is being played through it), the dimensions and acoustic properties of the room in which the speakers are heard, the location of the speakers (in relation to the listener), and the listener.

8.6 SPEAKER PLACEMENT

In the radio production room, there may not be many options as to where the monitor speakers are located. Usually they are positioned one on each side of the audio console, but exactly how they are positioned after that is open to various schools of thought. If nothing else, you should try to achieve an acoustically symmetrical layout. Don't put one speaker in the corner next to a glass window and the other speaker in the middle of a wall that's covered with acoustic tiles. That would be a mismatched

acoustic environment for the two speakers, rather than a similar one. One thought is to mount the speakers in the wall. As long as the speakers are isolated from the wall structure—using rubber shock mounts, for example—this flush mount creates an infinite baffle that prevents back wave problems.

Large speakers can be built into the wall, providing a loud, clear sound with plenty of "heavy" bass; unfortunately, this type of installation is often not practical for a radio studio. Some production people feel the ideal sound is obtained when speakers are even with or a bit above ear level. This installation is called **near-field** or **close proximity monitoring** and can be accomplished by putting small speakers, such as those shown in Figure 8.3, on the audio console "bridge" or on short stands to the left and right of the console, about 3 feet apart. Keeping the speakers a couple of feet from the back wall will prevent any excessive bass boost. Since the speakers are so close to the listener, you hear mostly direct sound and don't need to worry much about the effect from room acoustics. Toeing in the speakers (angling them toward the listener) or pointing them straight away from the wall will control the treble, with speakers pointing toward you providing the greatest high-frequency response. Very clear detail and excellent stereo imaging are characteristics usually associated with near-field monitoring setups.

A new concern with monitor speaker placement, especially true of studios that employ near-field monitoring, has to do with the increased use of computer equipment in the broadcast studio. Unless the monitor speakers are magnetically shielded, they must be positioned far enough away from the screen of the computer equipment so that they don't distort the picture. Perhaps the most practical monitor installation in many production studios is when the speakers are hung from the ceiling or attached to the wall behind the audio console. For the best sound dispersion, the speakers should be hung toward the upper corners of the production room. Keeping them close to the wall prevents a great deal of reflected sound and should produce a full bass at a higher sound level than other possible positions.

When speakers are placed closer to a wall, there is more bass sound produced because the usual omnidirectional sound field is cut down, and the sound is concentrated into a smaller dispersion area. Putting speakers totally into the corners of a room (such as the upper corners) may result in too much bass boost, but this is not an uncommon location. Hung speakers also keep counter space available for other production room equipment, and this is an important consideration in most broadcast settings.

Regardless of where the speakers are ultimately placed, the location of the operator in relation to the speakers also plays a role in how they sound, especially with stereo programming. Ideally, the operator is located directly between the two speakers and far enough back from them so that an equilateral triangle is formed if a line were drawn from speaker to speaker and from operator to speaker (see Figure 8.6). If the layout of the production room positions the operator closer to one speaker than the other, the source of all the sound appears to shift toward that one speaker. As a production person, you may not have any control over the speaker placement, but it's important that you realize the effects of speaker placement on the sound you hear.

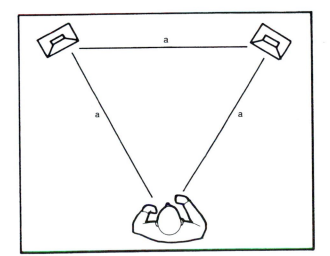

FIGURE 8.6 The most basic rule of speaker placement dictates that the distance between the speakers equals the distance from speaker to listener.

8.7 PHASE AND CHANNEL ORIENTATION

The concept of **phase** was previously mentioned in Chapter 4, "Microphones." Wiring monitor speakers incorrectly can also cause phase problems. Each speaker is fed its sound signal from the audio console monitor amp (and sometimes an external amp) by a positive and negative wire. If the wires are reversed on one of the speakers (i.e., the positive wire is connected to the negative terminal), the two speakers will be out of phase. As the driver moves the cone of one speaker in and out, the driver on the other speaker is moving out and in, so that the two speaker sounds are fighting each other and tend to cancel out individual sounds, diminishing the overall sound quality. This would be especially noticeable if the speakers were reproducing a mono signal.

Another concern about speaker wiring is channel orientation. Most studio monitors are wired so that moving a balance control from left to right will shift the sound image from left to right *as you face the speakers*. In other words, while looking at the speakers, the left speaker is in line with your left hand. This is important for true stereo sound reproduction. For example, if you were listening to a classical music piece and the channel orientation was reversed, the violins would sound as if they were to the right of the sound stage, which would be contrary to normal symphony orchestra arrangement. However, since most speakers are wired by the station engineer, phase and channel orientation should not be a problem for the radio production person.

8.8 MONITOR AMPLIFIERS

As you've previously learned, the audio console has an internal monitor amp that provides the signal to drive the monitor speakers. Although this is adequate for many studio applications, some production rooms (and control rooms) are set up with external monitor amplifiers. These are merely more powerful amplifiers that provide higher volume levels and clearer reproduction of the sound signal. *Remember, the volume of the monitor speakers is only for the pleasure of the operator and has no relationship to the volume of the signal being broadcast or recorded.*

8.9 SPEAKER SENSITIVITY

A speaker's sensitivity is the amount of sound (output level) that a speaker can produce from a given input level, much like the sensitivity of a microphone studied in Chapter 4. It is measured in decibels of sound-pressure level (SPL), and a good-quality broadcast monitor will usually have a sensitivity of more than 90 db SPL measured at one meter with 1 watt of input level. There are speakers that range from low sensitivity to high sensitivity, but, in reality, this characteristic of a speaker has little bearing on its quality. What it does mean is that a low-sensitivity speaker will need more power to drive it to any given volume level than a high-sensitivity speaker.

There is also a relationship among speaker size, sensitivity, and bass response. To increase a speaker's low-frequency response, its enclosure can be made larger, or its sensitivity can be decreased. For most broadcast situations, a smaller speaker size offers a lot more flexibility in placement of the speaker and thus is preferred, even if it means a low-sensitivity speaker that might require a more powerful monitor amplifier.

8.10 HEADPHONES

Headphones are another type of monitor in that they are tiny speakers encased in a headset. Headphones are necessary in radio production because the studio monitor speakers are muted when the microphone is on, and the operator must be able to hear sound sources that are also on. For example, if you're talking over the introduction of a song or reading a commercial over the background of a music bed, headphones allow you to hear both the other sound and the microphone sound so that you can balance the two or hit appropriate cues. Headphones are also portable, so sounds can be monitored when an actual monitor speaker might not be available.

Like regular monitor speakers, headphones come in a variety of designs, styles, and prices. The two main types of headphones found in the production studio are closed cushion headphones and open-air or hear-through cushion headphones. **Closed-cushion headphones,** also known as **circumaural,** have a ring-shaped muff that rests on the head around the ear and not actually on the ear. The enclosure around the muff is solid or closed as shown in Figure 8.7. These headphones are probably the most common in radio since they usually provide a full bass sound and attenuate outside noise better than other styles. Closed-cushion headphones are also less likely to leak sound into the studio; however, they're often heavier and more cumbersome than other styles.

Hear-through cushion headphones, also known as **supra-aural** or **open-air,** have a porous muff, instead of an ear cushion, that rests directly on the ear (see Figure 8.8). The enclosure around the muff typically has holes or other types of openings to give it the open-air design. Often made of very lightweight material, this design can be very comfortable for the wearer. However, open-air headphones are subject to possible feedback because the audio signal can leak out if driven at high volume levels, so some broadcast production people avoid them.

Other headphone types include the tiny **earbud,** which is designed to fit in the ear; **electrostatic headphones,** which are extremely high priced and high quality and require external amplification and special couplers to hook up; and **wireless headphones,** which operate similarly to

FIGURE 8.7 Closed-cushion or circumaural headphones have a ring-shaped muff that rests on the head around the ear. (Image courtesy of AKG Acoustics.)

wireless microphones by transmitting an RF, or infrared, audio signal from the source to the headphones.

Unlike consumer headphones, many broadcast-quality headphones are purchased "barefoot"; that is, they have no end connector on them. Although most broadcast equipment that allows headphone use requires a standard $\frac{1}{4}$-inch phone connector, there are other situations as well, and the barefoot headphone allows the engineer to wire them as necessary.

Which headphone style is most appropriate is often determined by the personal taste of the announcer; however, broadcast-quality headphones should always feature large drivers and full (but comfortable) ear cushions and headband. One note of caution for all headphone users: *Listening at extremely high volume, especially for extended periods of*

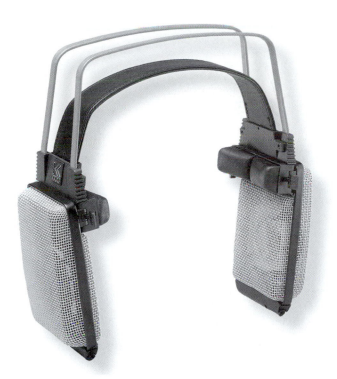

FIGURE 8.8 Hear-through cushion or supra-aural headphones have a porous muff that rests directly on the ear. (Image courtesy of AKG Acoustics.)

time, such as in a broadcast situation, can damage your hearing permanently. Good production practice (and common sense) dictates moderate volumes for headphone use.

8.11 HARDWIRING AND PATCHING

Audio equipment in the production studio is connected together by two methods: **hardwiring** and **patching**. Hardwired connections are somewhat permanent (such as the CD player directly connected to the audio console) and are usually soldered or wired by the engineer. Equipment that may, from time to time, be moved from one production area to another (such as an audio recorder) is often connected by male and female connectors known as plugs and jacks. More will be said about the typical broadcast connectors in the next few sections of this chapter.

Many pieces of audio equipment, and even two different production studios, are often connected together through the use of a **patch panel** or **patch bay,** as it is also called. Most patch panels are configured as two rows of 24 phone jacks in a one- or two-unit rack space as shown in Figure 8.9. The patch panel is located between the equipment and the audio console so that the input and output of each piece of equipment is wired to the patch panel.

There are often several modes that patch bays can be set to; however, in a typical setup, the top row of sockets on the panel is where the audio signal is coming from, and the bottom row of sockets is where the signal is going to. Putting a patch cord into the correct holes in the panel allows you to interconnect and reconfigure the various pieces of equipment or studios. Patch cords are available as either a single-plug cord or a double-plug cord. A double cord works well for stereo patch bays since it has two plugs at each end. One side of the plug casing will be marked (usually with a serrated or ribbed edge), so you can keep left and right channels correctly aligned on both the input and output sockets of the patch panel. Of course, single cords work fine, too—just remember to always plug in one cord from the top row right channel of the patch panel to the bottom row right channel before plugging in the left channel. That way you won't cross channels, which is easy to do if you plugged both left and right channels of the top row before plugging in the bottom row.

Figure 8.10 shows a portion of a patch bay (A) in which a cassette recorder and CD player are linked to two channels on an audio console. With no patch cord put into the panel, CASS 1 is linked to Channel 3 and CD 1 is linked to Channel 4. In patch panels, the top row is internally wired to the bottom row, and the audio signal flows in that manner. When it is unpatched like this, it's known as a "normalled" condition. Figure 8.10 shows another portion of a patch panel (B) that links the output of the audio console to audio recorders. When normalled, the PGM (program) output goes to REEL 1, and the AUD (audition) output goes to DAT 1. The PGM signal could be sent to DAT 1 (as shown) by putting a patch cord from the PGM position on the top row to the DAT 1 position on the bottom row. Now the signal flow has been changed, and that's the purpose of a patch panel—to allow flexibility in configuring the production studio. In this way the audio signals

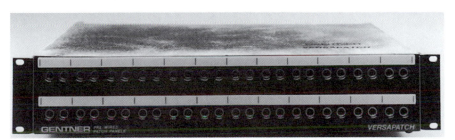

FIGURE 8.9 The patch panel simplifies rewiring individual audio components into an audio console or studio. (Image courtesy of Gentner Broadcast Systems.)

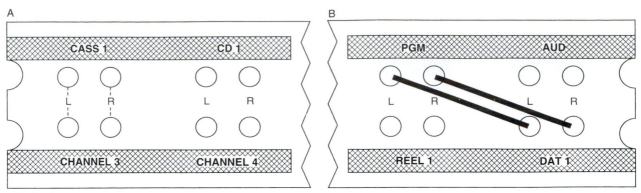

FIGURE 8.10   A portion of a patch panel that is "normalled" (A) and a portion of a patch panel that has been "patched" (B).

from various pieces of equipment can be sent to the audio console, and the audio console output can be sent to various pieces of equipment.

An alternative to the patch panel is the **audio routing switcher.** The router operates just like a patch panel by allowing several input sources to be switched to a single output (or sometimes multiple outputs); however, the switching is done electronically by selecting the appropriate switches or buttons, rather than by using patch cords. Most audio routers are centered around a matrix of "x" number of inputs times "x" number of outputs. Any one input can be sent to all the outputs, or all the outputs can be sent to one single input, or any combination can be configured. In other words, any input can be sent to any output. Similar types of audio distribution equipment, using CAT5 computer cable, are being used today to feed audio signals to multiple locations around the production studio.

8.12 COMMON BROADCAST CONNECTORS

In most broadcast situations, you'll be dealing with four types of audio connectors: RCA, XLR, phone, and mini-phone. In general, the female, or receiving, connectors are called **jacks** and the male connectors are called **plugs,** but often the terms "plugs," "jacks," and "connectors" are all used interchangeably.

The **RCA connector** is also known by the old time name, **phono connector.** Notice that it is *phono,* not phone. Most home stereo equipment uses this type of connector. In broadcast facilities that have turntables, this connector is often used to connect the turntable tone-arm assembly to the turntable preamp, and many CD players also utilize RCA connectors. This connector is always a mono connector, so two of them are needed for a stereo signal. Because of this, RCA connectors are often bundled in pairs and color-coded—red (right channel) and black or white (left channel). The male plug consists of a thin outer sleeve and a short center shaft that plugs into the female jack (see Figure 8.11). Although there are female in-line jacks, the female end is most often enclosed in a piece of equipment

(such as an audio recorder or preamp) so that the male end will just plug directly into the equipment. RCA connectors are used for unbalanced connections and are subject to picking up extraneous electrical noises, such as switch noise or hum.

The **XLR connector** is also known as the **Cannon connector** or **three-pin connector.** It's the most common microphone connector in broadcast production use and is also often used as the input–output connection on audio recorders. By convention, male XLR connectors are outputs and female XLR connectors are inputs. This connector attaches firmly and cannot be disconnected unless the latch lock is pressed. The three prongs of the male plug fit into the conductor inputs of the female jack. The guide pin on the female end fits into the slot for the guide pin on the male end so that the connector can't be put together improperly (see Figure 8.12). Like the RCA connector, the XLR connector is mono so that a stereo connection requires

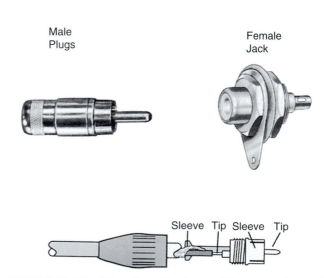

FIGURE 8.11   The RCA or phono plug is one of the common broadcast connectors. (Images courtesy of Switchcraft, Inc., a Raytheon Company; and Mackie Designs, Inc.)

Male Plug

Lock Release

Conductors

Female Jack (In Chassis)

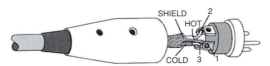

SHIELD 2
HOT
COLD 3 1

FIGURE 8.12 XLR connectors feature a locking latch that prevents them from being accidentally disconnected. (Images courtesy of Switchcraft, Inc., a Raytheon Company; and Mackie Designs, Inc.)

one XLR connector for the right channel and one for the left channel. The balanced three-conductor wiring of the XLR connector makes this a high-quality connection that is less likely to pick up noise through the cable.

The **phone connector** is also known as the ¼-inch **phone.** Notice it is called *phone*, not phono. Most broadcast-quality headphones are connected to the audio console with a phone plug, and most patch bays consist of female phone jacks into which phone plugs are inserted. The **miniphone connector** (also called a **mini**) is most often required to connect portable cassette recorders to other pieces of production equipment. The output of many portable cassette recorders is a female minijack. As you would expect, the miniphone is a smaller version of the phone connector. Although there are various sizes of miniphone connectors, the ones used most in broadcast production are ⅛ inch or 3.5 millimeters. The phone and miniphone plug consist of a tip and a sleeve, which go into the female jack. Male mono plugs have one insulating ring that separates the tip from the sleeve, and stereo plugs have two insulating rings, which actually define the ring portion of the connector (see Figure 8.13). If the signal is stereo, both the female and male connectors should be stereo. Again, the female end is often enclosed in a piece of equipment, but you can get in-line jacks if needed.

8.13 OTHER CONNECTORS AND CONNECTOR ADAPTERS

Most of the connectors mentioned so far are intended for analog inputs or outputs; however, much of the equipment

in the broadcast studio today has both analog and digital connections. Some digital connections utilize standard broadcast connectors—specifically the XLR and RCA plugs and jacks—and other digital inputs and outputs use different types of connectors. When XLR connectors are used for digital audio, you may see an input or output labeled AES-EBU. This denotes the digital standards set by the Audio Engineering Society and the European Broadcasting Union. Digital RCA connectors follow the S/PDIF (Sony-Philips Digital Interface Format) standards.

Two others that are often used for digital hookups include the BNC and Toslink connectors. The Toslink connector was developed by Toshiba and is the most common optical connector for digital audio. The connectors are usually molded plastic with a fiber-optic glass cable and are more common in audiophile applications than in broadcasting. BNC connectors (see Figure 8.14) feature a locking design along the lines of the XLR and are designed for use with 75-ohm cable. Used extensively for years in video applications, BNC connectors are now being developed specifically for audio use with radio's digital equipment.

Instead of using the connectors previously mentioned, some equipment manufacturers use a nonstandard connector for the input and output signals. For example, some tape recorders use a multi-pin connector, similar to the one shown in Figure 8.15, that includes input and output, as well as remote start and cue functions.

Something else in the connector realm that is very handy to have in a radio production studio is a supply of **connector adapters.** These enable you to change a connector from one form to another. Let's say, for example, that you need to connect an RCA output to a phone connector input, but

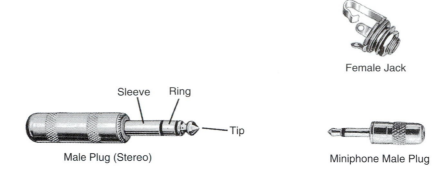

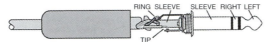

Sleeve   Ring

Tip

Male Plug (Stereo)

Female Jack

Miniphone Male Plug

RING SLEEVE   SLEEVE RIGHT LEFT

TIP

FIGURE 8.13   Phone and miniphone connectors can be either stereo or mono. (Images courtesy of Switchcraft, Inc., a Raytheon Company and Mackie Designs, Inc.)

the only cable you can find has an RCA connector at both ends. You can convert one of the RCA connectors to a phone connector with an adapter. This is a single piece of metal, which in this case houses a female RCA input at one end and a male phone output at the other (see Figure 8.15). When the male RCA connector is inserted into the female end of the adapter, the signal is transferred from the RCA

connector to the phone connector, and from there it can go to the phone input. Adapters usually come in most handy in emergency situations when some connecting cable fails, so having a variety of them around is good production practice.

8.14 BALANCED AND UNBALANCED LINES

The cable most often used in broadcasting consists of two stranded-wire conductors that are encased in plastic insulation plus a third uninsulated shield wire, all encased in a foil wrapping and another plastic sheathing as shown in Figure 8.16. For most wiring practices, the inner wires are designated + (red) and – (black); the uninsulated wire is the shield or ground wire. The audio signal is carried on the positive and negative conductors. This type of cable is referred to as three-wire, or **balanced cable,** and often requires the XLR connector, because that is the one designed to connect three wires and is also utilized by many types of broadcast equipment.

Another type of cable is two-wire, or **unbalanced.** In this configuration, the negative wire also acts as a ground. An unbalanced cable is not as good as a balanced cable because unwanted audio interference, such as that created by a nearby electric motor, can creep into the two-wire system. Also, balanced cables can be longer than unbalanced cables without encountering degradation of the signal. Finally, equipment that utilizes unbalanced cable generally outputs a lower level signal than equipment that employs balanced wiring. Ideally, balanced and unbalanced cable

FIGURE 8.14   Some digital input and output connections require the use of connectors not normally associated with the wiring of radio broadcast audio equipment. (Image courtesy of Neutrik USA.)

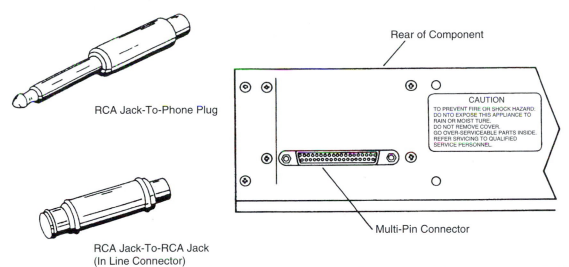

FIGURE 8.15 Connector adapters allow you to change from one type of connector to another, and the multi-pin connector may replace some of the standard broadcast connectors.

should not be mixed in the same audio setup, but sometimes this can't be avoided because different pieces of equipment are built for different cabling.

Wiring digital equipment is going to bring some new cabling concerns to broadcasters. On the one hand, since the digital signal carries both stereo channels on a single data stream, wiring digital equipment will actually take less cable than a normal installation. However, except for fairly short runs, ordinary audio cable should not be used for digital applications. As already noted, Toslink connectors are "wired" with fiber-optic cable that easily handles a digital signal. RCA cables used for digital should be 75-ohm impedance and coaxial in design, i.e., the signal wire and shield wire are aligned along the same axis. This usually means the audio signal wire goes down the center of a surrounding shield. Cables following AES-EBU standards utilize normal XLR wiring configurations, but the actual wire should be 110-ohm impedance. Some digital studio setups today are connecting an audio console interface with an audio engine using CAT5 wiring. Taken from the computer industry, CAT5 consists of four twisted pairs of copper wire using an RJ45 connector. It's likely that more nontraditional

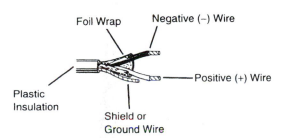

FIGURE 8.16 Typical broadcast audio cable is designed for a balanced wiring scheme. (Image courtesy of Cooper Industries, Belden Division.)

wiring will be seen in the production studio as digital becomes the standard.

8.15 MICROPHONE, LINE, AND SPEAKER LEVELS

Equipment inputs and outputs can be one of three levels: microphone, line, or speaker. You can think of these levels as very low for microphone level (which usually must be pre-amplified to be used further), normal for line level (most equipment will use line levels), and very high for **speaker levels** (designed to drive a speaker only). Problems arise when various levels are mismatched. For example, if you tried to feed an audio recorder from a speaker-level source, you would probably distort the recording because the speaker-level source is too loud, and there is no control to turn it down. Another problem would occur if you fed a microphone-level signal into a line-level input. In this case, the signal would be too low to be usable because microphone levels must be pre-amplified to a usable level. Most broadcast equipment inputs and outputs are clearly designated as microphone, line, or speaker level, and good production practice dictates sending only the proper output to the proper input.

Fortunately, most of the cabling of production room equipment will have been done by the engineer, and all the connections of various pieces of equipment will have been worked out so that everything matches.

8.16 STUDIO TIMERS

Timers have already been mentioned because some audio consoles have them built-in, but it is not uncommon to

FIGURE 8.17 A broadcast studio timer provides accurate timing for radio production work. (Image courtesy of Radio Systems.)

FIGURE 8.18 As less tape-based equipment is used, the bulk eraser or degausser may be hard to find in the production studio. (Image courtesy of Audiolab Electronics, Inc.)

find a separate studio timer in the radio production room (see Figure 8.17). Since the timing of radio production work is so important, an accurate timing device is crucial. Most studio timers are digital, showing minutes and seconds, and include at least start, stop, and reset controls. Many timers can be interfaced with other equipment (such as audio recorders and CD players) so that they automatically reset to zero when that piece of equipment is started. Shorter timers (10 minutes) are usually adequate for radio production work; however, 24-hour timers are often found in the studio.

8.17 OTHER STUDIO ACCESSORIES

The audio tape **degausser,** or **bulk eraser,** is merely a strong electromagnet used to erase audio tape in the production studio. Since equipment such as the reel-to-reel recorder and audio tape cart recorder is being used less and less in the production studio, the tape degausser will not be needed in the future. However, if you use a tape-based recording medium, it's good production practice to erase all audio tapes prior to use, even though some recorders have built-in erase heads. Some bulk erasers are designed for tabletop use (see Figure 8.18), and others can be handheld.

Erasing tapes is a simple operation, but it's often done improperly by beginning production people and studio pros alike. Make sure to extend the tape to be erased an arm's length away from the degausser and then turn the degausser on. If the tape is already sitting on the degausser when you turn it on, the transient surge of turning the unit on will put a click on the audio tape that can't be erased by normal operation of the eraser. Rotate or slide the tape over the top of the eraser two or three times on both sides and then move the tape an arm's length away from the degausser before you turn it off. Since the degausser is a strong electromagnet, it's a good idea to keep your watch out of close contact with it when erasing tapes. Also, keep tapes (diskettes and

zip disks) you don't want erased away from the degausser when it is operating. Once a tape is erased, it can't be restored except by rerecording the material.

Cleaning supplies are common broadcast accessories, many of which have to do with the care of CDs. Many stations use simple CD-cleaning cloths and sprays to remove dirt, dust, and fingerprint smudges from the CD surface. A Discwasher CD Hydrobath uses hydrodynamic principles to remove dirt and dry the CD while spinning it at high speed. This type of "no contact" cleaning prevents any accidental damage to the disc surface that could happen with hand cleaning. Other CD accessories include a laser lens cleaner and CD repair kits to remove scratches.

With more and more computer equipment making its way into the radio production studio, cleaning supplies for the monitor screen and keyboard need to be included as a broadcast accessory. Older basic supplies include cotton swabs and head cleaner, which are used to keep audio tape recorders clean. The swabs are not Q-Tips, but long wooden sticks with a cotton tip on one end that are excellent for getting at hard-to-reach tape heads. Expensive head-cleaning solvents can be replaced by denatured alcohol, but avoid using lower-quality isopropyl, or rubbing alcohol, because of its water content.

Stations usually have a supply of empty plastic cases for CDs, known as **jewel boxes** or **jewel cases.** These are needed because many promotional CDs come to radio stations in paper jackets rather than cases, and regular CD cases do break from time to time. Good production practice dictates keeping the CD in its case when not in use to prevent scratches or problems from dust and dirt.

PRODUCTION TIP #8
Proper Vinyl Storage

Most production facilities still have a stack of vinyl LP records around, such as an old sound effects library or a production music bed library. Of course, some radio stations still have a collection of music on records. If you're looking to store your vinyl for the long term, do it the right way. Use a conventional wooden enclosure, designed for record storage, that is appropriate for the size of your collection. The most important point about vinyl storage is to keep the records absolutely vertical. If you do, the only weight at the edge of the record will be the record itself. If you allow the records to lean to one side or the other, then the weight will be unequal and it could cause the disc to warp. Also be careful of storing records in either very dry locations, which will cause the paper record jackets to crumble, or very damp locations, which will cause mildew. A temperature between 65 and 70 degrees Fahrenheit with relative humidity between 30 and 40 percent offers the best environment for storing vinyl.

8.18 TELEPHONE INTERFACE

A simple **telephone interface,** or **telephone coupler** (see Figure 8.19), is a piece of equipment designed to connect telephone lines to broadcast equipment. In a basic configuration, the telephone goes through the interface and comes into the audio console on its own channel (just like a CD player, for example). The caller volume is controlled with that channel's fader, in addition to a caller volume control on the interface. Once a call is taken by the announcer and the interface is switched on, the announcer talks to the caller through the studio microphone, not the telephone instrument (which can be hung up at this point) and hears the caller through the headphones. The interface electronically maintains an isolation between the studio "send" signal and the caller "return" signal, providing a high-quality, clear telephone signal.

In addition, many radio stations have installed high-quality digital (ISDN) services that give a clearer signal than the older analog systems. Since the telephone becomes just another audio input, it can be easily recorded (and later edited), mixed with other sound sources, and otherwise manipulated for production use.

8.19 CONCLUSION

Often, monitor speakers and studio accessories are given little or no thought. Some production people are only concerned with making sure sound comes out of the speakers and that some accessory items are available. But, as you now understand, the role of the monitor speaker in radio production is not as minor as one might initially believe. And although not every accessory used by the professional radio broadcaster has been mentioned in this chapter, you have been introduced to the most common items used in the production studio, so you're less likely to run across something that makes you ask, "What's this for?"

FIGURE 8.19   The telephone interface allows mixing an audio signal and a telephone signal. (Image courtesy of Comrex Corporation.)

Self-Study

1. What components make up a two-way speaker system?

   a) tweeter, woofer, and midrange speaker
   b) tweeter, woofer, and crossover
   c) tweeter and woofer
   d) tweeter, woofer, and two crossovers

2. What is the transducing element of a speaker called?

   a) a tweeter
   b) a crossover
   c) a woofer
   d) a driver

3. Which speaker enclosure design utilizes a tuned port to provide a highly efficient system with a full bass sound?

   a) acoustic suspension
   b) bass reflex
   c) bass boom
   d) sealed box

4. Which individual speaker is designed to reproduce higher frequencies?

   a) woofer
   b) crossover
   c) tweeter
   d) bass reflex

5. For proper stereo sound, the listening angle formed between the speakers and the listener should be 90 degrees.

   a) true
   b) false

6. Which broadcast connector has a guide pin?

   a) RCA
   b) phone
   c) XLR
   d) phono

7. Which is the most practical place to locate monitor speakers in a production room?

   a) near the upper corners, close to the wall
   b) on the counter
   c) not in the room at all, but in an adjoining room
   d) in the middle of the wall, close together

8. Which is true if two speakers are out of phase?

   a) The bass sounds will be generated at the rear of the cones.
   b) Both negative wires will be connected to negative terminals.
   c) Both positive wires will be connected to positive terminals.
   d) The cone of one speaker will be moving out while the cone of the other speaker is moving in.

9. Which broadcast connector is always mono?

   a) phone
   b) miniphone
   c) ¼-inch phone
   d) RCA

10. Which type of monitor speaker will most likely be found in the production studio?

    a) ribbon speaker
    b) electrostatic speaker
    c) dynamic speaker
    d) condenser speaker

11. Which component of a speaker system divides the incoming audio signal into different frequencies and sends the proper frequencies to the appropriate driver?

    a) pigtail leads
    b) tweeter
    c) woofer
    d) crossover

12. Which type of headphone is designed with a porous muff that rests directly on the ear?

    a) closed-cushion headphone
    b) circumaural headphone
    c) earbud
    d) supra-aural headphone

13. Unbalanced audio cables are more susceptible to interference than balanced cables.

    a) true
    b) false

14. Having a high-power, external monitor amplifier in your production studio will allow you to record or broadcast a louder signal than using the internal monitor amp in the audio console.

    a) true
    b) false

15. Small speakers set on short stands, placed left and right of the audio console so the listener hears mostly direct sound at ear level, are known as which type of monitors?

    a) dynamic
    b) near-field
    c) acoustic suspension
    d) out-of-phase

16. When a patch panel is normalled, a patch cord is used to link broadcast equipment assigned to the top row of the panel to the equipment assigned to the bottom row.

    a) true
    b) false

17. Which broadcast connector has a sleeve, ring, and tip?

    a) RCA
    b) Cannon
    c) XLR
    d) phone

18. Which connector is most likely to be used for a patch bay?

    a) phone
    b) miniphone
    c) RCA
    d) multi-pin connector

19. What is a connector adapter used for?

    a) to transfer a signal in a patch bay
    b) to change a connector from one form to another
    c) to make a balanced line unbalanced
    d) to change a telephone signal to an audio signal

20. Which configuration describes a balanced cable?

    a) two wires
    b) three wires
    c) three ground wires
    d) two ground wires

21. The normal outputs of a CD player produce which level of audio signal?

    a) microphone
    b) line
    c) speaker
    d) none of the above

22. Which production room accessory is used to protect compact discs?

    a) Discwasher
    b) degausser
    c) jewel box
    d) timer

23. By convention, male XLR connectors are outputs and female XLR connectors are inputs.

    a) true
    b) false

24. Which production room accessory is used to connect telephone lines directly to broadcast equipment?

    a) audio routing switcher
    b) telephone coupler
    c) patch panel
    d) XLR connector

25. What would be the best type of monitor when you need to use a microphone in the production studio to record a voice over music?

   a) headphones
   b) a tweeter
   c) an acoustic suspension
   d) a bass reflex

ANSWERS

If You Answered A:

1a. No. This speaker complement would be in a three-way system. (Reread 8.3.)

2a. No. A tweeter is a speaker designed to produce high frequencies. (Reread 8.2 and 8.3.)

3a. No. The acoustic suspension design is relatively inefficient. (Reread 8.4.)

4a. Wrong. The woofer is designed to reproduce the lower frequencies. (Reread 8.3.)

5a. No. This would put the listener directly in front of one of the speakers, and all the sound would appear to be coming out of that speaker. (Reread 8.6; check Figure 8.6.)

6a. No. (Review Figures 8.11 to 8.14; reread 8.12 and 8.13.)

7a. Correct. This gives the operator good sound and also leaves the counter clear for other equipment.

8a. No. You're confusing this with speaker enclosures. (Reread 8.4 and 8.7.)

9a. No. The phone connector can be either stereo or mono. (Review Figures 8.11 to 8.14; reread 8.12 and 8.13.)

10a. No. Ribbon speakers are generally too exotic in design and too expensive for broadcast use. (Reread 8.2.)

11a. Wrong. You may be confused because this is a part of an individual speaker that receives an input signal, but after it has been divided into the proper frequencies. (Reread 8.3.)

12a. No. This is a headphone with a ring-shaped ear cushion designed to encircle the ear and rest on the head. (Reread 8.10.)

13a. Right. This is a true statement because one wire conducts the signal and also acts as a ground, so unbalanced cables are more likely to pick up unwanted noise.

14a. Wrong. A monitor amp has no relation to the broadcast or recorded signal; it only controls the volume of the monitor speakers. (Reread 8.8.)

15a. Although they may be dynamic speakers, this term usually refers to the speaker driver. There is a better answer. (Reread 8.2 and 8.6.)

16a. Wrong. A normalled patch panel is actually unpatched, so no patch cords are used. (Reread 8.11.)

17a. No. The phono connector only has an outer sleeve and tip. (Review Figures 8.11 to 8.14; reread 8.12 and 8.13.)

18a. Right. A male phone plug is the most likely connector to use with a patch bay.

19a. No. You would be very unlikely to use an adapter with a patch bay. (Reread 8.11 and 8.13.)

20a. No. Two wires would be unbalanced. (Reread 8.14.)

21a. Wrong. Microphone level is a low output level, which must be pre-amplified to be usable, and is primarily produced by microphones, as the name implies. (Reread 8.15.)

22a. No. You're close because Discwasher has a CD-cleaning system that helps keep dust and fingerprints off the disc, but there's a better answer. (Reread 8.17.)

23a. Correct. This is a true statement.

24a. Wrong. An audio router can be involved in selecting various inputs and outputs, but it can't connect a telephone line by itself. (Reread 8.11 and 8.18.)

25a. Yes. Headphones would prevent feedback and allow the operator to hear the music when the speakers are muted because the microphone is on.

1b. Correct. These are the basic components of a two-way speaker system.

2b. Wrong. The crossover divides the electrical signals and sends them to the speaker drivers. (Reread 8.2 and 8.3.)

3b. Right. This answer is correct.

4b. No. The crossover is not a speaker but an electronic device for sending various frequencies to different speaker drivers. (Reread 8.3.)

5b. Correct. This is false because an angle of about 60 degrees should be formed between the listener and the speakers for the best stereo sound.

6b. No. (Review Figures 8.11 to 8.14; reread 8.12 and 8.13.)

7b. No. The sound can be good, but the speaker takes up counter space that could be used for something else. (Reread 8.6.)

8b. No. One negative wire connected to a positive terminal would put them out of phase. (Reread 8.7.)

9b. No. The miniphone connector can be either stereo or mono. (Review Figures 8.11 to 8.14; reread 8.12 and 8.13.)

10b. No. Electrostatic speakers are generally too exotic in design and too expensive for broadcast use. (Reread 8.2.)

11b. Wrong. This is a part of a speaker system that reproduces high frequencies. (Reread 8.3.)

12b. No. This is another name for the closed-cushion headphone, which has a ring-shaped ear cushion designed to encircle the ear and rest on the head. (Reread 8.10.)

13b. Wrong. This is a true statement (Reread 8.14.)

14b. Correct. This is the right response because monitor amps have no relation to the broadcast or recorded signal.

15b. Yes. Some production people feel the best sound is heard through near-field monitoring.

16b. Yes. When a patch cord is put into a patch panel, it is no longer normalled.

17b. Wrong. Cannon is just another name for the XLR connector. (Review Figures 8.11 to 8.14; reread 8.12 and 8.13.)

18b. No. You're warm but not correct. (Reread 8.11 and 8.12.)

19b. Correct. It transfers the signal so that another form of connector can be used.

20b. Right. There are three wires: positive, negative, and ground.

21b. Right. Line-level outputs are standard for most broadcast production equipment, such as CD players and audio recorders.

22b. No. This has nothing to do with compact discs. (Reread 8.17.)

23b. No. This is a true statement. (Reread 8.12.)

24b. Correct. This is the best answer.

25b. No. This is only part of a monitor speaker. (Reread 8.3 and 8.10.)

If You Answered C:

1c. No. You're close though, but you've left out one component. (Reread 8.3.)

2c. No. A woofer is a speaker designed to reproduce low frequencies. (Reread 8.2 and 8.3.)

3c. Wrong. There's no such enclosure design. (Reread 8.4.)

4c. Correct. The tweeter is the speaker designed to reproduce high frequencies.

6c. Right. The XLR jack has a guide pin that prevents it from being connected incorrectly.

7c. No. You couldn't hear them if they were in another room. (Reread 8.6.)

8c. No. One positive wire connected to a negative terminal would put them out of phase. (Reread 8.7.)

9c. No. A ¼-inch phone or phone connector can be either stereo or mono. (Review Figures 8.11 to 8.14; reread 8.12 and 8.13.)

10c. Yes. The dynamic speaker is found most often in the production studio.

11c. Wrong. This is a part of a speaker system that reproduces low frequencies. (Reread 8.3.)

12c. No. This is a type of headphone that is designed to fit into the ear. (Reread 8.10.)

15c. Wrong. Although they may be acoustic suspension speakers, this term is usually associated with the speaker enclosure. There is a better answer. (Reread 8.4 and 8.6.)

17c. No. (Review Figures 8.11 to 8.14; reread 8.12 and 8.13.)

18c. No. (Reread 8.11 and 8.12.)

19c. No. Adapters are not related to balance. (Reread 8.13 and 8.14.)

20c. No. Although there are three wires, they aren't all ground wires. (Reread 8.14.)

21c. No. Speaker level is quite high and is designed to drive a monitor speaker. Most production equipment, like a CD player, would have to have its output signal amplified to reach speaker level. (Reread 8.15.)

22c. Yes. Jewel boxes are plastic protective cases for compact discs.

24c. Wrong. A patch panel could be involved in wiring a telephone line to an audio console, but it can't connect a telephone line by itself. (Reread 8.11 and 8.18.)

25c. No. You're confusing monitors and enclosures. (Reread 8.4 and 8.10.)

If You Answered D:

1d. Wrong. Only a single crossover is required in a speaker system. (Reread 8.3.)

2d. Yes. The driver transforms electrical signals into mechanical energy and thus audible sound.

3d. No. This is another name for an acoustic suspension speaker, which is relatively inefficient. (Reread 8.4.)

4d. No. Bass reflex describes a speaker enclosure design, not an individual speaker. (Reread 8.3 and 8.4.)

6d. No. Phono is just another name for the RCA connector. (Review Figures 8.11 to 8.14; reread 8.12 and 8.13.)

7d. Wrong. This would really limit sound dispersion and any stereo imaging. (Reread 8.6.)

8d. Right. The sounds will be fighting each other when this happens.

9d. Correct. You must use two RCA connectors for stereo, one for each channel.

10d. No. You might be thinking of a microphone; there is no such speaker. (Reread 8.2.)

11d. Correct. A crossover is a network of filters that divides the audio signal into different frequencies and sends it to the proper individual speaker.

12d. Yes. Also known as open-air or hear-through cushion headphones, supra-aural headphones are designed to rest directly on the ear.

15d. No. Out-of-phase speakers are miswired, and this has nothing to do with speaker placement. (Reread 8.6 and 8.7.)

17d. Correct. The miniphone connectors also have them.

18d. No. (Reread 8.11 to 8.13.)

19d. No. There are devices to do this, but they are interfaces, not connector adapters. (Reread 8.13 and 8.18.)

20d. Wrong. (Reread 8.14.)

21d. No. There is a correct answer and this isn't it. (Reread 8.15.)

22d. No. This has nothing to do with a compact disc. (Reread 8.17.)

24d. Wrong. You're quite confused if you chose this answer. (Reread 8.12 and 8.18.)

25d. No. You're confusing monitors with speaker enclosure designs. (Reread 8.4 and 8.10.)

Projects

PROJECT 1

Compare speaker/listener placement.

Purpose

To make you aware of how sound can change as the relationship between speaker and listener changes.

Advice, Cautions, and Background

1. If your studio is too small for you to hear any differences, just indicate this.
2. The most important thing for your drawings will be to show the relative dimensions of the studio and the position of the speakers.

How to Do the Project

1. Make three sketches of your control room, showing where the speakers are located.
2. On the first drawing, put an *X* where the production person usually sits. On the second drawing, put an *X* at another spot in the control room where you can stand and listen to the monitors. Do the same for the third drawing.
3. Play some music (you can use the music provided on the CD-ROM that accompanies this text) through the monitor speakers, and position yourself in each of the three places where you have placed *X*s. Listen for any differences in the way the music sounds at the three locations.
4. Write a short report detailing how the music sounded at each position.
5. Put your drawings and your report into a packet labeled with your name and the title, "Speaker–Listener Relationship." Give the packet to your instructor to receive credit for this project.

PROJECT 2

Inventory the broadcast accessories found in your production facility.

Purpose

To familiarize yourself with available accessory items.

Advice, Cautions, and Background

1. Design a form to conduct your inventory.
2. You can use items in any studio available at your facility, but note the exact locations.

How to Do the Project

1. List the brand name and model of each item, if possible.
2. Make sure you record the location of each item (e.g., Production Studio A or PDX 1).
3. Provide specifics about an item, if appropriate. For example, is the digital timer a 10-minute timer or a 24-hour timer?
4. Try to find as many accessory items as possible, such as headphones, patch bay, timer, cleaning supplies, and telephone interface.
5. If your production facility doesn't have a particular item mentioned in this chapter, indicate this on the form.
6. Turn in your inventory form to the instructor to receive credit for this project. Don't forget to put your name on it and label it "Broadcast Accessories Inventory Form."

Identify common broadcast connectors found in the production studio.

Purpose

To familiarize yourself with broadcast connectors and how they are used in the production studio.

Advice, Cautions, and Background

1. Figure 8.20 shows the broadcast connectors you'll use for this project.
2. If you have trouble identifying them, review Figures 8.11 to 8.13.

How to Do the Project

1. Draw four columns on a sheet of paper and label them "A," "B," "C," and "D."
2. Write the correct name for each connector beneath the appropriate letter. If the connector is also often called by another name, include both names.
2. Indicate whether this connector is mono, stereo, or can be both.
3. Now look around your studio and see how many instances you can find where each connector is used and note this on your list. Provide specifics on how the connector is being used. For example, "the output of the CD player uses RCA connectors for the left and right channel."
4. Try to find at least one instance of use for each connecter, but be aware that some connectors may be used numerous times in the studio.
5. Label your form with your name and the title, "Broadcast Connectors." Turn it in to your instructor to receive credit for this project.

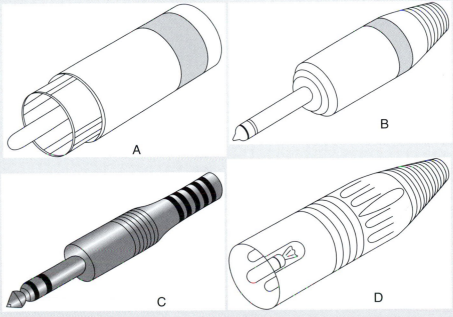

FIGURE 8.20 Common broadcast connectors.

9

ANALOG AUDIO PRODUCTION

9.1 INTRODUCTION

In a number of production and broadcast studios you'll still find a combination of analog and digital equipment. However, some equipment that was once a mainstay of audio production is now relegated to secondary status. For example, while it is no longer the primary playback source, many facilities still employ a turntable for playback of specialty material that is only available on vinyl recording. **Audio tape recorders** found in the radio production facility, such as the reel-to-reel or cassette, are in a similar position as the turntable. In most audio studios, they're mostly gathering dust. This chapter looks at equipment and production techniques that are analog based. For those who have mostly digital studios, it will merely provide some historical insight into audio production as it was in an earlier time. For others who still work with a number of pieces of analog equipment, it may prove more valuable.

9.2 THE BROADCAST TURNTABLE

While many have abandoned vinyl altogether, there may still be a need for the broadcast turntable to incorporate vinyl recordings into digital production. In fact, some new turntables (see Figure 9.1) have a digital output to facilitate transferring vinyl discs to digital discs. Regardless of whether it's analog or not, the **turntable** has two basic functions: to spin a record at the precise speed at which it was recorded, and to convert the variations in the grooves of the record to electrical energy. In the production studio, a turntable's signal is usually first sent into a pre-amplifier to increase the level of the signal produced and then to the audio console for further amplification. Professional-grade turntables provide quick speed buildup and they maintain precise speeds. They can backtrack the platter for cueing and are housed in a sturdy base or cabinet designed for heavy-duty use.

9.3 BASIC TURNTABLE COMPONENTS

The basic parts of the broadcast-quality turntable include a platter (a metal plate about 12 inches across covered by a felt or rubber mat), a motor to turn the platter, a tone arm, a cartridge/stylus, and a pre-amplifier. In addition, most production turntables have an on/off switch, a speed selector switch, and a pitch control that work in conjunction with the motor. Most broadcast turntables use only the 45 **RPM** and 33-1/3 RPM (revolutions per minute) speeds. Even though a speed may be selected, if the turntable is "off," the operator can move the turntable in either direction by hand for cueing.

A **tone arm** is usually a metal tube attached to a pivot assembly near the back of the turntable. At the front is a **headshell,** which allows installation of the cartridge/stylus assembly. The function of the tone arm is to house the cartridge and stylus and allow them to move freely across the record as it is played. This is a fairly sensitive piece of equipment and should be handled carefully. Most tone arms have small handles on the headshell, next to the cartridge, that should be used to pick up the arm and place it on the record. The cartridge/stylus assembly is the working end of the tone arm that actually picks up the signal from the record. The **cartridge** receives the minute vibrations from the **stylus,** converts them into variations in voltage, then sends the signals to a pre-amplifier and ultimately the audio board. The stylus is a very small, highly compliant strip of metal. The end that touches the record groove is made of a hard material, usually diamond. It may be called a needle by the home consumer or beginning broadcaster, but stylus is the professional term.

Styli are either spherical or elliptical; spherical styli are preferred for broadcast use because they allow backtracking of the record (for cueing up) with a minimum amount of damage to the vinyl grooves. The stylus should not be touched with the fingers. If it's necessary to remove dust

FIGURE 9.1 The turntable gets limited use in the modern production studio. (Image courtesy of Denon Electronics.)

from the stylus, do this by blowing lightly on it, or use a special fine-hair stylus brush.

9.4 VINYL RECORDS—CARE AND CUEING

Vinyl records are thin plastic discs either 7 inches (the 45 RPM single) or 12 inches (the 33-1/3 RPM LP) in diameter. Some broadcast "singles" are produced on the 12-inch disc but are recorded at the 45 RPM speed. Beginning broadcasters have often played records at the wrong speed because they automatically assumed the 12-inch disc was a 33-1/3 RPM record. The music, or audio signal, is represented in an analog fashion by tiny wiggles in the walls (or sides) of the record groove. The 45 was originally designed to hold about 4½ minutes of music, and the LP could contain about 30 minutes of music on each side. By spacing the grooves closer together, these times have been increased.

Dust is probably the biggest problem for records and turntables, causing undue record and stylus wear. Ultimately, dust in record grooves develops permanent pops and scratches on the record. The static electricity produced by playing a record compounds the problem by attracting more dust. Use a good-quality record cleaner before playing records to help minimize the dust problem. Unlike CDs, records can be wiped clean with a cloth and record-cleaning fluid, using a circular motion following the record grooves. Records should be handled by the edges to avoid getting fingerprints on the grooved surface. Unless they're being played, keep records in their paper/plastic inner sleeve and cardboard jacket to keep dust off them. Both LPs and 45s should be stored in a vertical position to prevent them from warping.

In most broadcast and production situations, you'll want the sound to begin immediately when playing a record. Broadcasters cue the record to avoid any silence (**dead air**) between the start of the record and the first sound heard. To cue a record, gently place the stylus in the outer groove of

the record. Rotate the turntable platter clockwise until the first sound is heard, then backtrack the platter enough to avoid "wowing" the record—about a one-quarter turn. Make sure the speed selector switch is set to the proper speed and turn the on/off switch to "on" just before you want actual sound to begin. Another way to cue a record is known as **slip cueing** because you hold the edge of the record with a finger, using enough force to keep it from spinning when the on/off switch is turned to "on" (the turntable platter will be spinning below the record), and you release the record when you want the actual sound to begin. You can only attempt to slip cue if the turntable has a felt-type mat. The typical rubber mat on some professional turntables doesn't allow the platter to continue to spin as you hold the record edge. Slip cueing allows tighter cueing than conventional cueing, but it takes some practice to become proficient at it.

Both methods for cueing records cause some deterioration, known as **cue burns,** of the outer grooves of the record as the stylus moves back and forth. A common problem with turntables is improper playback speed, which results in a distorted reproduction of the original sound signal. **Wow** refers to changes in pitch caused by slow, regular variations in the playback speed, and the term is somewhat descriptive of the actual sound heard. It's commonly caused by not backtracking far enough when cueing a record, so the record wows as it builds up to speed when the turntable starts to play. Wow can also be heard because of a record defect (warp or off-center hole) or a turntable defect (worn motor bearings). In any case, wow should be avoided and never heard on the air.

PRODUCTION TIP #9
Dead Rolling

In production work it's frequently important to end a piece of music at an exact time. For example, at the end of a program you might want the music and closing narration to end at exactly the same time, or a radio show's musical theme to end right at the top of the hour so that a newscast can begin. Regardless of the situation, you won't often find music that fits exactly the time that you have to fill. One method of dealing with this is the **dead roll.** To dead roll means to begin playing a CD, record, or any sound source with the volume turned down. For example, if you use a piece of music that's 4½ minutes long but is needed to only fill 3 minutes before the top of the hour, you would dead roll the music starting at 55:30, and then fade in the music at 57:00. In other words, the first 1:30 of the music would not be heard, but because you dead rolled it, the music would end exactly as desired at the top of the hour. Obviously, you usually dead roll music that's instrumental, so it isn't noticeable that you have cut out part of the song, but you can also dead roll some vocal music.

9.5 AUDIO TAPE

Before digital recording, audio tape was the basic storage medium for the sound a radio production person was working with. You could erase unwanted segments or edit long segments into shorter, workable concepts, but it all started with getting something onto tape first. Although audio tape appears to be merely a thin ribbon, its physical makeup actually consists of three basic layers: a **plastic base** sandwiched between a **backing layer** and a **magnetic layer** (see Figure 9.2). The top layer of audio tape is composed of tiny slivers of magnetic oxides that are capable of storing an electromagnetic signal. The plastic base in modern audio tape is **tensilized,** or prestretched polyester or mylar. The back coating provides traction as the audio tape moves through a tape recorder transport, and it also provides protection from tape breakage and print-through.

Print-through is the transfer of the magnetic signal on one layer of tape to the magnetic signal on the next layer of tape, either above it or below it on the reel. Think of the sandwich concept again, and visualize a jelly sandwich stacked on top of a peanut butter sandwich. If the jelly soaks through the bottom piece of bread and onto the peanut butter, print-through has occurred. It's most audible when one of the tape layers contains a very loud sound and the adjacent layer contains a soft sound. Although most modern audio tape is not very susceptible to print-through, you can help prevent it by recording at normal levels (i.e., avoid recording "in the red") and by avoiding using audio tape less than 1.5 mils (thousandths of an inch) thick. Are digital tapes, such as DAT or DASH, subject to print-through? Yes, they are, but the digital playback system simply ignores it. In digital recording systems, the playback electronics detects only the presence of the digital signal and when the signal is too low (such as print-through would be); then the playback system doesn't detect it at all.

Audio tape thickness is measured in mils, or thousandths of an inch. Most tape used in radio production work is either 1 mil or 1.5 mil; the latter is preferred by broadcasters. There are thinner audio tapes available, such as those used in audio cassettes. The advantage of thinner tape is that you can get more tape on a reel, which gives you more recording time. But thin tape also stretches more easily, is more susceptible to print-through, and is very difficult to handle in splicing. Tape specifically designed for digital recording is usually thinner than standard audio tape because it only has to store digital data on it. The other physical dimension of audio tape that concerns production people is its width. The standard width for reel-to-reel audio tape is ¼ inch. Cassette tape is usually ⅛-inch wide (actually .15 inches), and some multi-track recorders found in the radio production studio use ½-inch tape. Most wider audio tape (1- and 2-inch) is only found in the recording studio.

Perhaps the biggest problem with audio tape is signal loss due to drop-out. **Drop-out** (see Figure 9.3) is a defect in the oxide coating that prevents the signal at that point from being recorded at the same level—or at all. Drop-out is a problem that occurs in the manufacturing process of audio tape, but it can also be caused by flaking of the oxide coating due to heavy use or abuse of the tape. There are a few other tape defects or problems that you're likely to encounter during production work, but almost every tape problem can be avoided by using high-quality tape for all your radio production work.

9.6 LEADER TAPE

Leader tape is plastic or paper tape that does *not* have a magnetic layer. It is sometimes clear plastic, but more often it's colored as well as marked, or timed, in 7½-inch segments. This timing enables the operator to use leader tape to accurately cue up an audio tape. Leader tape is usually put at the beginning of an audio tape to mark the exact start of the recorded sound. The beginning of a tape is called the **head** (tape is normally wound on a reel "heads out"), and white or green leader tape is commonly used to signify this. Another reason for putting leader tape at the beginning is to use it to thread the tape recorder and avoid wear and tear on the actual recorded portion. Leader tape can also be written

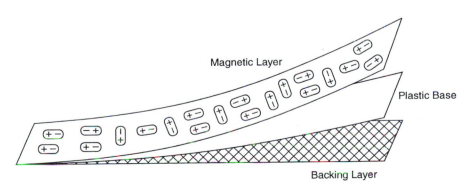

FIGURE 9.2 The basic "layers" of audio tape are the magnetic layer, the plastic base, and the backing layer.

FIGURE 9.3 Drop-out is an audio tape problem that can occur in the manufacturing process or through heavy use of the tape, which causes flaking of the oxide coating.

on; titles or notes can be put at the beginning of a tape this way. The end of an audio tape is called the **tail,** and if leader tape is put on the end of a tape, it will usually be yellow or red (often the leader tape is actually white, with the timing marks being green, red, etc.). Some audio tape (especially for prerecorded programs) is stored on reels **"tails out,"** or with the tail at the end of the recorded material. To play back a tape that is tails out, you would have to rewind the tape first.

In addition to being used at the beginning and end of an audio tape, leader tape is often used to separate various program segments. It's easier to cue up a tape when the operator can see the segments as they pass through the tape transport (even in fast forward) rather than having to listen for pauses between the segments. Cassette tapes also usually have leader tape at both ends of the tape reels. This keeps the actual audio tape within the plastic shell and not exposed at the open "head area" of the cassette. In addition, if the hub of the cassette (where the tape is attached) is slightly "out-of-round," it can cause sound quality problems at the beginning and end of the tape; however, the leader tape provides a cushion effect that helps prevent any adverse effect. Cassette leader tape is also used to activate an auto-stop or auto-reverse mechanism on some tape recorders.

9.7 AUDIO TAPE RECORDERS

Prior to the advent of digital recorders, analog audio tape recorders were the workhorse of the production room. The reel-to-reel and cassette recorders still see some production

studio use, but fairly limited compared to just a few years ago. The cartridge recorder is essentially obsolete in most broadcast facilities. The basic parts of a typical audio tape recorder consist of the tape recorder heads, the tape transport, and the electronics of the recorder.

9.8 TAPE RECORDER HEAD ARRANGEMENT

Tape recorders are devices that rearrange particles on magnetic tape so that sound impulses can be stored on the tape and played back later. This rearranging of particles is done by the recorder's **heads.** As noted above, the magnetic layer of tape consists of metallic particles. When a tape is unrecorded, the magnetic particles are not aligned and are on the tape in a random pattern (see Figure 9.4). Usually, professional-quality recorders have three heads: erase, record, and play. The erase head is always before the record head so that old material can be erased and new material recorded at the same time. With the play head behind the record head, it's possible to monitor what you've just recorded. When the machine is just in play, the erase and record heads are disengaged. The easiest way to remember the arrangement of heads in an audio tape recorder is to remember: "Every **R**ecorder **P**lays."

Because of the ERP head arrangement, you can't record one track in synchronization with a previously recorded track. For example, if you record one voice on one track and want to record another voice on another track on the same tape, you run into the following problem. As the previously recorded voice is playing, the sound signal is coming from the play head, but the second voice is recording at the record head. Because of the small distance between these two heads, you hear the previously recorded material a split second before you can record the second voice and therefore the two tracks would be out of sync when played back. To overcome this problem, one feature often found on audio tape recorders is **sel sync** (selective synchronization), also known as sound-on-sound, which makes the record

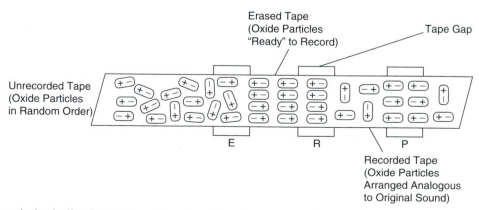

FIGURE 9.4 Tape recorder heads align the metallic particles of audio tape in a pattern analogous to the original sound.

head also act as the play head. Now you're hearing the previously recorded material at the same time as you're recording the new material, so there is no time difference between them, and you can easily synchronize the two recordings. This can be an important production tool, especially when you're doing multi-voice spots.

9.9 TAPE RECORDER HEAD FUNCTIONS

The erase, record, and play heads are very similar. Each head consists of a laminated metal core (see Figure 9.5) that is wound with an extremely fine wire coil at one end. At the other end of the core is a gap between the two magnet poles of the head. Tape recorder heads are merely small electromagnets; an electrical current through the coil creates a fluctuating magnetic field at the head gap. When recording, the audio tape is pulled across the head gap at a right angle. The sound signal is delivered to the record head from the record amplifier in the tape recorder and is transformed or converted from an electrical signal to a magnetic signal. This magnetic signal jumps the head gap and magnetizes the iron oxide layer of the audio tape passing by in a pattern analogous to the original sound signal (refer to Figure 9.4). Because the oxide coating on audio tape responds to magnetization differently at low and high input signal levels, **bias** current (an inaudible, high-frequency tone) is mixed with the audio signal during the recording process to raise the overall level to a point where the audio tape records sound more evenly.

During playback, the recording process is reversed. A recorded (magnetized) tape is drawn across the gap of the play head. The magnetic field of the tape (at the gap) passes into the core and then into the coil, creating an electrical current. This current is sent to a play amplifier in the recorder and is an exact reproduction of the original sound signal. Audio tape reproduces low and high frequencies at a softer level than the middle frequencies, and for that reason **equalization** is often used to compensate for this. Equalization affects the amount of amplification that is given to the highs and lows of the sound signal. Generally, the highs are boosted during recording and slightly decreased during playback; the low frequencies are increased during playback. The ultimate goal is a flat signal response.

The erase head is on during the recording process. A magnetic field is produced at the erase head gap that is so powerful, it demagnetizes the audio tape as it passes by. During the erase process, the random pattern of metallic particles on the unrecorded audio tape are arranged in a pattern that makes them ready to be recorded again (review Figure 9.4).

9.10 THE TAPE RECORDER TRANSPORT

Figure 9.6 shows the face of a typical reel-to-reel recorder found in the production studio. The **tape transport** is that part of the recorder that's involved with the actual motion of the audio tape as it passes the tape recorder heads. Starting with the tape reels, since the audio tape threads on a recorder from left to right, the left reel is the **supply reel**, or the **feed reel** (the reel that has audio tape on it as you begin to use the recorder). The right reel is the **take-up reel**, which starts out empty. Behind each reel (inside the tape recorder) are motors that help drive the tape from one reel to the other and help maintain proper tape tension. The standard reel sizes used in radio production facilities are 5-inch, 7-inch, and 10½-inch reels.

The audio tape is kept in line with the tape heads by various tape guides and tension arms. The **tape guides** are sometimes just stationary pins that provide a track or groove the width of the audio tape. The **tension arms** are generally movable. As the audio tape threads through them, they provide some spring, or tension, against the tape. One of these tension arms is usually an **idler arm;** if the tape breaks, this arm drops down into an "off" position, and the reel-to-reel recorder stops running.

The heart of the tape transport is the capstan and pinch roller. Normally located just to the right of the tape heads, the **capstan** is a metal shaft, and the **pinch roller** is a rubber wheel. The audio tape must pass between these two

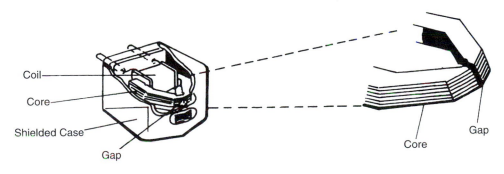

Internal View

FIGURE 9.5 Audio tape recorder heads function as small electromagnets.

FIGURE 9.6 The basic components of an audio tape recorder consist of the tape recorder heads, the tape transport, and the electronics of the recorder. (Image courtesy of Tascam.)

components. When the recorder is running, the pinch roller holds the tape against the revolving capstan. The capstan controls the speed of the tape as it passes the heads.

The final components of the tape transport are the actual controls of the audio tape recorder. Typically, recorders have an on/off button, rewind and fast-forward buttons, a play button, a stop button, a pause button, a cue button, and a record button. Most of these functions are obvious and merely control the direction and speed of the audio tape through the transport. Reel-to-reel tape recorders found in the production studio can record at different speeds ranging from 15/16 IPS (inches per second) to 30 IPS. The most common are 7½ IPS and 15 IPS. Of course, you must play back the tape at the same speed at which it was recorded. If you don't, it will have a speeded up "Donald Duck" sound or a slow, "groggy" sound. A tape machine operating at 7½ IPS means 7½ inches of recording tape go past the head each second. The more tape that goes past the head, the better the recording, because an audio signal with greater frequency response can be put on the tape with a better signal-to-noise ratio. You'll find that if you are editing audio tape, the faster the tape recorder speed, the easier it is to edit the tape. (Obviously, the pauses between words or other sounds will be longer at the faster speed.) A tape recorder speed of 3¾ IPS is usually acceptable for recorded material that is voice only.

The cue button allows the tape to stay in contact with the tape heads during rewind and fast forward or even in the stop position, so you can aurally find a certain spot on the tape. Usually, the tape is lifted away from the heads in the rewind or fast-forward position to save wear and tear on the heads. Some tape recorders require the operator to depress both play and record to put the machine into the record mode, but some will go into record when just the record button is pressed. Most audio tape recorders have a built-in timer or tape counter.

Modern machines have a digital timer that gives an accurate count of the minutes and seconds. Some machines have a mechanical counter that counts up from "0000," but the numbers have no relationship to time and are merely a gauge as to where you are on the tape. Most timers and counters also have a "zero set" that allows you to rewind to an exact location. For example, at the beginning of a voice track you're recording, you set the timer (or counter) to "00:00" and enable the zero set button. When you complete the recording, just push the rewind or memory button and it will rewind to the point where you set the "00:00." Timers are also useful to get a timing of a longer radio program. You don't have to listen to the program in real time since most timers work in the fast-forward mode of the recorder. An accurate timing of a half-hour radio show may only take a few minutes in fast forward; just reset the timer to "00:00" at the first sound at the beginning of the tape, fast forward to the last sound at the end of the tape, and look at the timer reading.

9.11 TAPE RECORDER ELECTRONICS

The electronics of the audio recorder include record-level and play-level pots, VU meters, and a source/tape switch. The **record-level pots** adjust the volume or level of the incoming sound signal. If the signal is being fed from an audio console, there is a pot, or channel, on the console that also controls the incoming volume. The best recording procedure is to make sure the level indicated on the audio board VU is near 100 percent, and then fine-tune the volume with the record-level pot on the audio tape recorder. The **play-level pot** controls the volume of the sound signal as it's being played from the audio tape. Again, there is also a volume control that adjusts the output volume of the recorder as it plays through the audio console. These pots should adjust closely together so that you don't have the tape recorder pot turned way down and then need to turn the audio console pot for the tape recorder way up to get a good signal level. The VU meter indicates the signal level, just like the VU meters on the audio console that were noted in Chapter 3.

What signal you see on the audio tape recorder VU meter is dependent on where the **source/tape switch** is set. The source position is sometimes labeled "record," "input," or "source," and the tape position is sometimes labeled "play," "reproduce," "output," "tape," or "monitor." In the "source" position, the VU meter shows the volume of the incoming signal at the record amplifier, usually just before the bias current is added. If this switch is set at the "tape" position, the VU meter shows the output level of the reproduced signal at the playback head, so it only indicates the level when you are actually recording. You can use the source/tape switch to make comparisons between the two levels. If the tape recorder is properly calibrated, there should be very little level change as you switch between the source and tape positions.

9.12 TRACK CONFIGURATION

Another important thing to understand about tape recorders is the recording patterns ("tracks") on the audio tape. Various audio tape recorders record differently by using different portions of the tape. There are four typical track configurations that conventional reel-to-reel recorders use. They differ in the number of signals put on the ¼-inch tape and the placement of the signals. Some recorders are **full-track**; that is, they essentially use the whole ¼-inch space to record one mono signal. Also, full-track recording can occur in only one direction (see Figure 9.7A). There is also **half-track mono** recording on ¼-inch tape. In this instance, the top of the tape is recorded on as it moves from left to right. When the end of the tape is reached, it can be flipped over. The two signals would then go in opposite directions because the tape has been flipped (see Figure 9.7B).

Most recorders used in radio production today are stereo or multi-track. Stereo can use ¼-inch tape, but it requires two tracks for each recording—one for the right channel and one for the left. When recording in **two-track stereo** (sometimes called **half-track stereo**), each of the two tracks uses half the tape, and both go in the same direction as shown in Figure 9.7C. Recording can only be in one direction because the two tracks use the entire width of the audio tape. This is probably the most common recording method found in the radio production facility.

There is also a **quarter-track stereo** recording method. Tracks 1 and 3 (the top one and the next-to-bottom one) are used for the first side, going from left to right. Then the tape is flipped and tracks 2 and 4 are recorded. The two recordings go in opposite directions (see Figure 9.7D). The track widths naturally have to be narrower, since four tracks have to fit on the ¼-inch audio tape. **Multi-track recorders** are also common in the radio production facility. For example, a **four-track recorder** uses four separate tracks all going in one direction (see Figure 9.7E).

There are two basic cassette tape-recording methods. One is half-track mono, which is like half-track mono on a ¼-inch tape except that it records the bottom of the tape first (see Figure 9.7F). The other recording method for cassettes is quarter-track stereo as shown in Figure 9.7G. This is not the same as ¼-inch quarter-track stereo; rather, the bottom two tracks are used for one side going in a left-to-right direction. When the tape is turned over, the top two tracks are

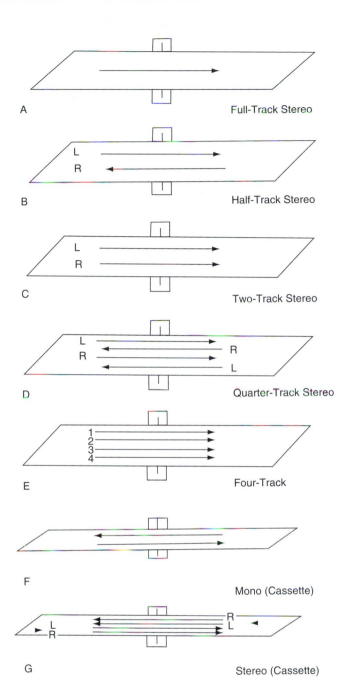

FIGURE 9.7 Audio tape track configurations include: (A) Full-Track Mono; (B) Half-Track Mono; (C) Two-Track Stereo; (D) Quarter-Track Stereo; (E) Multi-track (Four-Track, shown here); (F) Cassette Mono; and (G) Cassette Stereo.

recorded going in the opposite direction. Cassettes were designed this way so that mono and stereo cassettes would be compatible.

9.13 CROSS TALK AND COMPATIBILITY

All the stereo and multi-track recording heads have **guard bands**—small portions of blank tape between each track and at the edges to prevent cross talk. **Cross talk** occurs when the signal from one track is picked up simultaneously with the signal from an adjacent track. Another important consideration is compatibility. Quarter-inch tapes recorded on one machine can play on a different machine. In other words, a tape recorded on a quarter-track stereo machine can be played on a full-track mono recorder. All the tracks will be heard; however, there will be recorded material going both forward and backward, and the resulting sound will be a garble. If the stereo tape were recorded only on one side, then playback on the mono full-track would be intelligible, but, of course, it would not be stereo and probably would have some noise from nonrecorded sections. Certainly the best production practice would be to not mix track configurations, even though some are compatible to a degree.

9.14 THE CARTRIDGE TAPE RECORDER

For many years, the **cartridge recorder** (shown in Figure 9.8) was used to play commercials, public service announcements, station promos, and jingles that you heard on the radio. For some radio stations, even the music was transferred from LP record or CD to cartridge. The audio tape cartridge is constructed as a plastic container with a continuous loop of tape inside. The tape pulls from the inside and winds on the outside of the spool. Audio carts could put an inaudible **cue tone** just in front of the recorded information so that when music or a spot was played, the tone signals the machine to stop before it repeats itself. This automatic re-cueing also allows for putting several different spots on one cartridge and playing one without fear of playing another before stopping the machine. Most cart machines can also put secondary and tertiary cue tones on the cartridge that can be used to indicate the end of a spot, to start another cart machine, to engage warning lights in the studio, and to activate other programming features often found in automated situations. The audio cartridge recorder is essentially defunct in modern production environments.

9.15 THE CASSETTE TAPE RECORDER

The **cassette recorder** found its way into the broadcast facility mainly because of its portability and ease of use, but also because a professional-quality cassette recorder could offer high-quality recordings. Tape machines like the one shown in Figure 9.9 might still be found in the radio studio today. Portable units are also used, primarily in the news area, to record events or conduct interviews. From time to time, however, a cassette recorder also comes in handy for production work. For example, you might not have a sound effect that you need on record or CD, but you can easily record your own on a portable cassette. Most portable cassette recorders have a built-in microphone. Avoid using this microphone for broadcast work because it often picks up as much internal noise (tape recorder motor, for example) as the sound you want. Use a good-quality microphone like those mentioned in Chapter 4. Some other features that should be part of a professional-quality cassette machine are a VU meter, three heads (rather than two), XLR, balanced inputs, and durable construction.

The audio **cassette** tape is a small, ⅛-inch reel-to-reel tape housed in a plastic case (see Figure 9.10). A short **leader tape** is attached at each end, and both ends of the tape are permanently attached to the reels. When recording onto cassettes, it's important to remember the leader tape, because if you're at the very beginning of the cassette, the actual recording will not begin for a few seconds, until you are past the leader tape. Another feature of the cassette is the knock-out tabs on the back edge of the cassette shell. These two little plastic tabs (one for each side of the cassette) allow the recorder to go into the record mode. If you wish to save an important cassette and be sure no one records over the tape, you can knock out the tab. If at a later date you want to record on this cassette, you can put a small piece of cellophane tape over the hole where the tab was, and it will work just as if the tab was there.

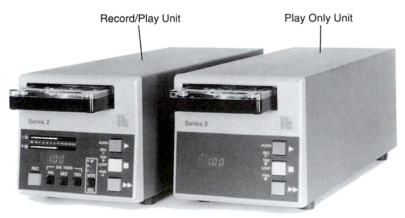

FIGURE 9.8 The cartridge recorder and player once played a major role in delivering the commercials, PSAs, promos, jingles, and music heard on the radio. (Image courtesy of International Tapetronics Corporation.)

FIGURE 9.9 Of all the analog tape recorders, the broadcast-quality cassette recorder is the most useful in the production studio today. (Image courtesy of Tascam.)

Audio cassettes are classified according to the kind of tape formulation used. The magnetic material used in standard cassettes is ferric oxide ("rust" in its natural form), and these cassettes are designated as **Type I** tapes. **Type II** tapes use a chromium-dioxide or a chrome-equivalent formulation. A **Type III** cassette tape, a ferrite and chrome dioxide combination, is no longer available. Cassette tapes that use a pure metal magnetic material, rather than an oxide compound, are known as metal or **Type IV** tapes. Type I and Type II tapes are most frequently found in the radio production studio situation. Although there isn't a huge quality difference between them, Type II tapes should produce a slightly better recording. Metal tapes (Type IV) actually provide the best quality but are expensive for day-to-day broadcast use. Each of the cassette tapes requires a different amount of **bias** (during recording) and **equalization** (during playback). Some cassette decks automatically set the bias and equalization, using special sensing cutouts on the plastic cassette shell, but many require the operator to set the correct tape type.

9.16 AUDIO TAPE RECORDER MAINTENANCE

Most tape recorder maintenance that a production person might be expected to handle is related to the heads themselves. The most common problem is, simply, dirty heads. When cut 'n' splice editing has been done in the studio, some residual grease from a grease pencil may have been left on the heads, and even normal use leaves some oxide material on or near the heads. It's good production practice to clean the tape heads before you begin any production work. The production studio usually has a supply of cotton swabs and head cleaner or denatured alcohol to gently clean any residue off the tape recorder heads.

One reason for keeping the tape path clean is to prevent wow and flutter. Both wow and flutter are tape recorder problems that are related to changes in the speed of the tape as it passes through the tape transport. **Wow** refers to slow variations in tape speed, and **flutter** refers to rapid variations. Both problems result in off-pitch sounds that are reflected in their names.

A final tape recorder maintenance concern is a buildup of magnetism on the tape recorder heads. After extended use, the tape heads will tend to become magnetized permanently. This could result in the heads actually erasing part of the signal that you don't want erased. Usually it will affect the high-frequency signals first. To prevent this, a **demagnetizer** is used to get rid of any built-up magnetism. This is typically part of the general maintenance done by the engineer, but in some production facilities this type of maintenance, along with cleaning of the heads, is left to the operators. A demagnetizer is brought near to (but not in contact with) the heads, guides, and other metallic parts in the tape path. Since it operates like a bulk eraser, you must be sure to turn it on and off away from the heads.

Bulk erase audio tapes prior to production work with a **degausser.** In general, you don't need to worry about erasing anything that may already be on these tapes because the unwritten rule in most studios is that any tape left in the production studio is up for grabs. If you want to save something that you've recorded, take the tape out of the production studio. Look over the audio tape, too. If it's excessively worn or damaged in any way, throw it out. If you're using reel-to-reel tape, spool off a few feet from the front of the reel, and throw it away (unless it has leader tape on it). That part of the tape gets the wear and tear of threading and handling and will wear out before the rest of the tape. If you're producing something that's very important or something that you know will be aired over and over, start with fresh tape.

9.17 AUDIO TAPE EDITING: TOOLS OF THE TRADE

To manipulate audio in the modern production studio, cut 'n' splice editing has all but been replaced by computer editing. However, for those still working with tape-based editing,

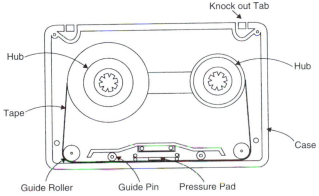

Knock out Tab

Hub

Hub

Tape

Case

Guide Roller   Guide Pin   Pressure Pad

FIGURE 9.10 The internal structure of an audio cassette tape.

here are the basic tools of the trade: a grease pencil, a splic- ing block, a razor blade, and splicing tape. A white or yellow **grease pencil**, or **china marker**, is used to physically mark on the back or unrecorded side of the tape the points where you're going to cut. When marking, make sure none of the grease pencil gets on the tape recorder heads or on the recorded side of the tape. A **splicing block** is a small metal or plastic block (see Figure 9.11) with a channel to hold the audio tape and two grooves to guide the razor blade when cutting the tape. The channel is designed so the audio tape snaps down into it. The tape can easily be slid in the chan- nel by the operator, but it won't move on its own.

The cutting grooves are usually at 45-degree and 90- degree angles to the audio tape. For almost all production work, you'll use the diagonal cut for two reasons. First, it provides more surface for contact with the splicing tape at the point of the edit, and thus a stronger bond or splice is made. Second, the diagonal cut provides a smoother sound transition. For example, if you are splicing together two pieces of music, rather than an abrupt change from one piece to another at the edit (such as a 90-degree splice could produce), you will have a short blend of the music pieces at the edit.

Although broadcast supply companies offer industrial- grade razor blades, almost any standard *single-edged* razor blade will work for cutting audio tape. Be careful! Razor blades are sharp and will cut your fingers as easily as they cut audio tape. **Splicing tape** is commercially available and is specially designed so that its adhesive material does not soak through the audio tape and gum up the heads of the tape recorder. Never use cellophane tape or other office tape to do editing work. Splicing tape is slightly narrower than audio tape so that any excess adhesive material will not protrude beyond the edge of the audio tape. In addition to rolls of splicing tape, you can get splicing tabs—precut pieces of splicing tape on applicator strips, designed to make the splicing process easier.

9.18 MARKING EDIT POINTS

Audio tape editing is really a two-step process: marking the edit points and then splicing. Since audio tape passes through the recorder from left to right, sounds are recorded on the tape in the same manner. For example, the phrase "editing is really a two-step process" would be recorded on

FIGURE 9.11 A splicing block is one of the tools used in analog audio tape editing. (Image courtesy of Xedit Corporation.)

audio tape in this manner: "ssecorp pets-owt a yllaer si gnitide"—the rightmost word ("editing") would be recorded first. If we wanted to edit out the word "really" in this phrase, we would make two edit points, one on each side of the word. The edit point is always made in front of the word (or sound) that you wish to edit *out* on the one side, and in front of the word (or sound) that you're leaving *in* on the other side. It's important that you always mark in front of words to maintain the proper phrasing of the speech.

For marking purposes, find the playback head because this is where you'll make your marks, and then find the dead center of that head. Remember that audio tape will be covering the actual head gap, so look for some kind of ref- erence above and below this portion of the head that will allow you to find this spot consistently. Every time you make an edit mark, make it *slightly to the right* of dead cen- ter. (Marking to the right compensates for the split second it takes you to actually press the stop button when listening to the audio tape to find where to make an edit.) You can also cue to your edit point by manually rocking the tape reels back and forth with the recorder in the stop position— that is, "scrubbing" the tape to find an exact sound. Your goal should be to make the same edit over and over and have each one sound the same. That is uniformity in edit- ing, and it's a skill you want to have.

9.19 BASIC STEPS IN SPLICING TECHNIQUE

If you've marked the audio tape at two points, it's time to perform the actual cut 'n' splice. Normal splicing technique follows these steps:

A. *Position the tape at the first edit mark in the splicing block.* (See Figure 9.12.) The unrecorded side of the tape should be facing up in the splicing block, and the edit mark should be exactly at the 45-degree cutting groove.

B. *Cut the tape at your first mark.* A simple slicing motion with the blade through the groove should cut the tape cleanly. If a razor blade doesn't slice cleanly through the audio tape, it's already dull and you should get a new one. Because the metal blade cuts through the magnetic layer of the audio tape, over a period of time it will become magnetized. If you need to dispose of a "dull" or magnetized razor blade, put a piece of masking or cellophane tape just a bit beyond the blade edge before you toss it so people who are emptying the trash won't cut themselves.

C. *Repeat steps A and B at the second edit mark.* Remove the unwanted piece of audio tape, *but don't discard it yet.* It's good production practice to hang on to cut-out tape until after you're sure the splice has been accom- plished as you want it. It's possible (although difficult) to splice the cut-out piece of tape back in and try the splice again if you've made a mistake.

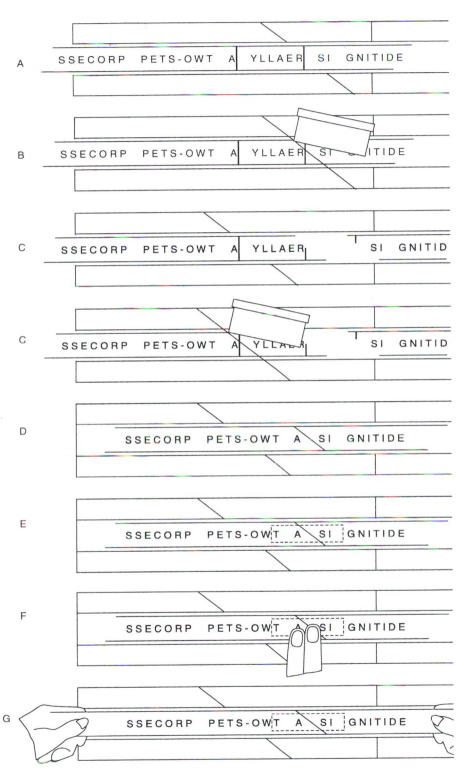

FIGURE 9.12 To edit audio tape: (A) Position tape at first edit mark. (B) Cut tape at first mark. (C) Position and cut tape at second edit mark. (D) Butt tape ends together. (E) Apply splicing tape. (F) Smooth out splicing tape. (G) Remove audio tape from splicing block.

D. *Butt the remaining tape ends together.* Move both pieces of the tape slightly left or right so that you don't butt them together directly over the cutting groove.

E. *Apply the splicing tape on the edit.* If you're using splicing tape from a roll, a piece about ¾ inch in length is ample. Splicing tabs are precut at the appropriate length. The splicing tape should be centered at the edit. Make sure it's positioned straight along the channel of the splicing block. Since the splicing tape is narrower than the audio tape, it should not protrude over either edge of the audio tape.

F. *Smooth out the splicing tape.* Be sure to get air bubbles out from under the splicing tape for a strong bond. Rubbing your fingernail over the splice will usually take care of this.

G. *Remove the audio tape from the splicing block.* Never do this by grasping one end and lifting; the edges of the channel can damage the audio tape. The proper procedure is to grasp both ends of the tape just beyond the splicing block, apply slight pressure to the tape by pulling your hands in opposite directions, and lift straight up. The tape will pop right out of the block, and you will have completed your splice.

It's best not to fast rewind the tape until you've played it, to help secure the splice, so manually wind the tape on the feed reel until you're past the splice. Then, thread the tape on your recorder, and listen to the edited tape. If it came out as you wanted, you can discard the unwanted tape section. Sometimes you may find it necessary to shave a piece of the edit by splicing off one edge of the tape. If you've made a good edit mark, however, you'll rarely have to do this.

9.20 SPLICE PROBLEMS

Beginning audio tape editors often encounter problems with their first few splices. These are usually overcome with practice and experience, but it's not uncommon to see splicing errors in manipulating the splicing tape itself and in manipulating the audio tape. One of the most common problems with splicing-tape manipulation is simply using too much; a piece of splicing tape that's too long is difficult to position properly on the audio tape and makes the tape too stiff at the edit, which prevents proper contact with the tape recorder heads. On the other hand, a piece of splicing tape that's too short may not hold the audio tape together during normal use. Another cause of an edit not holding is the splicing tape being poorly secured on the audio tape. For example, air bubbles or dirt or grease (from fingerprints or excessive marking with the grease pencil) may be under the splicing tape, preventing it from adhering to the audio

tape. Other problems arise when the splicing tape is put on crooked; a portion of the splicing tape will hang over the edges of the audio tape, making it impossible for the tape to glide through the tape recorder transport properly.

One of the most common problems with audio tape manipulation during the editing process is leaving a gap as you butt the two tape ends together. Obviously, a gap at the edit point will be heard as an interruption of sound or too long a pause. On the other hand, if you overlap the two tape ends as you butt them together, the splice won't occur where you thought it would.

9.21 DUB EDITING

Dubbing is another form of audio tape editing. This type of editing requires the use of two tape recorders. As you dub or copy from one to the other, the "master" tape recorder is in the play mode, and the "slave" tape recorder is in the record mode. Using our previous example (the phrase, "editing is really a two-step process"), you would dub "editing is" from the master to the slave tape recorder, and then stop both recorders. Next, you'd cue up the master tape recorder past the word "really" and then dub "a two-step process" from the master to the slave tape recorder. Dub editing requires a good deal of coordination because you manipulate the two machines so that they start at the same time. Usually dubbing produces a glitch at the edit point that can range from barely noticeable to terrible, depending on the tape recorders used.

Straight dubbing is frequently used in radio production work for purposes other than editing. Often a master tape is dubbed onto a working tape before splicing so that the original tape isn't cut during the editing process. You can also dub from one tape format to another. For example, you may have a news tape that was recorded on cassette, but you want to put it on reel-to-reel so that you can edit it down or perhaps equalize it to improve quality. Finally, dubbing can be used simply to make duplicate copies of any existing tape.

9.22 CONCLUSION

For years, turntables and audio tape recorders were the primary workhorses in most radio production studios and cut 'n' splice was the only way to edit audio tape. With the advent of digital equipment and the quality and convenience it offers, the use of older analog equipment and production techniques continues to diminish. However, many studios still use some of this equipment, and a good solid background in the main analog components will not hurt your future production studio work.

Self-Study

1. Which of the following could be a proper head arrangement for an audio tape recorder, assuming the tape goes from left to right?

   a) erase–record–play
   b) record–erase–play
   c) play–record–erase
   d) erase–play–record

2. If you put a 7-inch reel of tape on a reel-to-reel recorder at 7½ IPS, another 7-inch reel on a recorder at 15 IPS, and a third 7-inch reel on a recorder at 3¾ IPS, and start all the recorders at once, which one will run out of tape first?

   a) the reel at 3¾ IPS
   b) the reel at 7½ IPS
   c) the reel at 15 IPS
   d) they would all run out of tape at the same time

3. Which of the following prevents cross talk?

   a) sel sync
   b) the pinch roller
   c) leader tape
   d) guard bands

4. Which of the following is the term for an unwanted effect of the magnetic signal involving adjacent layers of audio tape?

   a) tensilize
   b) drop-out
   c) tails out
   d) print-through

5. Which thickness of audio tape is preferred by broadcasters?

   a) .5 mil
   b) 1.0 mil
   c) 1.5 mil
   d) 2.0 mil

6. Which of the following is true about the erase head of an audio tape recorder?

   a) It rearranges the iron particles, so they're in a random pattern.
   b) It is on during the recording process.
   c) It closes the gap on the metal core, so the signal jumps to magnetic energy.
   d) It rearranges the iron particles analogous to the original sound.

7. In most production situations, which type of edit is preferred?

   a) diagonal cut
   b) vertical cut
   c) horizontal cut
   d) none of the above

8. Which of the following is an adjustment that changes the amount of amplification given to highs and lows of the sound signal?

   a) digital
   b) bias
   c) equalization
   d) sel sync

9. What problem can be created if you use splicing tape that is too long?

   a) It will be difficult to position it properly.
   b) It will create a gap.
   c) It will misalign the recording tape.
   d) It will overlap the recording tape.

10. Referring to Figure 9.6, which of the following controls the speed of the tape as it passes the head?

    a) feed reel
    b) tape guide
    c) capstan
    d) take-up reel

11. What would happen if a two-track stereo tape were played back on a half-track mono recorder?

    a) Both stereo tracks would be heard, but one would be going backward.
    b) The tape would be intelligible, but the lower track's material would be missing.
    c) Four sounds would be heard—two going forward and two going backward.
    d) No sound would be heard.

12. If the source/tape switch on a tape recorder is in the "source" position, what does the VU meter show?

    a) a zero signal
    b) the outgoing signal that has been recorded
    c) the signal that was erased
    d) the incoming signal that is being recorded

13. Which term describes having the end of the material recorded on an audio tape at the outside of the reel?

    a) tails out
    b) tails in
    c) leader out
    d) none of the above

14. What would happen if a stereo cassette recorded on both sides were played on a mono cassette recorder?

    a) Two sounds would be heard, one going forward and one going backward.
    b) The stereo tape would be intelligible but would not be stereo.
    c) There would be a garbled sound.
    d) There would be no sound since they're not compatible.

15. Which describes a colored or clear plastic or paper tape that has the same dimensions as audio tape and is often used in audio tape editing?

    a) splicing tape
    b) scotch tape

c) cellophane tape

d) leader tape

16. Which term means to begin a record (or any sound source) with the volume control turned down?

a) cue

b) wow

c) dead air

d) dead roll

17. Which of the following is a function of the turntable?

a) spinning a record at the proper speed

b) allowing the cartridge/stylus to move freely across the record

c) amplifying the signal

d) none of the above

18. Which part of the turntable changes vibrations into variations in voltage?

a) cartridge

b) stylus

c) diamond tip

d) tone arm

19. Both splicing and dubbing can be easily accomplished with any audio tape recorder.

a) true

b) false

20. Which tape defect is a problem due to flaking of the oxide coating of the audio tape?

a) print-through

b) crosstalk

c) drop-out

d) flutter

ANSWERS

If You Answered A:

1a. Right. This is the most common head arrangement for broadcast recorders.

2a. No. (Reread 9.10.)

3a. Wrong. (Reread 9.8 and 9.13.)

4a. Wrong. To tensilize is to prestretch audio tape. (Reread 9.5.)

5a. No. Thinner audio tape stretches too easily and is more susceptible to print-through. (Reread 9.5.)

6a. No. It rearranges them into an orderly pattern making them "ready" to record. (Reread 9.9.)

7a. Right. The diagonal cut or 45-degree cutting groove is used in audio tape editing because it gives a smoother sound transition and a stronger edit.

8a. No. This is a recording technique using binary technology. (Reread 9.9.)

9a. Right. A long piece of editing tape will be difficult to position; shorter tape will make for better edits.

10a. Wrong. This is the reel that the tape is placed on, but it doesn't really control tape recorder speed. (Reread 9.10.)

11a. No. At first glance, this looks logical, but it's not. A half-track mono only plays back half a tape at a time. If it played back the full track, it would play back both sounds of its own tapes. All that is played back is the top half of the tape. (Reread 9.12.)

12a. No. There would be a reading on the VU meter. (Reread 9.11.)

13a. Right. The end of an audio tape is called the tail.

14a. No. (Reread 9.12.)

15a. Wrong. Splicing tape is used in audio tape editing, but it does not have the same dimensions as audio tape. (Reread 9.6 and 9.17.)

16a. No. To cue a record is to prepare it for air play, but this doesn't describe what's happening here. (Reread 9.4 and the Production Tip for this chapter.)

17a. Correct. This is one function of the turntable.

18a. Right. It's the cartridge that converts vibrations into voltage.

19a. Wrong. For all practical purposes, cassette and cart tapes can only employ dubbing techniques. (Reread 9.19 and 9.21.)

20a. No. Print-through is the transfer of the magnetic signal on one layer of tape to the magnetic signal on an adjacent layer. (Reread 9.5.)

If You Answered B:

1b. No. Erase must be before record. (Reread 9.8.)

2b. No. (Reread 9.10.)

3b. Wrong. (Reread 9.10 and 9.13.)

4b. Wrong. Drop-out is a defect in the oxide coating. (Reread 9.5.)

5b. You're close. 1-mil audio tape may be used by broadcasters, but it's not the best choice. (Reread 9.5.)

6b. Right. It is on so that the tape can be erased just before it's recorded on again.

7b. No. The 90-degree cut is normally only used when putting leader tape on an audio tape. (Reread 9.17.)

8b. No. Bias improves frequency response and provides a distortion-free signal during audio tape recording. (Reread 9.9.)

9b. No. The length of splicing tape has nothing to do with this. (Reread 9.19.)

10b. No. This guides the tape through the recorder mechanism but not at any particular speed. (Reread 9.10.)

11b. Correct. Half-track mono only plays back the top half of the tape.

12b. No. The tape position would do that. (Reread 9.11.)

13b. Wrong. (Reread 9.6.)

14b. Right. Cassette mono tape and stereo tape can each be played on the other recorder and be understood.

15b. No. Scotch tape should not even be used in audio tape editing. (Reread 9.6 and 9.17.)

16b. Wrong. Wow is an off-speed problem associated with records, but it's not this situation. (Reread 9.4 and the Production Tip for this chapter.)

17b. You're close. The tone arm (which is part of a turntable) houses the cartridge/stylus and allows it to move across the record. (Reread 9.2 and 9.3.)

18b. No. The stylus picks up the vibrations. (Reread 9.3.)

19b. Right. For all practical purposes, cassette and cart tapes can only employ dubbing techniques.

20b. No. Cross talk is a problem associated with audio signals being picked up on adjacent tracks. (Reread 9.5 and 9.13.)

If You Answered C:

1c. No. Erase must be before record. (Reread 9.8.)

2c. Yes. It goes through the recorder the fastest and so would run out first.

3c. Wrong. (Reread 9.6 and 9.13.)

4c. Wrong. Tails out refers to a reel of audio tape with the end program or recording at the outside of the reel. (Reread 9.5 and 9.6.)

5c. Yes. Audio tape that is 1.5 mil thick is most often used by broadcasters.

6c. No. (Reread 9.9.)

7c. No. (Reread 9.17.)

8c. You are correct.

9c. No. The editing tape shouldn't affect the position of the audio tape. (Reread 9.20.)

10c. Right. This, in conjunction with the pinch roller, pulls the tape through at a uniform speed.

11c. No. There are only two tracks on two-track stereo, so it couldn't play back four. (Reread 9.12.)

12c. No. It does not show the signal that was erased. (Reread 9.11.)

13c. Wrong. Although there may be leader tape at the end of the audio tape, this is not the correct term. (Reread 9.6.)

14c. No. (Reread 9.12.)

15c. Wrong. Cellophane tape (also known as Scotch tape) should not even be used in audio tape editing. (Reread 9.6 and 9.17.)

16c. Wrong. You're close because dead air equals silence, but it's not correct for this situation. (Reread 9.4 and the Production Tip for this chapter.)

17c. No. A turntable itself doesn't amplify. Amplification is done through the pre-amplifier and audio console. (Reread 9.2 and 9.3.)

18c. No. This is part of the stylus. (Reread 9.3.)

20c. Yes. Drop-out occurs when the oxide coating of audio tape flakes off; if there's no recording material on the tape, the audio signal drops out at that point.

If You Answered D:

1d. No. This is not a common head arrangement. (Reread 9.8.)

2d. No. You might be confused because they all have the same size reel. (Reread 9.10.)

3d. Right. Guard bands help prevent cross talk.

4d. Right. Print-through occurs when the magnetic signal of one layer of audio tape affects an adjacent layer.

5d. No. This is not a standard thickness for audio tape. (Reread 9.5.)

6d. No. You're getting this confused with the record head. (Reread 9.9.)

7d. No. There is a better response. (Reread 9.17.)

8d. Wrong. This allows you to record one track in synchronization with a previously recorded track. (Reread 9.8 and 9.9.)

9d. Wrong. The editing tape shouldn't cause the recording tape to overlap. (Reread 9.20.)

10d. No. As the tape goes past the heads it is taken up by this reel, but it doesn't really control the speed. (Reread 9.10.)

11d. Wrong. Although there is not full compatibility between two-track stereo and half-track mono, some sound would be heard. (Reread 9.12.)

12d. Correct. "Source" shows the source audio signal.

13d. No. (Reread 9.6.)

14d. No. Stereo and mono cassettes are compatible. (Reread 9.12.)

15d. Right. This accurately describes leader tape.

16d. Yes. This describes the term "dead roll."

17d. No. (Reread 9.2.)

18d. No. (Reread 9.3.)

20d. Wrong. Flutter is a problem associated with off-speed audio tapes. (Reread 9.5 and 9.16.)

Projects

PROJECT 1

Dub taped material between cassette and reel-to-reel recorders.

Purpose

To make sure you are able to do even, clear dubbing.

Advice, Cautions, and Background

1. The material you are to dub (which can be taken from the CD-ROM that accompanies this text) was not recorded properly in that it is not all at the same level. You are to make it as much at the same level as possible. On professional equipment, there are sophisticated meters to help you. On less-expensive equipment, you will have to do this by practicing a few times and getting the feel of it.
2. If you're unsure of what you're doing, get help rather than risk damage to the equipment.
3. You will need some analog equipment in your studio to complete this project.

How to Do the Project

1. Make sure you know how to operate a cassette and reel-to-reel recorder. If in doubt, ask the instructor.
2. Transfer the material from the CD-ROM to your reel-to-reel recorder without making any level adjustments.
3. Listen to the material, noting where the level changes are, and decide on a strategy for dubbing it so that it's all at one level.
4. Rewind the tape, and connect the cable from the proper audio output on the reel-to-reel to the proper audio input on the cassette recorder. If your equipment is already connected through an audio console, just be sure the switches and knobs are set properly so that you can record from reel-to-reel to cassette.
5. Place a tape in the cassette recorder.
6. Put the reel-to-reel recorder in play. Monitor the recording, and at the same time, adjust the volume on one of the recorders so the level will be even.
7. Rewind the reel-to-reel recorder, and set the cassette recorder so that it will record and the reel-to-reel recorder so that it will play. The audio will then go from the reel-to-reel to the cassette recorder.
8. Practice your dub several times, adjusting levels until you get the feel of how much you need to vary the volume. Then make the dub.
9. Now you're ready to make your dub from cassette back to the reel-to-reel recorder. Place a different tape on the reel-to-reel recorder.
10. If necessary, change cables so that one goes from the proper audio output on the cassette to the proper audio input on the reel-to-reel. (Again, you may just have to set the proper switches and knobs on your audio console.)
11. Decide on a volume for both recorders, and put the cassette recorder in play and the reel-to-reel recorder in record mode.
12. Make your dub. This time you shouldn't have to adjust levels. Listen to the dub to make sure it recorded properly.
13. Label the tape with your name and "Tape Dub." Turn it in to the instructor to get credit for this project.

Make two edits by splicing an audio tape.

Purpose

To enable you to feel comfortable editing a vocal audio tape with analog reel-to-reel equipment.

Advice, Cautions, and Background

1. If you're not sure of what you're doing, ask the instructor for assistance. Don't take the chance of damaging the equipment.
2. Remember, you are to do two edits, not just one.
3. You'll be judged on the cleanness of your edits, so don't try to edit something that is too tight.

How to Do the Project

1. Familiarize yourself with the operation of the reel-to-reel tape recorder in your production studio. If you have questions, ask your instructor.
2. Assemble the editing tools and supplies that you will need, including splicing block, razor blades, grease pencil, and splicing tape.
3. You can use the material provided on the CD-ROM that accompanies this text, or you can record something of your own.
4. Do your edits as follows:
   a. Press the play button and listen to what is recorded.
   b. Select something you wish to edit. Write down on a piece of paper the part you plan to edit with a few words before and after it. Put parentheses around what you plan to take out. For example, for the CD material, you could write: "Today's weather calls for (sunny skies and) a temperature of seventy degrees."
   c. Stop the tape recorder so it's at the exact place you wish to edit—in our example, just in front of "sunny."
   d. Listen to the tape on the play head; make your edit mark just right of dead center. Be careful *not* to get any grease pencil on the actual tape recorder heads.
   e. Continue playing the tape until you get to the end of your edit—in our example, just before "a."
   f. Using the grease pencil, make your edit mark just as you did before.
   g. Spool out enough tape so that your edit marks can be positioned in the splicing block. Cut the audio tape at the first edit point, according to proper splicing procedure.
   h. Position the other edit mark in the splicing block, and cut the tape as before. You should now have a loose piece of tape (the unwanted words "sunny skies and") and two pieces of tape with diagonal cuts that are both connected to the two tape reels.
   i. Butt the two tape ends and apply a proper amount of splicing tape. Make sure there are no twists in the audio tape.
   j. Rethread the tape in the recorder, and rewind it a ways by hand. Push "play" and listen to your edit.
5. Repeat the above steps for your second edit. If using the CD material, you can edit out "seventy-two in Philadelphia" so the vocal says "it will be sixty-six in Chicago and seventy-six in New York."
6. Label the tape with your name and "Edited Audio Tape." Turn in the tape to your instructor to receive credit for the project.

Record several generations of an audio signal, using analog and digital recording processes.

Purpose

To enable you to hear the loss of signal quality inherent in the analog recording process, but not in digital.

Advice, Cautions, and Background

1. This project assumes that you have both analog and digital equipment in your production facility.
2. As you make the analog recordings, watch the levels and other elements that might introduce a poor-quality recording due to operator error.

How to Do the Project

1. Review the material on digital recorders and recording in Chapter 5, "Digital Audio Players/Recorders."
2. Use a CD as your original sound source or use music on the accompanying CD-ROM.
3. Make a dub of the music onto an analog audio tape recorder. This will be the first-generation recording.
4. Now, *using the tape that you just made* as the sound source, make another analog tape recording. This will be the second-generation recording.
5. *Using the second-generation recording* as the sound source, make another dub, or a third-generation recording.
6. Listen to and compare the three recordings you just made with the original sound source (the CD). You should notice a loss of sound quality plus increased noise and distortion, among other things.
7. Repeat steps 2 through 6, using a digital audio recorder.
8. Listen to and compare the digital recordings with the original sound source.
9. Write a one-page report that summarizes the differences between the analog and digital recordings.
10. Turn in your report labeled "Analog/Digital Recording," along with both the analog and digital recordings, to your instructor to receive credit for completing this project.

10

PRODUCTION SITUATIONS

10.1 INTRODUCTION

Producing "spots" or commercials is the greatest concern of the production person, but the next few pages also offer production tips that apply to particular types of radio programming—namely, music shows, news, public affairs programs, call-in talk shows, play-by-play sports programs, and radio drama. Entire books have been written about each of these types of programming, so you won't be given the in-depth knowledge you would need to perfect any of the program forms. This chapter will, however, get you started in the right direction. Experience and advanced training can then propel you into more specialized skills. Although music shows, news, public affairs programs, call-in talk shows, play-by-play sports, and radio drama are the most common forms of radio programming, other forms certainly do exist. For example, some stations air children's programs, and others produce documentaries. Still others are no doubt open to new forms of programming that may become popular in the future.

10.2 BASIC RADIO PRODUCTION ELEMENTS

Radio production centers on sound, but you must stimulate the listener's imagination to truly get them to listen to your message. Radio has been called "theater of the mind," and the production person must be able to convey a "picture" of what's going on. To accomplish this there are four basic production elements: the announcer's voice, background music, sound effects (or natural sound), and silence.

Most productions mix several of these production elements together, but remember to keep the vocal track a bit louder than any of the other elements. The announcer's voice is generally the most important element because it conveys the basic information of the production. That's one reason the vocal track is often

produced first when putting a production project together. If the vocal track isn't good, do it again until it's just the way you want it. Both music and sound effects are used in productions to help set the mood of the spot, convey action, or emphasize a special copy point. While not all production work needs background music, it is a way to readily set the tone of the spot. For example, the strum of a Hawaiian guitar immediately transports the listener to a tropical island. Most facilities have a production music library filled with CDs of original music, often timed to 30 or 60 seconds, composed in a wide range of musical styles—everything from swanky symphonies to hard-core rock 'n' roll.

Sound effects also help set the scene of a production, but they are often used to help to visualize action taking place. For example, the sound of a telephone ringing or door opening creates an instant mental image. In audio productions, sound effects are often either "atmospheres" or "stingers." Atmosphere sounds are employed to create a natural environment, such as using sea gull cries and crashing waves to set the scene at the ocean shore. Sound effect stingers are individual, short, sharp sounds designed to capture immediate attention, such as glass crashing, a gun shot, or an alarm going off. Like production music, there are libraries of sound effect CDs that offer the production person every imaginable sound. In addition to using "canned" sounds, there may be times when you just record natural sound live as part of the overall production or simulate a sound yourself, such as crinkling cellophane near a microphone to create a "fire" sound. The rule of thumb regarding the use of any sound effect is that the sound must be instantly recognized by the listener.

The final production element is silence or a dramatic pause. If you're trying to highlight a specific copy point, don't be afraid to pause a little longer than normal before saying that phrase. Just remember that too long a pause will be perceived as **dead air** and a problem rather than the effect you're trying to achieve.

10.3 COMMERCIAL PRODUCTION

Much of what has been detailed in this text applies to producing a 60-second or shorter commercial. Most radio production people are involved with producing commercial or station promotional spots. At some stations it's a full-time position, and at many stations the disc jockeys spend a portion of their workday doing commercial production work. At their simplest level, commercials are simply straight copy that the announcer reads over the air. At their most complex level, they are highly produced vignettes that include several voices, sound effects, and music. In between are commercials that feature celebrity testimonials, dialogue between two announcers, and an announcer reading over a music bed, to name a few.

Commercials are usually exactly 30 seconds or exactly 60 seconds. Because they are inserted within other programming elements, they must have exact times. Otherwise part of the commercial will be cut off if it runs long, or there will be dead air if it runs short. At some stations, commercials are brought on and taken off the air by computers, which are very unsympathetic to anything that's too long or too short.

Anyone reading commercial copy should use a natural, sincere style. Reading commercials in a condescending manner is definitely uncalled for. Commercials pay station salaries and should be treated with respect. If you're to read commercial copy live, you should read it over ahead of time to avoid stumbling on words. If the commercial involves both reading live and playing a prerecorded segment, make sure you rehearse the transition between the two. Sometimes a prerecorded spot sounds like it's ending, but it actually contains additional information—perhaps new store hours or a bargain price. If you're to read material after the recording ends, make sure you don't read on top of the recorded information.

Probably the most basic form of commercial you'll produce involves an announcer reading over a **music bed** or sound effects. The usual format for a commercial with music is that the music bed begins at full volume for a few seconds and then fades under and holds as the announcer begins reading the spot. The voice-over is read on top of the music bed, and then the music bed is brought up to full volume at the end of the voice-over for a few seconds until it fades out or ends cold. Although this seems simple enough, it won't come easily until you've practiced and accomplished it many times. Not only must you be concerned with timing, you also have to determine how much music to use to establish the spot, balance the levels between voice and music bed, select appropriate music, and correctly manipulate the broadcast equipment. Often you do a lot of this at the same time, although it is possible to record the voice-over and mix it with music at a later time. Reading over sound effects is similar to reading over music in that the sound will need to fade up and down.

Sound effects are usually short, however, so often they need to be looped (recorded over several times) in order to cover the 30-second length of the commercial. This is easy to accomplish with computer editing. The sound can simply be copied and laid on the time line as many times as needed. Highly produced spots usually take a relatively long time to prepare. Minidramas, which start with music and involve two people bantering to the accompaniment of sound effects, involve a great deal of preproduction, rehearsing, mixing, and editing. They are among the most challenging, creative products a radio production person handles. Often different parts of them are recorded at different times. The talent will record their parts and then leave, especially if they're highly paid talent. Then the production person will mix the talent skit with music and sound effects.

As you can see, mixing complex commercial spots (or any type of production) can be complicated. As you've learned by reading this text, production work of this type can be accomplished much more easily by using a multi-track recorder and/or digital editing.

PRODUCTION TIP #10
Music Punctuators

Many radio spots consist of a mixture of the announcer's voice and a background music bed. The voice should be dominant and in the foreground as it conveys the important information of the spot. The music is in the background and helps convey the mood of the spot. You can make this basic radio production more interesting for the listener by raising the volume level of the background music slightly during natural pauses in the vocal track. This will move the music from the background to the foreground momentarily. The listener will pay attention to this because our ears "follow" movement and will focus on this subtle shift. Make sure you turn down the background music when the vocal starts again. You can punctuate key phrases or concepts in your spot with this technique, and your production work will sound more lively than just keeping the music constantly in the background.

10.4 MUSIC ANNOUNCING

Music constitutes the largest percentage of radio station programming and is usually introduced and coordinated by a **disc jockey.** If you become a disc jockey, you'll be spending most of your time in the on-air studio doing your production work live. This is actually a more challenging production situation than that in the production studio, where you have the time and luxury of rerecording until you get things just the way you want. On-air broadcasting is fast paced, pressure packed, and, for most people, a lot of fun.

Although the main element of the programming is music, the main duty of the disc jockey is talking. Much of this talk involves introducing music. For this, your announcing style must fit the format of the radio station. For example, fast-paced, high-energy, rapid-fire speech is not appropriate for a classical music or big band format but may be required at a contemporary hit or rock radio station. Develop a variety of ways of getting into and out of the music. Many beginning announcers latch onto one record introduction and use it over and over ("Here's a classic from The Beatles . . ."; "Here's a classic from Bob Dylan . . ."; "Here's a classic from . . ."). If you have trouble thinking of clever material, read the liner notes on the CD or record. This will often give you an idea for something to say that's unusual or informative. Additional ad-lib material can be found in music trade publications, Internet "show prep" sites, and artist or record label Web sites. Your station may have certain policies regarding what you say and how you say it. For example, some stations require you to talk over the beginning and ending of every record. Other stations have particular slogans ("All hit radio") that they want repeated at regular intervals, or you may be required to say the station call letters every time you open the microphone.

As a disc jockey, you'll also be talking about things other than music. For example, you may need to give the time, temperature, commercials, weather, news, or traffic reports. Or you may introduce other people, such as the newscaster, who will give some of this information. Station policy will probably dictate whether you must be very formal about these introductions or have the latitude to banter with the other person. At some stations, the good-natured joking between, say, a disc jockey and helicopter traffic reporter is part of what keeps listeners tuned in.

Regardless of what's going on within the live production situation, always assume the microphone may be open. Don't say anything that you wouldn't want to go out over the air. This includes personal conversations and, of course, indecent language. Many studios have an on-air light *inside* the studio as well as the one outside the door. This inside light is to alert the announcer to the fact that the microphone is live, but the best rule is to assume the microphone is always on.

Obviously, as a disc jockey, you need to be proficient at operating the equipment so that you can cue up and play tapes and CDs. But this involves more than just equipment manipulation since you're normally operating equipment and talking. It means you have to plan ahead. For example, if you have to join a network, you must know exactly when and how to do it. If you aren't sure whether you've cued up a CD, redo it. You must have everything cued up and ready to go, and have a routine for what you are doing. It's also good practice to have an alternative if something goes wrong. If the CD player you want to play doesn't start, have in mind what you'll do immediately. A good announcer can

FIGURE 10.1 The radio disc jockey manipulates all the broadcast equipment and adds the element of live announcing within the style of the radio station's format. (Image courtesy of Alan R. Stephenson.)

overcome most miscues so that the listening audience doesn't even know that anything went wrong.

Make sure you have previewed your music, especially to know how songs begin and end. This will insure that you avoid **walking over** (beginning to "outro" a song before it's really over) a false ending. Previewing also helps you know how much instrumentation there is at the beginning of the record before the vocal starts. This will enable you to talk over the instrumental but not the vocal part of the beginning. Sometimes timing information is provided on the CD, and this helps you with **voice-overs** on the intro and outro of the song. In any case, there is no excuse for a disc jockey playing a CD on the air that he or she isn't completely familiar with. Plan how you'll get from one piece of music to the next if you play them consecutively. You might want to review the sound transitions mentioned in Chapter 3, "The Audio Console." Remember to use a variety of ways rather than the same method time after time. Listen to the on-air monitor frequently, if not continuously. Most audio consoles allow the announcer to hear the program line, the audition line, or the on-air signal; however, only the on-air signal allows you to hear exactly what the listener hears.

When your shift is over, clean up around the studio. It's also thoughtful to pull the first couple of songs or the first commercial break material for the next announcer so that he or she can get off to a smooth start. Playing music on the radio is a hectic but rewarding job. Disc jockeys are, in every sense of the word, production people. Not only do they have to manipulate all the broadcast equipment, but they must also add the element of announcing and present it all live within the fast pacing of the radio station's format.

10.5 VOICE TRACKING

Over the past few years, the practice of **voice tracking** in radio has grown. Voice tracking is simply when an announcer prerecords the vocal portion of his or her air shift (such as song introductions, time checks, etc.) that will be mixed with the music, commercials, jingles, and other programming elements later. Often computer software that allows a station to automate its programming also facilitates voice tracking. In this way, rather than do a four-hour air shift in real time, it can be recorded in a much shorter period of time—often about one-quarter of the time. The announcer can then record other shifts or do other production or operations work for the station. Announcers can record several shifts both for the local station and perhaps for other stations in other markets. It is not uncommon for an air personality to voice-track a number of different formats for stations in several markets in one session.

Voice tracking is not really new, although current technology has made it easier than ever to accomplish. The "count-down" shows heard on radio have long been voice-tracked. The host records the various song introductions and later an engineer mixes them with the appropriate songs when mastering the final tape, vinyl record, or CD on which the show is delivered to stations. Syndicated radio formats, delivered on tape or via satellite, are also voice-tracked. However, the practice has become more controversial as the cyber jocks who create this "virtual radio" have replaced "live and local" announcers. Using "cheat sheets" listing local names, places, and events, a voice-tracking announcer can sound like he or she is in Portland, Maine, when the announcer is really in Dallas, Texas. Many listeners may not even realize their favorite "local" announcer has never been to their market. As a result of voice tracking, since one announcer can cover several air shifts, DJ jobs are being lost. On the other hand, top-quality DJs from larger markets can be heard on smaller-market stations, and stations can save money through voice tracking. There are pros and cons to this method of creating radio content, but it is a practice that anyone wishing to become a radio announcer should be familiar with and become proficient at.

10.6 NEWS ANNOUNCING

If you're involved with radio production, you're likely to do news work at some point. In some instances the disc jockey may just **rip and read** from the news service on the hour or half hour. In a worst-case scenario, the announcer would literally just rip some news copy off the wire and read it on the air. Of course, most radio news is now read directly off a computer screen so "rip 'n' read" just refers to the practice of reading a newscast cold or with no preparation. As we'll note in a moment, this is *not* good broadcast practice. At the other extreme are all-news stations, which usually have sep-

arate on-air people for news, weather, sports, traffic, commentaries, business news, and the like. This is a complicated format that necessitates using people who are very knowledgeable in their specialties and who have established themselves and their voices as personalities. Whatever situation you find yourself in, some knowledge about newscasting will prove useful.

Even if you're expected to simply read a short newscast each hour, you should give some time and thought to your news presentation. First, you must decide which news to present. Of course, you probably have a station news format to follow, but you should also try to select those items that are most likely to be of interest to your listeners.

You may find that you need to do some rewriting of the wire service news and write some transitions to take the listener from one story to the next. Timing is important on a newsbreak. Make sure you read your news copy in the time prescribed. Sometimes beginning newscasters run out of news to read before the newscast time is up. To prevent this, you should pad your newscast with some extra stories that you can cut if you have to, but that provide a cushion if you need extra material. You'll usually need to get commercials in at an appropriate time during a newscast, so make sure you know when this happens and are prepared for it. Don't ever read a newscast cold. Read it over first so that you're familiar with the material. Rewrite anything that isn't natural for you, such as tongue-twisting phrases that you might trip over. Also rewrite if there are long sentences that make you run out of breath before you finish them. Avoid too many numbers or facts jammed into a single sentence. Whenever something is unclear, rewrite

FIGURE 10.2 In the modern studio, radio newscasters write, edit, and read the news directly from a computer screen. (Image courtesy of Alan R. Stephenson.)

to make it simple and easy to understand. Remember, broadcast news should be conversational and written for the ear, not the eye.

When a news story includes the actual voice of the person in the news, such as the mayor commenting on the new city budget, that segment is called an **actuality**. Most radio news operations strive to include many actualities within a newscast because these bring life to the news. It's more interesting to hear the mayor's comments than the voice of an announcer telling what the mayor said. Actualities are best reserved for opinion or reaction. The reporter can give the facts about the story, and then the newsmaker can say what he or she thinks about the subject. Obviously, many news actualities are gathered in the field with portable audio recorders; however, you can also make use of the phone to gather them. Many small radio stations have one-person news departments, and in these cases the phone actuality is especially crucial. In some situations, newsroom phones are semi-permanently hooked up to an audio recorder. But if not, you can use a contact microphone that's specifically made to attach to the phone for this purpose. You must obtain permission to record someone for broadcast use, and your station newsroom probably has specific guidelines to follow for doing this.

Actualities generally need to be edited. For this, you should use all the editing techniques presented in Chapter 6, "Digital Editing and Multi-Track Recording," and then add one very important rule: Make sure that when you edit, you don't change the meaning of what someone has said. Ethical news procedures dictate that a great deal of care be taken in this area because the elimination of a single word can significantly alter a news report. For example, "The mayor did not agree with the city council's decision . . ." could easily become just the opposite if the word "not" were edited out, leaving, "The mayor did agree with the city council's decision . . ." When you're editing and need to eliminate part of what a person said, either because it's too long or it's irrelevant, try to match voice expressions where the statement leaves off and where a new one begins. For example, don't make an edit that would jump from an excited, fast-paced explanation a speaker was making to a slow, measured response he or she was formulating. Edits are usually best if made at the end of thoughts, because a person's voice drops into a concluding mode at that point. Be careful not to edit out all the breaths the person takes because this will destroy the natural rhythm. People do breathe, and actualities without any breathing sound unnatural. If an edit is going to be too tight because the person runs words together, add in a little background noise, or add a breath from a different place on the tape. Either of these will make for a natural-sounding pace between two edit points. Try to maintain a constant background level throughout the actuality. To do this, you may have to mix in background noise from one part of the tape into another part. If you mix narration with an actuality, known as a voice actuality, make sure you maintain the same level for both, and try to have background noises that are similar—or at least not jarring.

Whether you're a disc jockey reading a few newscasts or a broadcast journalist at an all-news station, you may wish to consult one of several good books available on techniques and ethics of gathering, writing, editing, and presenting news. Some of these books are listed in the Suggested Reading section at the end of this book.

10.7 PUBLIC AFFAIRS PROGRAM HOST

Public affairs programming usually consists of long programs that explore a news or community issue in depth. Some public affairs programs take a lighter tone and profile an individual or group. The typical public affairs show is a half-hour interview or discussion between host and guest(s). Although some stations have a specific public affairs host, many stations delegate this responsibility to a newsperson or an announcer. The key to good public affairs programming is proper preparation. The host needs to research the subject and the guest before doing the program. Not only will this provide background, but it should also enable the host to generate a list of questions to ask. Asking the right questions really means asking *good* questions. For example, ask questions that require more than a simple yes or no answer. Rather than asking, "Do you agree with the mayor's new policy regarding the police?" ask, "What do you think of the mayor's new policy regarding the police?" Ask short, simple, and direct questions. The question, "Given the salaries of employees and the possible raises they will receive, what do you think the effects will be on the social security system and the GNP?" will most likely get a response of, "Huh?"

FIGURE 10.3 Radio newspersons can often find themselves recording actualities in the field for use in a later newscast. (Image courtesy of Alan R. Stephenson.)

Break complex questions down into a number of questions such as, "How do you think increasing salaries five percent will affect the GNP?" Ask questions that don't require long answers. Don't ask, "What would you do to improve the city?" Instead ask, "What is the first thing you would do to improve the city?"

Asking good questions also means knowing how to handle the answers you get. For example, if the answer is too wordy, ask the person to summarize the response. If the answer is muddy or unclear, ask the question over again in smaller parts. If the answer is evasive, come back to it later, or ask it again from a different angle. If the response gets off track, redirect. And if the response goes on and on, interrupt politely and redirect. Listen carefully to what the guest says so that you can ask appropriate follow-up questions. Sometimes interviewers become so engrossed in thinking about the next question that they miss an important point the guest has made that could lead to something significant. Although you should write questions ahead of time so that you remember to cover all important points, don't slavishly stick to those questions. In all probability, when you ask question one, the guest will also answer questions three and seven, so you must constantly flow with the conversation. The more you can lead off what the guest says, the more natural the interview will appear. But make sure you do get the information you want.

If you're going to be recording the program at a remote location, make sure all the equipment works before you leave the station. This also holds true for recording in the studio; check everything out before your guest arrives. You may be using a single microphone, so talk at the same level as the interviewee. As a broadcast professional, your voice may be stronger than the interviewee's, in which case lower your voice or else keep the microphone farther away from yourself than from the guest. If you're talking with several guests, move the microphone back and forth as each person talks. Also, follow speakers if they move their heads. Never let the guest take the microphone. He or she probably won't know how to use it properly, and you'll lose control of the conversation. When you have a number of different guests, identify them frequently because the listener has difficulty keeping track of the various voices. Even a single guest should be reintroduced during a 30-minute program. Not only does this remind listeners who your guest is, but it introduces him or her to those listeners who joined the program while it was in progress.

When you record at a remote location, listen to at least part of the tape before you leave to make sure you have actually recorded something. It's more than a little embarrassing to get back to the station and discover that you have nothing on the tape or disc, and it can be impossible to rearrange the interview for another time. If you're doing the interview in the studio, make sure you have a recording before the guest leaves. Many public affairs programs are aired live or "as taped," but sometimes it's necessary to

FIGURE 10.4 The public affairs program often involves an interview or discussion between the program host and a studio guest. (Image courtesy of Alan R. Stephenson.)

edit the tape. If you're going to be editing extensively, make a log of the material so that you know what is on the tape and where it is. An understanding of the public affairs programming concepts and techniques, especially interviewing, will help you handle many types of production situations.

10.8 TALK SHOW HOST

Not everyone is cut out to handle hosting a call-in talk show. You must be fast on your feet and able to ad-lib in an entertaining and effective manner. For many programs, you're expected to have more than broadcast production knowledge. For example, a sports program or radio psychology show requires a host with some expertise in those areas. Sometimes the telephone talk show host has an engineer handling the equipment and a producer screening the calls so that the host can concentrate on dealing with the callers on the air, but this is not always the case, especially in a smaller-market radio. A telephone talk show host has to be able to handle people tactfully (or, in some cases, abrasively, if that's the style of the program). As when interviewing for public affairs programs, the host must remain in charge of the program. Many of the other principles of public affairs interviewing also apply to call-in shows. If you have a guest to whom people are posing questions, you should give information about the guest and redirect questions if they're not understandable. The host must be able to establish good communication, without the aid of body language.

PRODUCTION TIP #11
Trade Publications

If you're serious about having a career in radio broadcasting, you might want to subscribe to some of the following publications to keep abreast of current events in the industry. Subscription information can be found at the publications' Web sites, which are given at the end of this "tip." *Broadcasting & Cable* is considered by many to be the "bible" of the radio, television, and cable industry. In addition to the top news stories of the week, *Broadcasting & Cable* focuses on programming issues and technology developments, and it features a classified section. Those interested in the music aspects of the industry will want to check out *Billboard* for music charts in all formats and for music news. *Radio & Records* (known in the industry as *R&R*) is a publication that provides both music and business information in a newspaper style format. Another publication for the latest news and information of the radio industry, with emphasis on technical aspects, is *Radio World*. If you meet certain publisher qualifications, you can get *Radio World* on a complimentary basis. These aren't the only trade magazines, by any means, but any one of them will provide valuable reference knowledge for someone interested in the radio industry.

Broadcasting & Cable—www.broadcastingcable.com
Billboard—www.billboard.com
Radio & Records—www.rronline.com
Radio World—www.rwonline.com

10.9 SPORTS ANNOUNCING

Many announcers also handle some sports broadcasting duties, and **play-by-play** (**PBP**) announcing skills can be a valuable asset for anyone entering the radio business. As a radio sports announcer, you must keep up the chatter, and you must describe completely what is happening. Since the listeners don't have the video image of TV, you have to be their eyes. Sports announcers often work in a team, with one announcer providing the play-by-play while another offers color commentary along with game statistics. The PBP sportscaster operates remote equipment designed for sports broadcasting. Most of it is similar to studio equipment but extremely portable. A small audio console and headset microphone make up the bulk of sports remote equipment. The headset microphone arrangement allows the sportscaster the use of both hands and keeps the counter or tabletop free for equipment and "stat sheets." The signal is sent from a remote console to the station by phone line or a remote pick-up unit or RPU (portable transmitter) that relays the signal to a special receiver at the station. You

should also have some other way of communicating with the studio, such as a separate telephone line. This way you can talk with the station about production matters that should not be heard by the audience. For example, commercials are usually played from the station, and you might need to coordinate when and how many will be played during a break in the action. Many remote consoles have some type of talkback feature that allows off-air communication with the radio station.

Pre-game preparation is very important for sports broadcasting. Gather all the information and facts about the teams and players, make sure all the equipment is ready to go, and get to the game in plenty of time to check out the broadcast booth, so you know everything is in order, especially the phone line connection. Sportscasting is one of the most glamorous types of radio production, but it is time consuming and requires quick thinking plus a thorough knowledge of the sport.

10.10 RADIO DRAMA

Drama isn't produced very often on radio anymore, but when it is undertaken, it employs the use of many production skills, such as microphone techniques and the blending of sound effects and music into the production. Quite often, radio commercials are really a short form of the radio drama. In any radio drama, the talent, sound effects, and music must convey the setting and action. Drama is best recorded with one microphone, but you may need to have

FIGURE 10.5 Sports announcers often work in a team, with one announcer providing the play-by-play while another offers color commentary along with game statistics. (Image courtesy of Alan R. Stephenson.)

people with louder voices position themselves a little farther away from it. It's also important to keep **perspective** during a production. In other words, people who are coming toward the supposed location of the play should sound far away at first and then sound nearer. The best way to do this is for the talent to walk away from or toward the microphone. You can mark the studio floor as to where they should start or stop talking to be on or off the microphone.

Sometimes one actor performs several parts. The actor needs to be able to create a number of distinct voices in order to do this. In fact, all voices used within a drama should be as distinct as possible because audience members have trouble distinguishing one character from another. Talent should avoid using an affected radio voice but rather should talk in their character's natural, conversational style.

As noted earlier, sound effects can be simulated in the studio, usually on a different microphone from the one the talent is using. Or they can be prerecorded or taken from a sound effects CD and edited into the production at a later time. They can be used to establish locale, tell the time, create mood, indicate entries and exits, and establish tran-

sitions. Music is also an effective way to create mood and establish transitions. Most radio dramas open and close with music that's appropriate to the overall theme of the drama.

10.11 CONCLUSION

Whether producing a commercial, disc-jockeying a radio show, calling play-by-play sports action, or performing any of the other forms of programming, audio production is an exciting aspect of the radio business. The various types of programming allow for a great deal of variety in your day-to-day occupation and for numerous opportunities to be creative and innovative. Most people who enjoy radio production find it difficult to call it "work." You should have gained insight into the basic procedures, techniques, and concepts of modern radio production by this time. Now you need to continue working in the studio, gaining the practical, hands-on experience that will help you develop into an experienced radio production person.

Self-Study

1. A fast-paced announcing style would be most appropriate for a disc jockey working at which type of radio station?

   a) contemporary hit radio format
   b) classical music format
   c) big band format
   d) all-news format

2. How would a radio DJ "walk over" a false ending of a song?

   a) by leaving the microphone open when it should be off
   b) by recueing a CD
   c) by beginning the outro of a song before it is really over
   d) by imitating other announcers heard on the radio

3. What does the term "actuality" refer to?

   a) the voice of a person in the news
   b) a pad for a newscast
   c) wire service copy
   d) the voice of the news announcer

4. Which of the following is true about the content of radio news copy?

   a) It should contain as many facts and numbers as possible.
   b) It should be written in simple, easy-to-understand sentences.
   c) It should contain tongue-twister phrases.
   d) It should be written using long, explanatory sentences.

5. Which of the following would not be a good reason for editing a news actuality?

   a) to cut out a cough
   b) to cut out material that is irrelevant
   c) to change the meaning of the story
   d) to shorten the length of the story

6. Which of the following is true of a basic 30-second radio commercial produced with a music bed?

   a) It is usually 35 seconds long because of the music.
   b) It is usually read live by the disc jockey.
   c) It is usually produced with a voice-over on top of the music.
   d) It is usually recorded with two announcers and sound effects mixed in.

7. How long should it take an announcer to record a four-hour air shift by voice tracking?

   a) one-quarter hour
   b) one hour
   c) two hours
   d) four hours

8. Which of the following describes good radio interviewing technique?

   a) Let the interviewee hold the microphone.
   b) Ask all your questions in the order you have them written down.
   c) Ask follow-up questions based on the interviewee's response.
   d) Ask complex questions so you cover the topic thoroughly.

9. Which of the following is *true* regarding radio sports announcers?

   a) They usually project an abrasive announcing style.
   b) They cue up commercials while the game is in progress.
   c) They usually work in teams.
   d) They require very little preparation prior to the game.

10. How is radio drama often recorded?

    a) at a remote location
    b) with a single microphone for the entire cast
    c) without regard for the "perspective" of sound
    d) with announcers using an "affected" radio voice

11. Which basic production element should be kept slightly louder than the others?

    a) music bed
    b) vocal track
    c) sound effect
    d) silence

12. Which of the following would be the best radio interview question?

    a) Do you favor capital punishment?
    b) What do you think will be the outcome of the present attempt to outlaw capital punishment?
    c) What do you think will happen regarding an amendment against capital punishment being added to the Constitution after it has been discussed by the state legislature in light of the case pending in Florida at the present time and the one recently decided in Illinois?
    d) You favor capital punishment, don't you?

13. Which term describes a short, sharp sound effect designed to capture the listener's immediate attention?

    a) actuality
    b) dead air
    c) stinger
    d) voice-over

14. Which term describes the practice of an announcer prerecording the vocal portion of his or her air shift that will later be mixed with the music?

    a) rip and read
    b) play-by-play
    c) dead air
    d) voice tracking

15. Which of the following would be the *least likely* reason for using music in an audio production?

    a) to set the mood of the spot
    b) to convey action in the spot
    c) to underscore a copy point in the spot
    d) to fill time at the end of a spot

ANSWERS

If You Answered A:

1a. Right. Most rock music formats utilize a fast-paced announcing style.

2a. No. While the microphone needs to be open, this doesn't describe what a walk-over is. (Reread 10.4.)

3a. Right. Actualities are statements from the people involved in a news event.

4a. No. Too many facts and numbers in radio news stories can be confusing because the listener can't refer back to them. (Reread 10.6.)

5a. No. Cutting out a cough or vocal stumble would be a reason to edit an actuality. (Reread 10.6.)

6a. Wrong. Commercials must be exact lengths; a 30-second spot is 30 seconds, and this includes the music bed. (Reread 10.3.)

7a. No. This would be too short a period of time. (Reread 10.5.)

8a. No. You can lose control of the interview if you let the interviewee take the microphone. (Reread 10.7.)

9a. No. While a few are abrasive, most sports announcers are not; radio talk show hosts are more likely to have this demeanor. (Reread 10.8 and 10.9.)

10a. No. Radio drama is best produced in the controlled environment of the studio. (Reread 10.10.)

11a. No. While music helps convey the mood of the spot, it is usually in the background. (Reread 10.2.)

12a. No. This type of question can be answered with a simple yes or no response, which would be a conversation-stopper. (Reread 10.7.)

13a. Wrong. An actuality is the actual voice of a person in the news. (Reread 10.2 and 10.6.)

14a. No. Rip and read refers to the bad practice of reading a newscast without any preparation. (Reread 10.5 and 10.6.)

15a. Wrong. Music helps set the mood or tone of a radio spot. (Reread 10.2.)

If You Answered B:

1b. No. Classical music announcers are generally more subdued. (Reread 10.4.)

2b. Wrong. Cueing a CD has nothing to do with a walk-over. (Reread 10.4.)

3b. No. A pad refers to extra news stories used if the news announcer comes up short with his or her timing. (Reread 10.6.)

4b. Correct. Radio news copy should be easily understood.

5b. No. Cutting out unimportant or irrelevant material would be a reason for editing a news story. (Reread 10.6.)

6b. No. Commercials with music beds are usually recorded before they are aired, not read live. (Reread 10.3.)

7b. Yes. Usually an announcer can produce an air shift in about one-quarter of the actual time by voice tracking.

8b. No. An interview can become very stilted if you ask every question in order from a list. You need to be prepared to deviate from any order of questions based on the interviewee's responses. (Reread 10.7.)

9b. Wrong. Commercials, during a sports broadcast, are usually played from the studio. (Reread 10.9.)

10b. Correct. A single microphone is often sufficient for recording radio drama.

11b. Yes. Since the vocal conveys the important information of the spot, it should be dominant.

12b. Yes. This is the best interview question.

13b. Wrong. Dead air is a period of silence in radio that generally occurs when there is a problem. (Reread 10.2 and 10.3.)

14b. No. Play-by-play refers to the sport announcer who calls the action of a sports event. (Reread 10.5 and 10.9.)

15b. Wrong. Music, as well as sound effects, can help convey action in a radio spot. (Reread 10.2.)

If You Answered C:

1c. No. Announcing for a big band format is usually more laid back. (Reread 10.4.)

2c. Correct. This describes what a walk-over is.

3c. Wrong. Wire service copy is not an actuality. (Reread 10.6.)

4c. No. These would be difficult for a newscaster or any announcer to read, so they should be avoided. (Reread 10.6.)

5c. Yes. This is a definite ethics violation, and not a reason for editing an actuality. (Reread 10.6.)

6c. Correct. This describes the basic music bed commercial.

7c. No. This would be more time that most announcers would need. (Reread 10.5.)

8c. Yes. During an interview, you should listen carefully and ask appropriate follow-up questions.

9c. Right. One person does the actual play-by-play while the other adds color commentary.

10c. No. In radio drama you must be careful to ensure the correct perspective is maintained during recording. (Reread 10.10.)

11c. No. While sound effects help set the scene or convey action, they shouldn't be the loudest element. (Reread 10.2.)

12c. No. This question is much too complex and convoluted. (Reread 10.7.)

13c. Correct. This is the term for this type of sound effect.

14c. No. Dead air refers to a period of unintentional silence in radio. (Reread 10.3 and 10.5.)

15c. Wrong. Music can highlight a specific copy point in a radio spot. (Reread 10.2.)

If You Answered D:

1d. Wrong. The disc jockey is normally associated with music formats and a fast pace isn't the best announcing style for news. (Reread 10.4 and 10.6.)

2d. No. This has nothing to do with a walk-over and it's not something you'd want to imitate. (Reread 10.4.)

3d. No. An actuality isn't the voice of the news announcer; in fact, it's just the opposite. (Reread 10.6.)

4d. Wrong. Although radio news copy must explain the elements of the news story, long, complex sentences should be avoided. (Reread 10.6.)

5d. No. Editing is essentially shortening, and news stories often have to be a specific length, so this is a reason to edit. (Reread 10.6.)

6d. Wrong. This type of commercial may include a music bed, but you're getting confused with a highly produced radio vignette in which all these elements are employed. (Reread 10.3.)

7d. No. If it took this long, there would be no advantage to voice tracking. (Reread 10.5.)

8d. No. Complex questions should be broken down into simpler, easy-to-follow questions. (Reread 10.7.)

9d. Wrong. Pre-game preparation is extremely important and is the key to good sports announcing. (Reread 10.9.)

10d. No. Radio drama announcers use a natural-sounding, conversational voice even when the announcer is playing the role of a particular character. (Reread 10.10.)

11d. No. Silence can't be louder. (Reread 10.2.)

12d. No. This is just a rewording of the first question. It can be answered with a simple yes or no response and also is leading the interviewee. (Reread 10.7.)

13d. Wrong. A voice-over is when an announcer speaks over some other programming element, such as music. (Reread 10.2 and 10.4.)

14d. Yes. This is the practice of voice tracking.

15d. Correct. While music can be used to "trail out" a radio spot, a well-written spot should not have much time to fill at the end, and that really shouldn't be why you use music in the spot.

Projects

PROJECT 1

Record an air-check tape.

Purpose

To instruct those interested in doing on-air broadcasting in how to make an audition or demo recording, something required when applying for a job.

Advice, Cautions, and Background

1. To apply for on-air jobs in broadcasting, you will send your resume and an air-check recording to many stations. An air-check is a recording of less than 5 minutes that shows how you handle on-air broadcast situations.
2. Ideally, an air-check is an edited-down sample of your actual on-air work, but if you aren't on the air on a regular basis, a simulated air-check can be put together in the production studio.
3. Try to make the recording as general as possible so that it could be sent to several different types of stations.
4. Put those things you do best at the beginning. Many potential employers don't have time to listen past the first 30 seconds and will rule you out if they don't like the beginning. Don't structure the recording so that it builds to a climax because probably no one will listen that far.
5. Feel free to use things you've done for other projects for this assignment.
6. Keep the pace moving. Don't do any one thing for too long.

How to Do the Project

1. Plan what you intend to include in your recording. An air-check format might include ad-lib introductions to a few songs (either fade out the music after a few seconds, or edit to the end of the songs so that the listener doesn't have to hear the whole song), some production work (commercials, station promos, etc.), and a short newscast. If you can do play-by-play, you might want to put a short example at the end. There is no standard format, so do whatever showcases your talent best.
2. Plan the order of your recording. Make it sound like a continuous radio show as much as possible.
3. Record the project and listen to it. Redo it if it doesn't present good broadcast skills.
4. On the recording, write your name and "Air-Check Project." Turn in the completed recording to the instructor to receive credit for this project.

PROJECT 2

Record a 5-minute radio interview show in which you are the interviewer.

Purpose

To prepare you for this very common type of broadcasting situation.

Advice, Cautions, and Background

1. Your interview must be exactly 5 minutes. Meeting the exact time without having an awkward ending will probably be the hardest part of the project, but it's a lesson worth learning because broadcasting is built around time sequences.

2. Don't under-prepare. Don't fall into the trap of feeling that you can wing this. In 5 minutes you must come up with the essence of something interesting, and you can't do this unless you have an organized list of questions in mind. You'll also only be able to record the interview once. You can't redo this project, so you need to get it right the first time.
3. Don't over-prepare. Don't write out the interview word for word. It will sound stilted and canned if you do.
4. Five minutes is actually a long time; you'll be amazed at how much you can cover in this time.
5. As the interviewer, don't talk too much. Remember, the purpose is to convey the ideas of your guest to the audience, not your own ideas.

How to Do the Project

1. Select someone to interview. If you're taking a course, it will probably be easier to do this project with someone in class.
2. Decide what the interview will be about. You may select any subject you wish. You could talk about some facet of a person's life or his or her views on a current subject, or you could pretend the interviewee is a famous person.
3. Work up a list of questions. Generate more than you think you'll actually need, just in case you run short.
4. Think of a structured beginning and ending for the show, since those will probably be the most awkward parts.
5. Discuss the interview organization with your guest so that you are in accord as to what is to be discussed, but don't go over the actual questions you're going to ask.
6. Record the interview, making sure you stop at 5 minutes. Listen to it, and check that it has recorded before your guest leaves. You are finished with the project once the interview is recorded. Even if it didn't come out as you had hoped, do *not* redo this project.
7. On the recording write "Interview Project" and your name. Give the interview to your instructor to receive credit for this project.

PROJECT 3

Record a radio drama with several other students.

Purpose

To allow you to practice your dramatic skills and to give you the experience of performing radio dramas.

Advice, Cautions, and Background

1. Make sure you have a group of congenial, dependable people. You don't want to start rehearsal and then have to switch cast members.
2. Sound effects will probably give you the most trouble. Make sure you have all that you need. Some are available on the CD-ROM that accompanies this text.
3. Participants can get credit for this assignment without being on the air. For example, you might want to have one person in charge of sound effects, one in charge of engineering, and one as the director.
4. If you want to write a play rather than use one that's already written, this is fine.
5. One person can play more than one role in radio by changing voices, but all voices used in the drama should be distinct.

How to Do the Project

1. Select the group and choose a director.
2. Have the director or the group select a play. The following are some books you may be able to find in a library that contain radio plays:
   a. Carol Adorjan et al., *WKID: Easy Radio Plays*, 1991
   b. Alonzo Cole and David Siegel, *The Witch's Tale: Stories of Gothic Horror from the Golden Age of Radio*, 1998
   c. Metheun Books, *Best Radio Plays of 1985*, 1986
   d. David Pownall, *Radio Plays*, 1998
   e. Emil Sher, *Making Waves: Three Radio Plays*, 1998
3. Decide what each person is going to do for the production.
4. Check with the instructor about what you're planning to do and what problems you can expect to experience.
5. Make sure that everyone gets a copy of the script. You can check with the instructor about ways to get the script duplicated.
6. Have set times to rehearse. Rehearse section-by-section, both with and without microphones, and then put the whole thing together. Rehearse music and effects as well as dialogue.
7. When the production is polished enough, record it. Listen to it, and if it's good enough, label and give the finished recording to the instructor (see 8 and 9 below). If not, redo it.
8. On the recording write "Radio Drama Project" and the names of all the people who were involved.
9. On a sheet of paper, list the names of all involved, and write what each did for the production. Give this sheet and the completed recording to the instructor to receive credit for this project.

11

INTERNET RADIO AND OTHER DISTRIBUTION TECHNIQUES

11.1 INTRODUCTION

Digital technology has changed not only the production techniques of radio but the very nature of the industry itself. Radio stations have found that in order to keep up with the times, they must align themselves with the Internet. For many stations this means building **Web pages** that tie to their programming by promoting contests, concerts, and special events. Many also **netcast** their broadcast signal over the Internet, broadening their audience from a local area to potentially the whole world, as well as allowing office workers to listen to the radio station of their choice on their computers throughout the work day.

The Internet has been important to radio at colleges and universities. College radio stations that have existed as over-the-air FM stations can now have an international audience. This has been a particular benefit to broadcasting students who go away to college because their friends and relatives back home can now hear their radio programs. Alumni can use Internet radio to stay informed about their school, perhaps listening to the sports events. In addition, colleges that have not had stations in the past due to lack of funds or lack of available frequencies in their particular area can now create radio stations that are Internet only.

In fact, any group or individual with the proper equipment can now program a radio station that can be heard throughout the world. With the growth in Web radio listenership expected to surpass 20 million per week in 2005, existing radio broadcasters and neophytes alike are hoping to attract listeners and increasing advertising dollars.

This chapter will look at the techniques for creating an Internet radio station and will then discuss, in briefer fashion, other radio distribution techniques, both new and tried-and-true.

11.2 WEB PAGES

While many listeners to your Web radio program will access it directly through a media player, such as Real One or Microsoft's Media Player, chances are that at some point or another they will want to visit the station's Web page in a browser. The Web page can provide information about the station's content, as well as have links to additional content.

The **home page** (see Figure 11.1) will, of course, contain a hyperlink that will allow listeners to hear your station live. However, in addition to live content, many stations provide previously recorded **on-demand** content of program material from the past or even program material that was never broadcast live. For example, one file might contain last night's basketball game, another file might be a talk show from a week ago, and another might contain an unedited version of an interview that was only broadcast in its abridged form. When listeners click on those files, they hear the programming from the past, not what is currently being programmed.

Your home page can contain a list of all the on-demand files, but if there are many of them you may want to lead the listener to other Web pages where they can get more information. For example, you might say, "Click here for Sports Programs" on your home page and then have a list of seven or eight on-demand sports programs on a different page with brief summaries of each. Many sites that offer voluminous on-demand content now also have internal search engines so that listeners can type in key words to search for content on a specific topic. You may also want to include written information about your disc jockeys, contests, program schedule, and other features. How you organize your Web pages is largely up to you and is beyond the purview of this book. There are many programs (Microsoft FrontPage, Adobe GoLive, and Macromedia DreamWeaver and Flash) that you can use to build eye-catching Web pages. We will concentrate on what you need to create the audio portion of your Internet radio station.

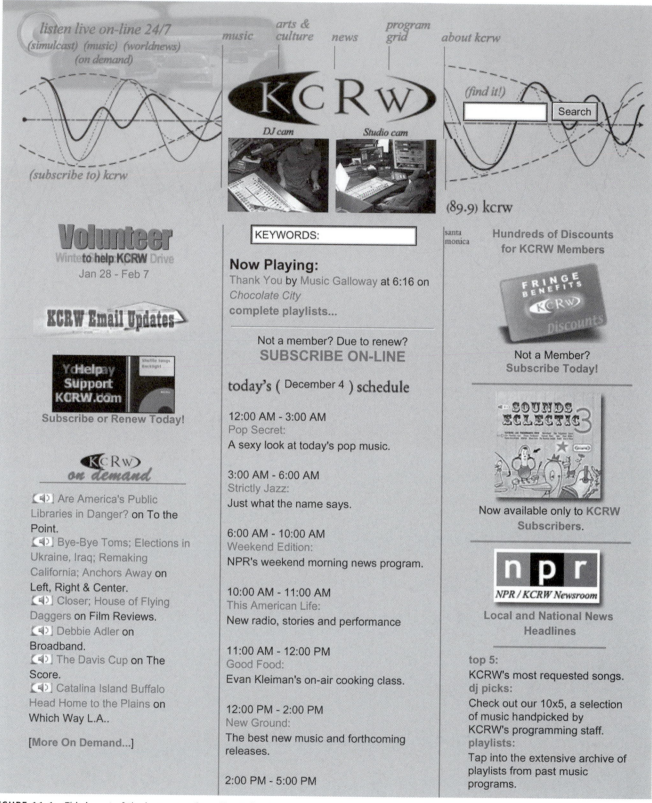

FIGURE 11.1   This is part of the home page for radio station KCRW, operated from Santa Monica City College. Note the area for listening on-air as well as the daily schedule and the archived programs that can be listened to on-demand. (Image courtesy of Santa Monica College-based National Public Radio station KCRW; 89.9FM; KCRW.com)

11.3 OVERVIEW OF THE AUDIO PROCESS

To undertake real-time **streaming audio** of a live broadcast, you need to get the output of your on-air console to the **sound card** (also called an **audio card**) of a computer that contains encoding software. This **encoder** system translates the analog audio from the sound card into a digital streaming format and sends it to a **server,** which is a much larger computer. The server sends the audio data stream over the Internet to the **player** software on the listener's computer, where it is decoded and played out over the analog speakers attached to the listener's computer (see Figure 11.2). The sound must be changed from analog to digital because analog audio cannot stream. It must be converted back to analog because the human ear cannot hear digital.

Connecting the output of the audio console to the computer sound card is fairly simple. As we discussed in Chapter 3, most consoles have several outputs, so one can be designated for the Internet. The signal can still go out over the airwaves. The input to consumer-grade sound cards is usually a **miniphone** connector, and the input on professional-grade sound cards is either **RCA, XLR,** or a digital connection that can be made from a digital mixer. There are also FM radio sound cards that can pick up an on-air FM signal and bring it into the computer.

To place files on the Internet that can be accessed on-demand, you can simply create a **soundfile** using audio editing and encoding software. The size and quality of the soundfile must be considered carefully to ensure that listeners can play it easily and that your server will have the bandwidth capacity necessary to serve it to listeners. While broadband connections are becoming de rigueur, there are still many people in the United States and many more abroad who access the Internet via low bandwidth, dial-up telephone connections of 56 kilobytes per second or less. These potential listeners will be turned off if files they try to listen to cannot download fast enough to be heard uninterrupted.

Different types of audio content require different settings to maximize quality and minimize size. For example, a soundfile that contains only talk may be encoded with much lower quality (and size) than a musical soundfile, where a broader frequency range is desired. Some sites choose to offer several different-sized files of the same material. This way, people who are connecting via dial-up can select a smaller file, and those connected through broadband can listen to a higher-quality file. Some file types, such as RealMedia's G2, allow audio to be encoded with several different versions of the content saved within the same file. When the file starts to download onto the visitor's computer, it determines the visitor's connection speed and switches to the highest quality file that the connection speed will allow.

There are two different ways to listen to on-demand sound files—streaming and non-streaming. Streaming begins to play sound on the listener's computer soon after the listener clicks on the link to it. Streaming provides near-instant access to material, but playback may be interrupted if the speed of the listener's Internet connection cannot consistently keep up with the amount of information that needs to be transmitted per second to keep sound playing.

With non-streaming listening, the file must be completely downloaded before it begins to play. This allows even listeners on dial-up connections to listen to uninterrupted, high-quality audio files, if they are patient enough to wait through long download times.

11.4 ENCODERS

The sound card in the computer that encodes is used to translate an analog signal into a digital format. The signal is sampled and then compressed so it can be sent efficiently over the Internet and be received by people who are using DSL, cable, or dial-up **modems** that can operate anywhere from 28 to 300 kilobytes per second or even higher. (A "T1" or "T3" 1,540 or 45,000 kilobyte connection, using fiber-optic cable, is available, but is still very expensive, and is usually only used by commercial entities with large computer networks. This high bandwidth is more appropriate to transmit simultaneous streams of Internet radio than to receive it.)

Many audio operations strive to have their Internet files be CD-quality. As you learned in Chapter 5, CDs are encoded using a **sampling** rate of 44.1 kHz. In other words, they are sampled at 44,100 times per second. In addition, each sample has a **bit depth** of 16 bits. One way to look at bit depth is to relate it to **signal-to-noise ratio** (see Chapter 1, "The Production Studio Environment"). The higher the number of bits, the higher the signal-to-noise ratio, and hence the better the signal. You get approximately 6 **decibels (dB)** of signal to noise for each bit, so 8-bit audio is about 48 dB of signal to 1 dB of noise, and 16-bit audio is a very respectable 96 dB. A 44.1, 16-bit signal uses a lot of bandwidth—roughly 1.4 megabits per stereo second

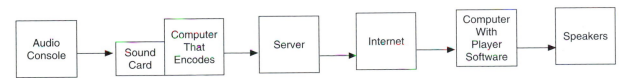

FIGURE 11.2 This diagram shows how the sound goes from the on-air console through the encoder, server, and player to the listener's speakers.

(44,100 samples per second, times 16 bits per sample, times 2 for stereo, equals 1,411,200 bits).

When data is sent over the Internet, it needs **overhead** (more bandwidth) so that the packets it is sent in arrive at their destination properly. What all this means is that in order to receive pure CD-quality sound, a listener might need a connection to the Internet that operates at approximately 1.7 *mega*bytes per second. Most people have modems that operate from 56 to 300 *kilo*bytes per second. Another way to look at this is that it could take as long as 2 hours to download a 3-minute piece of CD-quality music using a 56K modem. Somehow the bandwidth used by an audio signal being sent over the Internet must be reduced.

There are several ways to handle this reduction. One solution is to send a monaural signal instead of a stereo one. That cuts the bandwidth needed in half. Another method is to employ **compression,** which is the method used by most of the encoding systems. It does degrade the quality of the signal somewhat, but it gets the bandwidth down to about one-tenth of what is needed for pure CD-quality sound. Most compression systems use some form of **perceptual coding** that is based on characteristics of the human ear. For example, there are certain sounds humans cannot hear (e.g., those below 20 Hz or above 20,000 Hz). These can be eliminated. Similarly, there are also sounds human ears hear better than others. If two sounds are playing at the same time, we hear the louder one but not the softer one. By taking human hearing into account, a great deal of what is in a normal sound signal can be eliminated without much damage to the quality. Some compression systems also deal with silence. They take out the silent places within the audio and insert a code that places the silence back in when the sound is **decompressed** before it gets to the listener's audio speakers.

11.5 SERVERS

Computers used as servers must run audio software that is specially designed to handle sending out multiple audio data streams simultaneously. Bandwidth again comes into play. Unlike over-the-air radio service, where one signal can reach an infinite number of listeners, for Internet service you must provide a separate audio stream from the streaming server for each listener. This can take up large amounts of bandwidth, especially if audio is encoded in high quality (and size); therefore Internet radio stations must limit the number of listeners who can tune in at any one time. Sometimes this number is as small as 10, but other stations choose to incorporate multiple servers with high bandwidth connections to the Internet that can handle 1,000 or more listeners simultaneously.

Most colleges, universities, and other educational institutions now have servers that connect to the Internet. The most common procedure for a college Internet radio station is to use part of the space on the university server. It is pos-

sible (although expensive) for a station to have its own server, or it can contract to use part of a server from an Internet Service Provider (ISP) or some other source. ISPs usually charge based on the amount of bandwidth a station occupies, so this is another reason to pay careful attention to bandwidth needs.

11.6 PLAYERS

The player software resides on the listener's computer. It receives the audio data stream from the server and decodes and decompresses it into analog sound that can be heard from the computer speakers. Most streaming audio does not stay on the listener's hard drive; it streams in and then is discarded.

What actually happens is that the initial compressed audio data is placed into a buffer area, analogous to a small storage tank. Once a certain amount of data has partially filled the "tank," the soundfile begins to play. Streamed audio is poured into the top of the tank while the playback audio is being drained from the bottom of the tank. The filling of the tank is slightly faster than the draining of the tank, so there is always enough in reserve to continue playing back the audio if the input stream is momentarily interrupted.

The player software is available to listeners for free or at a low price. They simply download it from the Web site of the company providing it or, in many cases, it comes preinstalled on store-bought computers.

11.7 SOFTWARE OPTIONS

Usually the company that provides the encoder and server software to a station is the same company that provides the listener with software. This can present a problem, especially for the listener who needs one brand of software to listen to one station and another to listen to a different station. Although both brands of software can be downloaded for free or for a minimal cost, the two may compete to be the dominant (default) software on the consumer's computer. This can create nasty incompatibility problems.

In addition, the players and software are always being updated. The major manufacturers in the market want to keep providing a better, more dependable product—thus siphoning off customers from the competition. The newest encoding software or file type might be very appealing for content providers, in terms of providing better-quality sound with smaller file sizes, thus allowing more simultaneous outgoing streams, but if visitors haven't upgraded or don't know how to upgrade to the latest version of software that can play the file type, they will only be frustrated by your jump to the cutting edge.

The major software players at present are Real from RealNetworks (www.real.com), Windows Media from

Microsoft (www.microsoft.com), and QuickTime from Apple (www.apple.com/quicktime). Others providing software are Winamp (www.winamp.com) and MusicMatch (www.musicmatch.com).

RealNetworks (see Figure 11.3), being the first audio player to enter the market in 1995, continued to dominate the streaming content market in the mid- to late 90s, but started to lose significant market share when Microsoft bundled its own player, Windows Media Player, with its nearly ubiquitous operating system, Windows (see Figure 11.4). Legal battles over this matter will probably continue for some time, but the fact remains that Windows Media Player with its proprietary audio format (.wma) has come from behind to become quite popular.

Apple's QuickTime player (see Figure 11.5), though supported by both PC and Mac computers, has always remained a distant third. Many users claim, however, that the Windows Media Player, and especially Real's media

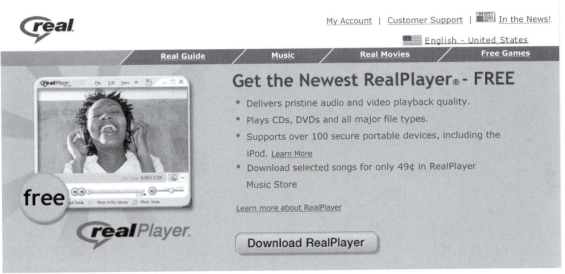

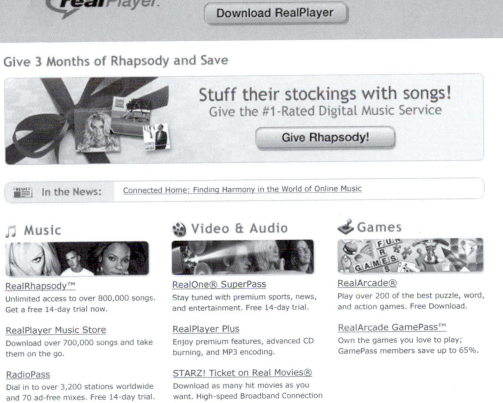

FIGURE 11.3 RealNetworks' Web page allows you to download its player easily, though it has been criticized for making it difficult to actually find the "free" version of its program, which is touted so loudly on their home page. (Web page courtesy of RealNetworks, copyright 1995–2004 RealNetworks, Inc., all rights reserved. RealNetworks, Real.com, RealOne, RealArcade, RealAudio, RealVideo, RealMedia, RealPlayer, RealRhapsody, RealProducer, Helix, the HelixDesign, DNA, SureStream, TurboPlay, PerfectPlay, Listen.com, and the Real bubble are the trademarks or registered trademarks of RealNetworks, Inc.)

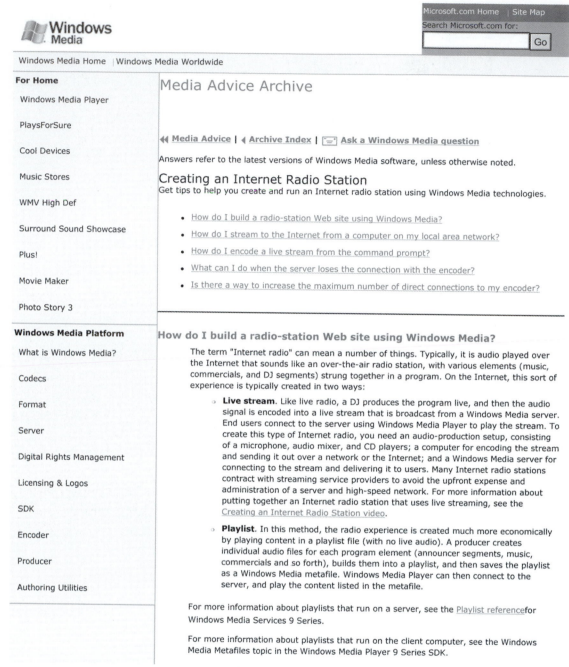

FIGURE 11.4 This page is an outline of some of the material Microsoft provides to help customers get their Internet radio stations up and running. (Image courtesy of Microsoft.)

players, have become too big for their britches. Some complain that, for the user who just wants to listen to an audio clip, the offerings from Real and Microsoft have confusing and overly complicated navigation schemes—some that seem designed to trick users into accidentally signing up for "premium" services that require payment. QuickTime, its adherents claim, provides a more no-nonsense and straightforward interface.

Many Internet radio sites now offer streams in all three of the proprietary formats: Windows, Real, and QuickTime. Others limit themselves to two formats or only one, usually either Real or Microsoft. Some sites have even made well-publicized switches from one format to another after users complained of being duped into paying for players because the link to the free version of the player was squirreled away several obscure clicks into the provider's Web site.

FIGURE 11.5 QuickTime's Web page emphasizes its video features as well as its audio. (Web page courtesy of Apple.)

PRODUCTION TIP #12
Internet Audience and On-Air Talent Interaction

The Internet, being a very flexible tool for exchanging information and communication, can be used to expand the product of any business—radio included. Allowing listeners to feel that they are a part of your radio station or show is a good way to assure they keep coming back, though it can backfire as well, so care must be taken in the introduction of such technologies and add-ons to your station.

The Internet and your webmaster can offer you countless cheap and easy ways to invite your listeners to get involved in your station: chat rooms, instant messaging, message boards with more threads than an unraveling sweater. Audience members can communicate directly with on-air talent, management, and other audience members—in either real time or through archived posts.

But it is important for users of such services to feel that the service is active, if they are to be encouraged to come back. If you set up a message board for your station with 20 different subcategories, and if many of the categories see little use and new postings, it will look to visitors like the whole site is dead and they will move on to greener pastures. Better to start out with just one category and then break it up after the site is already populated and when the main topics visitors are interested in discussing become evident.

Another concern is that Internet sites that allow users to interact with the site run the risk of being "flamed" by mischievous or malicious individuals who may post incendiary content to your site that could set off a "flame war," with different visitors trying to get in their last rancorous word. It is often a good idea to have a "moderator" for your site—someone who reviews posts for unwanted content before the content is posted to the site. However, if you plan to moderate your site, make sure you have the personnel to do so. Nothing that will so quickly turn off a visitor as posting to a site, only to find the post lingers in moderator purgatory for days before actually being added to the site.

11.8 ON-DEMAND FILES

As mentioned previously, one of the advantages of Internet radio is that you can place programs on the server that listeners can access at any time. This means listeners can hear your programming at times that are convenient for them.

When you record material that you want to place in an on-demand mode, you should take special care to make a high-quality recording because these files, too, go through encoding, compression, and other processes. The more useful audio information the system has to analyze, the better. You should try to record with minimal background noise and high-quality equipment.

In order to prepare on-demand material, you create soundfiles and then place these on your server so that your listeners can access them through their players. Most soundfiles end with .wav, .avi, .rm, .wma, or .mp3.

MP3 has received particular attention because of its use in downloading music files from the Internet. It is an audio file format that is supported by a large number of shareware applications that convert music from CDs. Basically, it is a compression system for audio. Its full name is MPEG-2, Layer 3. MPEG stands for Moving Picture Experts Group, the group that developed compression systems for video data. This MPEG system encompasses a subsystem for audio compression that is referred to as Layer 3; it is based on the "perceptual coding" discussed earlier.

The three major streaming providers (RealNetworks, Microsoft, and Apple) are now supporting this format in addition to their own proprietary systems. Some of the lesser-known players use MP3 as their streaming technology and do not have their own proprietary systems.

11.9 COPYRIGHT

Copyright in relation to the Internet has become a major concern. Because it is so easy to copy digital material, the copyright laws (written in the 1970s) either do not cover the concept or are ineffective in stemming the tide of illegal copying. Your Internet radio station must remain aware of the latest in copyright legislation and enforcement or it can find itself in major legal trouble.

There are three agencies that license music to radio stations—ASCAP, BMI, and SESAC. These organizations (see Figure 11.6) have been in business for many years and have negotiated license agreements that enable regular radio stations to play music without having to negotiate for each song. The agencies collect a set fee from each station and then have stations submit logs of what they play. They then distribute the money collected to composers and music publishers based on an approximation of how often each selection was played. There are three agencies because each of them handles different music, but a station that subscribes to all three can feel that it is playing music without violating copyright laws. These organizations have determined minimum annual fees for Internet broadcasting—$264 for ASCAP, $500 for BMI, and $50 for SESAC. Additional fees apply when your site turns a profit, and special arrangements are in place for stations broadcasting religious music. If you are starting an Internet radio station, you should make sure you contact these agencies (www.ascap.com, www.bmi.com, www.sesac.com).

Another Web site to consult regarding copyright is that of the Recording Industry Association of America (RIAA). Its Web address is www.riaa.org and it constantly updates information about copyright procedures (see Figure 11.7). This site will help you determine what licenses you need and how to obtain them.

11.10 INTERNET RADIO STATION LISTING SITES

Once you have established an Internet radio station, you want people to know about it. With all the material on the Internet, it would be hard for any but the most avid fans to find your station. To help solve this problem, there are Internet sites that list radio stations (see Figure 11.8). They list by format type, geographic area, and various other parameters and simply link to all the radio stations they list. Some charge for listing and some don't. You would be well

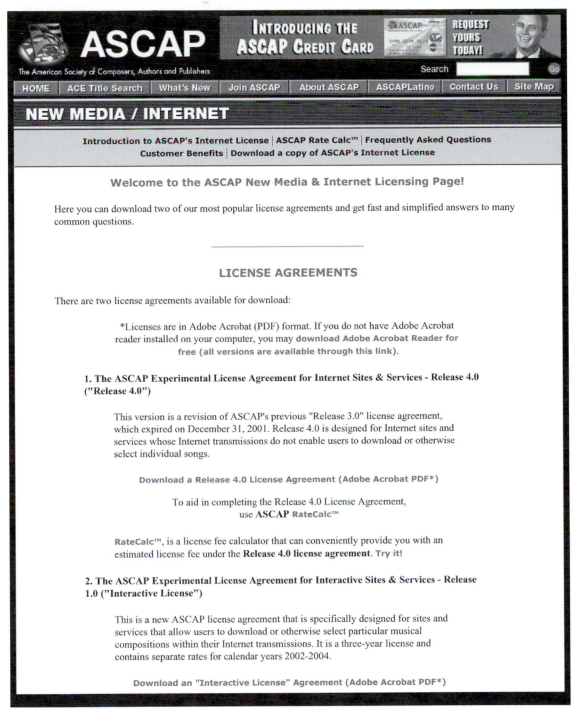

FIGURE 11.6 ASCAP's Web site. (Copyright © 2004 ASCAP. Reproduced with permission of the American Society of Composers, Authors and Publishers from www.ascap.com)

advised to contact as many of these as possible to see if they will list your station.

Most computer audio players now have a built-in radio station listing service, so that potential listeners no longer need to go through a browser or search engine to find radio stations. This can be both good and bad for radio stations. It allows listeners to easily find their station, but though it provides a link, it does not require listeners to visit the stations' Web sites, where additional advertising, appeals for support, and branding can occur.

So, for starters, it would be best to contact the companies that provide the encoder/server/player software. Other sites that list radio stations that you may want to check out are:

FIGURE 11.7 The Recording Industry Association of America updates its copyright information regularly. (Image courtesy of RIAA.)

www.radio-locator.com
www.radiotower.com
www.shoutcast.com
www.live-radio.net
www.virtualtuner.com
www.live365.com

Establishing and operating an Internet radio station can be a rewarding activity and a very good learning experience for anyone interested in a career in either traditional radio or new media technologies.

11.11 OTHER DISTRIBUTION MEANS

New distribution techniques, such as the Internet, are not unusual in radio programming. As each new form takes hold, the old ones undergo change, but the need for programming remains. Regardless of how the material is distributed, it must be produced in such a way that meets the entertainment and information needs of the public.

AM over-the-air entertainment broadcasting was started in the 1920s and was the dominant form of radio distribu-

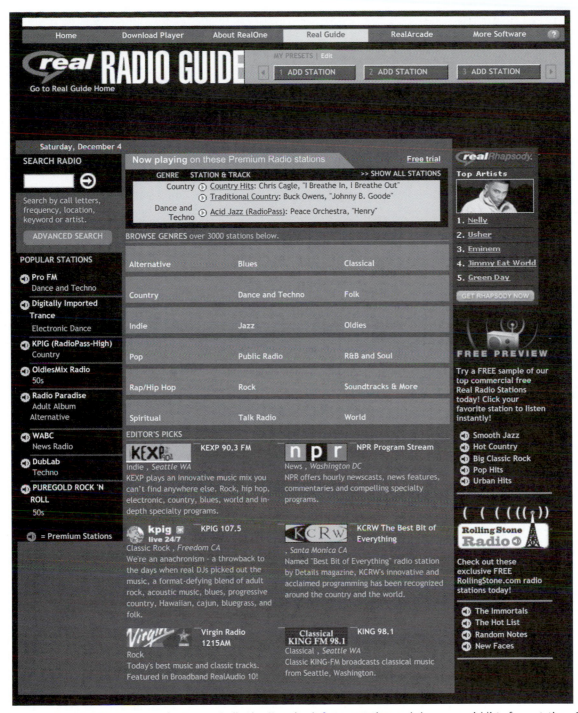

FIGURE 11.8   Here is part of the home page for Internet Radio List. Note that it features stations and shows a special list of new stations. It also covers stations from other countries. You can search by station name, country, language, and key word. (Copyright 2004 Jupitermedia Corporation. All Rights Reserved. Reprinted with permission from www.Internet.com)

tion for many years. FM was developed during the 1930s but did not come to fruition until the 1960s, and it later overtook AM as the favored listening form. When cable TV went through a growth spurt in the 1980s, it added audio-only services to its menu, but while many cable subscribers elect to utilize the service, it has never achieved the cache of AM or FM radio, being mostly a background music provider without disc jockeys or special events. However, a relatively new form of broadcasting that distributes directly from satellites to radio receivers has begun to create serious competition for traditional over-the-air AM and FM.

11.12 SATELLITE RADIO

Satellite radio, often called **digital audio radio service (DARS),** beams radio programming directly from a satellite to a home or car receiver. The signals are distributed nationally with no need for local stations that broadcast to a local area. Programming is up-linked from earth-based studios to satellites designed to transmit the signal back to earth and provide coast-to-coast coverage. If the satellite signal can be interrupted, such as in some urban areas, ground repeaters are used to beam the signal to listeners. Because DARS is a digital service, its signals are of higher quality than current FM broadcasting.

The FCC has granted two companies, Sirius Satellite Radio and XM Satellite Radio, the right to broadcast DARS. Both services charge consumers for access to approximately 120 channels, most of them narrowly focused to particular interests such as classical music, new popular releases, or auto racing (see Figure 11.9). Some of the offerings are commercial free (usually the music channels), others carry nominal commercials, while still others mirror the amount of advertisement time that terrestrial commercial radio has. In fact, some of the stations provided by the service, such as Los Angeles KIIS-FM, are just simultaneous broadcasts of terrestrial broadcasts with commercial breaks included. Some programming that was once available on traditional radio stations is now moving to satellite radio, such as NPR's Bob Edwards and the Opie and Anthony show. The services occupy different frequencies from current radio broadcasting, so anyone wanting to hear them needs to have a new radio receiver. The radios are relatively inexpensive, and both companies have working arrangements with auto manufacturers to have the radios offered as standard or optional equipment in new cars.

There are no definite plans to make any of the audio channels training grounds for students, but this type of service is something students should prepare for if they wish a career in radio. The multitude of channels and their narrow focus will provide an opportunity for creativity in both programming and production. With so many stations, programming to niche audiences is possible, such as is the case with Sirius's OutQ stations, catering to the taste and concerns of gays and lesbians.

11.13 CABLE RADIO

Many cable TV systems provide digital CD-quality audio services that are piped into the home along with the cable TV service. Obviously, these **cable radio** signals cannot be heard in the car but are limited to in-home listening. In some instances the cable systems charge extra for these services, and in other instances the services are part of the basic package. There are both commercial-free programs and ones that contain advertisements. Sometimes the audio is used as background for text channels listing local events or program schedules. Some of the companies providing these audio services also make them available to broadcast networks or commercial establishments such as doctors' offices. Sometimes a cable company will provide only one channel of audio services, whereas other companies may provide multiple channels. The offerings are varied, such as news programs from around the world, classical music, religious programming, and foreign language programming.

Many colleges operate public access cable channels and place student-produced audio on the channel, often behind a layer of character-generated announcements about the school. This is frequently the same programming that is going out over the Internet radio station or the on-air station, thus giving the student work a broader audience.

11.14 OVER-THE-AIR BROADCASTING

The most traditional way that radio programming is delivered is over the airwaves by local stations. The sound goes from the station's studio to the **transmitter.** Here it is **modulated,** which means the signal is superimposed onto a **carrier wave** that represents a particular station's frequency. Some stations operate in the **AM** band where the frequencies are 535 to 1,705 kilohertz, and others are in the **FM** band of 88 to 108 megahertz. These frequencies are much higher than sound frequencies (20 to 20,000 hertz) and can travel much further than sound. Once the sounds have been modulated, they are sent out of the station antenna into the air. The carrier wave can be picked up by a radio receiver that demodulates the signal and turns it back into sound that the ear can hear.

Technically, the difference between AM and FM involves how the on-air signal is modulated. AM stands for **amplitude modulation** and involves a method that varies the amplitude, or height, of the carrier wave in order to represent the sound. FM stands for **frequency modulation** and

XM Satellite Radio	Sirius Satellite Radio
The 60s (The Authentic 60s Sound)	*Totally 70s (The 70s)*
Nashville! (Round The Clock Country Hits)	*Spirit (Christian Hits)*
KISS (Pop Hits of The NOW Millenium!)	*The Vault (Deeper Classic Rock)*
The Heart (All Love Songs 24/7)	*Left Of Center (New/College/Indie Rock)*
U-Pop (From the World's Pop Charts)	*Reggae Rhythms (Reggae)*
Boneyard (Stadium Rock And Hairbancs)	*The Roadhouse (Classic Country)*
Squizz (Hard Alternative)	*Backspin (Old skool Rap)*
The Groove (Old School R & B)	*Slow Jamz (Soul Ballads)*
Frank's Place (Sinatra & Friends)	*Jazz Café (Smooth Jazz)*
Luna (Latin Jazz)	*Symphony Hall (Symphonic)*
CNN	*CNBC*
The Weather Channel	*Bloomberg Radio*
Sporting News Radio	*BBC World News Service*
NASCAR Radio	*ESPN Radio*
Laugh USA	*Sports Byline USA*
E! Entertainment Radio	*Radio Disney*
Sonic Theater	*Discovery Channel Radio*

FIGURE 11.9 A partial listing of music, information, and entertainment channels available on satellite radio.

is a process that changes the frequency of the carrier wave in order to represent the sound. Figure 11.10 shows a representation of the two types of modulation.

FM signals are better quality, in part because of the modulation techniques. For example, AM is more subject to static because static is most likely to occur at the bottom and top of the carrier wave. For FM, that part of the wave can just be cut off to eliminate static, but for AM the top and bottom must remain because they are the key to how the modulation occurs. There are many other reasons why FM is better quality. One is that FM signals occupy more bandwidth than AM because bandwidth was not given a great deal of consideration when AM was developed in the 1920s.

Fortunately for colleges, most student-operated radio stations are in the FM band. This has nothing to do with modulation or bandwidth; it has more to do with politics. Many early AM stations were operated by educational institutions, but as radio's popularity grew and frequencies were in short demand, the universities lost out to commercial interests. When FM was established, the educators convinced the FCC to reserve some of the frequencies (88.1 to 91.9) for noncommercial use so that commercial stations could not operate in that band. Today, many of these frequencies are licensed to colleges and universities that use them for public radio programming or as student stations. As previously mentioned, sometimes the programming going out to the community from the FM antenna also goes over the Internet or over a cable TV system.

11.15 DIGITAL AUDIO BROADCASTING

In 2002, the FCC approved "in band, on channel" (**IBOC**) technology to permit existing AM and FM radio stations to transmit a digital signal. The sole developer of the technology is iBiquity Digital Corporation. HD Radio, as digital radio is also known, promises FM radio that will be CD-quality and AM radio that will rival the quality of current FM radio, making traditional radio broadcasting more competitive with satellite-delivered radio. Already hundreds of stations are on the air broadcasting a digital signal, and digital receivers are offered by JVC, Kenwood, Panasonic, and other electronics manufacturers.

Figure 11.11 shows how HD radio works. The analog signal is sandwiched between digital information (1) and along with the audio program, text (such as artist and song information) can be transmitted. Once the digital signal layer is compressed (2) using iBiquity's HDC compression technology, the combined signal is transmitted (3) on the station's regular frequency. HD radio receivers will pick up the digital signal and older, analog radios will receive the

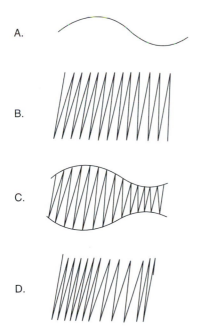

FIGURE 11.10 (A) An electrical wave that represents original sound. (B) The carrier wave of a radio station that is of a much higher frequency. (C) How the carrier wave is changed for amplitude modulation. Note that the height of the carrier wave is varied to take into account the characteristic of the sound wave. (D) How the carrier wave is altered for frequency modulation. Note that the frequency or distance between the waves is varied to relate to the original sound wave—the frequency is decreased where the sound wave is lowest.

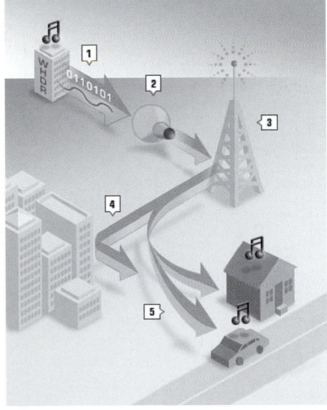

FIGURE 11.11 How HD Radio Works. (Image courtesy of iBiquity Digital Corporation.)

regular AM or FM signal (5). Multipath distortion (common radio interference) can occur when part of a signal bounces off an object (4) and arrives at the receiver at a different time than the main signal. HD radio receivers are designed to sort through reflected signals and reduce static, hiss, pops, and fading. In the future, surround sound broadcasting or multiple audio services could also be offered. With this possibility of more than one programming signal, HD radio should open the door for additional program distribution using the terrestrial radio system.

11.16 DIGITAL DISTRIBUTION NETWORKS

Another way digital technology has impacted radio and radio production is the ability to deliver CD-quality audio to radio stations using **digital distribution networks.** DG Systems is one company that provides such a service by linking radio stations with ad agencies, production houses, and record companies.

Under traditional analog techniques, radio spots were recorded onto audiotape masters, then dubbed to tape copies, and finally delivered by mail or courier to individual stations. A digital distribution network features PC-based servers in the ad agency, production house, or record company onto which audio files are loaded. This audio is sent via phone line to network headquarters, and then, with appropriate instructions, sent to receivers at client stations (see Figure 11.12).

Since they employ broadband digital lines, these networks offer fast, even instantaneous delivery of digital quality audio to stations around the country. They have been used to send commercials, newly released singles, and other production material. Digital distribution networks have also been used to facilitate simultaneous recording from two different locations.

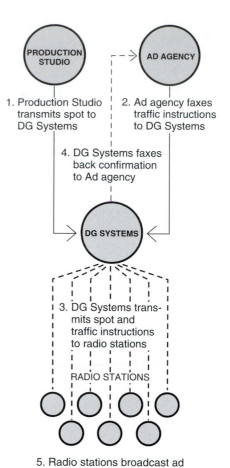

FIGURE 11.12 A digital distribution network delivers CD-quality content, such as commercials, music singles, and news actualities to radio stations. (Image courtesy of DG Systems.)

11.17 CONCLUSION

At present there is a wealth of outlets for student audio work. In addition to stations operated by colleges and universities, there are Internet sites, cable services, and broadcast stations that accept individual programs produced by students. Anyone wishing to get experience and exposure, while a student, can certainly find a distribution outlet for quality audio work.

Self-Study

QUESTIONS

1. How has the Internet been important to college radio?

   a) Stations can have an international audience.
   b) Alums can keep in touch by listening to the college radio station over the Internet.
   c) Colleges that could not have a station because of lack of available frequencies can now have one.
   d) All of the above.

2. Which of the following defines on-demand programming?

   a) programming that is streamed live over the Internet
   b) files of programmed material that can be accessed over the Internet
   c) the icon that listeners click on to receive live streaming
   d) a home page as opposed to a Web page

3. Which of the following aspects of Internet radio is on the listener's computer?

   a) encoder
   b) server
   c) player
   d) overhead

4. Which type of soundfile allows listeners with low-bandwidth connections to the Internet to still listen to high-quality, on-demand soundfiles?

   a) streaming
   b) non-streaming
   c) FM
   d) Flash

5. Someone with a modem operating at 56 kilobytes per second can easily receive uncompressed, analog audio signals from the Internet.

   a) true
   b) false

6. The greater the bandwidth of a signal means which of the following will occur?

   a) the faster the system will operate
   b) the lower the signal-to-noise ratio will be
   c) the greater the frequency of the sound will be
   d) the higher the quality of the sound will be

7. Approximately how much does the signal-to-noise ratio improve with each additional bit when you are dealing with bit depth?

   a) 44.1 kilohertz
   b) 48 dB
   c) 6d B
   d) 1,411,200 bits

8. Which is true about perceptual coding?

   a) It takes into account what sounds the human ear can't hear.
   b) It involves sending a mono signal instead of a stereo one.
   c) It is a compression system that increases the amount of bandwidth a signal uses.
   d) It places more silence in a signal so it can be easily decompressed.

9. Computers that serve Internet radio stations do not need to have as much bandwidth as those that receive the signal.

   a) true
   b) false

10. What is one difference between Internet radio and over-the-air radio?

    a) Internet radio stations do not need to pay license fees to play music.
    b) Internet radio covers a smaller geographic area than over-the-air radio, enabling only people who are close to its server to receive its signal.
    c) Each listener is served individually for Internet radio, but an over-the-air signal can be picked up by anyone who has a radio within the service area.
    d) Internet radio was developed earlier than over-the-air radio.

11. Streamed audio stays on a listener's computer in a large buffer area that acts like a storage tank.

    a) true
    b) false

12. Which two audio streaming formats are currently used by the most stations?

    a) QuickTime & Real
    b) Windows Media & QuickTime
    c) Real & WinAmp
    d) Real & Windows Media

13. Which of the following major audio players has the simplest interface?

    a) MusicMatch
    b) Windows Media Player
    c) QuickTime
    d) Real Player

14. What is the audio compression system based on the one developed by the Moving Picture Experts Group known as?

    a) WAV
    b) MP3
    c) QuickTime
    d) AVI

15. Which of the following is a music licensing agency?

    a) ISP
    b) RIAA
    c) ASCAP
    d) MPEG

16. Which of the following delivers CD-quality radio content, such as commercials, to radio stations around the country?

    a) digital audio workstation
    b) digital distribution network
    c) digital audio card
    d) digital audio editor

17. Which of the following was developed the earliest?

    a) AM radio
    b) FM radio
    c) cable radio
    d) satellite radio

18. Which mobile form of radio requires a subscription and a special receiver?

    a) cable radio
    b) Internet radio
    c) FM radio
    d) satellite radio

19. Which company has established a satellite radio service?

    a) Apple
    b) RealNetworks
    c) Sirius
    d) Microsoft

20. What is one difference between AM and FM?

    a) AM stations have greater bandwidth than FM stations.
    b) AM stations modulate by varying the height of the carrier wave, whereas FM stations modulate by varying the frequency of the carrier wave.
    c) FM stations are more subject to static than AM stations.
    d) More college radio stations are on the AM band than are on the FM band.

ANSWERS

If You Answered A:

1a. This is basically correct, but there is a better answer. (Reread 11.1.)
2a. No. By definition, on-demand is not streamed live. (Reread 11.2.)
3a. No. An encoder would be used by the station. (Reread 11.3, 11.4, and 11.6.)
4a. Wrong. A quality streaming soundfile will not play easily on a computer with low bandwidth. (Reread 11.3.)
5a. Wrong. (Reread 11.4.)
6a. No. It is the opposite. (Reread 11.4.)
7a. No. This relates to sampling, not bit depth. (Reread 11.4.)
8a. You are right. Perceptual coding takes into account what a human can hear.
9a. No. It is the opposite. (Reread 11.4 and 11.5.)
10a. Wrong. They must both pay. (Reread 11.5 and 11.9.)
11a. No, not on the listener's computer. (Reread 11.6.)
12a. No. These are not the top two. (Reread 11.7.)
13a. No. This is not one of the major players on the market. (Reread 11.7.)
14a. No. This can indicate a soundfile, but not a compressed one. (Reread 11.8.)
15a. No. (Reread 11.5 and 11.9.)

16a. No. A DAW could be utilized to produce a commercial, but it is not used to send spots around the country. (Reread 11.16.)

17a. Yes, in the 1920s.

18a. No. The cable TV system is not mobile. (Reread 11.12 and 11.13.)

19a. Wrong. This is computer oriented. (Reread 11.7 and 11.12.)

20a. Wrong. It is the other way around. (Reread 11.14.)

If You Answered B:

1b. This is basically correct, but there is a better answer. (Reread 11.1.)

2b. Correct. A listener can click on a file on a Web page.

3b. No. A server would be used by the station. (Reread 11.3, 11.5, and 11.6.)

4b. Correct. Non-streaming files can be downloaded and then listened to.

5b. Right. Data must be compressed or the information would take forever to download.

6b. Wrong. This has more to do with bit depth. (Reread 11.4.)

7b. No. This number was used in reference to 8-bit sound. (Reread 11.4.)

8b. No. That is a form of bandwidth reduction, but it is not related to perceptual coding. (Reread 11.4.)

9b. Yes. You are correct.

10b. Wrong. It would be the opposite. (Reread 11.5 and 11.14.)

11b. Correct. It does not stay on the listener's computer.

12b. No. These are not the top two. (Reread 11.7.)

13b. No. This is considered a more complicated player. (Reread 11.7.)

14b. Yes. This stands for MPEG-2, Layer 3.

15b. No. This organization has been involved with copyright disputes, but it doesn't license music. (Reread 11.9.)

16b. Yes. This is the correct response.

17b. No. There is a better answer. (Reread 11.11.)

18b. No. Internet radio sometimes requires a subscription, but it is not mobile. (Reread 11.12.)

19b. Wrong. This is a software company. (Reread 11.7 and 11.12.)

20b. Correct. You understand the modulation well.

If You Answered C:

1c. This is basically correct, but there is a better answer. (Reread 11.1.)

2c. No. The program is not an icon, and they would not click to stream. (Reread 11.2.)

3c. Yes. The listener's computer has the player.

4c. No. FM is not a soundfile. (Reread 11.3 and 11.14.)

6c. Wrong. Bandwidth and frequency are not related here. (Reread 11.4.)

7c. Yes. This answer is the correct choice.

8c. No. This is wrong for a lot of reasons, one of which is that compression does not call for an increase in bandwidth. (Reread 11.4.)

10c. Right. Internet radio requires a separate stream for each listener.

12c. No. Winamp is not a file format. (Reread 11.7.)

13c. Correct.

14c. No. This is Apple based. (Reread 11.7 and 11.8.)

15c. Correct. ASCAP is one of the music licensing agencies.

16c. No. A digital audio card is part of a desktop radio system. (Reread 11.16.)

17c. Wrong. This didn't come along until much later than some of the other choices. (Reread 11.11.)

18c. No. FM radio, though mobile, does not require a subscription. (Reread 11.12 and 11.14.)

19c. Yes. And so has XM Satellite Radio.

20c. No. It is the other way around. (Reread 11.14.)

If You Answered D:

1d. Yes, this is the correct answer. All of the answers apply.

2d. No. On-demand programming could be placed on a home page or Web page, but it is not either of them. (Reread 11.2.)

3d. Wrong. Overhead is not a relevant term here. (Reread 11.3, 11.4, and 11.6.)

4d. Wrong. While Flash is capable of transmitting sound, it does not allow users to download files onto their computers for later use. (Reread 11.2 and 11.3.)

6d. Correct. More bandwidth equals higher quality.

7d. No. This huge number was used in relation to a minute of stereo sound. (Reread 11.4.)

8d. No. This answer does not relate to perceptual coding. (Reread 11.4.)

10d. No. (Reread 11.5 and 11.11.)

12d. Correct. Real and Windows Media are the top two.

13d. Wrong. Real's player is considered more complex with its numerous options. (Reread 11.7.)

14d. No. This can indicate a soundfile, but not the right one. (Reread 11.8.)

15d. Wrong. This is an organization dealing with compression. (Reread 11.8 and 11.9.)

16d. No. A digital audio editor could be used to produce a commercial, but it's not used to send spots around the country. (Reread 11.16.)

17d. No. This is very new. (Reread 11.11.)

18d. Correct. Satellite radio or DARS (Digital Audio Radio Service).

19d. No. Microsoft, though it seems to have its fingers in most businesses, is not directly in charge of a satellite radio company. (Reread 11.12.)

20d. Wrong. That is not the band where college radio is located. (Reread 11.14.)

Projects

PROJECT 1

Report on the differences and similarities among six radio station Web sites.

Purpose

To give you a feel for how stations are currently utilizing the Internet.

Advice, Cautions, and Background

1. Try to select different types of stations—for example, ones that are Internet only, ones that are both broadcast and Internet, AM stations, and FM stations.
2. Consider both the audio and visual elements as you do your analysis.

How to Do the Project

1. Find six different stations that have Web pages on the Internet. Feel free to use the Internet sites that list radio stations, as mentioned in section 11.10.
2. Go to one of the Web sites and click on a soundfile or on the live streaming. If necessary, download the player software.
3. Make notes about the appearance of the site and about the type of audio material that is available. Look at the various pages and see the types of materials that are included. You might want to consider such facets as how much material is on the home page; whether or not the site contains live streaming and on-demand files and, if so, what types of on-demand files are included; the color scheme of the pages; the organizational principles around which the pages are presented; the extent to which on-air personalities are featured; and so on.
4. Do the same for five more sites.
5. Write a report that compares and contrasts the radio station presentations. See if you can find trends or recurring features. For example, do music stations tend to use the Internet in different ways than talk stations? Are there things that Internet-only stations include that broadcast stations do not? Do most of the station sites include daily schedules?
6. Put your name on your report and label it "Web Site Analysis." Give the report to your instructor to receive credit for this project.

PROJECT 2

Compare and contrast XM and Sirius.

Purpose

To enable you to learn more about satellite radio.

Advice, Cautions, and Background

1. If you happen to subscribe to satellite radio or have a friend that does, you can incorporate your experience or your friend's into your report.
2. You can consider information on the Web sites and also information that has been written up about the companies in various trade magazines or the popular press.

How to Do the Project

1. Go to an Internet search engine and type in "Sirius Satellite Radio," and then go to the various sites that you think will give you pertinent information. Be sure to visit Sirius' site at www.sirius.com.

2. Jot down basic information. You might want to consider:
    a. What are the programming options?
    b. What kind of programming is free and what must you pay for?
    c. How can you sign up for the service?
    d. When did the service start?
    e. Where is the company headquarters?
    f. How many subscribers does the service have?
    g. How many satellites does it use to broadcast?
3. Go to the same Internet search engine and type in "XM Satellite Radio," and then go to the various sites that you think will give you pertinent information. Be sure to visit XM's site at www.xmradio.com.
4. Jot down the same type of basic information that you did for Sirius.
5. Look over your notes and see how the two services compare and contrast. Write a report of your findings.
6. Put your name and "Satellite Radio" on your report and hand it in to your instructor to get credit for this assignment.

PROJECT 3

Tour a broadcast radio station transmitting facility.

Purpose

To enable you to see a broadcast transmitter firsthand and better understand the broadcast process.

Advice, Cautions, and Background

1. Although you may have toured a radio station already, you may not have seen the transmitter facility because many broadcast studios are physically separated from the transmitter site.
2. Try to arrange to talk with an engineer, as that is the person who can give you the most information.
3. Make sure that before you go you have some ideas about what you want to find out.
4. Your instructor may have set up a tour for the entire class, or the engineer at your college FM station may offer a tour of your own station. Either case is fine for completing the project.

How to Do the Project

1. Select a station. (If the instructor has arranged a station tour for the whole class, skip to Step 4.)
2. Call someone at the station, tell him or her you would like to see the station's transmitter site and talk with someone about it so you can write a report for a radio production class, and ask if you may visit.
3. If the answer is yes, set a date; if not, call a different station.
4. Think of things you want to find out for your report. For example:
    a. How does the line out of the audio console get to the transmitter?
    b. Is there any signal processing equipment at the transmitter site?
    c. Does the station use amplitude modulation or frequency modulation, and exactly where is this modulation equipment located?
    d. What is the physical layout of the transmitter site?
    e. How does the signal get from the transmitter to the antenna?
5. Go to the station transmitter site. Tour to the extent the station personnel will let you and ask as many questions as you can.
6. Write a report about what you found out.
7. Put your name and "Transmitter Site Report" on your report and hand it in to your instructor to get credit for this assignment.

GLOSSARY

A-B miking A method of stereo miking where one microphone feeds the right channel and another microphone feeds the left channel.

Absorption The process of sound going into the walls, ceilings, and floors of a studio.

Absorption coefficient The proportion of sound a material can absorb in relation to the sound it will reflect back. A coefficient of 1.00 means all sound is absorbed in the material.

Acoustic suspension A speaker enclosure design that consists of a tightly sealed box that prevents rear sounds from disrupting main speaker sounds.

Actuality A voice report from a person in the news rather than from the reporter.

Adaptive Transform Acoustic Coding A data compression system used for minidiscs.

Adhesion A condition that occurs when one layer of audio tape sticks to another.

ADSR Attack, decay, sustain, and release; the change in sound volume over a period of time.

Aliasing Unwanted frequencies that can be created during the sampling process and mixed with the sound signal.

AM Amplitude modulation.

Amplify To make louder.

Amplitude The strength or height of a sound wave or radio wave.

Amplitude modulation A form of radio transmission in which the amplitude (height) of a carrier wave is varied according to the characteristics of the sound signal being broadcast.

AMS See *automatic music sensor*.

Analog A recording, circuit, or piece of equipment that produces an output that varies as a continuous function of the input, resulting in degradation of the signal as material is copied from one source to another.

Announce booth See *performance studio*.

Anti-aliasing Filtering the input signal during the digital process to prevent the creation of unwanted frequencies.

ATRAC See *Adaptive Transform Acoustic Coding*.

Attack The time it takes an initial sound to build up to full volume.

Audio card A connection between a computer-based audio workstation and other audio equipment.

Audio chain The route through various pieces of equipment that sound takes in order to be broadcast or recorded.

Audio console The piece of equipment that mixes, amplifies, and routes sound.

Audio routing switcher A type of patch panel that allows audio inputs to be switched to various outputs electronically.

Audio signal A sound signal that has been processed into an electromagnetic form.

Audio tape recorder A device that rearranges particles on magnetic tape in order to store sound.

Audition An output channel of an audio console.

Automatic music sensor A button on a digital audio tape recorder that allows the operator to skip forward or backward to the start of a new song.

Aux See *auxiliary*.

Auxiliary An output channel of an audio console.

Backing layer The back side of audio tape—the side that does not have a magnetic coating.

Balance control A knob on stereo input channels used to determine how much sound goes to the right channel and how much sound goes to the left channel.

Balanced cable A cable with three wires—plus, minus, and ground.

Band cut filter See *band reject filter*.

Band pass filter A filter that cuts all frequencies outside a specified range.

Band reject filter A filter that allows all frequencies to pass except a specified frequency range.

Bass reflex A speaker enclosure design that has a vented port to allow rear sounds to reinforce main speaker sounds.

Bass roll-off switch A switch that turns down bass frequencies to counter the proximity effect.

Bias   A high-frequency signal that improves frequency response of a recording and cuts down distortion.

Bidirectional   Picking up sound from two directions; usually refers to a microphone pickup pattern.

Binary   A number system that uses two digits, 1 and 0.

Bit depth   Number of data bits used to encode a digital sample.

Blast filter   See *windscreen*.

Boom arm   A microphone stand for use in the radio studio, consisting of metal rods designed somewhat like a human arm; one end goes into a base that can be mounted on a counter near the audio console, and the other end supports the microphone.

Boom stand   A stand that can be placed away from an announcer; usually it consists of one vertical pipe with a horizontal pipe at the top of it.

Bouncing tracks   A multi-track recording technique that combines two or more tracks and transfers them to a vacant track.

Boundary microphone   See *PZM microphone*.

Bulk eraser   See *degausser*.

Cable   Wire that carries audio signals.

Cable radio   Music services offered by cable TV systems.

Cannon connector   See *XLR connector*.

Capacitor microphone   Another name for a condenser microphone.

Capstan   A metal shaft that controls the speed of a tape recorder.

Cardioid   Picking up sound in a heart-shaped pattern; usually refers to a microphone pickup pattern.

Carrier wave   A radio wave that is constant in amplitude or frequency but can be modulated by some other audio signal; used to deliver a radio broadcast signal.

Cartridge   A device that converts the vibrations from the turntable stylus into variations in voltage; also, the endless-loop tape container used in a tape recorder.

Cartridge recorder   A tape recorder that uses tape that is in an endless loop.

Cassette   A plastic case containing ⅛-inch audio tape.

Cassette recorder   A tape recorder that records and plays back ⅛-inch tape housed in a plastic case.

CD   See *compact disc*.

CD player   The piece of equipment that uses a laser to play back compact discs.

CD-R   See *CD recorder*.

CD recorder   A type of CD machine that can record as well as playback compact discs.

CD-RW   A CD format that can be recorded on more than once.

Channel   The route an audio signal follows; also, a grouping of controls on an audio console associated with one input.

China marker   A pen-type device used to mark edit points on audio tape.

Chorusing   A multi-track overdubbing technique in which an announcer reads the same script on several different tracks to give a "chorus" effect.

Circumaural   See *closed cushion headphones*.

Closed cushion headphones   A ring-shaped muff that rests on the head, not the ear, through which a person can hear sound.

Close proximity monitoring   See *near-field monitoring*.

Coding   In digital technology, assigning a 16-bit binary "word" to the values measured during quantizing.

Coincident miking   Using multiple microphones with pickup patterns that overlap; usually refers to a stereo microphone technique.

Cold ending   A natural, full-volume ending of music or a song.

Combo   The working procedure in which the radio announcer is also the equipment operator.

Compact disc   A round, shiny disc onto which sound is recorded digitally so that it can be read by a laser.

Companders   Signal processing equipment that compresses dynamic range during recording and expands it during playback.

Compression   A sound wave characteristic that occurs when the air molecules are pushed close together; also, a system for encoding digital data bits so fewer can be placed on a disc or tape yet still represent the original data.

Compressor   A volume control usually associated with the transmitter that boosts signals that are too soft and lowers signals that are too loud.

Condenser microphone   A microphone that uses a capacitor, usually powered by a battery, to respond to sound.

Connector adapters   Freestanding connector parts that allow one connector form to be changed to another.

Connectors   Metal devices to attach one piece of audio equipment to another.

Control board   See *audio console*.

Cross-fade   To bring up one sound and take down another in such a way that both are heard for a short period of time.

Crossover   An electronic device that sends low frequencies to the speaker woofer and high frequencies to the tweeter.

Cross-pair miking   See *X-Y miking*.

Cross talk   The picking up on a tape track of the signal from another track.

Cue   To preview an input (such as a CD or audiotape) before it goes over the air; also, to set up an audio source at the point where it is to start.

Cue burn   Damage to the outer grooves of a record caused by backtracking the record.

Cue defeat   Switch on a cart recorder that can be set so that a cue tone is not put on the audio tape during recording; used for editing purposes.

Cue talent   A signal given to talent that means, "You're on"; it is given by pointing the index finger at the talent.

Cue tone A tone that cannot be heard that is put on a cartridge tape to stop it automatically.

Cue wheel Part of a CD player that allows the operator to find the exact starting point of the music.

Cupping The turning up of the edges of audio tape.

Curling The twisting of audio tape from front to back.

Cut A hand signal given to talent at the end of a production; it is given by "slicing your throat" with your index finger.

DARS See *digital audio radio service*.

DASH See *digital audio stationary head*.

DAT See *digital audio tape*.

Data compression See *compression*.

DAW See *digital audio workstation*.

dB The abbreviation for decibel.

dbx® A noise-reduction system that compresses both loud and soft parts of a signal during recording and then expands them during playback.

Dead air A long pause on a broadcast when no sound is heard.

Dead roll To play music with the volume turned down at first to shorten the piece's duration.

Dead studio A studio with very little echo or reverberation, caused by a great deal of absorption of the sound.

Decay The time it takes a sound to go from full volume to sustain level.

Decibel A measurement to indicate the loudness of sound.

Decompressed The process of restoring an audio signal that has been encoded with some type of data compression system.

De-esser A processor that gets rid of sibilant sounds without affecting other parts of the signal.

Degausser A magnetic unit that erases tapes.

Demagnetizer A device to remove magnetic buildup on a tape-recorder head.

Desk stand A microphone stand for a person in a seated position.

Diffusion Breaking up sound reflections by using irregular room surfaces.

Digital A recording, circuit, or piece of equipment in which the output varies in discrete on–off steps in such a way that it can be reproduced without degradation of the signal.

Digital audio editing Using computer software to manipulate audio.

Digital audio editor Equipment that uses standard or proprietary computers to edit sound.

Digital audio radio service See *satellite radio*.

Digital audio stationary head A digital recording system that records horizontally on reel-to-reel recorders.

Digital audio tape High-quality cassette tape that can be dubbed many times without degradation because of the sampling process of its recording method.

Digital audio workstation A computer-based system that can create, store, edit, mix, and send out sound in a variety of ways, all within one basic unit.

Digital cartridge recorder A piece of equipment that operates similarly to an analog cart machine but stores sound on a computer disc.

Digital delay A unit that holds a signal temporarily and then allows it to leave the unit.

Digital distribution network A network that links ad agencies, production houses, or record companies with radio stations to deliver CD-quality audio via PC-based servers and phone lines.

Digital reverb A unit that produces reverberation electronically.

Digital signal processor A type of electronic audio card used for computer editing.

Digital Versatile Disc A data storage format that has the capacity to hold a feature-length movie on a compact disc-styled medium. It can also be used for music and computer data.

Direct-drive turntable A system in which a turntable platter sits on top of the motor.

Direct sound Sound that goes straight from a source to a microphone.

Disc jockey A person who introduces and plays music for a radio station. The term arose because the person plays recorded discs and "rides gain" on the audio board.

Distortion A blurring of sound caused by overamplification or other inaccurate reproduction of sound.

Dolby A noise-reduction system that raises the volume of the program signal most likely to be affected by noise during production, then lowers it again during playback so that the noise seems lower in relation to the program level.

Dovetailing A multi-track overdubbing technique in which a single announcer appears to have a dialogue with himself or herself by recording different parts of a script on different tracks.

Drop-out A flaking off of oxide coating from audio tape so that the total signal is not recorded.

DSP See *digital signal processor*.

DSP audio card A necessary component in order to use standard computers to edit audio.

Dubbing Electronically copying material from one tape to another.

Dub editing Audio editing in which portions of one tape are copied onto another tape.

Duration The time during which a sound builds up, remains at full volume, and dies out.

DVD See *digital versatile disc*.

Dynamic microphone A microphone that consists of a diaphragm, a magnet, and coils. It is extremely rugged and has good frequency response, so it is used often in radio.

Dynamic range   The volume changes from loud to soft within a series of sounds; also, the amount of volume change a piece of equipment can handle effectively.

Dynamic speaker   A speaker with a cone attached to a voice coil. Electrical current in the voice coil creates a magnetic force that moves the cone.

Earbud   A headphone that fits in the ear.

Echo   Sound that bounces off one surface.

Editing   Splicing or dubbing material to rearrange or eliminate portions of it.

Electret microphone   A type of condenser microphone with a permanently charged capacitor.

Electromagnetic speaker   Another name for a dynamic speaker.

Electrostatic headphones   Headphones that require external amplification.

Electrostatic speaker   A rarely used type of monitor speaker.

Encoder   In streaming audio, a computer or software that converts the analog signal into a digital format.

Envelope   The stages that sound goes through during its duration from full volume to silence.

EQ   The general process of equalization.

Equalization   The adjustment of the amplification given to various frequencies such as high frequencies or low frequencies.

Equalized   Audio sound that has had the amplification of its various frequencies adjusted.

Equalizer   The unit that adjusts the amount of amplification given to particular frequencies such as high or low frequencies.

Equalizer/filter switch   A switch on a turntable to eliminate scratchy noises in the record.

Equal loudness principle   The principle that humans hear the midrange frequencies better than high or low frequencies.

Eraser/splice finder   A degausser that looks like a cart machine; audio carts that are inserted into it are erased and stopped just past where the tape was joined together.

Event   The start point to end point for an edit; usually associated with digital audio editors.

Fade   To gradually increase or decrease the volume of music to or from silence.

Fade in   To bring sound up from silence to full volume.

Fade out   To take sound from full volume to silence.

Fader   Part of an audio console that moves up and down to control volume.

Feedback   A howling noise created when the output of a sound (usually from a speaker) is returned to the input (usually a microphone).

Feed reel   See *supply reel*.

Filter   A unit that cuts out a particular frequency range of the audio signal.

Flanger   A device that electronically combines an original signal with a slightly delayed one.

Flat   See *flat frequency response*.

Flat frequency response   The quality of a frequency curve wherein all frequencies are produced equally well.

Floor stand   A microphone stand for a person in a standing position.

Flutter   Fast variations in sound speed.

FM   See *frequency modulation*.

FM microphone   A microphone that does not need a cable because it consists of a small transmitter and receiver.

Four-track recorder   A machine that records four signals on a tape, all going in the same direction.

Frame   The housing for a computer chassis, power supply, and motherboard.

Frequency   The number of cycles a sound wave or radio wave completes in one second.

Frequency modulation   A form of radio transmission in which the frequency (wave length) of a carrier wave is varied according to the characteristics of the sound signal being broadcast.

Frequency response   The range of highs and lows that a piece of audio equipment reproduces.

Full-track   A recording method that uses the whole tape for one monophonic signal.

Fundamental   A basic tone and frequency that each sound has.

Gain control   A knob or fader that makes sound louder or softer.

Gain trim   Controls on an audio board that are used to fine-tune the volume of each input.

Give mic level   A signal given to talent to tell them to talk into the microphone so the audio engineer can set controls properly. It is given by "chattering" one hand, with the palm down and the thumb under the second and third fingers.

Graphic equalizer   An equalizer that divides frequency responses into bands that can then be raised or lowered in volume.

Grease pencil   A crayon-like substance used to mark edit points on a tape.

Guard bands   Small portions of blank tape between each recorded track and at the edges of the tape.

Half-track mono   The recording of two separate mono signals on a tape, one going to the left and one going to the right.

Half-track stereo   See *two-track stereo*.

Hand signals   Method of communication that radio production people use when a live microphone prohibits talk or when they are in separate rooms.

Hard disk drive   A storage medium built into a computer.

Hardwiring   Connecting equipment in a fairly permanent manner, usually by soldering.

Harmonics   Exact frequency multiples of a fundamental tone.

Head An electromagnet that rearranges iron particles on tape; also, the beginning of an audio tape.

Headphones Tiny speakers encased in something that can be placed in, or close to, the ear.

Headshell The front part of a turntable tone arm where the cartridge and stylus are installed.

Heads out Having tape on a reel, with the beginning of the audio tape facing out.

Hear-through cushion headphones See *open-air headphones*.

Hertz (Hz) A measurement of frequency based on cycles of sound waves per second.

Hiss A high-frequency noise problem inherent in the recording process.

Home page The initial or index page for an Internet Web site.

Hum A low-frequency noise problem caused by leaking of the 60-cycle AC power current into the audio signal.

Hyper-cardioid Picking up sound well from the front, but not the sides; usually refers to a microphone pickup pattern.

IBOC In-band, on-channel; a method of digital audio broadcasting used by terrestrial radio stations.

Idler arm A tension part of a reel-to-reel tape recorder that will stop the recorder if the tape breaks.

Imaging The apparent space between speakers and how sounds are heard within the plane of the speakers.

Impedance The total opposition a circuit offers to the flow of alternating current.

Indirect sound See *reflected sound*.

In phase A combination of two sound waves such that their crests and troughs exactly align.

Input selectors Switches that are used to choose microphone or line positions on an audio board.

Insert edit See *punch in*.

In the mud Operating volume consistently below 20 percent on the VU meter.

ISDN Integrated Services Digital Network; a type of digital phone line for audio and data transmissions.

Jacks Female connectors.

Jewel box A plastic case for a CD.

KiloHertz (kHz) 1,000 cycles per second.

Laser An acronym for "light amplification by simulated emission of radiation"; a narrow, intense beam in a compact disc that reads encoded audio data.

Laser diode A semiconductor with positive and negative electrons that converts an electrical input into an optical output.

Lavalier microphone A small microphone that can be attached unobtrusively to an announcer's clothing.

Leader tape Plastic tape that does not contain iron particles to record. It is used primarily before and after the recording tape so that the tape can be threaded.

LEDE See *live end/dead end*.

Limiter A compressor with a large compression ratio that won't allow a signal to increase beyond a specified point.

Linear In relation to audio editing, a process that works in a sequential fashion.

Line level An input that has already been pre-amplified.

Liner notes Information found on the back of vinyl albums or inside compact discs about the songs, artists, writers, and so forth; often used by announcers to provide ad-lib information.

Live bouncing A multi-track recording technique that combines two or more tracks plus a live recording and transfers them to a vacant track.

Live end/dead end A studio where one end of the studio absorbs sound and the other end reflects sound.

Live studio A studio with a hard, brilliant sound caused by a great deal of reverberation.

Low cut filter A filter that eliminates all frequencies below a certain point.

Low pass filter A filter that allows all frequencies below a certain point to go through unaffected.

M-S miking See *mid-side miking*.

Magnetic layer The part of the tape that contains the iron oxide coating.

Magneto-optical design A recordable CD that records on a magnetic alloy and uses laser light to play back.

Master fader The control that determines the volume of the signal being sent from the audio console.

MD See *minidisc*.

Mic level An input that has not been pre-amplified.

Microphone A transducer that changes sound energy into electrical energy.

MIDI See *musical instrument digital interface*.

Mid-side miking A method of stereo miking where three microphones are arranged in an upside-down T pattern.

Mini See *miniphone connector*.

Minidisc A 2.5-inch computer-type disc that can hold 74 minutes of digital music.

Miniphone connector A small connector with a sleeve and a tip.

Modem Device used for communication of computer data over standard telephone lines; converts digital signals to analog and vice versa.

Modulated A radio wave whose frequency or amplitude has been changed according to the characteristics of another audio signal to broadcast that signal.

Monaural One channel of sound coming from one direction.

Monitor amplifier A piece of equipment that raises the volume level of sound going to a speaker.

Monitor speaker A piece of equipment from which sound can be heard.

Moving-coil microphone Another name for a dynamic microphone.

Moving-coil speaker A monitor speaker that used a wire coil within a magnetic field as part of its internal sound-generating structure.

MP3 A compression system for audio that is a subsystem of the video MPEG compression format.

Multidirectional microphone A microphone that has switchable internal elements that allow it to employ more than one pickup pattern.

Multiplay A type of CD player that can hold up to 200 CDs and access material on them according to a prescribed pattern.

Multiple-microphone interference Uneven frequency response caused when microphones that are too close together are fed into the same mixer.

Multi-track recorder A machine that can record four, eight, or more tracks, all going in the same direction.

Musical instrument digital interface A communication system that allows musical instruments, other electronic gear, and computers to communicate with and control each other.

Music bed Background music used in commercial production to convey the tone or mood of the commercial.

Mute switch Control on an audio console that prevents the audio signal from going through a channel; similar to an on/off button.

Near-field monitoring Placement of monitor speakers on a counter on each side of an audio console so they are extremely close to the announcer.

Netcast To "broadcast" radio programming or similar material using audio streaming on the Internet.

Noise Unwanted sound in electronic equipment.

Noise gate A signal processing device that reduces noise by suddenly turning way down any audio signal below a set threshold point.

Noise reduction Methods of eliminating unwanted sound from a signal.

Nondirectional Another word for omnidirectional; usually refers to a microphone pickup pattern.

Nonlinear In audio editing, a process that can occur in any order or at any location; i.e., random access.

Notch filter A filter that eliminates a narrow range of frequencies or one individual frequency.

Octave A sound that doubles in frequency; for example, sounds at 220 hertz and 440 hertz are an octave apart.

Omnidirectional Picking up sound from all directions; usually refers to a microphone pickup pattern.

On-air lights A signal that comes on to indicate that a live microphone is on in the studio.

On-air studio The studio from where programming is broadcast.

On-demand Programming that can be accessed at any time.

Open-air headphones Devices to hear sound that fit onto the ear.

ORTF miking A method of stereo miking where two microphones are crossed in a precise manner determined by a French broadcasting organization.

Out of phase A phenomenon that occurs when the sound wave from one microphone or speaker is up and the sound wave from a second microphone or speaker is down; the combined result is diminished or canceled sound.

Output selectors Buttons that determine where a sound goes as it leaves the audio console.

Overdubbing Adding new tracks to something that is already recorded; usually a multi-track recording technique.

Overhead Additional bandwidth that is available if necessary for audio streaming on the Internet.

Overtones Pitches that are not exact frequency multiples of a fundamental tone.

Pan knob The part of an audio board that controls how much sound goes to the right channel of a stereo system and how much goes to the left channel.

Pan pot See *pan knob*.

Parametric equalizer An equalizer that can control the center frequency and the bandwidth that will have its volume raised or lowered.

Patch bay See *patch panel*.

Patching Connecting equipment together through the use of jacks and plugs.

Patch panel A board that contains jacks that can be used to make connections with plugs.

PBP See *play-by-play*.

Peaking in the red Modulating a signal so that it reads above 100 percent on the VU meter.

Pegging the meter Operating sound so loudly that the needle of the VU meter hits the metal peg beyond the red area.

Penetration Sound going through a surface and being transmitted into the space on the other side of the surface.

Perceptual coding Data compression based on characteristics of human hearing.

Performance studio A studio used primarily by actors or musicians that has microphones but no other production equipment.

Perspective The spatial relationship of sound; for example, sounds that are supposed to be distant should sound distant.

Phantom power Power that comes from a recorder or an audio board through a microphone cable to a condenser microphone.

Phase The up and down position of one sound or radio wave in relation to another.

Phone connector A connector with a sleeve and a tip.

Phono connector See *RCA connector*.

Photodiode The part of a CD player that provides the data signal that will be converted to an audio signal.

Pickup pattern The area around a microphone where it "hears" best.

Pinch roller   A rubber wheel that holds tape against the capstan.

Pin connector   See *RCA connector*.

Ping-ponging tracks   See *bouncing tracks*.

Pinning the needle   See *pegging the meter*.

Pitch   Highness or lowness of a sound determined by how fast its sound wave goes up or down.

Planar-magnetic   A rarely used type of monitor speaker.

Plastic base   The middle part of audio tape, usually made of polyester.

Plate microphone   See *PZM microphone*.

Platter   The part of the turntable on which the record rests.

Play-by-play   A term designating sports broadcasting from the scene.

Player   In relation to audio streaming, the software or computer used to decode and play back audio on the listener's computer.

Play level pot   A fader or potentiometer that controls the volume of a sound signal that is being played back.

Playlist   An order into which edit events are assembled; usually associated with audio tape editors.

Plugs   Male connectors.

Polar pattern   A two-dimensional drawing of a microphone's pickup pattern.

Pop filters   See *windscreen*.

Pot   See *potentiometer*.

Potentiometer   A round knob that controls volume.

Pre-amplification   The initial stage at which volume is boosted.

Pressure microphone   Another name for a dynamic microphone.

Pressure pads   Small, soft elements that keep cartridge tape pressed against the tape heads.

Pressure zone microphone   A flat microphone that, when set on a table or other flat surface, uses that surface to collect the sound waves and therefore can pick up audio levels from a fairly widespread area.

Print-through   The bleeding through of the magnetic signal of one layer of tape to an adjacent layer of tape.

Prism system   The part of a CD player that directs the laser to the disc surface.

Production studio   The place where material for radio is produced before it is aired.

Program   An output channel of an audio console.

Proximity effect   A boosting of bass frequencies as a sound source gets closer to a microphone.

Punch in   Editing by recording over one section of a track but leaving what was before and after the edited section intact; a technique associated with multi-track recording.

PZM microphone   See *pressure zone microphone*.

Quantizing   In digital technology, determining how many levels or values each sample will be broken down into; the standard for most digital recording is 65,536 quantizing levels (16-bit).

Quarter-inch phone   See *phone connector*.

Quarter-track stereo   The recording of two stereo signals on one tape in which two signals go to the left and two go to the right.

R-DAT   See *rotary head digital audio tape*.

Radio microphone   Another name for an FM microphone.

Rarefaction   A sound wave characteristic that occurs when the air molecules are pulled apart.

RCA connector   A connector with an outer sleeve and a center shaft.

Record-level pot   A control that adjusts the volume of an incoming sound signal.

Reel-to-reel recorder   A tape recorder that uses open reels of tape placed on a feed reel and a take-up reel.

Reflected sound   Sound that bounces back to the original source.

Region   In digital audio editing, a common designation for a section of audio that is to be edited or saved for later use.

Regulated phase microphone   A microphone that consists of a wire coil impressed into the surface of a circular diaphragm that is suspended within a magnetic structure.

Reinforced sound   Sound that causes objects to vibrate at the same frequency as the original sound.

Release   The time it takes a sound to die out from sustain level to silence.

Remote start switches   Buttons that enable a piece of equipment to be operated from a distance.

Reverb   See *reverberation*.

Reverberation   Sound that bounces off two or more surfaces.

Reverb ring   The time it takes for a sound to go from full volume to silence.

Reverb route   The path a sound takes from a source to a reflective surface and back again.

Reverb time   See *reverb ring*.

Reverse echo   A production technique used to punctuate a key word.

RF microphone   Another name for an FM microphone.

Ribbon drive speaker   A rarely used type of monitor speaker.

Ribbon microphone   A microphone that consists of a metallic ribbon, a magnet, and a coil. Because it is bulky, heavy, and fragile, it is rarely used in radio anymore.

Riding levels   See *riding the gain*.

Riding the gain   Adjusting volume during production.

Rip and read   To read news copy from the wire service machine with very little editing.

Rotary head digital audio tape   Another name for digital audio tape.

RPM   Revolutions per minute.

SACD   Super audio compact disc; a higher-quality compact disc format.

Sampling   In digital technology, the process of taking readings from the original sound source to convert to binary data.

Sampling rate   The number of times per second that a reading of the sound source is taken in order to convert it to binary data.

Satellite radio   Beaming radio programming from a satellite directly to home or auto receivers.

Scattered wind   When tape does not spool up evenly on a reel.

Sealed box   See *acoustic suspension*.

Segue   To cut from one sound at full volume to another sound at full volume.

Sel sync   Selective synchronization; a tape recorder feature that makes a record head act as a play head.

Sensitivity   A microphone's efficiency in terms of its ability to pick up various volumes.

Server   A powerful master computer used to store and distribute files on demand.

Shock mount   A microphone holder that isolates the microphone from mechanical vibrations.

Shotgun microphone   A highly directional microphone that consists of a microphone capsule at one end of a tube or barrel that is aimed toward the sound source.

Signal processing   Manipulating elements of sound, such as frequency response and dynamic range, so that the resulting sound is different from the original sound.

Signal-to-noise ratio   The relationship of desired sound to inherent, unwanted electronic sound. The higher the ratio, the purer the sound.

Slider   See *fader*.

Slip cueing   Preparing a record to play by having the turntable motor on and holding the edge of the record until it should be played.

SMPTE time code   An electronic language developed for video that identifies each picture frame.

S/N   See *signal-to-noise ratio*.

Solid-state recorder   An audio recorder that uses compact flash or other solid-state storage devices as its recording medium.

Solo switch   A button that allows one particular audio board sound to be heard on the monitor.

Sound card   See *audio card*.

Sound file   A segment of audio recorded on a hard disk; usually associated with digital audio editors.

Soundproofing   Methods of keeping wanted sound in the studio and unwanted sound out of it.

Sound signal   A noise that has not been processed into an electromagnetic form.

Source/tape switch   A switch that allows someone to monitor either the input or the output of a tape recorder.

Spaced-pair miking   See *A-B miking*.

Speaker   A transducer that converts electrical energy into sound energy.

Speaker level   An input that has been amplified several times in order to drive a speaker.

Speed selector switch   On a turntable, the control that determines whether the record plays at 33 1/3 RPM or 45 RPM.

Splice editing   A form of editing in which audio tape is physically cut and spliced back together.

Splicing block   The device that holds audio tape during editing.

Splicing tape   Special tape used for holding together audio tape in the editing process.

Split-pair miking   See *A-B miking*.

Stacking   A multi-track overdubbing technique in which an announcer "sings harmony" to a previously recorded track.

Standby   A signal given to talent just prior to going on-air by holding one hand above the head with the palm forward.

Standing wave   A combination of a sound wave going in one direction and an identical sound wave going in the opposite direction.

Stereo   Sound recording and reproduction that uses two channels, one coming from the right and the other from the left, to imitate live sound as closely as possible.

Stereo microphone   A microphone that incorporates small, multiple sound-generating elements as part of a single microphone housing that can record sound in such a way that when it is played back, it sounds like it is coming from two areas.

Stereosonic miking   A method of stereo miking in which two bidirectional microphones are placed one on top of the other.

Stereo synthesizer   A device that inputs a monophonic audio signal and simulates a stereo output signal.

Streaming audio   Using the Internet to transfer audio data from one computer to another so that it can be heard in real time.

Stylus   A small, compliant strip of metal that vibrates in record grooves.

Super-cardioid   Picking up sound well from the front but not the sides; usually refers to a microphone pickup pattern.

Supply reel   The reel on the left-hand side of a reel-to-reel or cassette tape recorder that holds the tape before it is recorded or played.

Supra-aural   See *open-air headphones*.

Surface-mount microphone   See *PZM microphone*.

Surround sound   A multi-channel audio format that refers to five full-bandwidth channels (right, left, center, right rear, left rear) and one limited-bandwidth channel (bass subwoofer).

Sustain   The amount of time a sound holds its volume.

Sustain ending   Music or songs that end with the last notes held for a period of time, then gradually faded out.

Tail   The end of an audio tape.

Tails out   Having tape on a reel with the end of the audio tape facing out.

Take-up reel   The reel on the right-hand side of a reel-to-reel or cassette tape recorder that holds the tape after it is recorded or played.

Talk-back switch   A simple intercom on an audio console that allows the operator to talk with someone in another studio.

Tape guide A stationary pin that leads tape through the transport system of a reel-to-reel recorder.

Tape loop A piece of audio tape spliced together so that it plays around and around in a continuous circle.

Tape transport The part of a tape recorder that moves the tape from the supply reel to the take-up reel.

Telephone coupler See *telephone interface*.

Telephone interface A piece of equipment that connects telephone lines to broadcast equipment.

Tensilize To pre-stretch an audio tape.

Tension arm A moveable guide for tape on a reel-to-reel recorder.

Three-pin connecter See *XLR connector*.

Three-way system A monitor speaker that divides sound not just to a woofer and tweeter, but also to another driver such as a midrange.

Threshold of hearing The softest sound the human ear can hear, noted as 0 decibels.

Threshold of pain The loudness level at which the ear begins to hurt, usually about 120 decibels.

Timbre The distinctive quality of tone that each voice or musical instrument has, composed of the fundamental tone, plus overtones and harmonics.

Timer A mechanism with a series of numbers that can be used to indicate how long something is recorded.

Tone See *timbre*.

Tone arm The device that holds the turntable cartridge and stylus.

Tone control A control that increases the volume of the high frequencies or the low frequencies.

Tone generator An element in an audio board or other piece or equipment that produces a tone that can be set to 100 percent to calibrate equipment.

Track sheet A format for keeping notes of what material is recorded on what tracks of a multi-track recording.

Transducer A device that converts one form of energy into another.

Transmitter Equipment used to broadcast a radio signal.

Tray The area where the CD sits so that it can spin and be read by the laser.

Trim control See *gain trim*.

Turntable A device for spinning a record and converting its vibrations into electrical energy.

Tweeter The part of a speaker that produces high frequencies.

Two-track stereo The recording of two tracks on one tape, both going in the same direction to produce stereo sound.

Two-way speaker system A speaker that has a woofer, a tweeter, and a crossover to send the sound to each.

Type I A cassette tape that uses ferric oxide as its magnetic material.

Type II A cassette tape that uses chromium dioxide or a chrome equivalent as its magnetic material.

Type III A cassette tape format that is no longer available.

Type IV A cassette tape that uses pure metal magnetic material.

Ultra-cardioid Picking up sound well from the front, but not the back or sides; usually refers to a microphone pickup pattern.

Unbalanced cable Cable with two wires, of which one is positive and the other is combined negative and ground.

Under-modulated An audio signal or recording in which the volume of the signal is too low, causing noise to be more noticeable.

Unidirectional Picking up sound from one direction; usually refers to a microphone pickup pattern.

Unity-gain A device whose circuits do not make the output signal louder or softer than the input signal.

User interface A device, such as a keyboard or mouse, that allows a person to interact with a computer.

Variable resistor A device that controls the amount of signal that gets through the audio console, and thereby controls the volume.

Vented box See *bass reflex*.

Vocal stripping Removing the lyrics from a song by manipulating the recorded channels.

Voice actuality See *actuality*.

Voice doubling A multi-track overdubbing technique in which an announcer reads the same script on two different tracks to give a double voice effect.

Voice-over Speech over something else, such as music.

Voice tracking The practice of a radio announcer recording various vocal elements that will later be incorporated into a regular on-air shift, often by some type of automation.

Volume Loudness.

Volume control See *gain control*.

VU meter A unit that gives a visual indication of the level of volume.

Walking over Talking over the vocal portion of a song, such as when an announcer is introducing a record. Normally, an announcer only talks over the instrumental portion.

Waveform The shape of an electromagnetic wave.

Wavelength The distance between two crests of a radio or sound wave.

Web page A screen that can be called up on the Internet using a computer browser.

Well See *tray*.

Windscreen A ball-shaped accessory placed over the microphone to reduce plosive sounds.

Wireless headphone A device to hear sound that transmits an RF, or infrared, audio signal from the source to the headphone.

Wireless microphone Another name for an FM microphone.

Woofer The part of the speaker that produces low frequencies.

Wow Slow variations in sound speed.

XLR connector A connector with three prongs.

X-Y miking A method of stereo miking in which two microphones are placed like crossed swords.

SUGGESTED READING

Adams, John J. *Complete Guide to Audio.* Indianapolis, IN: Howard W. Sams, 1998.

Albarran, Alan B., and Pitts, Gregory G. *The Radio Broadcast Industry.* Needham Heights, MA: Allyn Bacon, 2000.

Alten, Stanley R. *Audio in Media,* 6th ed. Belmont, CA: Wadsworth, 2002.

Barnard, Stephen. *Studying Radio.* New York: Oxford University Press, 2000.

Connelly, Donald. *Digital Radio Production.* Boston: McGraw-Hill, 2004.

Crook, Timothy. Radio Drama: *Theory and Practice.* London and New York: Routledge, 1999.

Dominick, Joseph R., Sherman, Barry L., and Messere, Fritz. *Broadcasting, Cable, the Internet, and Beyond,* 4th ed. Boston: McGraw-Hill, 2000.

Fong-Torres, Ben. *The Hits Just Keep Coming: The History of Top 40 Radio.* San Francisco: Miller Freeman, 1998.

Godfrey, Donald G., and Leigh, Frederic A., editors. *Historical Dictionary of American Radio.* Westport, CT: Greenwood Press, 1998.

Hausman, Carl, Benoit, Philip, Messere, Frank, and O'Donnell, Lewis. *Modern Radio Production: Production, Programming, and Performance,* 6th ed. Belmont, CA: Wadsworth, 2003.

Hyde, Stuart. *Television and Radio Announcing,* 10th ed. Boston: Houghton Mifflin, 2004.

Keith, Michael C. *Talking Radio: An Oral History of American Radio in the Television Age.* Armonk, NY: M.E. Sharpe, 2000.

Keith, Michael C. *The Radio Station,* 6th ed. Boston: Focal Press, 2004.

Lynch, Joanna R., and Gillispie, Greg. *Process and Practice of Radio Programming.* Lanham, MD: University Press of America, 1998.

McLeish, Robert. *Radio Production: A Manual for Broadcasters,* 4th ed. Boston: Focal Press, 2000.

Nachman, Gerald. *Raised on Radio.* New York: Pantheon, 1998.

Neer, Richard. FM: *The Rise and Fall of Rock Radio.* New York: Villard, 2001.

Olszewski, Mike. *Radio Daze: Stories from the Front in Cleveland's FM Air Wars.* Kent, OH: Kent State University Press, 2003.

Perebinossoff, Philippe, Gross, Lynne S., and Gross, Brian. *Programming for TV, Radio and the Internet.* Boston: Focal Press, 2005.

Pohlmann, Ken C. *Principles of Digital Audio.* New York: McGraw-Hill, 2000.

Priestman, Chris. *Web Radio: Radio Production for Internet Streaming.* Boston: Focal Press, 2001.

Reese, David E., Beadle, Mary E., and Stephenson, Alan R. *Broadcast Announcing Worktext,* 2nd ed. Boston: Focal Press, 2005.

Sauls, Samuel J. *The Culture of American College Radio.* Ames: Iowa State University Press, 2000.

Shingler, Martin, and Wieringa, Cindy. *On Air: Methods and Meanings of Radio.* New York: Oxford University Press, 1998.

Sterling, Christopher, editor. *The Museum of Broadcast Communications Encyclopedia of Radio.* New York: Fitzroy Dearborn, 2004.

Warren, Steve. *Radio: The Book,* 4th ed. Boston: Focal Press, 2004.

White, Ted. *Broadcast News Writing, Reporting and Producing,* 4th ed. Boston: Focal Press, 2005.

PRODUCTION TIP #13—AUDACITY

Audacity offers a free audio editor that you can download for Windows, Mac, and some other operating systems at www.audacity.source-forge.net. Many of the key features found in professional programs and mentioned throughout this text are made available in the Audacity program. You can record audio or digitize (analog sources) in 16-bit, 24-bit, or 32-bit (floating point) resolution and up to 97 kHz sampling rate. Basic audio editing commands include cut, copy, paste, and delete with undo and redo functions. The program facilitates audio effects like pitch change, noise reduction, equalization, echo, phasing, and more. Audacity can import and export several common sound file formats such as MP3, WAV, and AIFF.

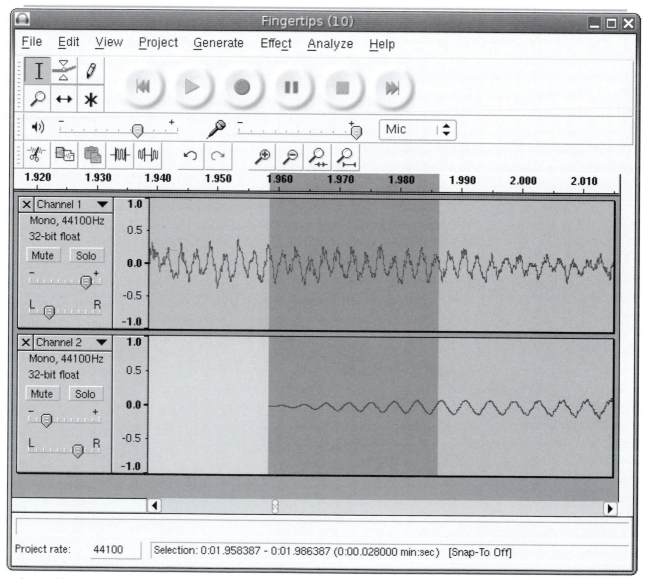

The main screed for the Audacity audio editor. (Copyright © 2005 Members of the Audacity Development Team. "Audacity" is a trademark of Dominic Mazzoni.)

Audacity is free software released under the terms of a GNU General Public License. Users of this open source software can use the program, as well as study, copy, modify, and redistribute it under the terms of the license.

INDEX

ELSEVIER LICENSE AGREEMENT

PLEASE READ THE FOLLOWING AGREEMENT CAREFULLY BEFORE USING THIS ELECTRONIC MEDIA PRODUCT. THIS ELECTRONIC MEDIA PRODUCT IS LICENSED UNDER THE TERMS CONTAINED IN THIS ELECTRONIC MEDIA LICENSE AGREEMENT ("Agreement"). BY USING THIS ELECTRONIC MEDIA PRODUCT, YOU, AN INDIVIDUAL OR ENTITY INCLUDING EMPLOYEES, AGENTS AND REPRESENTATIVES ("You" or "Your"), ACKNOWLEDGE THAT YOU HAVE READ THIS AGREEMENT, THAT YOU UNDERSTAND IT, AND THAT YOU AGREE TO BE BOUND BY THE TERMS AND CONDITIONS OF THIS AGREEMENT. ELSEVIER INC. ("Elsevier") EXPRESSLY DOES NOT AGREE TO LICENSE THIS ELECTRONIC MEDIA PRODUCT TO YOU UNLESS YOU ASSENT TO THIS AGREEMENT. IF YOU DO NOT AGREE WITH ANY OF THE FOLLOWING TERMS, YOU MAY, WITHIN THIRTY (30) DAYS AFTER YOUR RECEIPT OF THIS ELECTRONIC MEDIA PRODUCT RETURN THE UNUSED ELECTRONIC MEDIA PRODUCT AND ALL ACCOMPANYING DOCUMENTATION TO ELSEVIER FOR A FULL REFUND.

DEFINITIONS

As used in this Agreement, these terms shall have the following meanings:

"Proprietary Material" means the valuable and proprietary information content of this Electronic Media Product including all indexes and graphic materials and software used to access, index, search and retrieve the information content from this Electronic Media Product developed or licensed by Elsevier and/or its affiliates, suppliers and licensors.

"Electronic Media Product" means the copy of the Proprietary Material and any other material delivered on Electronic Media and any other human-readable or machine-readable materials enclosed with this Agreement, including without limitation documentation relating to the same.

OWNERSHIP

This Electronic Media Product has been supplied by and is proprietary to Elsevier and/or its affiliates, suppliers and licensors. The copyright in the Electronic Media Product belongs to Elsevier and/or its affiliates, suppliers and licensors and is protected by the national and state copyright, trademark, trade secret and other intellectual property laws of the United States and international treaty provisions, including without limitation the Universal Copyright Convention and the Berne Copyright Convention. You have no ownership rights in this Electronic Media Product. Except as expressly set forth herein, no part of this Electronic Media Product, including without limitation the Proprietary Material, may be modified, copied or distributed in hardcopy or machine-readable form without prior written consent from Elsevier. All rights not expressly granted to You herein are expressly reserved. Any other use of this Electronic Media Product by any person or entity is strictly prohibited and a violation of this Agreement.

SCOPE OF RIGHTS LICENSED (PERMITTED USES)

Elsevier is granting to You a limited, non-exclusive, non-transferable license to use this Electronic Media Product in accordance with the terms of this Agreement. You may use or provide access to this Electronic Media Product on a single computer or terminal physically located at Your premises and in a secure network or move this Electronic Media Product to and use it on another single computer or terminal at the same location for personal use only, but under no circumstances may You use or provide access to any part or parts of this Electronic Media Product on more than one computer or terminal simultaneously.

You shall not (a) copy, download, or otherwise reproduce the Electronic Media Product in any medium, including, without limitation, online transmissions, local area networks, wide area networks, intranets, extranets and the Internet, or in any way, in whole or in part, except that You may print or download limited portions of the Proprietary Material that are the results of discrete searches; (b) alter, modify, or adapt the Electronic Media Product, including but not limited to decompiling, disassembling, reverse engineering, or creating derivative works, without the prior written approval of Elsevier; (c) sell, license or otherwise distribute to third parties the Electronic Media Product or any part or parts thereof; or (d) alter, remove, obscure or obstruct the display of any copyright, trademark or other proprietary notice on or in the Electronic Media Product or on any printout or download of portions of the Proprietary Materials.

RESTRICTIONS ON TRANSFER

This License is personal to You, and neither Your rights hereunder nor the tangible embodiments of this Electronic Media Product, including without limitation the Proprietary Material, may be sold, assigned, transferred or sublicensed to any other person, including without limitation by operation of law, without the prior written consent of Elsevier. Any purported sale, assignment, transfer or sublicense without the prior written consent of Elsevier will be void and will automatically terminate the License granted hereunder.

TERM

This Agreement will remain in effect until terminated pursuant to the terms of this Agreement. You may terminate this Agreement at any time by removing from Your system and destroying the Electronic Media Product. Unauthorized copying of the Electronic Media Product, including without limitation, the Proprietary Material and documentation, or otherwise failing to comply with the terms and conditions of this Agreement shall result in automatic termination of this license and will make available to Elsevier legal remedies. Upon termination of this Agreement, the license granted herein will terminate and You must immediately destroy the Electronic Media Product and accompanying documentation. All provisions relating to proprietary rights shall survive termination of this Agreement.

LIMITED WARRANTY AND LIMITATION OF LIABILITY

NEITHER ELSEVIER NOR ITS LICENSORS REPRESENT OR WARRANT THAT THE INFORMATION CONTAINED IN THE PROPRIETARY MATERIAL IS COMPLETE OR FREE FROM ERROR, AND NEITHER ASSUMES, AND BOTH EXPRESSLY DISCLAIM, ANY LIABILITY TO ANY PERSON FOR ANY LOSS OR DAMAGE CAUSED BY ERRORS OR OMISSIONS IN THE PROPRIETARY MATERIAL, WHETHER SUCH ERRORS OR OMISSIONS RESULT FROM NEGLIGENCE, ACCIDENT, OR ANY OTHER CAUSE. IN ADDITION, NEITHER ELSEVIER NOR ITS LICENSORS MAKE ANY REPRESENTATIONS OR WARRANTIES, EITHER EXPRESS OR IMPLIED, REGARDING THE PERFORMANCE OF YOUR NETWORK OR COMPUTER SYSTEM WHEN USED IN CONJUNCTION WITH THIS ELECTRONIC MEDIA PRODUCT.

If this Electronic Media Product is defective, Elsevier will replace it at no charge if the defective Electronic Media Product is returned to Elsevier within sixty (60) days (or the greatest period allowable by applicable law) from the date of shipment.

Elsevier warrants that the software embodied in this Electronic Media Product will perform in substantial compliance with the documentation supplied in this Electronic Media Product. If You report a significant defect in performance in writing to Elsevier, and Elsevier is not able to correct same within sixty (60) days after its receipt of Your notification, You may return this Electronic Media Product, including all copies and documentation, to Elsevier and Elsevier will refund Your money.

YOU UNDERSTAND THAT, EXCEPT FOR THE 60-DAY LIMITED WARRANTY RECITED ABOVE, ELSEVIER, ITS AFFILIATES, LICENSORS, SUPPLIERS AND AGENTS, MAKE NO WARRANTIES, EXPRESSED OR IMPLIED, WITH RESPECT TO THE ELECTRONIC MEDIA PRODUCT, INCLUDING, WITHOUT LIMITATION THE PROPRIETARY MATERIAL, AND SPECIFICALLY DISCLAIM ANY WARRANTY OF MERCHANTABILITY OR FITNESS FOR A PARTICULAR PURPOSE.

If the information provided on this Electronic Media contains medical or health sciences information, it is intended for professional use within the medical field. Information about medical treatment or drug dosages is intended strictly for professional use, and because of rapid advances in the medical sciences, independent verification of diagnosis and drug dosages should be made.

IN NO EVENT WILL ELSEVIER, ITS AFFILIATES, LICENSORS, SUPPLIERS OR AGENTS, BE LIABLE TO YOU FOR ANY DAMAGES, INCLUDING, WITHOUT LIMITATION, ANY LOST PROFITS, LOST SAVINGS OR OTHER INCIDENTAL OR CONSEQUENTIAL DAMAGES, ARISING OUT OF YOUR USE OR INABILITY TO USE THE ELECTRONIC MEDIA PRODUCT REGARDLESS OF WHETHER SUCH DAMAGES ARE FORESEEABLE OR WHETHER SUCH DAMAGES ARE DEEMED TO RESULT FROM THE FAILURE OR INADEQUACY OF ANY EXCLUSIVE OR OTHER REMEDY.

U.S. GOVERNMENT RESTRICTED RIGHTS

The Electronic Media Product and documentation are provided with restricted rights. Use, duplication or disclosure by the U.S. Government is subject to restrictions as set forth in subparagraphs (a) through (d) of the Commercial Computer Restricted Rights clause at FAR 52.22719 or in subparagraph (c)(1)(ii) of the Rights in Technical Data and Computer Software clause at DFARS 252.2277013, or at 252.2117015, as applicable. Contractor/ Manufacturer is Elsevier Inc., 360 Park Avenue South, New York, NY 10010-5107 USA.

GOVERNING LAW

This Agreement shall be governed by the laws of the State of New York, USA. In any dispute arising out of this Agreement, you and Elsevier each consent to the exclusive personal jurisdiction and venue in the state and federal courts within New York County, New York, USA.